Connective Action and the Rise of the Far-Right

JOURNALISM AND POLITICAL COMMUNICATION UNBOUND

Series editors: Daniel Kreiss, University of North Carolina at Chapel Hill, and Nikki Usher, University of San Diego

Journalism and Political Communication Unbound seeks to be a high-profile book series that reaches far beyond the academy to an interested public of policymakers, journalists, public intellectuals, and citizens eager to make sense of contemporary politics and media. "Unbound" in the series title has multiple meanings: It refers to the unbinding of borders between the fields of communication, political communication, and journalism, as well as related disciplines such as political science, sociology, and science and technology studies; it highlights the ways traditional frameworks for scholarship have disintegrated in the wake of changing digital technologies and new social, political, economic, and cultural dynamics; and it reflects the unbinding of media in a hybrid world of flows across mediums.

Other books in the series:

Journalism Research That Matters
Valérie Bélair-Gagnon and Nikki Usher

Voices for Transgender Equality: Making Change in the Networked Public Sphere
Thomas J Billard

Reckoning: Journalism's Limits and Possibilities
Candis Callison and Mary Lynn Young

News After Trump: Journalism's Crisis of Relevance in a Changed Media Culture
Matt Carlson, Sue Robinson, and Seth C. Lewis

Press Freedom and the (Crooked) Path Towards Democracy: Lessons from Journalists in East Africa
Meghan Sobel Cohen and Karen McIntyre Hopkinson

Data-Driven Campaigning and Political Parties: Five Advanced Democracies Compared
Katharine Dommett, Glenn Kefford, and Simon Kruschinski

Borderland: Decolonizing the Words of War
Chrisanthi Giotis

The Politics of Force: Media and the Construction of Police Brutality
Regina G. Lawrence

Authoritarian Journalism: Controlling the News in Post-Conflict Rwanda
Ruth Moon
Imagined Audiences: How Journalists Perceive and Pursue the Public
Jacob L. Nelson

Pop Culture, Politics, and the News: Entertainment Journalism in the Polarized Media Landscape
Joel Penney

The Invented State
Emily Thorson

Democracy Lives in Darkness: How and Why People Keep Their Politics a Secret
Emily Van Duyn

Building Theory in Political Communication: The Politics-Media-Politics Approach
Gadi Wolfsfeld, Tamir Sheafer, and Scott Althaus

Media and January 6th
Khadijah Costley White, Daniel Kreiss, Shannon C. McGregor, and Rebekah Tromble

Connective Action and the Rise of the Far-Right

Platforms, Politics, and the Crisis of Democracy

Edited by
STEVEN LIVINGSTON
MICHAEL MILLER

Oxford University Press is a department of the University of Oxford.
It furthers the University's objective of excellence in research, scholarship,
and education by publishing worldwide. Oxford is a registered trade mark of
Oxford University Press in the UK and in certain other countries.

Published in the United States of America by Oxford University Press
198 Madison Avenue, New York, NY 10016, United States of America.

© Oxford University Press 2025

This is an open access publication, available online and distributed under the terms of a Creative
Commons Attribution-Non Commercial-No Derivatives 4.0 International license (CC BY-NC-ND 4.0),
a copy of which is available at https://creativecommons.org/licenses/by-nc-nd/4.0/.
Subject to this license, all rights are reserved.

Inquiries concerning reproduction outside the scope of the above should be sent
to the Rights Department, Oxford University Press, at the address above.

You must not circulate this work in any other form
and you must impose this same condition on any acquirer.

CIP data is on file at the Library of Congress

ISBN 9780197794944
ISBN 9780197794937 (hbk.)

DOI: 10.1093/oso/9780197794937.001.0001

Paperback printed by Marquis, Canada
Hardback printed by Bridgeport National Bindery, Inc., United States of America

Contents

Foreword: *The Conservative Dilemma in the Digital Age*   vii
Daniel Ziblatt

Preface   xiii
Steven Livingston and Michael Miller

Author Biographies   xxvi

1. Technological and Institutional Roots of Democratic
   Backsliding in the United States   1
   W. Lance Bennett and Steven Livingston

2. Unraveling the Big Lie: Participatory Disinformation
   and the 2020 Election   32
   Kate Starbird

3. How QAnon Developed from a Fringe Group to a
   Digital Surrogate for the GOP   62
   Josephine Lukito, Yunkang Yang, and Sang Jung Kim

4. The Democratic Decay Within: The US Republican
   Party and QAnon as a Digital Surrogate   90
   Daniel Kreiss and Aaron Sugarman

5. In-Groups and Outrage: How Narratives and Affect
   Shape Digital Surrogate Networks and Radicalize
   Right-Wing Parties   122
   Curd Knüpfer and Ulrike Klinger

6. Japan's *Netto Uyoku* and the Crisis of Transnational
   Digital Surrogate Organizations   146
   Julia R. DeCook and Brett J. Fujioka

7. Advocates and Authoritarians: Surrogate Management
   and Asymmetric Party Development in American Politics   169
   Adam Hilton

CONTENTS

8. Exploring the Motivations of the MAGA Movement 191
   Christopher Sebastian Parker and Rachel M. Blum

9. The Rise of Conservative Illiberalism and the Parallel
   Ascendance of Right-Wing Surrogates 207
   Steven Feldstein

10. Hating the Other as a Cross-Cutting Issue: Assessing
    the Role of Media Surrogate Organizations 230
    Babak Bahador and Daniel Kerchner

11. Demographic Determinism, Republican Identity, and
    Democratic Backsliding 251
    Andrew Ifedapo Thompson

12. Digital Death Spiral: How Analytics Hastened the
    Republican Party's Descent into Trumpism 268
    David Karpf

13. Conclusion 286
    Steven Livingston and Michael Miller

Foreword
Daniel Ziblatt
The Conservative Dilemma in the Digital Age

What has given rise to the growth and endurance of illiberal right-wing radicalism in established democracies? Most scholarly attention in the social sciences has framed this question in what might be thought of as a "bottom-up" way. Whether one emphasizes the impact of economic dislocation, the perceived cultural threat brought by new waves of immigration, or sweeping technological innovation, a shared assumption is that the forces driving our politics come from deep societal changes, representing a sharp break from the past. What I want to offer in this forward is a different angle on our current political moment. What we are witnessing may not represent a sharp break from the past, but instead the return of an old and reoccurring dilemma of democratic politics—what I have elsewhere called "the conservative dilemma" (Ziblatt 2017).

What is the conservative dilemma? As modern democracies were built in the nineteenth century, traditional conservative parties represented the nexus of power, wealth, and prestige. In short, their core constituency was upper-income voters (Gibson 2001). Conservative parties could easily thrive under the predemocratic restrictions of the mid-nineteenth century, where competition was between elitist parties of Liberals and Conservatives. But under conditions of full suffrage, where the median voter was relatively poorer, winning over middle-class and especially lower-class voters posed an existential challenge. And given this challenge, conservatives before World War II found that they had to offer something else to voters. And they did. They stumbled into a new strategy that was premised on highlighting *noneconomic* or identity appeals. This was the core of the late nineteenth century British Tory Party's defense of "empire and crown." This, too, is also partly why German conservatives found themselves as the self-identified defenders of the German nation. This dynamic shaped the competition between right and left in the early years of democracy. Nonclass "identity" electoral appeals, in the hands of nineteenth and early twentieth-century conservatives, relied not only nationalism but also fear of national decline

viii FOREWORD

and traditional religious identities. Such appeals could become aggressively malignant, at times drawing on, and accentuating racial, ethnic, or racial divisions. With strong emotional and mobilizing potential, however, these identities proved extremely useful to conservatives in the early years of democratic electoral competition.

In the decades after World War II, the tactics of mobilizing cross-cutting issues did not disappear entirely. But a remarkable development in the period between 1945 to about the 1990s, was that the conservative dilemma, while never fully disappearing from view in Western Europe and North America, was significantly submerged (Urwin 1997). The modern center right itself began to campaign on economic issues. Consider the West German Christian Democratic Party (CDU). In the 1950s, it made mostly traditional appeals and disagreements over economic policy were rife, and the party's identity was one as primarily a pro-democratic defender of traditional ways of life. But by the 1960s, the CDU also conceived of itself as defender of a particular variant of market capitalism (Spick 2007). It was an economic identity that held together in no small measure the German center-right. A similar story can be told of the British Conservative Party. Under the leadership of Anthony Eden, the British Tory entered the postwar period deploying the slogan of a "property owning democracy"—a useful concept that stitched together the middle class and the wealthy core of its base into a potentially broad economic coalition (Rothwell 1992). The key facilitating condition however, for the success of both of these conservative moderating efforts was this: in the postwar period income inequality was shrinking, and the gap between the richest and middle-income voters in a society was less pronounced. It was therefore easier for conservatives to appeal to middle-class voters on economic grounds when the gap between rich and middle class was not as severe. Put simply, the sharpness of conservative dilemma was diminished as long as economic inequality was lower.

No longer. The conservative dilemma has returned in the twenty-first century with a vengeance. Propelled by levels of inequality that only match pre–World War I levels, we have gone "back to the future" (Hacker and Pierson 2020). Over the past 30 years, as income inequality has again begun to skyrocket, just as it did before World War II, the conservative dilemma has returned. And conservatives, seeking to hold together much more economically heterogeneous coalitions, once again shape their campaigns on identity issues This has been at the core of the Republican's electoral strategy since at least the presidency of Barack Obama—and going back to the 1980s. The reinjection of race and fear of immigration into electoral politics has fueled the Republican Party electoral strategy for several decades, heightening in recent years (Levitsky and Ziblatt 2023). There is evidence of this also in the Republican response to the Biden administration's COVID relief bill, infrastructure bills, proposals to tax big corporations at a higher rate, and to raise taxes on the high-end income earners in society. These were large, and for the most part, popular economic measures. Republicans responded to this not by making counterarguments on the economic policy proposals but instead they've responded by trying to change the topic entirely. They try drawing attention instead to cancel culture, diversity, equity, and inclusion (DEI), Black Lives Matter, and immigration. It is on cultural issues that Republicans think they can win. This is a sign the conservative dilemma has returned.

Under conditions of high economic inequality, the revival of the conservative dilemma and the concomitant rise of identity issues may be an inherent feature of democracy. However, this dynamic is exacerbated by one further development: the transformation of established political parties across established democracies.

We live in increasingly civil society landscapes in which political parties have "hollowed out." This latter development has made our democracies more, not less vulnerable to the rise of demagogues and illiberal political forces. In short, what we are experiencing has one further uncanny echo from the past: weakened political parties and mainstream politicians can more easily lose control of the identity issues. One of the key lessons of my own research on pre–World War II conservatives is exactly that; when mainstream political parties lose control of the issues to outside surrogate groups, interest groups, advocacy groups, and radical civil society groups, the tail begins to wag the dog. This is what I documented in my research on conservative parties in Imperial and early Weimar Germany—before the rise of Nazism. In Weimar Germany it was nationalists and radical-right civil society groups, veterans' groups, antisemitic groups, various nationalist pressure groups, powerful media moguls, and rural agrarian leagues that pushed German conservative parties further to the right and, ultimately, into the fascist regime. The weakness of the German conservatism mean it relied on a strategy of organizational "outsourcing" of mobilization to narrow interest groups and ideological pressure groups. The result of course was calamitous.

X FOREWORD

A worrying parallel is visible today especially in the United States. Theda Skocpol's research on the role of the outside surrogate groups like Americans for Progress on the Koch Network on the Republican Party has made this clear (Skocpol forthcoming). So too has the research of Jacob Hacker and Paul Pierson made it plain that groups like the NRA and others have rotted out the organizational foundation of the Republican Party. Finally, most recently, the scholars Daniel Schlozman and Sam Rosenfeld have developed the thesis of the "hollow parties"—how political parties have become shells of their former selves, becoming reliant on outside surrogate groups to mobilize voters. The dangers of these developments, the past should teach us, are two-fold. First, political parties historically serve as gatekeepers, keeping demagogues from power; they may now be losing that capacity. Second, as political parties weaken, especially on the right, this opens the door to more radical, narrow interest groups that can hijack political parties or clear the way for the emergence of anti-system political parties to dominate the civil society landscape.

Why this is happening should be a major area of research but *that* it is happening—and not just in the United States—is clear. For example, nearly everywhere, the emergence of social media has eroded the influence of the establishment media. My coauthor of *How Democracies Die* (Steve Levitsky), visited Brazil at the beginning of that country's 2018 presidential election campaign. While he was there he met with business leaders, most of whom backed the established center-right candidate. Even though the candidate was down in the polls at the time Levitsky was visiting, business leaders were convinced the traditional candidate would win because he was backed by a broad mainstream coalition. This gave the candidate a huge advantage, which according to Brazil's elections laws, also gave him a huge advantage in allocated television time. He had access to free nightly television time whereas the right-wing candidate, Bolsonaro, had extremely limited airtime each night. No one that Levitsky spoke with in Sao Paulo mentioned WhatsApp or YouTube. But Bolsonaro used WhatsApp and YouTube to bypass the television networks and traditional parties. And of course he won the election.

In Germany today, a similar story can be told: the radical right Alternative for Germany (*Alternative für Deutschland*, AfD) doesn't necessarily need mainstream media institutions, let alone a traditional party structures. I was recently told by a journalist writing for a major German publication that the AfD no longer agrees to be interviewed by the mainstream media.

He said, "They don't need us." The AfD has its own YouTube channel that it can use to communicate directly with voters. They also dominate social media (including TikTok). In the six months before the 2019 European Parliament elections, Trevor Davis, Matthew Hindman, and Steven Livingston (2019) analyzed 220 million Facebook interactions and found that 86% of all Facebook shares of German political pages and 75% of comments of political news were connected to the AfD. The radical right dominated social media, at least in the 2019 elections. The establishment parties were seriously overshadowed, as the outsider party, the AfD, is reaching voters outside of traditional media channels. This continues today.

In sum, what all of this means is that politicians don't need the establishment political parties of the right as much as they once did. They can raise money online, and they can reach voters via social media platforms. And they can hijack political parties through primaries, as Donald Trump did in the United States. Or, in multiparty systems, they can create their own parties, such as the Five Star Movement in Italy or the AfD in Germany. For politicians, especially outsider politicians, this is quite liberating. It's much easier to bypass the established parties of the right than it was 50 years ago. This scenario, however, leaves us more vulnerable to demagogues, many of whom, once in office, to assault democratic institutions. When we combine institutional porousness with the return of the conservative dilemma, and the emergence of new online organizations such as QAnon, we find ourselves in dangerous terrain.

We sometimes think that more democracy means fewer rules. This might not be the case. In fact, more democracy might require *more rules*. Like today, the early twentieth century was also marked by the rise of new technologies, including radio. These technologies opened the door to demagogues. The response to this new reality in the United States was the invention of new regulatory structures like the Federal Communications Commission in the 1930s to combat some of these developments and the emergence of the Fairness Doctrine in 1949 to guarantee balance in the airwaves. We need the equivalent regulatory structures for our own age. Democracy is certainly about making political and social institutions more inclusive. It is also about making our institutions arenas of fairer and freer competition. But to make such institutions endure, we need to recognize that democracy contains vulnerabilities. One of these is demagogues who use the very institutions of democracy to attack it. With new threats, we need to develop new rules, new regulations to protect ourselves and our institutions.

In the 1880s, James Russell Lowell, editor of *The Atlantic Monthly*, was looking back to the US Civil War some two decades earlier. He regarded it as having triggered a breakdown in faith in American democracy. He wrote, "After our Constitution got fairly into working order, it really seemed that we had invented a *machine that would go of itself*. And this begot a faith in our luck which even the Civil War itself but momentarily disturbed." Lowell knew it was dangerous to think of democracy as a machine that would go of itself. Democracy is not some kind of perpetual motion machine. It requires mending, new rules, and new regulations, to make it endure. This seems to me to be the central agenda facing all of us as we think about the new threats facing democracy. This Social Science Research Council project led by Steven Livingston and Michael Miller helps us understand the scope of the problems that arise from broad economic and social inequality and conservative party surrogate organizations, both on and offline.

References

Gibson, Edward. 2001. *Class and Conservative Parties: Argentina in Comparative Perspective.* Baltimore: Johns Hopkins University Press.

Hacker, Jacob, and Paul Pierson. 2020. *Let them Eat Tweets: How the Right Rules in an Age of Inequality.* New York: Liveright.

Levitsky, Steven, and Daniel Ziblatt. 2023. *Tyranny of the Minority: Why American Democracy Reached the Breaking Point.* New York: Crown Books.

Rothwell, Victor. 1992. *Anthony Eden: a Political Biography, 1931–1957.* Manchester, UK: University of Manchester Press.

Skocpol, Theda. Forthcoming. "The Trumpist Turn in U.S. Politics." In Andrew Rudalevige, Julia Azari, and Bert Rockman, eds., *The Trump Legacy.* Lawrence: University of Kansas Press.

Spick, Mark. 2007. *Selling the Economic Miracle: Economic Reconstruction and Politics in West Germany, 1949–1957.* New York: Berghahn Press.

Urwin, Derek. 1997. *A Political History of Western Europe Since 1945.* New York: Routledge.

Preface
Steven Livingston and Michael Miller

This book's origins are found in workshops organized by the Social Science Research Council (SSRC) in New York and by the Institute for Data, Democracy, and Politics (IDDP) at George Washington University in Washington, DC. The first virtual meeting in 2021 featured keynote presentations by political historian Daniel Ziblatt (2021) of Harvard University and data scientist Kate Starbird (2021) of the University of Washington. A second meeting of invited contributors was convened in Washington, DC in March 2022. These meetings continued the work of an earlier SSRC working group co-led by Lance Bennett and Steven Livingston. It produced *The Disinformation Age*: *Politics, Technology, and Disruptive Communication in the United States* (2019).

Selecting a well-regarded political historian and a renowned data scientist as featured speakers at our inaugural meeting signals the book's central ambition. We believe explaining democratic backsliding in the twenty-first century requires cross-disciplinary engagement. Ziblatt and other democracy scholars describe the necessary social and economic conditions for a healthy democracy. Starbird and other data scientists and media scholars tell us something about the role of digital platforms in the realization (or not) of these same conditions. In this volume, these two broad research traditions are woven together to create an analytical framework we believe explains a core threat to democracy in the twenty-first century. We argue that the threat to democracy comes from the organization of illiberal movements, both on and offline. Put differently, we argue that democratic backsliding is the consequence of *far-right connective action*. "Digital surrogate organizations" or networks are entwined with more conventional organizations aligned with conservative parties, which are themselves facing a uniquely precarious position in democracies that are mired in social and economic inequality. To explain what is happening to liberal democracy in the twenty-first century requires us to draw on the insights of several research fields. Here is our vision of the joint effort.

Democracy scholars, or what we shall call in this volume *institutionalists* or the "institutionalist model," constitute an interdisciplinary field that includes economists, sociologists, historians, and political scientists who respectively emphasize the critical role of economics, elites, and organized interests in society, historical contingency, and political parties when considering the threats to liberal democracy. Institutionalists look outward to society when searching for an explanation of backsliding.

A technocentric model of democratic backsliding is an interdisciplinary field involving data scientists, computational social scientists, sociologists, political communication researchers, and computer scientists. Technocentric explanations of democratic backsliding look to features of digital networks (affordances) and their effects on individual-level cognitive processes. To date, despite their shared intellectual focus on democracy, there has been little overlap between these two fields of study. For the institutionalists, digital space is terra ignota; for media scholars, long-established democracy theory is something akin to codices. Yet the skills and insights of both traditions are essential to any serious effort to explain democratic backsliding in the twenty-first century. As Jürgen Habermas notes in a 2022 reflection on the political public sphere in an era of digitized politics, media scholars must remain attentive to social context.

> For it is only against *the backdrop of the complex causes of the crisis tendencies of capitalist democracies* in general that we can assess the limited contribution that the digitalization of public communication may add to the *other relevant causes of an impairment of deliberative opinion and will formation.* (Habermas 2022, emphasis added)

How can we understand the role of digital platforms and networks in the context of the crisis tendencies of democratic capitalism? In this volume, we assess the effects of digitized public communication on democracy without losing sight of social and economic power structures. In this preface, we begin with a brief primer on the main contours of the institutionalist research literature. After that, we review the plan of the book.

Institutionalist Approach to Explaining Democratic Consolidation and Backsliding

While there is nothing like a consensus among the historians, political scientists, and economists who study democracy, much of the debate revolves around a handful of factors that are thought to be associated with democratic consolidation or backsliding. In some measure, much of the debate involves differences in the allocation of weight that should be given to one or another of these factors (Lust and Waldner 2015; Bernhard and O'Neill 2021; Andersen 2019; Carothers and Press 2022). While some democracy scholars emphasize economics, others emphasize the effects of civic culture, elites, political parties, or various combinations of each. The focus on parties, civic associations, elites, and economic disparities comes together in Daniel Ziblatt's conservative dilemma model, used in this volume as a centerpiece of the institutionalist literature (2017).

According to Ziblatt's conservative dilemma model, as he explains in the forward to this volume, conservative parties such as the Tories in the United Kingdom or the Republicans in the United States face daunting circumstances, especially during times of great social and economic inequality. They must on the one hand find ways to remain competitive in fair and free elections where majorities matter while *also* remaining loyal to economic elites, with whom they are most closely aligned. They must learn to "play the numbers game," as Ziblatt describes it. Put differently, while remaining loyal to the economic and social power structures, conservative parties must find ways to appeal to voters who are not economically privileged. *Parties do so by priming elections with nonmaterial issues that are intended to mobilize publics across class divides* (Eggert and Giugni 2015; Kriesi 2010; Hooghe and Marks 2018). So-called cross-cutting cleavage issues mobilize publics by tapping into existing social identity divisions. As Hacker and Pierson (2020, 22) note, to be effective, cross-cutting cleavage issues cannot be trivial or temporary: "In modern societies, the list of such 'cleavages' is short, and their history unpleasant." They are often "racially tinged, all involving strong identities and strong emotions—that draw a sharp line between 'us' and 'them'." Several of the chapters in this volume take close looks at the nature of cross-cutting issues.

Second, a conservative party must find allies—organizations that have manageable degrees of separateness from the party. Ziblatt calls these advocacy allies "surrogate organizations." They are often civil society groups, social movements, agrarian leagues, and media organizations. If all goes as expected, the dilemma is mitigated. As a conservative party gains confidence that it has a chance of winning fair and free elections, albeit elections that fail to address social and economic inequality and despair, it will be less inclined to turn to more direct anti-democratic measures in an effort to cling

xvi PREFACE

to power. Of course, all of this comes at a price: the conditions in greatest need of systematic redress—deep disparities in the life and well-being of citizens—remain sublimated by identity grievance issues.

But even in the more optimistic scenario, surrogates are a mixed blessing, as the institutionalist literature's ambivalence about civil society organizations suggests (Armony 2004; Almond and Verba 1963; Berman 1997; Bermeo 2003). Surrogates and the issues they promote can quickly drift into extremism. In some cases, surrogates can become more powerful and popular than the party itself. In this way, news organizations or other surrogate organizations can pull a party into uncompromising stances that fly in the face of democratic norms. Of course, some in the party are quite eager for this to happen (Bermeo 2003).

In sum, the health and vitality of democracy is, according to the institutionalist literature, affected by economic conditions, the nature of governing elites and their relationship with publics, the nature of civil society organizations, and by the issues they champion. What this research tradition has yet to do is give sustained thought to the ways social media and other digital platforms affect the organization of publics, the nature of civil society organizations, or the role of political parties as mediating organizations. Our goal is to fill that gap.

Digital Surrogate Organizations

The aim of this volume is to build on the conventional understanding of surrogate organizations with insights gained by media studies scholars about the nature of organizing and organizations in digital space. To the concerns about the potentially volatile combination of conventional surrogate organizations championing highly emotive issues, we add that organizations are now constituted online. W. Lance Bennett and Alexandra Segerberg put it this way: "Communication routines can, under some conditions, create patterned relationships among people that lend organization and structure to many aspects of social life." Beyond basic transmission of information, communication mechanisms, "establish relationships, activate attentive participants, channel various resources, and establish narratives and discourses" (2014, 304). Hashtags, Facebook groups, and subreddits emerge and facilitate patterned relationships among people online. In this way, "technology-enabled networks may become dynamic organizations in their own right (Bennett and Segerberg 2014, 297; see also Parsloe and Holton 2018; Vaast et al. 2017; Suk et al. 2021; Mirbabaie et al. 2021).

Unlike a conventional organization, digitally enabled organizations are in a constant state of *becoming*. They are liminal. Digitally enabled organizations are also less hierarchical, more fluid and organically reactive to exogenous stimuli, which is to say less bound by formal roles and rules. Participation is often motivated by social expressions of identity—or what Bennett and Segerberg call personal action frames. Lifestyle elements organize personalized political meaning concerning issues such as climate change (buy sustainably certified produces, recycle, and avoid single-use plastics), food production (buy fair trade labeled products). "Seemingly disparate issues become related as they fit into crosscutting demographics and consumer lifestyles" (Bennett and Segerberg 2014, 1502). Today, opposition to a vaguely defined "wokism" and non-normative lifestyle choices seem to constitute some of the far-right personal action frames.

How do digitally enabled organizational forms affect the stability of liberal democracy? If conventional surrogates are a mixed blessing, how might *digitally constituted organizations* affect the stability of democracy? Even conventional surrogates can "quickly and easily overrun and capture weak and institutionally porous parties" (Ziblatt 2017, 174). In this volume we ask how "digital surrogates" affect the stability of democracy during times of great social and economic inequality.

Plan of Book

In Chapter 1, W. Lance Bennett and Steven Livingston present the volume's framing argument. The "communication as organization" concept brings the institutionalist focus on social, economic, and political factors into the digital age. In addition to conventional surrogate organizations mobilizing cross-class coalitions with highly emotive issues, publics are now also mobilized online. As several of the chapters in this volume note, #QAnon or #StoptheSteal offer examples of digitally enabled surrogate organizations. At the same time, the connective action model Bennett and Livingston outline brings greater awareness of the role of social power structures to political communication scholars who tend to favor more technocentric explanations of democratic backsliding. In other words, social, political, and economic factors are imbraided with the explanations that attribute backsliding to technological factors.

xviii PREFACE

In Chapter 2, in her examination of events leading up to the Capitol Insurrection on January 6th, 2021, Kate Starbird illustrates Bennett and Livingston's far-right connective action framework. Conventional surrogate organizations operating from a top-down position propagated easily shared personal action frames, such as "rigged election" and "voter fraud." As Starbird notes, "Through repetition of these claims, which echoed across social media as well as partisan media outlets online and on cable television, President Trump set a frame and an expectation among his followers of a 'rigged' election. This frame became a lens through which his supporters interpreted the events of the 2020 US election, as it "provided the motivation and a pathway for them to participate." Participation involved everyday people gathering "evidence" that fits the personal action frame. These claims are then amplified by online networks and then echoed back down from elites and conventional surrogates, including members of Congress.

In Chapter 3, Josephine Lukito, Yunkang Yang, and Sang Jung Kim trace the emergence of QAnon on anonymous imageboards such as 4chan and 8kun. They soon evolved into a hybrid organization with links to the Republican Party. By tracking the emergence of the GOP/QAnon hybrid organization, Lukito and her colleagues show how "communication as organization" pulls conventional parties into illiberal terrain. As they remark, "As a digital surrogate for the GOP, an extremist online group must adapt its narratives, develop organizational capacities and resilience, and gain acknowledgment from the GOP. QAnon, therefore, makes for a useful case to study how online fringe groups develop into digital surrogates." Running through several of the chapters is a similar observation about the role of narratives—common themes across national cases—in forming what we call digital surrogate organizations.

Daniel Kreiss and Aaron Sugarman continue the focus on QAnon in Chapter 4 by analyzing the uptake of its symbols and narratives by Republican Party candidates. As a digital surrogate organization, QAnon offers a set of symbolic resources or narratives to Republican candidates that evoke white, Christian, and heteronormative identities. "We argue," says Kreiss and Sugarman, "that QAnon has created a rich cultural field of ideas encoded in discourse that Republican candidates draw from in their attempts to mobilize their electorates." They end with a sobering conclusion: if surrogate organizations of a conventional sort run the risk of pulling a conventional conservative party into illiberal terrain, as the conservative dilemma literature argues, the structure and debate occurring on online platforms is less governable and more likely to erode boundary spaces between a conventional conservative party and a radical fringe. Fringe candidates who might have once been held in check by institutional gatekeepers now have access to ungovernable digital platforms. This is illustrated by current GOP members of the US House of Representatives Marjorie Taylor Greene and Lauren Boebert, both of whom have embraced QAnon symbols. A more recent characterization of Representative Greene captures the point: she has been referred to as "the leader of the Outburst Caucus," someone who exemplifies "the struggles that (former) House Speaker Kevin McCarthy has in controlling the behavior, let alone the votes, of his conference" (Viser and Wang 2023).

One of the strengths of the institutionalist research literature is its historical comparativist approach. Ziblatt (2017), for example, draws on several European historical cases, while Bermeo (2003) focuses on cases from Latin America and Europe. While most chapters in this volume focus on the United States, two chapters offer case studies that draw on first German and then Japanese politics. Besides the deep scholarly interest and value found in the application of our connective action model to non-US cases, these chapters also offer points of contrast with our main cases. Like a relief sculpture projecting from a two-dimensional foundation, applying our connective action model to non-US cases helps us begin to ask questions about how well the model might explain a broad array of cases from around the world. For example, moving forward, one might ask questions about the comparative effects of differing civil society cultures, differing electoral or party systems, or differences emerging from national perspectives on social media content regulations. In such a limited space we can only begin to suggest the contours of a comparativist research agenda.

In Chapter 5, Curd Knüpfer and Ulrike Klinger draw attention to German politics in their analysis of the far-right *Alternative für Deutschland* (AfD). Along the way, they also make the point that similar analyses are possible for the Vox party in Spain and the Sweden Democrats, among others. The AfD began as a neoliberal political party supporting an unpopular economic agenda. To mobilize broader public support, it eventually turned anti-immigration narratives as "cross-cutting cleavage issues." This also involved taking advantage of the affordances of alternative media spheres and enlisting digital surrogate organizations. As the authors state, "Tapping into these networks ultimately also meant that the party surrendered autonomy to more extreme actor types and led to the increasing radicalization of its platform and leadership." At this point, even the ontological status of the networks is unclear, or as Knüpfer and Klinger put it, "without clearly identifying as actually existing persons or institutions." Yet they function as digital surrogate organizations, "active across various social media platforms where they are extremely prolific in amplifying the party's messages."

What holds digital surrogate organizations together? A meaningful and mutually shared *narrative* "establishes and maintains a discursive network's architecture." Like Bennett and Segerberg's personal action frames, narratives shape a collective sense of meaning and create ties between political actors and their audiences. This seems like Kreiss and Sugarman's observations about the role of "a rich cultural field of ideas encoded in discourse" in the pull of an extremist fringe on a conventional party structure. In a sense, narratives seem to have less to do with updating prior beliefs than they have to do with offering ritual spaces where common identities and shared meanings are reaffirmed (Carey 2009). In this respect, Ziblatt's (and Hacker and Pierson's references to "cross-cutting issues" might be better understood as "deep stories" about meaning and identity. They are stories, explanations that "feel true" to the observer (Hochschild 2016, 16). Narratives, Knüpfer and Klinger suggest, provide a broader analytical framework in which cross-cutting issues and surrogate organizations mobilize publics across class lines (Miskimmon et al. 2013). The thematic content of far-right narratives includes references to a global hegemonic cabal of progressive or leftist forces (often accompanied by antisemitic tropes) that suppress and vilify conservative ideas and actors who are themselves facing an existential threat to their very way of life. This powerful analytical framework is aligned with the arguments made by Parker and Blum on the narrative elements of the MAGA movement and with Bahador and Kerchner's findings concerning hate speech on conservative media in the United States.

Chapter 6 offers another opportunity to gauge possible differences in how our connective action model works outside the United States. Julia R. DeCook and Brett J. Fujioka offer a fascinating look at the rise of a Japanese far-right group, the *netto uyoku* (translation: the online far right). The *netto uyoku* are a leaderless, digital social movement that have had tremendous influence on mainstream beliefs. As they note, "Focusing on the U.S. context misses some critical history about the nature of online spaces in the formation of meaning and construction of political realities." Continuing with the focus on the role of narratives that has emerged in the chapters so far, DeCook and Fujioka argue that the crisis of social cohesion and the

PREFACE xxi

postmodern collapse of "grand narratives" help to explain the emergence of these alternative political groups, including surrogate organizations. Here they are echoing Bennett and Livingston's point in *The Disinformation Age* (2020) that carries over to this volume. The adoption of factually unanchored beliefs, including grand conspiracy theories like QAnon, is not only a matter of nefarious trolls, relentless bots, and sophisticated algorithms. There is also, as DeCook and Fujioka put it, "external social and cultural factors that influence these types of behavior and political action as well." Conspiracy theories fill the crisis of meaning that emerges from the erosion of trust and credibility of formally authoritative institutions and the social order they defined. We see this dynamic play out in Japan, the United States, and probably elsewhere around the world, irrespective of variations in political systems and legal regimes. As DeCook and Fujioka put it,

> In the West, the grand narratives that held society together came from the Enlightenment, democracy, capitalism, Christianity, Liberalism, Marxism, and modernism. For the Japanese, the postmodern period was defined by the collapse of high-economic growth, the oil shocks, the waning of the Season of Politics (the student protest movement), and a succession of domestic terrorist attacks beginning with the Asamo-Sanso incident by the United Red Army.

With Adam Hilton's contribution in Chapter 7, we return to the United States with questions concerning the divergent relationships the Democratic and Republican parties have with their respective surrogate organizations. What is it about the GOP that has made it susceptible to radicalizing surrogates, including now digital surrogates? Hilton notes that the literature on American party politics recognizes that the Republicans have shifted dramatically to the right while Democrats have moved only modestly to the left. Hilton argues that this is the result of the "unique and divergent developmental paths the parties have travelled for decades, specifically regarding their relationships with social movement organizations and interest group networks as surrogate organizations of the pre-digital age." One of the key contributions Hilton makes is his clarification as to what constitutes a strong party. Ziblatt's model contends that "weak conservative parties" are most susceptible to the pull of powerful surrogates. Hilton invites us to rethink our assumptions about what makes for a strong party.

xxii PREFACE

Christopher Sebastian Parker and Rachel M. Blum's contribution in Chapter 8 takes us back to a fascinating consideration of the nature of cross-cutting cleavage issues. The conservative dilemma model claims that to remain competitive, especially during times of social and economic inequality, conservative parties form alliances with surrogate organizations that help champion cross-cutting cleavage issues. As Knüpfer and Klinger astutely observe in their German case, such issues tend to have similar narrative structures. Parker and Blum argue that it is a status threat that drives MAGA adherence to disinformation and conspiracy theories, and to embrace illiberal politics. This observation aligns with the earlier chapters that emphasize the role of narratives in extending Ziblatt's notion of surrogate organizations with our friendly addendum concerning digital networks. As Parker and Blum conclude, "it appears that symbolic, identity-related explanations carry the day when it comes to understanding attachment to the MAGA movement, in both word and deed. . . . In terms of the model here, MAGA is a cross-class coalition, just as would be expected. Extensive research has found that Tea Party supporters were fueled more by cultural anxiety, not concerns over government spending."

In Chapter 9, Steven Feldstein follows with an important reminder: digital surrogate organizations are logical extensions of a much older conservative media infrastructure that remains a part of the broader digital networks now pulling the GOP into authoritarianism. As he puts it, "the synergies and connections between the mass media ecosystem and internet platforms have provided fertile ground for rightwing conservative entrepreneurs, acting as political surrogates, to seed narratives on talk radio or Fox News and to then exploit the virality of social media to disseminate disinformation on an industrial scale." The role of Fox News and right-wing talk radio in propagating conspiratorial narratives should not be overlooked.

In Chapter 10, Babak Bahador and Dan Kerchner offer an empirical examination of the nature of contemporary cross-cutting cleavage issues in the United States. Much in keeping with Parker and Blum's argument in Chapter 8, Bahador and Kirchner find that right-wing media outlets traffic in hate filled narratives. Blacks are vilified the most, followed by immigrants and Muslims. As they conclude, "The findings from this chapter and underlying study provide evidence to support claims that the conservative media, as surrogate organizations, were disproportionately focused on outrage narratives targeting protected status groups associated with their political opposition."

PREFACE   xxiii

In Chapter 11, Andrew Ifedapo Thompson raises interesting questions about the underlying logic driving GOP politics. According to the logic of the conservative dilemma model, conservative parties face a numbers challenge in democratic elections. On the one hand, they are most closely aligned with a status quo often defined by its vast social and economic inequality. Yet conservative parties must find a way to either win at the polls or undermine democracy. The former calls for an effort to prime the election on cross-cutting issues, on the grand narratives that several of this volume's contributors have pointed to in their respective chapters. But Thompson argues that Republican Party leaders have wrongly perceived coming racial demographic trends as *inevitably* supporting the Democratic Party. This is simply not the case, according to his research findings. As he notes, this false assumption has real-world political consequences: "The influence of this idea lays a foundation in which the party is significantly more susceptible to influence by surrogate organizations that can effectively advance ideas of racial threat *and, in turn,* push the party away from commitments to democracy."

Drawing on his previous work on the greater reliance on data analytics by advocacy organizations—broadly, elements of what we here are calling surrogate organizations, in Chapter 12 David Karpf explores "digital listening" and the rise of illiberal politics. If cross-cutting cleavage issues are, as Knüpfer and Klinger claim, a narrative or deep story about a global hegemonic cabal that suppress and vilify conservative ideas and actors facing an existential threat, how do variations on this theme emerge? One day the threat is from immigrant caravans, the next it's critical race theory, Antifa, or threats to a key element of the American way of life: "stores of gas"?. These can be seen as variations on a narrative theme, like a fugue of far-right fears.

In the concluding chapter, Steven Livingston and Michael Miller address some of the remaining questions. First, we discuss the inversion of two key components of Ziblatt's model. In simple terms, he argues that conservative parties join surrogate organizations (qua interest groups, media organizations, civic associations of various types) to promote issues that have the capacity to mobilize publics from across class divides. The danger in this is found in the possibility that surrogates might prove to be more popular than the party, and more radical in their embrace of far-right politics. The point of a cleavage issue is to exacerbate existing social cleavages around race, ethnicity, religion, and other nonmaterial ways societies divide themselves. In the connective action model presented in this volume, these relationships

xxiv PREFACE

are scrambled. Most especially, the relationship between "surrogate organizations" and cross-cutting cleavage issues is changed in a fundamental way. If one accepts Bennett and Segerberg's (2013) claim that routinized patterns of communication can be understood as constitutive of organization, one is led to the conclusion than online networks sustained by narratives *are surrogate organizations*. Narratives have the ontological status of surrogate organizations. And if online networks are largely leaderless and uncontrollable, what hope is there that a conservative party will find the means to maintain boundary spaces between its core principles and its fringe? We explore this question in the concluding chapter.

Before one can hope to find a solution to any problem one must specify the nature of the problem. Our ambition in this volume rests here, in coming to a clearer understanding of the causes of democratic erosion. In so doing, we hope to point the way to the development of solutions that fit the scope of the problem. On their own, the solutions that arise from a technocentric model of democratic backsliding—media literacy, fact checking, and content moderation—seem inadequate to the challenges to democracy that have been identified by institutionalists scholars.

References

Almond, Gabriel, and Sidney Verba. 1963. *The Civic Culture: Political Attitudes and Democracy in Five Nations*. New York: Sage Publishing.

Andersen, David. 2019. "Review of *Comparative Democratization and Democratic Backsliding: The Case for a Historical-Institutional Approach*, by Daniel Ziblatt, Stephan Haggard, Robert R. Kaufman, and Steven Levitsky." *Comparative Politics* 51 (4): 645–663.

Armony, Ariel C. 2004. *The Dubious Link: Civic Engagement and Democratization*. Stanford, CA: Stanford University Press.

Bennett, Lance W., and Steven Livingston. 2020. *The Disinformation Age: Politics, Technology, and Disruptive Communication in the United States*. New York: Cambridge University Press.

Bennett, Lance W., and Alexandra Segerberg. 2013 (2014 Kindle). *The Logic of Connective Action: Digital Media and the Personalization of Contentious Politics*. New York: Cambridge University Press.

Berman, Sheri. 1997. "Civil Society and the Collapse of the Weimar Republic." *World Politics* 49 (3): 401–429.

Bermeo, Nancy G. 2003. *Ordinary People in Extraordinary Times*. Princeton, NJ: Princeton University Press.

Bernhard, Michael, and Daniel O'Neill. 2021. "Comparative Historical Analysis." *Perspectives on Politics* 19 (3): 699–704.

Carey, James. 2009. *Communication as Culture*. Revised edition. New York: Routledge.

Carothers, Thomas, and Benjamin Press. 2022. "Understanding and Responding to Global Democratic Backsliding." October. Carnegie Endowment for International Peace Working Paper. https://carnegieendowment.org/files/Carothers_Press_Democratic_Backsliding_v3_1.pdf.

Eggert, Nina, and Marco Giugni. 2015. "Does the Class Cleavage Still Matter? The Social Composition of Participants in Demonstrations Addressing Redistributive and Cultural Issues in Three Countries." *International Sociology* 30 (1): 21–38.

Habermas, Jürgen. 2022. "Reflections and Hypotheses on a Further Structural Transformation of the Political Public Sphere." *Theory, Culture & Society* 39 (4). https://doi-org.proxygw.wrlc.org/10.1177/02632764221112341.

Hacker, Jacob S. and Paul Pierson. 2020. *Let Them Eat Tweets: How the Right Rules in an Age of Extreme Inequality.* New York: Liveright.

Hochschild, Arlie Russell. 2016. *Strangers in their Own Land: Anger and Mourning on the American Right.* New York: The New Press.

Hooghe, Liesbet, and Gary Marks. 2018. "Cleavage Theory Meets Europe's Crises: Lipset, Rokkan, and the Transnational Cleavage." *Journal of European Public Policy* 25 (1): 109–135.

Kriesi, Hanspeter. 2010. "Restructuration of Partisan Politics and the Emergence of a New Cleavage Based on Values." *West European Politics* 33 (3): 673–685.

Lust, Ellen, and David Waldner. 2015. "Unwelcome Change: Understanding, Evaluating, and Extending Theories of Democratic Backsliding." June 11. US Agency for International Development. https://pdf.usaid.gov/pdf_docs/PBAAD635.pdf

Mirbabaie, Milad, Felix Brünker, Magdalena Wischnewski, and Judith Meinert. 2021. "The Development of Connective Action during Social Movements on Social Media." *ACM Transactions on Social Computing* 4 (1): 1–21.

Miskimmon, Alister, Ben O'Loughlin, and Laura. Roselle (2013). *Strategic Narratives: Communication Power and the New World Order.* New York: Routledge.

Parsloe, Sarah M., and Avery E. Holton. 2018. "# Boycottautismspeaks: Communicating a Counternarrative through Cyberactivism and Connective Action." *Information, Communication & Society* 21 (8): 1116–1133.

Starbird, Kate. 2021. "A Changed Landscape: Conceptual and Institutional Foundations of the Conservative Dilemma." May 4. The Conservative Dilemma: Digital Surrogate Organizations and the Future of Liberal Democracy, SSRC/IDDP. https://www.youtube.com/watch?v=-ASzPcCcynI&t=109s.

Suk, Jiyoun, Aman Abhishek, Yini Zhang, So Yun Ahn, Teresa Correa, Christine Garlough, and Dhavan V. Shah. 2021. "# MeToo, Networked Acknowledgment, and Connective Action: How 'Empowerment Through Empathy' Launched a Social Movement." *Social Science Computer Review* 39 (2): 276–294.

Vaast, Emmanuelle, Hani Safadi, Liette Lapointe, and Bogdan Negoita. 2017. "Social Media Affordances for Connective Action: An Examination of Microblogging Use during the Gulf of Mexico Oil Spill." *MIS Quarterly* 41 (4): 1179–1206.

Viser, Matt, and Amy B. Wang. 2023. "Marjorie Taylor Greene Yells 'Liar' during Combative State of the Union." *Washington Post,* February 8. https://www.washingtonpost.com/politics/2023/02/08/state-of-union-hecklers-marjorie-taylor-greene/

Ziblatt, Daniel. 2017. *Conservative Political Parties and the Birth of Democracy.* New York: Cambridge University Press.

Ziblatt, Daniel. 2021. "A Deepening Crisis: The Role of 'Digital Surrogate Organizations' in Conservative Parties." May 3. The Conservative Dilemma: Digital Surrogate Organizations and the Future of Liberal Democracy, SSRC/IDDP. https://www.youtube.com/watch?v=Qq_jck6PMnM.

Author Biographies

Babak Bahador is a research professor at the School of Media and Public Affairs (SMPA) at George Washington University and senior fellow at the University of Canterbury in New Zealand. He holds a PhD in international relations from the London School of Economics. His research focuses on the overlap of media and politics/international relations, with primary focus on peacebuilding.

W. Lance Bennett is senior research fellow at the Center for Journalism, Media and Democracy, and emeritus professor of Communication and Political Science and at the University of Washington, Seattle. He has lectured and published on media and information systems, press-government relations, citizenship and civic engagement, digital activism, and problems of disinformation in democracies. He has held visiting professorships at Harvard, Uppsala, Stockholm, and Free University, Berlin, and was awarded honorary doctorates from Uppsala and Bern. He has received career achievement awards from the American Political Science Association, The International Communication Association, and the US National Communication Association, along with a German Humboldt Research Prize for distinguished international scholarship. Selected publications include *The Logic of Connective Action* (2013, with Alexandra Segerberg), *The Disinformation Age* (open access, 2020, with Steven Livingston), and *Communicating the Future: Solutions for Environment, Economy and Democracy* (2021).

Rachel M. Blum is assistant professor in the Carl Albert Congressional Research and Studies Center and the department of political science at the University of Oklahoma. She is the author of *How the Tea Party Captured the GOP: Insurgent Factions in American Politics* (2020). Her current projects include *The Enemy Within: MAGA and American Democracy* (with Chris Parker).

Julia R. DeCook (PhD, Michigan State University) is a former academic and independent scholar. Her research focuses on platform governance and policy, online hate groups and digital culture, and the affordances of web infrastructure. She currently works in the tech industry as a researcher and policy specialist.

Steven Feldstein is a senior fellow at the Carnegie Endowment for International Peace in the Democracy, Conflict, and Governance Program. He is the author of *The Rise of Digital Repression: How Technology is Reshaping Power, Politics, and Resistance* (2021), which is the recipient of the 2023 Grawemeyer Award for Ideas Improving World Order. Previously he was the holder of the Frank and Bethine Church Chair of Public Affairs and an associate professor at Boise State University. He has served in multiple foreign policy positions in the US government.

Brett J. Fujioka (MS, University of Illinois at Urbana Champaign) is an independent researcher and freelance writer. His research interests include Japanese media and culture. His work has appeared in a number of venues, including *NOEMA, Giant Robot Magazine,* and *Tablet Magazine.*

Adam Hilton is associate professor of politics at Mount Holyoke College. His research focuses on the intersection of institutional and contentious forms of politics, especially the dynamic interrelationship of parties and outside groups as co-evolutionary forces in American political development. His book *True Blues: The Contentious Transformation of the Democratic Party,* was published in 2021.

David Karpf is an associate professor in the George Washington University School of Media and Public Affairs. He teaches and conducts research on strategic political communication in the digital age. He is the author of *The MoveOn Effect* (2012) and *Analytic Activism* (2016).

Daniel Kerchner is a senior software developer and librarian at George Washington University (GWU). He holds an MS in systems engineering from the University of Virginia and a BS in applied and engineering physics from Cornell University. He is also a graduate student in health and biomedical data science with a concentration in bioinformatics, at GWU's Milken Institute School of Public Health.

Sang Jung Kim (PhD, University of Wisconsin-Madison) is an assistant professor of journalism and mass communication at the University of Iowa. She studies the interaction between technology, politics, and social identity, with

xxviii AUTHOR BIOGRAPHIES

particular attention to the mediating role of social media platforms and the spread of information to the public.

Ulrike Klinger is professor of political communication and journalism at the University of Amsterdam and the Amsterdam School of Communication Research ASCoR. Her research focuses on political communication, the transformation of digital publics, and the role of technologies in democratic societies.

Curd Knüpfer is an associate professor at the Digital Democracy Centre of the University of Southern Denmark. His research focuses on political communication, with a particular emphasis right-wing media, transnational information flows, and the digitalization of democratic media systems.

Daniel Kreiss is the Edgar Thomas Cato Distinguished Professor in the Hussman School of Journalism and Media at the University of North Carolina at Chapel Hill and a principal researcher of the Center for Information, Technology, and Public Life. Kreiss coedits the Oxford University Press book series Journalism and Political Communication Unbound and is an associate editor of political communication.

Steven Livingston is the founding director of the Institute for Data, Democracy, and Politics and Professor of Media and Public Affairs at George Washington University (GW) in Washington, DC. He is also a senior fellow in the Illiberal Studies Program at GW, and in 2023, a senior fellow at the Contestation of the Liberal Script Cluster of Excellence at the Freie Universität-Berlin. He has also been a Fulbright Scholar at the University of Helsinki (2021). He has also been a senior fellow at the Carr Center for Human Rights Policy at the Harvard Kennedy School, Harvard University.

Josephine Lukito ("Jo") is an assistant professor at the University of Texas at Austin's School of Journalism and Media. She is also the director of the Media & Democracy Data Cooperative and a senior faculty research affiliate for the Center for Media Engagement. Jo uses mixed methods and computational approaches to study political language in the multiplatform information ecology.

Michael Miller is the managing director of the Moynihan Center at The City College of New York (CCNY). Miller is a scholar of media, technology, and politics, with a focus on the ways that authoritarian regimes have adapted modes of information control—censorship, surveillance, and propaganda—to digital media environments. Prior to joining CCNY, Miller was a program director at the Social Science Research Council (SSRC), where he led the Media & Democracy program and the Just Tech program and served as chief editor for the Just Tech Platform. Miller received his PhD in political science from the Graduate Center at the City University of New York (CUNY).

Christopher Sebastian Parker is professor of political science at the University of California, Santa Barbara. He is the coauthor of *Change They Can't Believe In: The Tea Party and Reactionary Politics in America* (2013), and author of *Fighting for Democracy: Black Veterans and the Struggle against White Supremacy in the Postwar South* (2009). He is currently at work on *The Enemy Within: MAGA and American Democracy* (with Rachel Blum).

Kate Starbird is an associate professor in the Department of Human Centered Design & Engineering (HCDE), where she studies online rumors and disinformation campaigns. She is also a cofounder of the University of Washington's Center for an Informed Public, which formed in 2019 around a shared mission of resisting strategic misinformation, promoting an informed society, and strengthening democratic discourse.

Aaron Sugarman is a policy analyst who has worked with the Global Disinformation Index and other civil society organizations to address online harms, digital economies, and regulatory compliance. He received his MSc in media and communications governance from the London School of Economics and a BA with highest distinction in political science and peace, war, and defense from the University of North Carolina at Chapel Hill.

Andrew Ifedapo Thompson is an assistant professor whose research focuses on how perceptions of racial demographic change in the US drive democratic erosion. He shows in his book project and across a series of articles how there are key presumptions Americans make about the changing American landscape that are grounded in historical ideas about Black political enfranchisement that go on to cause conservative and Republican-minded Americans to turn away from the system of democracy. His current research goes about using different messaging frameworks that stem from these same ideas to reduce these same anti-democratic views.

Yunkang Yang (PhD, University of Washington) is an assistant professor of communication at Texas A&M University. He is also a faculty affiliate with A&M's Data Justice Lab and a fellow at the Weizenbaum Institute for the Networked Society. Yang's research focuses on US right-wing media, misinformation, and social media.

Chapter 1
Technological and Institutional Roots of Democratic Backsliding in the United States

W. Lance Bennett and Steven Livingston

In a 2021 report, V-Dem, a research institute at the University of Gothenburg in Sweden, concluded, "Advances in global levels of democracy made over the last 35 years have been wiped out. 72% of the world's population—5.7 billion people—live in autocracies by 2022" (V-Dem 2021. The Economist Intelligence Unit's (EIU's) *Democracy Index* offered similarly pessimistic conclusions. In 2020, 116 of 167 countries recorded a decline in their total democracy score compared with the previous year. The United States held steady as a "flawed democracy," unchanged from 2016 when it lost its "full democracy" status (EIU 2020). By 2022 the gloom hanging over the US had lifted a bit, but the EIU still observed that "social cohesion and consensus have collapsed in recent years as disagreements over an expanding list of issues fuel the country's 'culture wars'" (EIU 2020. The restoration of democratic processes and values was further impeded by Donald Trump's second election in 2024.

What accounts for this crisis of liberal democracy? We address this question by drawing on two distinct yet complementary research literatures. One perspective focuses primarily on the spread of disinformation and the algorithmic amplification of extremist content, while the other addresses the role of institutions and elites in restricting popular participation and promoting extremist ideas. We refer to the first approach as the *technocentric research paradigm* and the second as the *institutionalist research paradigm*. Both literatures provide incomplete yet complementary clues as to why anti-democratic tendencies are more pronounced among parties and voting publics on the right.

W. Lance Bennett and Steven Livingston, *Technological and Institutional Roots of Democratic Backsliding in the United States*. In: *Connective Action and the Rise of the Far-Right*. Edited by: Steven Livingston and Michael Miller, Oxford University Press. © Oxford University Press (2025). DOI: 10.1093/oso/9780197794937.003.0001

Our goals in this analysis are to 1) describe the logics of both explanations, 2) identify the gaps found in each, and 3) sketch a synthesis. Drawing on the "connective action" model, we argue that hitherto scattered and uncoordinated extremist elements cohere online into quasi-organizations, or what the research literature has referred to as "digitally constituted organizations." Because digital organizational forms tend to be more fluid, nonhierarchical, and leaderless, they also tend to be more resistant to distancing efforts by party leaders. Incorporating digitally constituted organizational forms into institutionalist arguments brings its analytical reach into the digital era as it simultaneously anchors technocentric arguments in broader historical, social, and economic contexts. We begin with a description of what we mean by liberal democracy and democratic backsliding. We then turn to the explanations of how "asymmetrical polarization" on the radical right contributes to democratic decline (Benkler et al. 2018; Bennett et al. 2018). Finally, we develop a more holistic *connective action model of democratic backsliding* that situates extremist digital networks in a broader institutionalist framework that sheds light on the rise of illiberal politics in both institutions and public communication spheres.

Democratic Backsliding

Just what is democratic backsliding? Several often-interchangeable terms are found in discussions of democratic backsliding, including illiberalism and de-democratization, along with references to hybrid regimes, populism, or soft authoritarianism (Collier and Levitsky 1997). For purposes of simplification we understand democratic backsliding as a movement away from liberal democratic ideals via "a series of discrete changes in the rules and informal procedures that shape . . . elections, rights, and accountability" (Lust and Waldner 2015, 2; Waldner and Lust 2018).[1] An opening question posed by political scientist Nancy Bermeo asks: "What kinds of concrete actions transform a regime from one type to another?" (2016, 5). Most scholars agree that rather than a sudden coup d'état, democratic backsliding today is more likely to involve a disjointed series of incremental developments. Steven Levitsky and Daniel Ziblatt note that the process of decline comes "slowly, in barely visible steps" (2018, 76–77). Marianne Kneuer refers to "democratic erosion" and offers a model of how these incremental changes

---

[1] The term "democratic backsliding" is used quite commonly in the research literature. See for example Alemán and Yang (2011), Erdmann (2011), and Finkel et al. (2012).

occur based on the interplay of agency, opportunity and sequencing (2021). Those changes to formal political institutions and informal practices and norms generally "attenuate the public's ability to make demands on the state without fear of reprisal" (Lust and Waldner 2015, 4).

Through practices such as gerrymandering and other barriers to voting, election fairness is limited without explicitly abolishing universal franchise. When able to govern through minority parties, and appoint judges, or obstruct judicial processes, political leaders become less constrained by accountability norms and threats of possible punishment. Oppositional politicians and parties are demonized, declared "enemies of the people," and in advanced cases of backsliding, threatened with violence, as happened to many honest state election officials following Donald Trump's defeat in the 2020 US presidential election. In extreme cases, opponents may be jailed or murdered (Bermeo 2003, 238; Levitsky and Ziblatt 2018, 21–24). Meanwhile, those responsible for such assaults on liberal democratic norms and practices usually cloak their actions in the rhetoric of institutional "reforms" that are defended as restoring "true democracy," which in many cases is a code term for white supremacy or ethnic nationalism.

The institutionalization of minority rule that continues to be advertised as "democratic" requires some mobilization of popular support to establish a veneer of legitimacy. That, in turn, entails various forms of media management. In self-proclaimed illiberal democracies such as Hungary, this may involve complicated schemes of media ownership and content coordination to promote right-wing policies and politicians such as Viktor Orbán. In a less consolidated illiberal system such as the US, more complex media flows involve a mix of broadcast outlets (e.g., Fox news and talk radio), political disinformation sites often funded by wealthy elites (e.g., Breitbart, Daily Caller), and social media platforms that connect and organize publics on the right. The interplay of these different media with institutional actors is important to understand (see Yang 2020). One of the key media-institution interactions that we explore in this chapter involves: 1) the amplification of disinformation, conspiracy, and hate, 2) which makes more extremist candidates viable in elections, and 3) which may result in conservative parties losing control of their own agendas. These dynamics will be discussed in more detail later, but for now the point is that there are important interactions between institutions and communication processes, with each contributing importantly to the transformation of democracies.

What are the benefits of our approach? We hope this synthesis offers a corrective to the sizeable number of books that have looked at institutional processes yet have had little to say about media and communication processes in general and social media in particular (Levitsky and Ziblatt 2018, Ch. 4). Many of these institutional explanations seem indifferent to the headlines and legislative hearings concerning the threat to democracy posed by social media platforms. The same can be said in reverse about the work done by scholars who focus on the role of media and social technologies in democratic decline (Persily and Tucker 2020). Few factors outside of technology itself can be found in their explanations of democratic decay (Kreiss 2021). More broadly, most of the technocentric literature ignores how the growing audiences for extremist content have been shaped by centuries of racial capitalism, or the catastrophic damage done to rustbelt communities by deindustrialization, and the resulting appeals of politicians to the accompanying crises of meaning and purpose visited upon millions of people (Robinson 2020; Case and Deaton 2020).

We begin with a review of technocentric explanations, highlighting some of the gaps that can be filled by institutionalist approaches.

Technocentric Approaches to Asymmetrical Polarization and Democratic Backsliding

Following the 2016 Brexit referendum in the United Kingdom and the presidential election in the United States, many observers pointed to the role of social technologies as the chief cause of these unexpected outcomes. Soon a broad consensus formed around the idea that a new and largely unexpected crisis of democracy had emerged, one principally fueled by social media platforms. "It seemed possible," noted Yascha Mounk (2018), "that the rise of digital technology, and the concomitant spread of essentially costless communication, have set up a direct clash between two of our most cherished values: freedom of speech and the stability of our political system." Resting on an intuitive logic, the technocentric argument has two parts.

First is the claim that the priorities of the social media behemoths are shaped not by a sense of collective civic responsibility or by a regard for democratic principles but by an insatiable appetite for financial growth and market domination, often fueled by the circulation of extremist content. The platforms rest on a business model that Shoshana Zuboff (2019, 8) terms "surveillance capitalism." She likens it to a manufacturing process, one beginning with the extraction of raw materials, arguing that a platform "unilaterally claims human experience as free raw material for translation into behavioral data, which become proprietary behavioral surplus." Predictions of future behaviors are then packaged and sold on a "behavior futures market" to other corporations for use in targeted marketing campaigns (Zuboff 2019, 7). To extract behavioral surplus, user attention must remain fixed on digital content, and nothing holds attention like algorithmically amplified fear and loathing. Surveillance capitalism is fueled by extremist content.

This logic is evident in the internal Facebook documents provided to news organizations and the US Securities and Exchange Commission in the fall of 2021 by whistleblower Frances Haugen (Horwitz 2021). They show that Facebook employees raised concerns internally about the spurious "Stop the Steal" content spread by Trump supporters both before and after the 2020 election. A Facebook data scientist discovered that as much as 10% of all US political views on the platform during the week after the election contained the false claim that the election was fraudulent (Mac and Frenkel 2021). Facebook also knew that extremist movements and groups on its site were "trying to polarize American voters before the election" (Mac and Frenkel 2021). Haugen made it clear that Facebook executives were fully aware of just how serious a problem algorithmic amplification of polarizing content was during the election.

A second part of the technocentric research paradigm emerges from the cognitive turn in political science in the closing decades of the twentieth century (Freelon and Wells 2020, 149). Here the focus is on the limitations of human information processing and the resulting susceptibility to emotionally soothing disinformation (Porter and Wood 2019). Citizens are understood to be pulled between conflicting motivations (Taber and Lodge 2006). On the one hand, are accuracy goals that lead individuals to seek out and carefully consider relevant evidence to reach factually sound conclusions (Baumeister and Newman 1994; Fiske and Taylor 1991). On the other hand, partisan goals involve motivations to seek out confirming information and to reason in support of prior beliefs (Kruglanski and Webster 1996; Kunda 1987, 1990; Bakshy et al. 2015; for a more recent treatment of this conclusion, see Brady et al. 2017; for a contrary perspective, see Boxell et al. 2017). Protecting existing beliefs rather than accuracy is the goal.

According to this understanding of the problem, a recursive downward spiral of democratic dysfunction is triggered by algorithmically amplified content that encourages selective exposure through curated newsfeeds

(Thaler 2021; Pennycook and Rand 2021). This leads to greater political polarization, which opens space for yet more disinformation, which then exacerbates polarization, and so forth. In this environment, ideologically temperate citizens are put off by highly polarized politics, leaving the political arena to divisive extremist voices. Rumors, innuendo, and conspiracy theories are ratcheted up in a reinforcement loop among online and cable news personalities and prominent political officials.

Layered over this dynamic is the disruptive influence of foreign actors who leverage social media affordances to their own political advantage (Sanovich 2018; Harold et al. 2021). For example, a 2023 study found that Russian disinformation concerning its invasion of Ukraine parroted rhetorical themes common with the American far right in an effort to undermine public support for US and NATO military aid to Ukraine. Onetime Fox on-air personality Tucker Carlson, far-right podcaster Steve Bannon, and several Republican congressional representatives all pushed the false narrative that Russia and Russian President Vladimir Putin were allies in backing traditional values and religion in the fight against "woke" ideas (Stone 2023).

This account describes the underlying logic of much of the backsliding-as-a-technology-problem (see Freelon and Wells 2020; Tucker et al. 2018; Wooley and Guilbeault 2017; Tsfati et al. 2020; and Boulianne 2015). It offers an elegant and intuitively logical explanation of polarization and democratic backsliding. Yet we believe it is also incomplete, especially in its inattentiveness to existing social and institutional power structures.

Institutional and Political Contexts of Disinformation and Democratic Disruption

Explanations that focus on the algorithmic amplification of polarizing content often neglect the erosion of trust in democratic institutions by media and political organizations that aim to undermine authoritative claims about shared realities. Reliance on cognitive models of *individual* radicalization creates blind spots to social and historical context. That erosion of trust in political institutions in the US began long before the advent of social media (Pew Research Center 2015). Decades of attacks on trusted public institutions and scientific authorities by the Republican Party and affiliated political, media, and business groups have created openings for the spread of disinformation (Bennett and Livingston 2018, 2020). Ironically, those attacks on shared authority and a national identity grounded in tolerance kindled a rebirth of white nationalism which aided the takeover of the GOP by Trump and his Make America Great Again (MAGA) movement. The Stop the Steal campaign following Trump's 2020 election loss has opened the path to even greater erosions of voting rights, including allowing partisan certification of elections in a number of Republican states. The resulting loss of trust in elections has added to political polarization and the spread of disinformation to justify the corruption of public institutions and protections. As Rachel Kuo and Alice Marwick observe, framing these problems only in technological terms "disconnects disinformation from the broader politics of knowledge production and systems of power that undergird it" (2021). In their view, purely technological solutions are "curiously depoliticized, framed as 'polluting' or 'infecting' an otherwise healthy information ecosystem" (2021, 1).

Furthermore, when understood mainly as a technnological or media problem, technical solutions are given priority, including AI solutions for content moderation, better bot detection, remedial citizen literacy programs, and fact-checking to clean up around the edges of an otherwise healthy information environment. Technical problems call for technical solutions. Yet as we have noted elsewhere, the current "information disorder" is rooted in the physical world where money and influence undermine the legitimacy of authoritative institutions. Or as Daniel Kreiss observes, "It is impossible to understand social media and democracy without accounting for the historical, racial, and institutional contexts that gave formative shape to our present politics, for they explain why disinformation and polarization take the specific forms they do" (Kreiss 2021, 5). With the technocentric approach, political, historical, economic, and social factors recede into the background (Kreiss and Reddi 2021).

Nor does the technocentric research paradigm account for the role of political organizations and operatives such as Robert Mercer and his daughter Rebekah as financial backers of the Breitbart political propaganda site, the Cambridge Analytica behavioral engineering company, and later, the far-right–friendly Parler social media platform that served as a coordinating platform for the January 6th insurrection, and housed a collection of hundreds of videos from participants documenting the events (Gold 2017; Lerman 2021). Nor do technocentric approaches account for a half-century of free market libertarian attacks on the credibility of scientific findings that signaled the need for market regulation or protections for public health and the environment. With billions of dollars spent over three decades, the Koch network has created hundreds of think tanks, free market university research programs, and a host of grassroots and astroturf social movements, and helped to refashion the Tea Party into a GOP power base to disrupt governance, defeat the regulatory state, and limit challenges to white elite power structures (Mayer 2016; Leonard 2019; Maclean 2017; for the Tea Party see Parker and Barreto 2013). To advance such an illiberal agenda, many long-known facts, such as the relationship between burning hydrocarbons and climate change, had to be dismissed and the scientists who produced such studies discredited (Powell 2011). Our post–fact era started well before Mark Zuckerberg created the precursor to Facebook in his Harvard dorm room. Our point is that *the relationships between disruptive technologies and historical patterns of institutional corruption need to be better understood and addressed.* Beyond offering more complete explanations of why the US is on an illiberal path, the interactions between politics, institutions, and communication may shed light on where that path may lead. As noted earlier, various post-democratic forms have emerged, with historical cases displaying different combinations of ethnic nationalism, crony capitalism, authoritarianism, fascism, violence, and anarchy. We pick up these national variations in the conclusion.

To advance our understanding of contemporary threats to democracy, at least one more question that must be addressed. Why is most of this disinformation and institutional corruption coming from the right? Intuitive understandings may suggest that there are more reactionary economic interests with more money driving these attacks on democracy. In addition, an inspection of right-wing movements around the world suggests that large publics are reacting against perceived challenges to their privileged statuses in society, as racial, religious, and marginalized gender identity groups assert democratic rights (Parker 2021). However, there remains a piecemeal quality to explaining the convergence of elite interests, public resentments, and disinformation, resulting from different varieties of democratic backsliding in different societies. *What overarching brokerage mechanisms or institutional processes organize this convergence of conservative business interests, disinformation, and popular unrest?* We propose that many of these elements of democratic backsliding have come together—with different configurations in different polities—based on the ways in which conservative political parties try to manage the dilemma of how to maximize their electoral success while advancing elitist and often unpopular economic agendas.

How Did We Get Here? Updating the Conservative Dilemma

What accounts for such transformations of political parties, and the resulting erosion of democratic institutions such as election integrity processes, independent press organizations and court systems? In *Conservative Parties and the Birth of Democracy*, Daniel Ziblatt (2017) argues that sustaining liberal democracy in nineteenth- and early twentieth-century Europe depended on the nature of conservative party efforts to dodge growing public demands for fairer and more equitable distributions of power and resources. As the scope of suffrage and the power of social movements grew, center-right parties faced what Ziblatt calls a *conservative dilemma*. To win elections, conservative parties must appeal to the working and middle classes while also remaining loyal to the economic elites with whom they are most closely aligned. How a party navigates this dilemma may determine both its political fate and its impact on democracy. In some of the cases he examines, compromises were reached, and democracy was sustained; in other cases, democracy was crushed as public passions were directed to distractive nationalism, racism, and xenophobia. The types of issues a party uses to mobilize support from nonelites, along with the stability of its relationships with allied "surrogate" civil society, business, and media organizations shapes the outcome.

Applying this model to the US Republican Party, Jacob Hacker and Paul Pierson argue that "other kinds of organizations—single-issue groups, cultural institutions such as churches, and certain kinds of media outlets" become *party surrogates*: "These organizations can focus on building strong emotional bonds with citizens and tapping shared identities" (2020, 23). Both in Ziblatt's historical analysis and in Hacker and Pierson's contemporary US case, party surrogates are understood in terms of conventional bureaucratic organizations. For example, Ziblatt notes the role of the Primrose League, a civic organization that served as a surrogate of the British Conservative Party in the early twentieth century by appealing to nonelites with a focus on opposition to Irish independence and support for the Anglican Church and the monarchy. These *cross-cutting issues* mobilized support across class divides. In the US, traditional surrogates include Christian evangelical churches, gun rights organizations, anti-abortion groups, and conservative media outlets like *National Review*, and more recently, Fox News and conservative talk radio (Hemmer 2016; Kruse 2015).

While surrogate organizations can help resolve the conservative party dilemma, they also present risks. Most concerning are cases where the interests of surrogates are at odds with party priorities, resulting in usurping organizational identity and ideological coherence. For example, in a desire for better ratings, an aligned media organization, such as Fox News, might appeal to key audience demographics by taking positions on issues or promoting politicians that spread destabilizing extremist rhetoric on immigration, minority gender identities, non-Christian religious sects, or "white replacement" theories. The sworn testimony provided by Fox News personalities, and Rupert Murdoch himself, in the Dominion Voting defamation case underscored that Fox News was more interested in preserving its market share among conservative viewers than it was in preserving trust in US elections. According to their private message exchanges, Sean Hannity, Tucker Carlson, and Laura Ingraham all expressed doubts about the "Stop the Steal" narrative, with Carlson at one point writing, "Sidney Powell is lying." Powell, of course, was a quasi-official member of Trump's legal team following his election loss. Still, despite the private misgivings, all Fox hosts continued to air the election fraud narrative (Ellison and Gardner 2023). When activated by opportunistic politicians, political foundations and interest groups, or media organizations, extremist factions represent votes for or against a conservative party. At the same time, appealing to such elements may risk electing more extreme representatives who threaten party agendas and stability. Surrogate organizations can be a mixed blessing. Social technologies, we argue, exacerbate the tendency toward party boundary maintenance challenges and the pull toward illiberalism.

Many extremist groups are typically scattered and poorly organized, and thus present more challenging problems to mobilize than traditional organizations such as churches. However, digital media platforms (both social media and political information sites) enable once fragmented extremist networks to grow and find each other. The ease of communicating with formerly marginalized fringe elements may attract opportunistic politicians, media sites, and political organizations that aim to mobilize them into voting blocks. When scattered extremists become organized into more coherent publics, conservative parties risk becoming destabilized and radicalized.

In sum, traditional approaches to the conservative dilemma in the US have focused mainly on formal interest organizations such as conventional religious groups, anti-abortion movements, or gun rights lobbies, along with more recent developments such as how Koch political organizations helped add the Tea Party to the Republican mix (Skocpol and Williamson 2016). What we would like to add is the emergence of increasingly organized grass-roots *online* extremist factions that now compete with traditional surrogate groups for control of the party and its political agenda, with even greater disruptions to larger democratic processes. In effort to understand how all of this happened in a seemingly short time, we address two questions:

First, what developments in the Republican Party's historic quest for power created conditions that opened the party to losing control over its own surrogates, resulting in rapid political transformation?

Second, what communication and institutional conditions enabled once fringe elements to become organized enough to reshape the fortunes of the party and accelerate the threat to core democratic institutions such as election processes?

Undermining Institutional Authority: The Historical Conservative Quest for Power

In 1964, Lyndon Johnson defeated Republican Barry Goldwater in one of the greatest landside victories in American political history. Not only did Johnson trounce Goldwater, but the Democratic Party also picked up 37 seats in the House of Representatives and two seats in the Senate, thereby capturing supermajorities in both chambers. After 1964 election, the GOP found itself in a position not unlike that of the British Conservative Party in 1906. Following the party's disastrous defeat in the 1906 Parliamentary elections, the Liberal-led government—holding 397 seats to the Conservative Party's 156—pioneered Britain's transformation into a modern welfare state (Wikipedia n.d.). The Liberal government also enacted an aggressive tax program aimed at the rich and landed aristocracy (Ziblatt 2017, 143). It was a bold frontal assault on the old order.

In response, Conservative Party leaders adopted a "combative, hard-edged and distinctly right-wing profile because the *party fell into the grips of its activist base*" (Ziblatt 2017, 143 Emphasis added). According to one historian's account, the British Conservative Party appeared "prepared to defy the laws and legislature of the land to resort to extra-parliamentary and nonconstitutional means, to preach violence and to practice it if needs be, and even to support rebellion and risk civil war, in an attempt to recover their position" (Cannadine 1999, 517). A similar outcome took longer to realize in the US, as the GOP first succeeded in adding less extreme surrogate groups who helped elect Ronald Reagan in the 1980s. However, an economic crisis and the election of a Black president in 2008 helped mobilize a racist Tea Party, followed by the election of Donald Trump in 2016 who brought even more extremist elements into the party (Parker and Barreto 2013).

The long road to Republican extremism began with the shock to the core party constituency of pro-free enterprise conservatives after 1964 when Johnson's Great Society programs turned federal government into an engine of renewal and progress for poor people, and especially for subjugated people of color. Johnson's signing of the Civil Rights Act in 1964 outlawed discrimination based on race, color, religion, gender, or national origin pushed unwanted change on the centuries-old racial caste system of the South (Civil Rights Act 1964). The Civil Rights Act also prohibited unequal application of voter registration requirements, and racial segregation in schools, employment, and public spaces. The Voting Rights Act the following year was intended to end Jim Crow impediments to African American voting rights. Of course, it wasn't until the heroic actions of those in the civil rights movement—who forced segregationist compliance with the law by putting their own bodies on the line—did the new laws begin to have the intended effects (Branch 1988). Meanwhile, the environmental, women's rights, and sexual rights movements, among others, added demands that government act to right grievous social and economic inequality and threats to life on the planet.

How did the GOP respond to these challenges? Following the logic of Ziblatt's conservative dilemma model, Hacker and Pierson (2020) review two GOP responses to the conservative dilemma: 1) voter suppression and manipulation of institutional rules to facilitate GOP minority control of state and national government; and 2) offering symbolic (e.g., moral, religious, and racial) appeals to distract from growing economic disparity issues. Before turning to our synthesis of the institutionalist and technocentric models of democratic backsliding, we review Hacker and Pierson's argument and then turn to a discussion of where it falls short. Although they offer a compelling explanation of the modern GOP's response to the conservative dilemma, their understanding of the nature of party organizational surrogates in the digital age causes problems for their overall analysis. This oversight leads them to underestimate the true depth of the threat posed to liberal democracy by the conservative dilemma in the US.

Voter Suppression

Various mechanisms of voter suppression continue to be the most democratically destructive GOP tactics for addressing the conservative dilemma, though of course Republican disinformation campaigns frame them in terms of election integrity. There is, however, no sound evidence in support of Republican claims about voter fraud (Levitt 2007; Bush 2020). Instead, "anti-fraud" measures are thinly disguised efforts to *suppress* voter participation, especially participation by the poor and people of color, just as poll taxes and literacy tests did in the Jim Crow era (Daniels 2020). Putting hurdles before Black people, poor people, and Democratic voters more generally becomes a.necessary supplement when the collection of surrogate organizations fails to deliver needed majorities. The level of open rigging of elections has become blatant. Of course, gerrymandering has remained a mainstay of voter suppression tactics, creating minority party rule in a number of states (Tausanovitch and Root 2020). In addition, many states have reduced the number of polling places in Democratic districts, particularly in African American and Latinx neighborhoods (Cohen 2020). In some states, photo identification requirements for voters accept gun club membership cards but not student IDs Lessig 2021). When a lawyer for the Republican National Committee was asked by Trump appointed conservative Supreme Court Justice Amy Coney Barrett why his party opposed legislation enabling more people to vote, his reply was because it "puts us at a competitive disadvantage" (Lessig 2021).

As Hacker and Pierson (2020) note, these many forms of voter suppression have become key pillars of GOP efforts to address the conservative dilemma. Fundamentally, it is an effort to undermine democracy. Voter suppression measures require the spread of growing volumes of disinformation to maintain the illusion of plausibility. Thus, voter suppression becomes "election integrity," and the partisan control of election certification is justified as a necessary response to election theft by the opposition (Stanley-Becker 2020). Disinformation in support of institutional

Issue Distraction

The second traditional GOP response to its conservative dilemma involves efforts to activate social divisions through noneconomic issues:

> Outflanked by the left on economic issues, *their survival depended on introducing or highlighting other social divisions.* And these divisions couldn't be trivial or temporary; they had to be strong enough to attract durable political support from the working and middle classes. In modern societies, the list of such "cleavages" is short, and their history unpleasant. There are racial, ethnic, and religious divisions. There is the call of nationalism or foreign military adventures. There are sectional loyalties. There is opposition to immigration. In short, there is a set of noneconomic issues—many racially tinged, all involving strong identities and strong emotions—that draw a sharp line between "us" and "them." (Hacker and Pierson 2020, 22, emphasis added)

Voter suppression and distraction are key pillars of Hacker and Pierson's analysis of how the Republican Party has responded to the conservative dilemma. However, we believe that there is another factor that adds an important element of volatility to these attacks on democracy—a development that makes it hard to predict just what form of rule might emerge following the possible demise of democratic governance in the United States. This critical element in the contemporary conservative dilemma involves expanding our understanding of what constitutes a surrogate organization in the digital age. In particular, we suggest that unlike traditional interest organizations or civil society surrogates, we now witness organized networks of formerly marginalized extremist groups that threaten anarchy, possibly followed by authoritarian consolidation. Unlike surrogates that align with parties as brokers for their issue agendas, digitally networked alignments of extremist, and potentially violent factions, can threaten party coherence and political order. *When such elements are cued by a combination of politicians inside parties, along with outside organizations, political operatives and media sites, a conservative party like the Republicans may well lose control of its own agenda and become an even more serious threat to democracy.* The rise of such organized extremism, and its central role in Trump's MAGA movement, bring us to our next question: How do communication processes enable the formation of digitally networked surrogate organizations that challenge the identity and control of the Republican Party itself?

Communication and the Organization of Networked Extremism

Hacker and Pierson (2020) generally overlook the effects of digital technology on both organizational forms and behavior. Manuel DeLanda (2006), Andrew Chadwick (2013), W. Lance Bennett and Alexandra Segerberg (2013), and Daniel Kreiss (2021a), among others, have noted that organizational forms based on digital platforms are markedly different from conventional organizations. These new forms can be fluid and composed of diverse networks connected around shared memes such as "stop the steal" or "deep state" conspiracies. These assemblages may be in constant flux and operate both online and offline, much as QAnon shifts issue focus and alignments with other groups, appears in diverse protests, and takes different transnational forms.

In *The Logic of Connective Action*, Lance Bennett and Alexandra Segerberg (2013) speak of *communication as organization*, whereas other scholars speak of hybrid organizations and digitally enabled organizations (Chadwick 2013; Livingston and Walter-Drop 2013). These terms point to the idea that social media platforms can enable new organizational forms. As Bennett and Segerberg note:

> Communication is often much more than a means of exchanging information and forming impressions, or an instrument for sending updates and instructions to followers. Communication routines can, under some conditions, create patterned relationships among people that lend organization and structure to many aspects of social life. As digital media become more prominent in contemporary contention, they too help to configure the protest space and the action that develops within it. Ultimately, technology-enabled networks may become dynamic organizations in their own right. (2013, 289, emphasis added)

Bennett and Segerberg array different organizational forms along a continuum anchored at one end by conventional organizations with buildings, staff, and budgets, and at the other, by technology enabled networked organizations with few of the outward trappings of more traditional bureaucracy. When Hacker and Pierson speak of surrogate organizations, they limit their understanding to conventional organizations with staff filling defined roles in a hierarchical bureaucratic structure. In failing to take theoretical account of digitally networked organizations, they underestimate the danger to democracy presented by a fracturing GOP that was transformed in a shockingly short time through interactions among social media networks, political information sites, reactionary organizations and foundations, and cues from opportunistic politicians inside the party itself. As a result, QAnon, the Boogaloo Bois, the Proud Boys, Christian white nationalist organizations, and dozens of other factions of the MAGA movement became surrogates of the Republican Party. Many Republicans might deny or resist this characterization, but this is exactly what we mean by digital surrogates creating new organizational boundary problems.

Much of the existing literature on connective action has focused on progressive or left-wing social movements. It is important to note that the kind of "asymmetrical polarization" that distinguishes the far left from the far right in many democracies reflects a different collection of political values and organizational styles that have become characteristics of the contemporary left. There have, of course, been impressive examples of massive mobilizations on the left based largely on forms of technology enabled organization. For example, the Occupy Wall Street protest networks in 2011–2012 became densely organized through processes of sharing memes that affirmed common identities (e.g., "We Are the 99%"), while crowds circulated and curated various connective resources such as protest tactics and advice on what to do when arrested. Those patterns of coordinated communication produced familiar organizational capacities such as making and sharing agendas, planning, taking action, and responding to external threats and opportunities (see Bennett et al. 2014).

Though impressive in many ways, these digitally networked organizations that operate outside of the conventional bureaucratic left of labor movements and environmental NGOs, tend to be fluid, relatively nonhierarchical, and difficult to sustain. Key factors contributing to the relative lack of stable movement and party formation on the technology-enabled left include diminished confidence in parties, and growing dissatisfaction with traditional movement organization based in ideology, collective identity, and conventional leadership. As a result, a continuing pattern of mobilization on the left involves creative uses of technologically to enable sometimes massive, but generally short-lived, protests and deliberative gatherings centered around principles of diversity, inclusion, and direct democracy (see Bennett et al. 2018).

Before their incorporation into the MAGA movement with its connection to the GOP, many fringe networks on the far right were also located at the "technology enabled" end of the Bennett and Segerberg organization continuum. The list of such organizations includes white nationalist and anti-immigrant groups, neo-Nazis, armed militias such as the Boogaloo Bois and the Proud Boys, wellness and anti-vaccination communities, patriarchal white male Christian identity organizations such as the Promise Keepers, various Tea Party remnants, conspiracy networks such as QAnon and the anti-globalists, and Stop the Steal activists, among other factions. A finer grained look reveals hundreds, if not thousands, of formerly scattered groups that have now become more connected to Republican Party politics. For example, a 2019 Southern Poverty Law Center report identified 576 extremist antigovernment organizations. By the fateful election of 2020, and the subsequent assault on the US Capitol to stop government officials from certifying the election, Facebook, YouTube, Twitter, Reddit, Pinterest, Instagram, and Telegram, among others, had become go-to organizational platforms for these groups.

What accounts for this shift toward greater coherence in movement organization on the right? In part, the smaller number of common core values such as racism, nationalism, and religion, makes common cause easier to create, in contrast with the proliferation of causes and identity politics on the left. An even more important explanation for the rapid organization of right-wing extremism is that factions on the right have received support from a variety of well-resourced political and media organizations (Mac and Lerer 2022; Derysh 2021).

The organizational transformation of right-wing extremism conforms to what Bennett and Segerberg call "organizationally enabled" networks which fall along the middle range of their continuum, in between conventional hierarchical organizations and more technology enabled distributed organizations. What accounts for this?

The scale and stability of right-wing networked organizations has been enabled by a mix of a) political media sites, b) tax exempt nonprofit political organizations, c) political operatives, and d) elected leaders, all promoting e) spreadable memes, narratives, and disinformation that connect different networks. After briefly describing these elements of organizationally enabled political surrogate networks, we will show how the various coordinating mechanisms, listed above, contributed to the January 6th insurrection at the US Capitol. That action, along with the behind the scenes plotting by Trump and his allies, constitutes a failed coup attempt. In the limited space here, we can only sketch brief illustrations of each type of organizational mechanism.

Political Media Sites

Media organizations have been instrumental in channeling messaging to and from audiences anchored in GOP surrogate organizations. In earlier years, talk radio and conservative television networks such as Fox News, communicated largely with traditional GOP surrogates such as evangelical Christian churches, family values NGOs, and gun rights groups. More recently, the appeals have included more extremist messages, as when Fox News personalities such as Tucker Carlson played up white replacement narratives already circulating in international radical right networks (Chait 2021). Such expansion of the bounds of conventional Republican ideas suggests that during the Trump years, Fox departed from its loyalty to mainstream party leadership. For example, hosts on Fox News such as Sean Hannity, Laura Ingram, and Tucker Carlson were once formerly more aligned with traditional GOP surrogates. However, their roles changed after Trump was elected and he became a celebrity guest on their programs. Their discussions on various issues such as trade, public health disinformation during the COVID-19 pandemic, and election integrity, moved those issues away from former GOP centers of gravity once established by party leadership and neoliberal surrogate organizations created by Charles Koch.

After the news side of Fox affirmed that Joe Biden had won the 2020 election, Trump directed the attention of his followers to other media organizations such as *One America News Network*, which held White House press credentials as a Trump administration surrogate, pushing the boundaries of the GOP public even farther to the extreme. However, after being taken down from Twitter and Facebook (until 2023), and failing with his own platform, Trump was soon back on Fox as his coterie of commentators gave him a platform to spread the Big Lie about the stolen election to a large audience.

Tax Exempt Political Nonprofits

Organizations funded by wealthy reactionaries also contribute resources, infrastructure and direction to the radical fringe. For example, former US Education Secretary Betsy DeVos's family funds the Michigan Freedom Fund and other far-right organizations in the Michigan Conservative Coalition (Wilson 2020). Those political organizations helped scattered local groups organize against the stay-at-home order in Michigan during the early days of the COVID pandemic. Those "Unlock Michigan" protests brought the far-right Proud Boys hate group and other Confederate flag-waving activists to the Michigan State House, and some militia members entered the Capitol carrying semiautomatic weapons. There were even calls to assassinate the governor of Michigan, and the FBI uncovered a plot to kidnap her and put her on trial. Eventually, the far-right militia members involved in the plot were given long prison sentences (Smith 2022). The DeVos family have also been principal contributors to the Koch network of more conventional Republican surrogate organizations (Mayer 2016, 205). The composition and organization of the Michigan occupation was seen by some observers as a dress rehearsal for the insurrection at the US Capitol on January 6, 2021 (Gray 2021).

Political Operatives

The "inside game" to overturn the election and install Trump as president was headed up by a coterie of Trump operatives and advisors who gathered in what they termed a "command center" at the Willard Hotel in the heart of Washington and communicated with White House officials, including the president (Alemany et al. 2021). Those operatives included Trump advisor and former Breitbart publisher Steve Bannon; Rudy Giuliani, Trump's personal lawyer and tireless advocate for overturning the election; and attorney John Eastman, who developed a legal theory that Vice President Mike Pence could stop the congressional certification of state electoral votes and either invite key states to select slates of electors favorable to Trump, or remand the decision to the House of Representatives, which had a majority of Republican states. In addition, Bannon used his popular *War Room* podcast to fuel doubt about the election results and to preview the events of January 6 with the promise that "all hell is going to break loose" (Neidig 2022).

Another member of the Willard command center was long-time Republican "dirty trickster" and Trump advisor Roger Stone, who was involved in staging the so-called Brooks Brothers riot when well-dressed Republican staffers disrupted the vote recount in Miami-Dade County Florida during the 2000 election. Stopping the count threw the outcome into the courts, where Bush was eventually declared the Florida winner in a 5–4 vote of the US Supreme Court, a decision that gave Bush enough electoral votes to make him president. Stone later coined the "Stop the Steal" meme ahead of the 2016 election, based on his assumption that Trump would lose, and that the election could be challenged. Stone's rallying cry was finally activated in 2020 and used by other political operatives and organizations to mobilize a number of state level protests leading up to the January 6th Capitol insurrection—all creating the appearance of public support for the coup attempt.

Cueing and Recognition by Elected Leaders

Consider the improbable rise of QAnon to national and international prominence. Several of the chapters in this volume document the rise and importance of the conspiracy in US and even German politics. A mysterious Q who claimed to be a high government official with Q-level security clearance alerted followers on 4chan that a ring of Democratic politicians and Hollywood elites were engaging in Satanic rites of child sex trafficking and cannibalism and suggesting that Donald Trump would save the children with a massive sting operation called "The Storm." Posts from Q appeared in late 2017, initially expanding upon the "Pizzagate" conspiracy theory from the 2016 election claiming that Democratic candidate Hillary Clinton and other top Democratic Party officials were conducting a demonic child sex trafficking operation from the (in reality, nonexistent) basement of a Washington pizza restaurant.

The updated pronouncements of Q were soon reposted on different platforms, and followers with Q signs and paraphernalia began showing up at Republican election rallies in 2018. During the 2020 presidential campaign, Trump disavowed knowing much about Q or QAnon, but he pledged to do what he could to save the children. More importantly, he recognized the movement during the 2020 campaign through his tweets. Trump retweeted at least 90 posts from 49 different QAnon conspiracy accounts, despite warnings from the Federal Bureau of Investigation that the network was "a potential source of domestic terrorism after several people radicalized by QAnon had been charged with crimes, ranging from attempted kidnapping to murder, all inspired by the conspiracy theory" (Nguyen 2020).

QAnon quickly gained visibility and entered the physical world through paraphernalia such as signs and shirts found at GOP rallies, and through activists such as the infamous Q shaman who became a signal player in the invasion of the US Capitol. Adherents to this and other conspiracy theories were elected to the US House of Representatives (Breland 2020). With high levels of social media engagement, legacy media attention, and recognition from politicians, the movement grew and intersected with other, once fringe, surrogate groups. Q signs soon appeared at right-wing rallies in Europe.

Memes, Narrative Elements, and Disinformation as Networking Mechanisms

With the help of various network brokers such as well-funded political organizations, operatives, media sites and elected politicians, once-isolated extremist networks began to join with more traditional Republican Party surrogates, such as anti-abortion groups and evangelical church organizations, around themes of patriotism and white Christian nationalism (Stewart 2019; Du Mez 2020; Gorski and Perry 2022). A collection of now familiar memes ("Stop the Steal," "Make America Great Again," "Build the Wall," "Lock Her Up") served as rallying cries that traveled across network boundaries to create common emotional bonds that united a large and volatile MAGA movement.

The themes that travel across different extremist networks can be cued top-down by media, politicians, political organizations, and operatives, but they can also travel from the bottom-up as networks generate their own content that various enabling actors may pick up and send back to confer recognition. This is essentially what Kate Starbird describes in Chapter 2 of this volume. Such interactive framing represents an organizational form that is difficult to command or control centrally. Hence the spiral of extremism.

Perhaps the biggest of many lies and deceptions of the Trump era was the claim that the election was stolen. That repeatedly falsified claim turned into a highly useful and disruptive mythology for many Republican voters. The widespread belief in the theft of the election, along with the mobilization of the Stop the Steal movement, would not have happened without the above elements working together to spread the disinformation, coordinate various action networks, and bring the resulting surrogates into the Republican Party. The Big Lie that the 2020 election was stolen later became the cover story for many state-level efforts to further limit voter participation, and even to grant control over election certification to Republican controlled state legislatures. These feedback loops have pushed the party's efforts to rig elections well beyond the bounds of decorum and democratic plausibility of earlier institutional corruption initiatives outlined by Hacker and Pierson and others.

The Fate of American Democracy and Future of the Republican Party

The density and extremism of the resulting MAGA movement organization that has changed the Republican Party is impressive. Consider just one brief phase of the Stop the Steal mobilization. A study by *Just Security* at New York University found that between September 1, 2020 and February 2, 2021 there were over 8,200 articles containing variations on the keywords "Stop the Steal":

> Those articles garnered more than 70,000,000 engagements on different platforms; more than 43.5 million of those engagements were registered in December 2020 alone. More than 83 percent (58.5 million) of total engagements were registered on YouTube videos, which appeared on multiple platforms, including Facebook, Twitter, Pinterest, and Reddit. YouTube videos containing "Stop the Steal" or "#StopTheSteal" garnered 21,267,165 views, 863,151 likes, and 34,091 dislikes in the time period analyzed." (Atlantic Council DFRLab 2021)

This networked organization linked grassroots citizens with media hubs, political organizations, and elected Republican officials—all joined in sharing convenient myths and disinformation. As a result, a collection of once isolated extremist factions has taken its place alongside traditional surrogate organizations to impact the identity and electoral future of the Republican

Party. As Sidney Tarrow (2021) has observed, when extremism develops into organized movements, those movements can take over parties, and in the case of the MAGA movement, push a conservative party into illiberal territory. This observation is aligned with the logic of Ziblatt's conservative dilemma model.

To put it mildly, this unfortunate outcome of the conservative dilemma in the US can be thought of as a failure of institutional gatekeeping. As Steven Levitsky and Daniel Ziblatt (2018, 36) argue, "protection against would-be authoritarians has not been (found in) Americans firm commitment to democracy but, rather, (in) the gatekeepers—our political parties." However, the scale of the party gatekeeping failure beggars the oft heard explanation in political science circles that the democratization of candidate selection processes after the civil unrest of the 1960s somehow later opened the door to Trump. That conventional wisdom is ironic in the sense that it blames too much democracy for the failures of Republicans. More importantly, it does not account for the long list of corrosive institutional actions and the related spread of disinformation over decades by Republican elites. While those party leaders and some of their backers, such as surrogates in the "Kochto-pus" network, may not have endorsed Trump in 2016, their own legacy of disinformation and erosion of institutional trust left them in no position to stop him or his insurgency once it took hold of the party.

This does not mean that the new Republican Party is one happy family or that its course, much less that of the nation's, are clear. Yet nearly everywhere one looks in the collection of Republican Party surrogates, one sees instability and boundary problems. For example, where are armed militia groups like the Proud Boys, the Boogaloo Bois, or the Patriot Prayer group taking party boundaries? What should we make of the evidence that local police departments and the US military have been infiltrated by far-right white supremacist militias (Levin 2020; Kennedy 2020; Burris 2020; Montgomery 2017)? As party boundaries are changing, the old strategies of "legalized voter suppression" are being supplemented by calls for violence, including attacks on elected Republican officials who do not cleave to the new more radical order.

Indeed, the embrace of violence by party operatives such as the Trump circle of Steve Bannon, Roger Stone, and Michael Flynn, is itself a key warning sign of democracy's threatened collapse. As Nancy Bermeo puts it (2003, 234, emphasis added): "Even profound polarization . . . is never, in itself, a sufficient condition for regime collapse. *Democracies will only collapse if actors deliberately disassemble them and the key actors in this disassembling process are political elites.*" Beyond those who condone violence in defense of their version of white nationalist democracy, many elected representatives have intensified efforts to dismantle voting rights and to replace secure election provisions with partisan control. This combination of accelerated institutional corruption and the failure of many Republican representatives to condemn and punish violence against state institutions and opponents, signals what Bermeo (2003, 238) refers to as a failure of the party's "distancing capacity."

> By this I mean the strength to distance a party and its members from acts of violence and lawlessness. This distancing involves condemning and prosecuting all those who engage in violence, even when they present themselves as current or potential party allies. The act of distancing serves as an antidote to the contagion of polarization. If parties can muster this sort of strength, they show themselves to be solutions to the problem of disorder and not contributing factors.

Trump and his enablers in the GOP have not just failed to distance themselves from violence, they have at times activity promoted it. During many political rallies, Trump called on his supporters to act violently against protesters and journalists (Cineas 2021; Sullivan 2019). In May 2020, one report found 54 cases of violence linked to Trump's rhetoric that were captured in court documents and police statements (Levine 2020). The chief example of Trump-inspired violence was his invitation to those attending his January 6 rally on the Ellipse Park near the White House to go to the Capitol and "fight like hell." Equally distressing was the action of newly elected Speaker of the House Kevin McCarthy, who gave the congressional security tapes of the insurrection to Fox personality Tucker Carlson in 2023. Carlson aired an edited version of peaceful visitors to the capitol behaving more like tourists than insurrectionists.

Conclusion

We hope that we have offered a friendly corrective to thinking about the nature and role of surrogates in the case of the contemporary US. In our account, the mobilization of online networks by the various enabling factors described earlier threatens the Republican Party's ability to control its own members, much less protect democratic institutions. We want to be clear that we do not believe that Trump's rhetoric, alone, is responsible for the increased use of violence in American politics. The organizational dynamics of networked extremism are interactive, with a circular flow of disinformation and support for illiberal actions among online extremist networks, opportunistic media, reactionary political organizations, party operatives, and elected politicians. The result is the movement of online network organizations into the physical world, embodying actions from electing ever more extreme representatives, to the occupation of the national Capitol (Karell 2021).

While Ziblatt's analysis seems to favor parties offering more coherent responses to the conservative dilemma, this may reflect the timeframe of his analysis which is set well before the digital age. It is less clear why Hacker and Pierson hedged the role of digitally mediated surrogates when speaking of the boundaries of institutional gatekeeping and illiberal political ideas in the United States. Our additions to these and other theories of democratic backsliding, suggests that institutional *boundary incoherence might make the conservative dilemma unresolvable for the GOP*. If this is the case, Marjorie Taylor Greene isn't an aberration; she's the future of the GOP. As the cycle of increasing extremism develops, the loudest and most violence prone elements of an increasingly incoherent party draw energy from failed efforts to reach an accommodation.

As networks of Republican surrogates have expanded to include armed militias and conspiracy theorists, and as political divisions are amplified by social media and the push and pull of billionaire donors, the ability of the Republican Party to control principles, core ideas, and even its own members, becomes much more challenging, if not impossible (Sottile 2020). What might that look like in the US in coming years? As party boundary problems lead to a splintering of the Republican Party due to a realignment of its surrogates, a period of instability seems likely. One path might feature relatively anarchic libertarianism and government instability. Another might include a more authoritarian white Christian nationalism.

These strains of the current situation may of course intermingle, along with other developing possibilities. Some of these outcomes will depend on how judicial institutions respond to the coming challenges to democratic integrity. The judiciary has played a role to date in both deciding elections and allowing voting rights standards to erode. Yet it is an open question as to how legal institutions will react to even more serious threats, given that the judiciary has itself been reshaped over decades as part of the longstanding

Republican minority rule strategy with guidance from Koch organizations and the Federalist Society, which has helped pack the courts with far-right judges, including a majority of the US Supreme Court justices (Vogel 2022).

This progression from conservative dilemma to party dysfunction more generally threatens the legitimacy of institutions and the coherence of public communication spheres. It is increasingly clear that these developments also present risks to the security of many citizens and public officials attempting to assert democratic values. While our account addresses the underlying institutional and communication factors at play in the contemporary United States, we invite scholars of democratic backsliding in both in the US and other nations to add to this account. Similar trends can be found operating in other democracies to different degrees, with the effects on democratic backsliding varying according to types of electoral systems (e.g., a proportional representation system in the US would surely limit the size of a MAGA party) and levels of corruption, among other factors. However, we offer the outlines of our framework as useful for thinking about other cases. At the very least, this analysis should make clear that it is hard to separate the institutional from the technological roots of attacks on liberal democracy in America and elsewhere.

References

Alemán, José, and David D. Yang. 2011. "A Duration Analysis of Democratic Transitions and Authoritarian Backslides." *Comparative Political Studies* 44 (9):1123–1151.

Alemany, Jacqueline, Emma Brown, Tom Hamburger, and Jon Swaine. 2021. "Ahead of Jan. 6, Willard Hotel in Downtown D.C. was a Trump Team 'Command Center' for Effort to Deny Biden the Presidency." *Washington Post*, October 23. https://www.washingtonpost.com/investigations/willard-trump-eastman-giuliani-bannon/2021/10/23/c45bd2d4-3281-11ec-9241-aad8e48f01ff_story.html.

Atlantic Council DFRLab. 2021 "#StopTheSteal: Timeline of Social Media and Extremist Activities Leading to 1/6 Insurrection." Just Security, February 10. https://www.justsecurity.org/74622/stopthesteal-timeline-of-social-media-and-extremist-activities-leading-to-1-6-insurrection/

Bakshy, Eytan, Solomon Messing, and Lada A. Adamic. 2015. "Exposure to Ideologically Diverse News and Opinion on Facebook." *Science* 348 (6239): 1130–1132.

Baumeister, Roy F., and L. S. Newman. 1994. "Self-Regulation of Cognitive Inference and Decision Processes." *Personality and Social Psychology Bulletin* 20 (1): 3–19.

Benkler, Yochai, Robert Faris, and Hal Roberts. 2018. *Network Propaganda: Manipulation, Disinformation, and Radicalization in American Politics*. New York: Oxford University Press.

Bennett, W. Lance, and Steven Livingston. 2018. "The Disinformation Order: Disruptive Communication and the Decline of Democratic Institutions." *European Journal of Communication* 33 (2): 122–139.

Bennett, W. Lance, and Steven Livingston. 2020. *The Disinformation Age: Politics, Technology, and Disruptive Communication in the United States.* New York: Cambridge University Press.

Bennett, W. Lance, and Alexandra Segerberg. 2013. *The Logic of Connective Action: Digital Media and the Personalization of Contentious Politics.* New York: Cambridge University Press.

Bennett, W. Lance, Alexandra Segerberg, and Curd B. Knüpfer. 2018. "The Democratic Interface: Technology, Political Organization, and Diverging Patterns of Electoral Representation." *Information, Communication & Society* 21 (11): 1655–1680.

Bennett, W. Lance, Alexandra Segerberg, and Shawn Walker. 2014. "Organization in the Crowd: Peer Production in Large-Scale Networked Protests." *Information, Communication & Society* 17 (2): 232–260.

Bermeo, Nancy G. 2003. *Ordinary People in Extraordinary Times.* Princeton, NJ: Princeton University Press.

Bermeo, Nancy G. 2016. "On Democratic Backsliding." *Journal of Democracy* 27 (1): 5–19.

Boulianne, Shelly. 2015. "Social Media Use and Participation: A Meta-Analysis of Current Research." *Information, Communication & Society* 18 (5): 524–538.

Boxell, Levi, Matthew Gentzkow, and Jesse M. Shapiro. 2017. "Greater Internet use Is Not Associated with Faster Growth in Political Polarization among US Demographic Groups." *Proceedings of the National Academy of Sciences* 114 (40): 10612–10617.

Brady, William, Julian Willis, John T. Jost, Joshua A. Tucker, and Jay Van Bavel. 2017. "Emotion Shapes Diffusion of Moral Content in Social Networks." *Proceedings of the National Academy of Sciences* 114 (28): 7313–7318.

Branch, Taylor. 1988. *Parting the Waters: America in the King Years, 1954–63.* New York: Simon and Schuster.

Breland, Ali. 2020. "QAnon Candidates Keep Winning Primaries and Top Republicans Keep Welcoming Them." *Mother Jones*, August 13. https://www.motherjones.com/2020-elections/2020/08/marjorie-taylor-greene-qanon-congressional-republicans.

Burris, Sarah K. 2020. "Boogaloo Militia Members Have Infiltrated the US Military—and They're Aiming to Overthrow the American Government." *Raw Story*, June 24. https://www.rawstory.com/2020/06/boogaloo-militia-members-have-infiltrated-the-us-military-and-theyre-aiming-to-overthrow-the-american-government/.

Bush, Daniel. 2020. "Trump-appointed Elections Commissioner Says 'No Real Evidence' of President's Claims About Voter Fraud." NPR, August 26. https://www.pbs.org/newshour/politics/trump-appointed-elections-commissioner-says-no-real-evidence-of-presidents-claims-about-voter-fraud.

Cannadine, David. 1999. *Decline and Fall of the British Aristocracy.* New York: Vintage Books.

Case, Anne, and Angus Deaton. 2020. *Deaths of Despair and the Future of Capitalism.* Princeton, NJ: Princeton University Press.

Chadwick, Andrew. 2013. *The Hybrid Media System.* New York: Oxford University Press.

Chait, Jonathan. 2021. "Tucker Carlson Endorses White Supremacist Theory by Name." *New York Magazine*, April 9. https://nymag.com/intelligencer/2021/04/tucker-carlson-great-replacement-white-supremacist-immigration-fox-news-racism.html.

Cineas, Fabiola. 2021. "Donald Trump is the Accelerant." *Vox*, January 9. https://www.vox.com/21506029/trump-violence-tweets-racist-hate-speech.

Civil Rights Act. 1964. https://www.ourdocuments.gov/doc.php?flash=false&doc=97&page=transcript.

Cohen, Seth. 2020. "Jim Crow 2.0? How Kentucky's Poll Closures Could Suppress Black Votes." *Forbes*, June 22. https://www.forbes.com/sites/sethcohen/2020/06/22/kentucky-and-jim-crow-2-dot-0/#526971cf2219.

Collier, David, and Steven Levitsky. 1997. "Democracy with Adjectives: Conceptual Innovation in Comparative Research." *World Politics* 49 (3): 430–451.

Daniels, Gilda R. 2020. *Uncounted: The Crisis of Voter Suppression in America*. New York: New York University Press.

DeLanda, Manuel. 2006. *A New Philosophy of Society*. New York: Continuum.

Derysh, Igor. 2021. "How One Billionaire Family Bankrolled Election Lies, White nationalism—and the Capitol Riot." *Salon*, February 4. https://www.salon.com/2021/02/04/how-one-billionaire-family-bankrolled-election-lies-white-nationalism—and-the-capitol-riot/.

Du Mez, Kristin Kobes. 2020. *Jesus and John Wayne: How White Evangelicals Corrupted a Faith and Fractured a Nation*. New York: Liveright Publishing.

Economist Intelligence Unit (EIU). 2020. "Democracy Index 2020: In Sickness and in Health?"https://pages.eiu.com/rs/753-RIQ-438/images/democracy-index-of the 21st century.

Ellison, Sarah, and Amy Gardner. 2023. "At Center of Fox News Lawsuit, Sidney Powell and a 'Wackadoodle' Email." *Washington Post*, March 16. https://www.washingtonpost.com/media/2023/03/16/sidney-powell-fox-news-dominion/.

Erdmann, Gero. 2011. "Decline of Democracy: Loss of Quality, Hybridization and Breakdown of Democracy." In Gero Erdmann and Marianne Kneuer, eds., *Regression of Democracy?* (pp. 21–58). Wiesbaden: Springer.

Finkel, Steven E., Jeremy Horowitz, and Reynaldo T. Rojo-Mendoza. 2012. "Civic Education and Democratic Backsliding in the Wake of Kenya's Post-2007 Election Violence." *Journal of Politics* 74 (1): 52–65.

Fiske, Susan, and Shelley Taylor. 1991. *Social Cognition*. 2nd ed. New York: McGraw-Hill.

Freelon, Deen, and Chris Wells. 2020. "Disinformation as Political Communication." *Political Communication* 37 (2): 145–156.

Gold, Matea. 2017. "The Mercers and Stephen Bannon: How a Populist Power base was Funded and Built." *Washington Post*, March 17. https://www.washingtonpost.com/graphics/politics/mercer-bannon/?itid=lk_inline_manual_3.

Gorski, Philip S., and Samuel L. Perry. 2022. *The Flag and the Cross: White Christian Nationalism and the Threat to American Democracy*. New York: Oxford University Press.

Gray, Kathleen. 2021. "In Michigan, a Dress Rehearsal for the Chaos at the Capitol on Wednesday." *New York Times*, January 9. https://www.nytimes.com/2021/01/09/us/politics/michigan-state-capitol.html.

Hacker, Jacob S., and Paul Pierson. 2020. *Let Them Eat Tweets: How the Right Rules in the Age of Extreme Inequality*. New York: Liveright Publishing.

Harold, Scott W., Nathan Beauchamp-Mustafaga, and Jeffrey W. Hornung (2021). "Chinese Disinformation Efforts on Social Media." RAND Corporation. https://www.rand.org/pubs/research_reports/RR4373z3.html.

Hemmer, Nicole. 2016. *Messengers of the Right: Conservative Media and the Transformation of American Politics*. Philadelphia: University of Pennsylvania Press.

Horwitz, Jeff. 2021. "The Facebook Whistleblower, Frances Haugen, Says She Wants to Fix the Company, Not Harm it." *Wall Street Journal*, October 3. https://www.wsj.com/articles/facebook-whistleblower-frances-haugen-says-she-wants-to-fix-the-company-not-harm-it-11633304122.

Karell, Daniel. 2021. "Online Extremism and Offline Harm." SSRC Items. June 1. https://items.ssrc.org/extremism-online/online-extremism-and-offline-harm/.

Kennedy, Bud. 2020. "A Paranoid Militia Infiltrating Texas Police is Bent on Rebellion, 'ready to rise up.'" *Fort Worth Star-Telegram*, February 28. https://www.star-telegram.com/news/politics-government/article240714426.html.

Kneuer, Marianne. 2021. "Unravelling Democratic Erosion: Who Drives the Slow Death of Democracy, and How?" *Democratization* 28 (8): 1442–1462.

Kreiss, Daniel. 2021. "Invited Review: *Social Media and Democracy: The State of the Field, Prospects for Reform*." *International Journal of Press/Politics* 26 (2): 1–8.

Kreiss, Daniel, and Madhavi Reddi. 2021. "How Identity Propaganda is Used to Undermine Political Power." Lawfareblog, August 11. https://www.lawfareblog.com/how-identity-propaganda-used-undermine-political-power.

Kruglanski, Arie, and Donna Webster. 1996. "Motivated Closing of the Mind: 'Seizing' and 'Freezing.'" *Journal of Personality and Social Psychology* 103 (2): 263–283.

Kruse, Kevin M. 2015. *One Nation Under God: How Corporate America Invented Christian America*. New York: Basic Books.

Kunda, Ziva. 1987. "Motivated Inference: Self-Serving Generation and Evaluation of Causal Theories." *Journal of Personality and Social Psychology* 53 (4): 636–647.

Kunda, Ziva. 1990. "The Case for Motivated Reasoning." *Psychological Bulletin* 108 (3): 480–498.

Kuo, Rachel, and Alice Marwick. 2021. "Critical Disinformation Studies: History, Power, and Politics." *Harvard Kennedy School Misinformation Review* 2 (4): 1–12.

Leonard, Christopher. 2019. *Kochland: The Secret History of Koch Industries and Corporate Power in America*. New York: Simon & Schuster.

Lerman, Rachel. 2021. "Major Trump Backer Rebekah Mercer Orchestrates Parler's Second Act." *Washington Post*, February 24. https://www.washingtonpost.com/technology/2021/02/24/parler-relaunch-rebekah-mercer/.

Lessig, Lawrence. 2021. "Why the US is a Failed Democratic State." *New York Review of Books*, December 10. https://www.nybooks.com/daily/2021/12/10/why-the-us-is-a-failed-democratic-state/.

Levin, Sam. 2020. "White Supremacists and Militias Have Infiltrated Police Across US, Report Says." *The Guardian*, August 27. https://www.theguardian.com/us-news/2020/aug/27/white-supremacists-militias-infiltrate-us-police-report.

Levine, Mike. 2020. "'No Blame?' ABC News Finds 54 Cases Invoking 'Trump' in Connection with Violence, Threats, Alleged Assaults." ABC News, May 30. https://abcnews.go.com/Politics/blame-abc-news-finds-17-cases-invoking-trump/story?id=58912889.

Levitsky, Steven, and Daniel Ziblatt. 2018. *How Democracies Die*. New York: Crown.

Levitt, Justin. 2007. "The Truth About Voter Fraud." Brennan Center for Justice at New York University School of Law. November 9. https://www.brennancenter.org/our-work/research-reports/truth-about-voter-fraud.

Livingston, Steven, and Gregor Walter-Drop. 2013. *Bits and Atoms: Information and Communication Technology in Areas of Limited Statehood*. New York: Oxford University Press.

Lust, Ellen, and David Waldner. 2015. "Theories of Democratic Change." USAID: Research and Innovation Grants Working Papers Series. https://www.iie.org/wp-content/uploads/2022/12/DRG-Center-Working-Paper-Yale-TOC.pdf.

Mac, Ryan, and Sheera Frenkel. 2021. "Internal Alarm, Public Shrugs: Facebook's Employees Dissect its Election Role." *New York Times*, October 22. https://www.nytimes.com/2021/10/22/technology/facebook-election-misinformation.html?smtyp=cur&smid=tw-nytimes.

Mac, Ryan, and Lisa Lerer. 2022. "The Right's Would-be Kingmaker." *New York Times*. February 14. https://www.nytimes.com/2022/02/14/technology/republican-trump-peter-thiel.html.

Maclean, Nancy. 2017. *Democracy in Chains*. New York: Penguin Books.

Mayer, Jane. 2016. *Dark Money*. New York: Doubleday.

Montgomery, Nancy. 2017. "Neo-Nazis Excluded from Military Service by Policy, but Concerns Persist." *Stars and Stripes*, August 18. https://www.rawstory.com/2020/06/boogaloo-militia-members-have-infiltrated-the-us-military-and-theyre-aiming-to-overthrow-the-american-government/.

30 CONNECTIVE ACTION AND THE RISE OF THE FAR-RIGHT

Mounk, Yascha. 2018. "Can Liberal Democracy Survive Social Media?" *New York Review of Books*, April 30. https://www.nybooks.com/daily/2018/04/30/can-liberal-democracy-survive-social-media/.

Neidig, Harper. 2022. "Bannon Predicted 'All Hell is Going to Break Loose Tomorrow' After Jan. 5 Call with Trump." *The Hill*, July 12. https://thehill.com/homenews/house/3556166-bannon-predicted-all-hell-is-going-to-break-loose-tomorrow-after-jan-5-call-with-trump/.

Nguyen, Tina. 2020. "Trump Isn't Secretly Winking at QAnon. He's Retweeting its Followers." *Politico*, July 12. https://www.politico.com/news/2020/07/12/trump-tweeting-qanon-followers-357238.

Parker, Christopher S. 2021. "Status Threat: Moving the Right Further to the Right?" *Daedalus* 150 (2): 56–75.

Parker, Christopher S., and Matt A. Barreto. 2013. *Change They Can't Believe it: The Tea Party and Reactionary Politics in America*. Princeton, NJ: Princeton University Press.

Pennycook, Gordon, and David G. Rand. 2021. "The Psychology of Fake News." *Trends in Cognitive Science*. May. https://www.sciencedirect.com/science/article/pii/S1364661321000516.

Persily, Nathaniel, and Joshua A. Tucker (eds). 2020. *Social Media and Democracy: The State of the Field, Prospects for Reform*. Cambridge: Cambridge University Press.

Pew Research Center. 2015. "Trust in Government: 1958–2015." November 23. https://www.pewresearch.org/politics/2015/11/23/1-trust-in-government-1958-2015/.

Porter, Ethan, and Thomas J. Wood. 2019. *False Alarm: The Truth about Political Mistruths in the Trump Era*. New York: Cambridge University Press.

Powell, James Lawrence. 2011. *The Inquisition of Climate Science*. New York: Columbia University Press.

Robinson, Cedric J. 2020. *Black Marxism: The Making of the Black Radical Tradition*. Chapel Hill: University of North Carolina Press.

Sanovich, Sergey. 2018. "Russia: The Origins of Digital Disinformation." In Samuel C. Woolley and Philip N. Howard, eds., *Computational Propaganda: Political Parties, Politicians, and Political Manipulation on Social Media* (pp. 21–40). New York: Oxford University Press.

Skocpol, Theda, and Vanessa Williamson 2016. *The Tea Party and the Remaking of Republican Conservatism*. New York: Oxford University Press.

Smith, Mitch. 2022. "Man Receives Nearly 20 Years in Prison for Plot to Kidnap Gov Gretchen Whitmer." *New York Times*, December 3. https://www.nytimes.com/2022/12/28/us/barry-croft-michigan-sentencing.html.

Sottile, Leah. 2020. "The Chaos Agents." *New York Times*, August 19. https://www.nytimes.com/interactive/2020/08/19/magazine/boogaloo.html.

Stanley-Becker, Isaac. 2020. "Disinformation Campaign Stokes Fears about Mail Voting, Using LeBron James Image and Boosted by Trump-aligned Group." *Washington Post*, August 20. https://www.washingtonpost.com/politics/disinformation-campaign-stokes-fears-about-mail-voting-using-lebron-.

Stewart, Katherine. 2019. *The Power Worshippers: Inside the Dangerous Rise of Religious Nationalism*. New York: Bloomsbury Publishing.

Stone, Peter. 2023. "Russia Disinformation Looks to U.S. Far-Right to Weaken Ukraine Support." *The Guardian*, March 16. https://www.theguardian.com/world/2023/mar/16/russia-disinformation-us-far-right-republicans-ukraine.

Sullivan, Margaret. 2019. "If Trump Doesn't Condone Violence Against Journalists, He Should Stop Inspiring It." *Washington Post*, October 14. https://www.washingtonpost.com/lifestyle/style/if-trump-doesnt-condone-violence-against-journalists-he-should-stop-inspiring-it/2019/10/14/f8cddb50-ee7e-11e9-8693-f487e46784aa_story.html.

Taber, Charles S., and Milton Lodge. 2006. "Motivated Skepticism in the Evaluation of Political Beliefs." *American Journal of Political Science* 50 (3): 755–769.

Tarrow, Sidney. 2021. *Movements and Parties: Critical Connections in American Political Development*. New York: Cambridge University Press.

Tausanovitch, Alex, and Danielle Root. 2020. "How Partisan Gerrymandering Limits Voting Rights." Center for American Progress. July 8. https://www.americanprogress.org/issues/democracy/reports/2020/07/08/487426/partisan-gerrymandering-limits-voting-rights/.

Thaler, Michael. 2021. "The Fake News Effect: Experimentally Identifying Motivated Reasoning Using Trust in News." July 22. https://ssrn.com/abstract=3717381or http://dx.doi.org/10.2139/ssrn.3717381.

Tsfati, Yariv, Hajo G. Boomgaarden, Jasper Strömbäck, Rozemarijn Vliegenthart, Alyt Damstra, and Elina Lindgren. 2020. "Causes and Consequences of Mainstream Media Dissemination of Fake News: Literature Review and Synthesis." Annals of the International Communication Association 44 (2): 157–173.

Tucker, Joshua A., Andrew Guess, Pablo Barberá, Cristian Vaccari, Alexandra Siegel, Sergey Sanovich, Denis Stukal, and Brendan Nyhan. 2018. *Social Media, Political Polarization, and Political Disinformation: A Review of the Scientific Literature*. Menlo Park, CA: William and Flora Hewlett Foundation.

V-Dem Democracy Report. 2021. "Autocratization Turns Viral." V-Dem Institute at University of Gothenburg. https://www.v-dem.net/documents/12/dr_2021.pdf

Vogel, Kenneth P. 2022. "Leonard Leo Pushed the Courts Right. Now He's Aiming at American Society." *New York Times*, October 12. https://www.nytimes.com/2022/10/12/us/politics/leonard-leo-courts-dark-money.html.

Waldner, David and Ellen Lust. 2018. "Unwelcome Change: Coming to Terms with Democratic Backsliding." *Annual Review of Political Science* 21: 93–113.

Wikipedia n.d. "1906 British Elections." https://en.wikipedia.org/wiki/1906_United_Kingdom_general_election#:~:text=The%201906%20United%20Kingdom%20general, landslide%20majority%20at%20the%20election.

Wilson, Jason. 2020. "The Rightwing Groups Behind Wave of Protests Against Covid-19 Restrictions." *The Guardian*, April 17. https://www.theguardian.com/world/2020/apr/17/far-right-coronavirus-protests-restrictions.

Wooley, Samuel C., and Douglas R. Guilbeault. 2017. "Computational Propaganda in the United States of America: Manufacturing Consensus Online." Working paper. The Computational Propaganda Project, Oxford University.

Yang, Yunkang. 2020. *The Political Logic of the Radical Right Media Sphere in the United States*. PhD dissertation, University of Washington.

Ziblatt, Daniel. 2017. *Conservative Parties and the Birth of Democracy*. New York: Cambridge University Press.

Zuboff, Shoshana. 2019. *The Age of Surveillance Capitalism*. New York: Public Affairs. (Kindle edition).

Chapter 2

Unraveling the Big Lie

Participatory Disinformation and the 2020 Election

Kate Starbird

Introduction

On January 6, 2021, an angry protest by supporters of President Trump turned into a violent attack on the US Capitol building—part of a multi-faceted effort to prevent the certification of Joe Biden as the winner of the 2020 US presidential election.

The day's events began at the Ellipse with organized protests from pro-Trump and conservative organizations featuring a range of speakers, including President Trump. As the speeches were winding down, and with urging from the president, who asserted he would be joining them, attendees began to trek to the Capitol. Many of the protesters were dressed in the red-white-and-blue of US patriotism—and Trump support. A small but significant number wore camouflage. A few had helmets and body armor. The January 6th Commission would later reveal that some of Trump's supporters were armed and planned to disrupt the certification of the Electoral College votes. There were hundreds of flags, including American flags, Trump flags, Blue Lives Matter flags, and Confederate flags. Eventually some would wave atop the Capitol, and others would be used as weapons against police as the crowd surged violently onto the grounds and eventually up the stairs (and walls) and into the building—where procedures to certify the Electoral College votes were disrupted.

Our understandings of the events of January 6—including how the violence that day began, how it was organized, and whom should be held responsible—have begun to crystallize in the intervening years. Arrests have been made and perpetrators have been tried and sentenced, in some cases to lengthy prison terms. Investigations from the House Select Committee on the January 6th attack on the US Capitol (US House 2022) revealed that the

---

Kate Starbird, *Unraveling the Big Lie*. In: *Connective Action and the Rise of the Far-Right*. Edited by: Steven Livingston and Michael Miller, Oxford University Press. © Oxford University Press (2025).
DOI: 10.1093/oso/9780197794937.003.0002

violence that took place that day was not a wholly emergent phenomenon from within an agitated crowd, but resulted at least in part from a pre-planned attack by organized militias. But there is little doubt, as evidenced by the signs and slogans of the protesters that day and the contemporaneous statements[1] from President Trump about a "stolen election," that the January 6 attack and insurrection attempt at the US Capitol was mobilized on top of the Big Lie—an amalgamation of hundreds of false, misleading, and unsubstantiated claims that sought to sow doubt in the results of the 2020 election.

Benkler et al. (2020) have described the early efforts to undermine trust in the 2020 election—particularly around mail-in voting—as an elite-driven disinformation campaign, highlighting the role of mass media. This chapter seeks to illuminate the role of social media within the production of this disinformation campaign, to explore the interplay between top-down and bottom-up dynamics, and to describe the collaborative relationship between elites and their audiences. Using examples from the digital record of social media activity during the lead up and following the 2020 election, and with particular focus on the #SharpieGate conspiracy theory, I present a model of *participatory disinformation* that explains how the Big Lie was coproduced by elites (conventional surrogate organizations) and their audiences (instantiations of digital surrogate organizations) and how elites mobilized those audiences, on top of that disinformation, through a series of calls to action that eventually led to the events on January 6.

In the terminology of the conceptual framework used in this volume, the top-down dynamics of participatory disinformation emerge from conventional surrogate organizations aligned with Trump and the GOP. According to the political science literature that informs this volume, a surrogate organization uses emotive issues and claims to mobilize publics on behalf of a political party (Hacker and Pierson 2020). Bottom-up production of disinformation occurs in our model through "digital surrogate organizations." The notion of a digital surrogate organization is derived from

---

[1] The statement referenced here was included in a tweet by President Trump's personal account (@realDonaldTrump) at 7:15 p.m. on January 6, 2022: "These are the things and events that happen when a sacred landslide election victory is so unceremoniously & viciously stripped away from great patriots who have been badly & unfairly treated for so long. Go home with love & in peace. Remember this day forever!" This tweet was deleted approximately one hour later. None of President Trump's tweets were accessible via the Twitter platform at the time of writing (2022), because his account had been suspended. However, a contemporaneous screenshot is included at the end of this chapter and ProPublica maintains a website with Trump's deleted tweets: https://projects.propublica.org/politwoops/user/realDonaldTrump.

Lance Bennett and Alexandra Segerberg's notion of "connective action" (2012). Bennett and Steven Livingston describe the concept in the opening chapter of this volume. Conventional surrogate organizations and digital surrogate organizations collaborate in the production of—and mobilization through—participatory disinformation.

Background

Defining Disinformation

To understand disinformation, we must first differentiate it from its less nefarious cousin, misinformation. Misinformation is information that is false, but not necessarily intentionally so (Jack 2017; Wardle and Derakhshan 2017). Disinformation, on the other hand, is false or misleading information, intentionally seeded or spread for a specific goal—such as a political, financial, or reputational one. The main distinction between mis- and disinformation, therefore, is one of intention. However, a historical view provides insight into and complicates those definitions.

Though the term has experienced broader use and taken on a somewhat blurrier definition in recent years, disinformation has its roots in Soviet "active measures" (Bittman 1985; Rid 2020). During the Cold War, the KGB and its allies in the Soviet sphere employed both passive (intelligence gathering) and active (information manipulation) measures as they pursued their geopolitical objectives (Bittman 1985; Rid 2020). Active measures included a suite of techniques to manipulate individuals and groups—from blackmail to forgery. Disinformation was one prominent tool in the Soviet active measures repertoire, and one that appears to be proliferating, appropriated by a wide variety of actors, in the internet age.

Disinformation is rarely just a single piece of false content. Instead, it takes shape as a series of information actions—that is, a *campaign* (Starbird et al. 2019). And rather than being outright false, it is often misleading. Bittman, a former practitioner, describes how effective disinformation is often built around a true or plausible core and then layered with exaggerations or distortions to create a false sense of reality (Bittman 1985). Additionally, though intention is core to the definition of disinformation, Bittman explains that disinformation campaigns and other active measures are designed to leverage the participation of "unwitting agents"—in many cases sincere believers of the distortions who may not be aware of their role in the campaign. Unwitting agents often work to disseminate, and in some cases even produce, disinformation.

Conceptualizing Disinformation as Participatory

From the perspective of US politics, the term disinformation rose to national awareness in the wake of the 2016 election, with researchers and journalists converging on the term to characterize efforts by Russia (and allied organizations) to manipulate US political discourse through both a hack-and-leak operation (Mueller 2019) and social media operations (e.g., Lukito et al. 2020; Freelon et al. 2020; Arif et al. 2018). The story of disinformation in 2016 was largely one of a foreign attack on the US, using inauthentic social media accounts to disseminate messages, and explicitly coordinated within an organization in St. Petersburg, Russia. In contrast, disinformation during the 2020 US election—especially the effort to undermine trust in the election process and results—was largely domestic, produced and promoted by authentic and in many cases "blue-check" or verified accounts, and hard to characterize as explicitly coordinated. Instead, the production and spread of false and misleading claims about the 2020 election appears to be a loose collaboration across a range of individuals and organizations, from political figures to hyperpartisan media outlets, to everyday people who became sincere believers and unwitting contributors to the Big Lie—or, in the terms used in this volume, surrogate organizations and networks.

My colleagues and I have described these collaborative dynamics previously in research on other recent disinformation campaigns (Starbird et al. 2019). Like propaganda more generally (Wanless and Berk 2019), disinformation is—and always has been if we reflect on the descriptions by Bittman (1985) and Rid (2020)—*participatory*. The affordances of social media, however, have enabled new pathways for participation and tighter feedback loops between elites and audiences (witting and unwitting agents)— paving the way for truly and fundamentally participatory disinformation campaigns.

Participatory Disinformation as Connective Action

Participatory disinformation is part of the broader phenomenon of political participation and political organizing that occurs online. Social media and other online platforms have been recognized for their capacity to bring people together, organize, and provide support for political movements—from the Arab Spring (e.g., Howard et al. 2011; Starbird and Palen 2012) to the Occupy Protests (Bennett and Segerberg 2012; Agarwal et al. 2014). Though initially celebrated by some for their potential to support pro-democratic movements, we are increasingly seeing the affordances of social media used—in part through the spread of disinformation—to organize and mobilize populist political action that supports authoritarian governance around the world. For example, Ong and Cabanes (2018) explain how "networked disinformation" in the Philippines leverages feedback between leaders and audiences to build a sense of collective grievance that fuels populist political movements. In that same context, journalist Maria Ressa has drawn attention to how the Duterte regime mobilized online troll networks to harass critics of that autocratic regime (Swisher 2019) and how similar dynamics of online political action played a role in the rise of recently elected President Ferdinand Marcos Jr. (Coronel 2022).

Similarly, the participatory disinformation campaign described in this chapter can be viewed as a social media-enabled political movement, or what Bennett and Segerberg call *connective action* (2012). Connective action is a form of political organizing that is shaped by technologies that enable people to connect and communicate—such as social media. Whereas traditional collective action requires formal organizing and hierarchical structure, connective action can be less hierarchical, relying on new vectors of participation enabled by online platforms. Connective action takes place as individual acts of personal expression that are shaped, echoed, and built upon by networks of connected people and organizations. As Bennett and Livingston note in the opening chapter, routinized patterns of communication online, such as hashtags in Facebook groups, can take on the quality of an organization. Or as Bennett and Segerberg put it, "Ultimately, technology-enabled networks may become dynamic organizations in their own right" (Bennett and Segerberg 2012).

To understand the dynamics of connective action, Bennett and Segerberg (2012) introduce the concept of "personal action frames." Frames are schemas of interpretation that shape how people make sense of information and experiences in the world (Goffman 1974). Through *framing*—that is, highlighting certain aspects of reality to promote a specific way or perceiving a problem, its cause, its moral interpretation, or its solution (Entman 1993)—communicators can shape how others interpret the world. Framing processes are important for social movements as they negotiate a shared understanding of a problem, its cause, and its potential solutions (Benford and Snow 2000). Within connective action, personal action frames are messages that are designed to be easily appropriated, personalized, and shared (Bennett and Segerberg 2012). In 2020, Trump's repeated and misleading message of voter fraud became a personal action frame through which his supporters could participate in a political effort to contest the outcome of the election. In this chapter, I explain how everyday Trump supporters collaborated with members of his campaign and other elites in conservative media and politics to create and then mobilized on top of a sense of grievance around a rigged election—eventually culminating in the events of January 6, 2021.

Methods

The insights presented here rely upon extensive analysis—by the author of this chapter along with numerous colleagues—of false and misleading claims that spread online in the lead up to, during, and for several months following the 2020 US election. This research incorporated real-time monitoring and rapid analysis conducted through the Election Integrity Partnership (Center for an Informed Public et al. 2021), which documented hundreds of incidents of problematic information about the 2020 election, including 356 false, misleading, exaggerated, or unsubstantiated claims that sowed doubt in election procedures or results (Kennedy et al. 2022).

Our team employed an interpretative, mixed-method approach to the investigation of "digital trace" data to understand how these misleading claims emerged and spread on social media and out through the broader information ecosystem. This grounded approach extends the qualitative methodology presented by Charmaz (2014) to include interpretative analysis of visual and quantitative representations of "big" social data. It builds upon methodological innovation from the field of crisis informatics (Palen and Anderson 2016) and the study of online rumors (Starbird et al. 2014; Maddock et al. 2015). Researchers iterate between macro-level views of information dynamics, such as using network and temporal graphs to identify patterns and anomalies, and micro-level views that rely on manual content analysis of social media posts to understand what those patterns and anomalies represent.

Though this chapter primarily focuses on a single case study (#Sharpie-Gate), the insights emerged from close inspection of dozens of cases—from misleading stories of mail-in ballots being discarded in dumpsters to false claims about voting machines systematically switching votes.

Trump Tweets Part I: Setting the Voter Fraud Frame

Viral claims of a rigged 2020 election began at the very top—in social media posts from then-President Donald Trump:

The tweet in Figure 2.1, posted by President Trump's Twitter account on June 22, 2020, claimed that the election would be rigged, that ballots would be "printed by foreign countries," and that it would be the "scandal of our times."

The post was retweeted more than 90,000 times and received nearly 300,000 likes, fairly typical engagement numbers for the @realDonaldTrump account at the time. At this point in the evolution of Twitter's ecosystem, Trump had a huge megaphone with tens of millions of followers, including a dedicated group who avidly and often systematically liked and retweeted his content.

This was one of many similar social media posts and other public statements—throughout the summer and into the fall election season, where President Trump pushed groundless claims of voter fraud. This voter fraud refrain was perhaps not surprising, considering Trump and some of his close

Figure 2.1 Screenshot of tweet from President Donald Trump's verified account on June 22, 2020.

supporters had made similar assertions in the lead up to the 2016 election (Roth 2016). And even after winning in 2016, President Trump claimed (and created a committee to investigate his claims) that he lost the popular vote due to large numbers of votes by noncitizen voters (Cottrell et al. 2018). In the summer of 2020, his poll numbers were consistently behind candidate Biden, and it is possible that he returned to this old refrain as reputational insurance against a likely loss.

Through repetition of these claims, which echoed across social media as well as partisan media outlets online and on cable television, President Trump set a frame and an expectation among his followers of a rigged election. This frame became a lens for his supporters to interpret the events of the 2020 US election—and provided the motivation and a pathway for them to participate.

The Elite-Driven Disinformation Campaign Targeting Mail-In Voting

It is important to note here that the election procedures heading into the 2020 US election were disrupted by the COVID-19 crisis. With infection (and death) rates rising and without access yet to protective vaccines, many states had adjusted voting procedures to include broader access to mail-in voting. Trump and many of his vocal supporters seized on these changes as an opportunity to sow doubt in the process—claiming (via tweet) that mail-in voting was vulnerable to fraud, and bizarrely considering the alternative of in-person voting, that drop-boxes could lead to the spread of COVID (O'Sullivan et al. 2020). These claims echoed through conservative and right-wing media, reinforcing the message that the election would be rigged against Donald Trump—and Republican voters.

In August and September, several stories ostensibly demonstrating the vulnerability of mail-in voting emerged and, in many cases, went viral—from claims about people receiving ballots at old addresses, to stories about ballots found with discarded mail in dumpsters or ditches (Center for an Informed Public et al. 2021). Some of these claims were outright false, like a viral photo pushed by right-wing media and amplified by Donald Trump Jr. with the framing that thousands of mail-in ballots had been found in a dumpster in Sonoma California.[2] Other claims, like those about discarded

---

[2] In reality, the photo featured ballot envelopes from the 2018 election that were being recycled according to election law. See Samanthat Putterman, "Ballots in California Dumpster Were Actually Old, Empty Envelopes from 2018 Election," Politifact, September 28, 2020, https://www.

mail-in ballots, were partially true, but misleading in that they exaggerated the impact or misattributed the cause (Kennedy et al. 2020). Though the production and spread of claims sowing (and reflecting) doubt in mail-in voting primarily spread through conservative and/or pro-Trump audiences, concerns about the vulnerability of mail-in ballots took root among audiences on the left as well—with rumors that the US Postal Service was intentionally sabotaging the process by taking mailboxes out of circulation (Kennedy et al. 2020).

Benkler and colleagues described this effort to discredit the mail-in voting process as an elite-driven "disinformation campaign" (2020). From all accounts, it was successful, manifesting in two parallel outcomes: 1) sowing doubt in the mail-in process generally; and 2) in states that had options for both mail-in voting and in-person voting, leading a larger proportion of Republicans to vote in-person rather than by mail (Stewart 2020).

This second outcome had other downstream effects—including some that were anticipated prior to Election Day. With more Democrats voting by mail and more Republicans voting in person on Election Day, and in combination with laws pushed by Republican legislatures to delay the processing and counting of mail-in ballots, it meant that there would be more uncertainty about the outcome of the election in the hours (and days) after the polls closed and that there would likely be a shift, in states that waited to count mail-in ballots, toward Democratic candidates as the mail-in votes were counted. About a week before the election, my colleagues and I posted an article explaining how the uncertainty and vote share shifts, in combination with the strategic amplification of false rumors and misleading narratives—the disinformation campaign noted by Benkler et al. (2020)— were likely to lead to an extensive spread of false, misleading, exaggerated, and unsubstantiated claims of voter fraud in the days following the election (Starbird et al. 2020).

Army for Trump: Staging Resources for a Disinformation Campaign

Repeatedly, and with help from conservative and right-wing media, President Trump set and reinforced the frame of a rigged election. In the weeks leading up to Election Day, his campaign also provided motivation for

politifact.com/factchecks/2020/sep/28/facebook-posts/ballots-california-dumpster-were-actually-old-empt/.

others to gather evidence to support that frame—and the mechanisms for sharing that evidence. One avenue was through the "Army for Trump."

As Election Day approached, the Trump campaign used their social media accounts and online presence (e.g., the Facebook post in Figure 2.2) to recruit and "train" informal poll observers. After repeatedly messaging that the election would be stolen from them, the Army for Trump provided an opportunity for Trump's supporters to take action and do something about it. Voters were encouraged to go to the polls and gather "evidence" of voter fraud. The campaign staged a website (defendyourballot.com) with a form that the "poll observers" could use to directly share their observations—and, as it turned out, their misinterpretations (Klasfeld 2020)—of issues at the polls. Pointers to this website circulated through social media, both through the accounts of the Trump campaign and high-level supporters and via links provided by everyday Trump voters letting others know that they could share their evidence using the form.

Another avenue for everyday Trump supporters to share with the Trump campaign's perceived evidence of voter fraud—or just speculation about something they or a friend (or a "friend of friend") saw on Election Day—was through social media. Online armies of "digital soldiers" combed

Figure 2.2 Screenshot of September 21, 2020 Facebook post from Team Trump, an official page of the Trump campaign, encouraging followers to join the "Army for Trump."

42 CONNECTIVE ACTION AND THE RISE OF THE FAR-RIGHT

through social media posts, amplifying claims that aligned or fitted with the frame of a rigged election, and "trading up" (Krafft and Donovan 2020) to larger influencers in the pro-Trump social media sphere. Social media users who shared claims of potential voter fraud were rewarded with attention (retweets) and reputational gains (follows) as their content echoed through the social network—eventually, in some cases, up to and through mega-influencer accounts. The potential of having "celebrity" accounts like @charliekirk11, @realJamesWoods, or @EricTrump notice and retweet them likely provided pro-Trump social media users additional motivation to participate. The rapid feedback loops provided by the affordances of social media, motivated and shaped the production of voter fraud claims during the mail-in voting period, and only accelerated on and after Election Day.

#SharpieGate: A Case Study of a False Voter Fraud Narrative

Our research team documented dozens of distinct claims about voter fraud on Election Day and even more in the days following. Perhaps one of the most salient was #SharpieGate—a rumor about Sharpie pens bleeding through ballots that soon grew into a conspiracy theory that the pens had intentionally been given to Trump voters as part of a Democratic election fraud scheme to disenfranchise them. Concerns about Sharpies bleeding through ballots first emerged during the early voting period, and election officials in some locations had even prestaged resources to address these concerns.[3] But that did not stop the claims from taking off on Election Day—and developing into a conspiracy theory of voter fraud that quickly went viral.

Early Amplification By a Conservative Media Pundit

On Twitter, the first concerns about Sharpie bleed-through were posted by a user in Chicago just half an hour after the polls opened (Figure 2.3, Label A). That first tweet appears to be one of sincere concern. It received no

---

[3] When marked ballots are rapidly fed into vote-counting machines, as they are on election day in many areas, the ink from ballpoint pens can smear the vote-reading instruments. Some election municipalities use fast-driving Sharpie pens to prevent this issue. In those cases, ballots are designed in a staggered way so that marks that bleed through from one side do not affect the voting areas on the other side of the ballot (MacDonald-Evoy 2020).

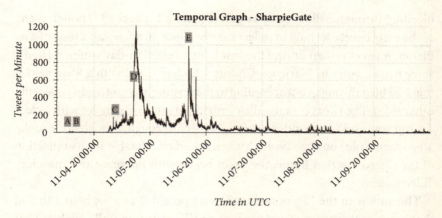

Figure 2.3 Temporal graph (tweets per minute) of tweets related to "ballots" and "Sharpies."

engagements. About 30 minutes later, a local host of a conservative radio show in Chicago (@AmyJacobson) posted the first of several tweets elevating concerns about Sharpies and encouraging her readers to "bring their own pens." Her retweets were retweeted about 400 times, bringing awareness of the perceived issue to a broad, but still limited audience. About 100 Twitter users quoted Jacobson's tweets, some with complaints about bad election management, but a few with the voter fraud frame:

@Anonymized (2020-11-03 13:33 UTC[4]):
They're destroying ballots. Voter suppression!
<quoted tweet>
   @AmyJacobson (2020-11-03 13:01 UTC, 7:01am Chicago time):
   If you are voting at LAKEVIEW HS bring your own black pen! Ballots are double sided and the sharpies they provide are bleeding through. Polling Marshal says there's nothing she can do. @MorningAnswer https://t.co/3j1hRwWgGg

From Concern to Suspicion to Accusation

Shortly after the polls opened in Arizona, users turned to social media (including both Twitter and Facebook) to share accounts of Sharpies

---

[4] For consistency of times across timezones, timestamps for the textual examples and graphs are in UTC time, which is five hours ahead of EST, seven hours ahead of MST (in Arizona).

bleeding through ballots there as well (Figure 2.3, Label B). Though many of the early tweets seemed to reflect sincere concern, a few had a tone of suspicion. A tweet posted during the first hour of election-day voting related a story from a voter in Maricopa County who had voted with a Sharpie pen that had bled through (but according to the posting account, didn't affect the other side). The tweet contained an embedded image of a ballot with a clear Trump vote and some evidence of slight bleed-through, though none in the area where votes on the visible side were marked. Notable for its reflection of the rigged election frame, the tweet began with the one-word question, "Electioneering?"

The author of the Electioneering? tweet posted it as a reply to a thread that began with a claim of violations at a polling place in Philadelphia. That thread was posted by @PublicSafetySME, a public safety columnist at the right-wing media outlet, Newsmax. @PublicSafetySME had only 1282 followers at the time. His tweet received thousands of retweets and hundreds of comments, eventually becoming a site where evidence of perceived voter fraud was aggregated and amplified—demonstrating the role that nano-influencers (and in this case, an up-and-coming hyperpartisan media outlet) played as a conduit between the stories provided by the online crowd and the massive megaphones of the pro-Trump elites.

As Election Day progressed in Arizona, stories about Sharpies spread through local groups on Facebook, along with directives to "bring your own pens." The latter may have set the stage for conflicts at the polls. Trump-supporting Arizonans who voted in the afternoon reported via social media posts on Twitter and Facebook that they had been "forced" to use Sharpie pens. In the evening, a little-known political activist posted a video, initially to a local Facebook group, of two women in Maricopa County describing the perception that Sharpie pens were invalidating votes, intentionally.

A Growing Theory to Explain a Trump Loss in Arizona

Initially, social media attention to tweets about Sharpies in Arizona and even to the provocative video claiming an intentional strategy of disenfranchise-ment through Sharpies was limited. On Election Day there were only about 2000 total tweets (including retweets) about Sharpie pens, and less than half were related to Arizona. But that changed on election night at about 11 p.m. Arizona time, shortly after Fox News called the presidential race in Arizona, announcing that Joe Biden was the presumptive winner there. On Twitter, after several hours with very few posts about Sharpies, the conversation began a slow but steady rise during the wee hours of the morning of November 4 (Figure 2.3, Label C)—as Trump's supporters, including members of his campaign as well as ordinary online activists, sought an explanation for why Trump had lost Arizona.

Much of this renewed activity consisted of 1) voters in Arizona recounting their experiences with Sharpies as evidence to support the growing theory and 2) online activists from Arizona and beyond amplifying that evidence and reinforcing the voter fraud frame. A micro-influencer (40,000 followers) from Arizona tweeted that election workers had distributed Sharpie pens knowing that they wouldn't work, capping off her tweet with an accusation of fraud, adding, "Dems are so desperate." That tweet had accumulated more than 1000 retweets in about two hours when social media mega influencer and head of the conservative political organization Turning Point USA, Charlie Kirk retweeted it out to his 1.8M followers. This was the first of three attempts by Kirk to amplify the emerging conspiracy theory.[5]

The election night video, originally posted to Facebook, began to spread on Twitter around this time through a handful of highly retweeted and quoted tweets. In one viral tweet, a micro-influencer who did not appear to have a local connection to Arizona, posted the video, with the framing that Sharpie pens had invalidated Trump voters' ballots, to her 50,000 followers. It received more than 15,000 amplifying engagements (retweets, quotes, retweets of quotes). Demonstrating the collaborative nature of the production of #SharpieGate, one of those quote tweets was from a low-follower account (<300 followers), operated by a voter in Arizona who seemed sincerely concerned about election procedures in her community, and who asserted, "Arizona has a massive voter fraud issue." Her tweet received nearly 9,000 retweets—a number more than 30 times the size of her follower count—from pro-Trump accounts, including conservative activist Charlie Kirk. This flood of attention can be exhilarating—and possibly was a motivating factor in some of the participation during this time, as local accounts angled for amplification from large-audience influencers.

---

[5] This first attempt was unsuccessful because Twitter suspended the retweeted account shortly after Kirk boosted it.

Going Viral through Elites and Mega Influencers

Around 10 a.m. Arizona time, #SharpieGate took off. This is the first massive spike on the graph in Figure 2.3 (Label D), surging from 200 to 1,200 tweets per minute. With that burst, the center of gravity in the conversation shifted from local voters and micro-influencers (and occasional boosting by Charlie Kirk) to elites in conservative and pro-Trump media and politics. Immediately precipitating that spike is the following tweet, from long-time conservative operative Matt Schlapp:

> @mschlapp (2020–11-04 ~16:51 UTC):
> AZ update: apparently the use of sharpie pens in gop precincts is causing ballots to be invalidated. Could be huge numbers of mostly Trump supporters. More to come

The speculative tweet summarized and amplified the earlier discourse about Sharpies invaliding the ballots of "mostly Trump supporters." It included an expression of uncertainty ("apparently") that allowed its author to repeat unsubstantiated claims while shielding himself from taking responsibility for their veracity (Starbird et al. 2016). And it quickly echoed through the pro-Trump media ecosystem—up to mega-influencers and then out to their audiences. Less than 10 minutes later, Fox News contributor @SaraCarterDC (1.3M followers) quote-tweeted Schlapp, saying that she was hearing the same thing from "friends" in Arizona and making a call to action, that "we need to investigate this." Ten minutes later, Townhall editor and Fox New contributor @KatiePavlich (865,000 followers) posted a retweet of Schlapp. And not long after that, Trump's two adult sons, @EricTrump and @DonaldJTrumpJr., retweeted Schlapp's unsubstantiated claims out to their millions of followers as well. In less than two hours, more than 80,000 Sharpie-related tweets were posted.

The volume of Sharpie-related tweets receded a bit after the initial spike, but the conversation persisted. Local Arizonans continued to post tweets with their own stories about being given Sharpies, voting with Sharpie pens, and having their Sharpies bleed through ballots—and many of these received outsized attention due to boosts from more influential accounts.

An Epidemic of Canceled Ballots

One of the more interesting dimensions of #SharpieGate involved an effort by Arizona voters to substantiate their claims of disenfranchisement. Many social media users shared a link to a website where voters could ostensibly go to check the status of their ballot. Unfortunately, the website listed provided the status of mail-in ballots. For people who had voted in-person, the site announced that their ballots had been canceled (which would not be surprising, because their mail-in ballots would have been canceled when they voted in person). But most did not, at first, catch the distinction.

For many, this message confirmed what they already believed, that they had been disenfranchised by being forced to use a Sharpie pen. The digital record reveals dozens of tweets like the one in Figure 2.4 (receiving thousands of retweets), often with screenshots of the online form, where people express anger and outrage due to their ballots being "canceled." These people weren't just told that they would be or had been cheated, but many Arizona Trump voters experienced (via this viral misinterpretation) being cheated. We can imagine that this politically and emotionally charged experience was a powerful one—and one that would be difficult to ever correct completely, even when they would later learn that their in-person vote was counted.

In its first 48 hours, #SharpieGate went from a perceived issue in polling places around the country to a viral conspiracy theory that provided a politically expedient explanation for Trump's loss in Arizona. A conservative media outlet was an earlier amplifier of the claims—possibly planting some of the specific seeds of doubt that would grow throughout the data. Likely influenced by repeated messaging of a rigged election, voters in Arizona (and elsewhere) went to the polls looking for evidence of cheating and misinterpreted their experiences there (and later their experience with an online form) through that lens. Motivated by the reputational economy of social media, they shared their experiences, which bounced around and eventually moved up the chain of politically active influencers. Within 24 hours of the polls closing, elites in politics and media, including members of the Trump family and Trump campaign, played a significant role in helping the nascent conspiracy theory take root and propagate widely.

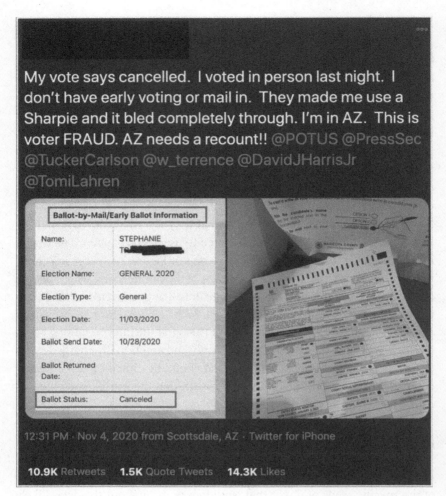

Figure 2.4 Anonymized screenshot of tweet posted on November 4, 2020 purporting to show that the account owner's in-person ballot had been invalidated due to a Sharpie pen, but instead showing that their mail-in ballot had been cancelled.

StopTheSteal: Mobilizing on Disinformation

#SharpieGate became wrapped up within the broader election fraud discourse. Elites in conservative media and politics helped to synthesize disparate claims around voting issues into a meta-narrative of systematic election fraud (by Democrats, against Trump). The following tweet, posted on

November 5 by Fox News pundit Maria Bartiromo, provides an illustrative example:

> @MariaBartiromo (2020–11-05 16:20:15 UTC):
>
> - 4am dump/Wisconsin 65,000 votes 100% for Biden
> - 4am dump/Michigan 138,499 votes 100% 4Biden
> - AZ poll workers forcing voters to use sharpies thereby invalidated ballots
> - Trump leading in GA, NC, PA, WI, MI & they stop counting before the vote fairy visits overnight...

By this time, election officials in Arizona had debunked the false rumors (with help from mainstream media) and some of the voters in Arizona who had shared early concerns with Sharpies had pulled back from those claims. But Bartiromo overlooked those corrections (or simply failed to look for them), bringing the false claims about Sharpie pens in Arizona together with claims about perceived statistical anomalies with vote counting in other states, and tweeting them out to her 850,000 followers—echoing these emergent claims back to the online audiences that had created them. The post went viral, receiving more than 60,000 amplifying engagements (retweets, quotes, retweets of quotes), and creating that second spike in our data (Figure 2.3, Label E).

On social media, one center of gravity for this synthesized discourse was the #StopTheSteal hashtag. The "Stop the Steal" slogan was originally created in 2016 by GOP operative Roger Stone. On the morning of November 3, 2020, it re-emerged as a hashtag, serving as a clearinghouse for dozens (and eventually hundreds) of different claims about election fraud in 2020. On Election Day and over the course of the days and weeks that followed, many disparate claims around perceived voting issues were reposted with the #StopTheSteal hashtag, implicitly invoking the voter fraud frame. For example, in a highly retweeted tweet, political operative Matt Schlapp tweeted the following, which connected misinterpretations of canceled ballots to the #StopTheSteal framing:

> @mschlapp (2020–11-04 17:34 UTC) This is one example of a Trump voter who had his legal ballot invalidated in AZ. He happened to check. How many others?

#SharpieGate
#StopTheSteal
<link to an image indicating a "canceled" early ballot>

As online Trump supporters, from everyday accounts to mega-influencers, began to converge around claims of voter fraud as an explanation and potential remedy for Trump's election loss, a number of calls to action began to circulate in connection with #SharpieGate and other claims. These included directions for checking ballot status (which led to more canceled confusion), instructions for calling lawyers, links for donations, and advertisements for in-person rallies and protests.

In Maricopa County, Arizona, several high-profile conservative political leaders and media figures played prominent roles in organizing, promoting, and/or taking part in protests. On the evening of November 4, just after #SharpieGate had gone viral, Senator Paul Gosar spoke at a rally near the Arizona Capitol and, in response to a question from the crowd about Sharpie pens, urged Trump supporters to go online and track their ballots. Afterward, Gosar turned to his social media accounts to promote his attendance. One tweet featured a statement of support for President Trump, along with an emerging refrain of "count all votes." Another included a video of his speech at the rally, with Gosar urging attendees to "email, text, tweet, everything you can possibly do to get the information out. . . make sure people know we are fighting, this is our Alamo."[6]

In the early hours of November 5, in response to a tweet asserting that his #SharpieGate claims were "easily debunked," Matt Schlapp doubled down on his voter fraud narrative, reporting that he and others planned to go to Arizona to, as Gosar had stated earlier, "count every legal ballot." Likely connected to the effort Schlapp mentioned, a second, larger gathering took place in Phoenix on November 6, 2020. That gathering, branded as a "Protect the Vote" rally, was advertised by other political influencers, including Charlie Kirk, who had played an early role in the spread of the false/misleading claims around Sharpie pens. Both Kirk and Gosar tweeted about the rally, positioning it as an attempt to stop Democrats or "the left" from "stealing the election" from President Trump and/or his supporters.

Over the course of November and December, #StopTheSteal messaging began to metastasize within online communities, with organizations (new

---

[6] Paul Gosar, Twitter, Nov 4, 2020, https://twitter.com/DrPaulGosar/status/13241922580825 70242.

UNRAVELING THE BIG LIE 51

and old) using that refrain to draw in supporters, garner donations, and make various calls to action. A series of protests were organized in other locations—including Georgia and Washington, DC.

The #StopTheSteal organizing efforts culminated in a final event in Washington, DC on January 6, 2021—timed to coincide with Congress's certification of Biden's electoral victory. In advance of the event, President Trump urged his followers to attend a "big protest" and asserted that it would be "wild," a message that echoed enthusiastically through pro-Trump social media spaces. Thousands of Trump supporters gathered at the Ellipse, south of the White House. The event was organized—at least in part—by Amy and Kylie Jane Kremer, a mother-daughter duo who were leading voices within the #StopTheSteal movement. Their accounts are among the most retweeted in #StopTheSteal tweets, and the Kremer's organization, Women for America First, held the permit for the rally. At the rally, high-profile Trump supporters took the stage, including others who were active in the voter fraud and #StopTheSteal social media discourse. Speakers—including then President Trump—repeatedly invoked the false narrative of a rigged election and urged the audience to take action, specifically calling on them to march to the Capitol and "fight like hell."

By the time Trump concluded his over one-hour speech, sections of the crowd had already begun to make the two-mile trek from the Ellipse to the Capitol. There they converged with other protesters and militia members who violently attacked police, overtook the Capitol grounds, and invaded the US Capitol building, disrupting the certification process as lawmakers were evacuated, hid, and sheltered in place.

Trump Tweets Part II: A Sacred Landslide Victory Stripped Away from Great Patriots

In the immediate wake of the violence on January 6, as the National Guard continued to clear the US Capitol Building and lawmakers prepared to reconvene to certify the election, at 6:01pm (EST) Donald Trump posted what would be his final tweet before his account was suspended:[7]

In this final message to his supporters (Figure 2.5), President Trump reiterated the core claim of the Big Lie—referring to "a sacred landslide

[7] As of the writing of this chapter (May 2022), Donald Trump's Twitter account is still suspended indefinitely. Later, following Elon Musk's purchase of Twitter, Trump's Twitter (X) account was reestablished.

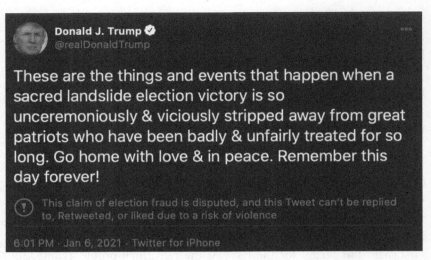

Figure 2.5 Screenshot of tweet posted by President Donald Trump's verified account in the evening of January 6, 2021.

election victory" that had been "so unceremoniously and viciously stripped away from great patriots who have been badly and unfairly treated for so long." His message acknowledged that he heard and appreciated the words and actions of his supporters and served to reinforce their sense of collective grievance.

A Model of Participatory Disinformation

Below, I present a model of *participatory disinformation* (Figure 2.6) that allows us to explore the dynamics between political elites and audiences in production of disinformation—specifically during the 2020 US election. This model emerges from extensive analysis of false, misleading, exaggerated, and unsubstantiated claims about election fraud in 2020, including the examples presented here as well as hundreds of other incidents that our research team tracked and analyzed (Center for an Informed Public et al. 2020).

First (Step 1 in Figure 2.6), political elites—including then-President Trump, members of his family and campaign, conservative political pundits, hyperpartisan media outlets on the political right, and others—repeatedly spread the message of a rigged election. This messaging set an expectation, among Trump supporters and other receptive audiences, of election fraud.

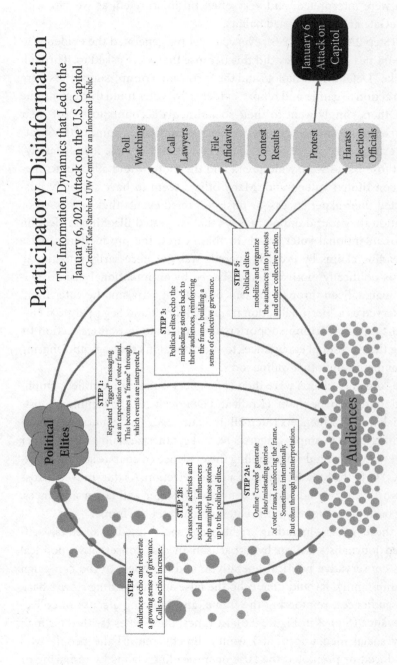

Figure 2.6 A model for participatory disinformation.
Credit: Kate Starbird, Center for an Informed Public.

It became a frame through which events leading up to and following the election were interpreted, and very often misinterpreted, as we saw with #SharpieGate and the canceled ballots.

Next (Step 2A in Figure 2.6), everyday people generated the evidence to fit these frames. In part, they did this because they were asked to. Through efforts like "Defend Your Ballot" and the "Army for Trump," supporters were called to action to gather and report "evidence" of voter fraud through online forms. Others simply went to their social media accounts to report their own—or amplify others'—experiences with voting issues. Some of these voters had experienced or witnessed legitimate issues but were led to (falsely) believe those issues were widespread and therefore would affect outcomes and/or constituted voter fraud. Many others seem to have sincerely misinterpreted their experiences—or misinterpreted events they witnessed or information they found online in ways that suggested illegitimate election results or intentional voter fraud. In these cases, the production of false or misleading claims by everyday people was not necessarily intentional, but it was politically motivated and shaped by an intentional disinformation campaign. Seen through the lens of political activism, the voter fraud refrain served as a "personal action frame" (Bennett and Segerberg 2012)—an opportunity for Trump supporters to participate in political action by adapting their personal experiences to the campaign's message and sharing via social media and other online tools.

These "organic" claims were then (often very quickly) identified, amplified, and "traded up the chain" (Krafft and Donovan 2020) by online activists and social media influencers (Step 2B in Figure 2.6). These motivated influencers functioned to amplify, aggregate, and synthesize claims into broader narratives of voter fraud—assembling the evidence (disparate stories of voting issues) to fit the broader frame of a rigged election. As they moved across the network, they would reach accounts with larger and larger audiences, filtering back up to the very same elites who had set the frame.

And those elites—including right-wing social media all-stars, self-described journalists within hyperpartisan media, conservative political pundits, conservative political operatives, and members of the campaign and Trump family—would then echo the false and misleading stories back to their audiences, reinforcing the frame, and building a sense of collective grievance (Step 3 in Figure 2.6). At times, these elites (with their high visibility social media accounts) would directly reward the people who had produced or promoted the false or misleading claims by resharing or retweeting their content.

Historically, one challenge for collective action has been a lack of visibility for individual contributions—which reduces motivation for participation (Olson 1965). Bennett and Segerberg (2012, 749) explain: "He (Olson) held that in large groups in which individual contributions are less noticeable, rational individuals will free-ride on the efforts of others: it is more cost-efficient not to contribute if you can enjoy the good without contributing." In the logic of traditional collective action, formal organizations are needed to overcome that barrier. But with technology-mediated connective action like the voter fraud disinformation campaign, the reputational-economy of social media provides a new motivational pathway that circumvents the need, to some extent, for formal organization. Individual contributions are spotlighted (Zhou et al., 2023) through a process of influencer-based amplification—functioning both to reward those contributing their personal stories of voter fraud with attentional and reputational gains and to motivate others to participate in the shared production of voter fraud claims.

After reaching and being broadcasted from the massive megaphones of influential elites, these false and misleading claims and narratives were then taken up by the audiences who grew increasingly agitated, as the cycles repeated themselves, around a shared sense of grievance (Step 4 in Figure 2.6). Calls to action increased, including demands for audits and recounts, and suggestions that the election should be overturned.

Political organizers, including established operatives and emergent influencers from both social and hyperpartisan media, soon began to mobilize on top of the misleading narratives and shared sense of grievance (Step 5 in Figure 2.6). There were instructions to help comb through online evidence to build new conspiracy theories, to call lawyers, to file affidavits, and eventually to mobilize physically through rallies and protests. Many individuals and organizations also used the voter fraud rhetoric to fundraise, calling for contributions via social media posts, websites, and email lists (Goldmacher and Shorey 2021). Eventually, this organizing culminated in the rallies and then the march and attack on the US Capitol on January 6, 2021.

In terms of applying this model to #SharpieGate specifically, after being asked to go to the polls looking for evidence of voter fraud (Step 1), we can see disparate claims on Election Day about Sharpies bleeding through ballots being shared by concerned voters (Step 2A), and shortly thereafter those claims being amplified by accounts of grassroots political activists as well as conservative and/or pro-Trump social media influencers and media personalities (Step 2B). On election evening, the claims were synthesized with help from political and media elites into a false conspiracy theory about the pens being used to intentionally disenfranchise Trump voters (Step 3). As it went viral, the conspiracy theory was leveraged by the Trump campaign and picked up by its supporters to question the results of the election in Arizona. In the social media record, we can see on the days following the election—from both elites (Step 3) and their audiences (Step 4)—calls to action, instructions for checking ballot status and calling lawyers, demands for recounts, and a growing sense of grievance about being cheated. Within two days, political protests were organized on top of those claims (Step 5), staged outside of the vote counting facilities and in tandem with chants to "Stop the Steal."

Discussion/Conclusion

In this chapter, I examine the false narrative of 2020 election fraud—now commonly known as the Big Lie—as a participatory disinformation campaign. This campaign was both top-down and bottom-up. The top-down organizational morphologies map onto what Ziblatt refers to as surrogate organizations. These are the more formally organized surrogates that help a party champion issues that are intended to mobilize support for the party and its standard bearer, in this case Donald Trump. We have shown that this part of our model set in motion the Stop the Steal frame many months prior to the election. Through repeated messaging of a rigged election, President Trump and his allies created both an expectation and a pathway for participation—via a personal action frame (Bennett and Segerberg 2012)—through which his supporters could adapt their experiences to fit a collective frame, and then share those experiences with their political community. The reputational economy of social media provided additional motivation, structure, and support for that participation. Mid-level influencers (1) synthesized disparate claims of perceived voting issues; (2) added the voter fraud framing (where it wasn't already present); and then (3) both echoed the claims and narratives back to their audiences, and (4) helped those unique messages move up the chain to more prominent influencers with larger audiences; often through the social media accounts of high level Trump supporters, including the president himself and his two adult sons. The early stages of this activity look a lot more like connective action (Bennett and Segerberg 2012) rather than collective action—that is, more like the Occupy movement than a traditional political campaign. The bottom-up dynamic captures the role of digitally constituted organizations which we are calling in this volume digital surrogate organizations or networks, or what Bennett and Segerberg call crowd enabled networks. However, the most salient features of this participatory disinformation campaign were that it was built on top of a false narrative and culminated with an anti-democratic (and violent) political act.

We are seeing similar dynamics across the globe—with participatory propaganda and participatory disinformation used to mobilize political action, often in service of anti-democratic outcomes. In the Philippines, online tools and platforms have been used to harass journalists (Swisher 2019), perpetrate networked disinformation campaigns (Ong and Cabanes 2018), and have most recently led to the rewriting of history and the return of the Marcos family to political power (Coronel 2022). In Brazil, the Bolsonaro family has employed similar techniques to the ones documented in this paper, spreading false and misleading messages for political gain (Soares 2021), and even participated (via multiple tweets) in the participatory disinformation campaign described in this paper. In the United States, a substantial portion of the Republican Party have refused to retreat from the Stop the Steal platform, choosing instead to rely upon the participatory disinformation dynamic, which may indeed represent the keys to power in the modern, connected world.

But how is participatory disinformation different from mobilizing on legitimate grievances? Researchers of political action have explained that the grievances upon which political movements mobilize are never wholly organic—in other words, they do not arise automatically from "naturally occurring conditions" or "specifiable material conditions"—but instead emerge through the interactive work of signifying and interpretation (Snow 2007). Does it matter that the core grievance in this case, the claim of election fraud, is entirely manufactured?

Mobilizing on false narratives removes constraints of reality and provides infinite possibilities for crafting and mobilizing on top of grievances. And some research suggests that the novelty of misinformation can make it more compelling than factual information and therefore lead to more engagement online (Vosoughi et al. 2018). From that perspective, this kind of organizing appears to be a powerful mechanism for short-term political wins in an ostensibly democratic system. However, the pervasive use of these tactics may undermine democracy—perhaps profoundly.

The foundations of democracy include an informed citizenry, empowered to organize and make their voices heard, to vote and make laws, to build coalitions, and to protest. Pomerantsev and Weiss (2014) explain how disinformation is an indirect threat to democracy, because it undermines trust in information and thereby reduces agency among a citizenry who can no longer trust their own grasp of reality. Disinformation, in their view, works in service to authoritarianism by jamming the systems of information-sharing and demotivating political action. Rid (2020) describes how democratic societies are inherently vulnerable to disinformation, because on the one hand disinformation exploits commitments to freedom of speech and transparency, and on the other, democratic societies cannot use the techniques of disinformation without undermining their own foundations. Farrell and Schneier (2018) argue that because it undermines the common knowledge about what the rules of democracy are: who the actors and coalitions are, and how elections work, disinformation works in service of autocratic, rather than democratic, political order. Synthesizing these perspectives, participatory disinformation leverages core democratic commitments to freedom of speech, association, and assembly, but simultaneously functions to undermine the institutions—like elections—that support democratic order.

Relating this case and the concept of participatory disinformation back to the theme of this volume, further underscores this threat. The central point of the conservative dilemma is that the use of cross cutting cleavage issues—with the assistance of surrogate organizations that tend to be more extreme than the party they are attached to—can drag the party itself into illiberal or authoritarian terrain. Short-term political tactics intended to win elections and hold on to power can lead to long-term destabilization of democratic institutions. Their result is democratic backsliding. The participatory disinformation campaign documented here, and its culmination with the events of January 6, 2021, is a striking example of these dynamics.

Acknowledgments

This essay emerged from collaborative research through the Election Integrity Partnership, including significant contributions from a range of researchers and support staff at the UW Center for an Informed Public and the Stanford Internet Observatory (SIO). I want to particularly recognize SIO for leading that effort and collaborators Renee DiResta and Mike Caulfield for helping to home in on the details of this case study and flesh out the concept of participatory disinformation. And I want to thank the many students and postdoctoral scholars that contributed to the real-time and posthoc work to curate the data used in the analysis presented here.

The Election Integrity Partnership—through which the initial work was conducted to identify and document this case study—was funded by the John S. and James L. Knight Foundation, William and Flora Hewlett Foundation, Craig Newmark Philanthropies, and Omidyar Group. Subsequent research to generate the participatory disinformation model and write this paper was funded by an NSF CAREER Grant to the author.

References

Agarwal, Sheetal D., Lance W. Bennett, Courtney N. Johnson, and Shawn Walker. 2014. "A Model of Crowd Enabled Organization: Theory and Methods for Understanding the Role of Twitter in the Occupy Protests." *International Journal of Communication* 8: 646–672.

Arif, Ahmer, Leo G. Stewart, and Kate Starbird. 2018. "Acting the Part: Examining Information Operations within #BlackLivesMatter Discourse." *PACMHCI. 2, Computer-Supported Cooperative Work (CSCW 2018).* Article 20. https://dl.acm.org/doi/pdf/10.1145/3274289

Benford, Robert D., and David A. Snow. 2000. "Framing Processes and Social Movements: An Overview and Assessment." *Annual Review of Sociology* 26 (1): 611–639.

Benkler, Yochai, Casey Tilton, Bruce Etling, Hal Roberts, Justin Clark, Robert Faris, Jonas Kaiser, and Carolyn Schmitt. 2020. "Mail-in Voter Fraud: Anatomy of a Disinformation Campaign." *Berkman Center Research Publication* 2020–2026. https://cyber.harvard.edu/publication/2020/Mail-in-Voter-Fraud-Disinformation-2020.

Bennett, Lance W., and Alexandra Segerberg. 2012. "The Logic of Connective Action: Digital Media and the Personalization of Contentious Politics." *Information, Communication & Society* 15 (5): 739–768.

Bittman, Ladislav. 1985. *The KGB and Soviet Disinformation: An Insider's View.* Washington: Pergamon-Brassey's.

Center for an Informed Public, Digital Forensic Research Lab, Graphika, & Stanford Internet Observatory. 2021. *The Long Fuse: Misinformation and the 2020 Election.* Stanford Digital Repository: Election Integrity Partnership. https://purl.stanford.edu/tr171zs0069.

Charmaz, Kathy. 2014. *Constructing Grounded Theory.* Los Angeles: Sage.

Coronel, Sheila. 2022. "The Triumph of Marcos Dynasty Disinformation is a Warning to the U.S." *The New Yorker.* May 17. https://www.newyorker.com/news/dispatch/the-triumph-of-marcos-dynasty-disinformation-is-a-warning-to-the-us.

Cottrell, David, Michael C. Herron, and Sean J. Westwood. 2018. "An Exploration of Donald Trump's Allegations of Massive Voter Fraud in the 2016 General Election." *Electoral Studies* 51: 123–142.

Entman, Robert M. 1993. "Framing: Towards Clarification of a Fractured Paradigm." *Journal of Communication,* 43(4): 51–58.

Farrell, Henry, and Bruce Schneier. 2018. "Common-Knowledge Attacks on Democracy." *Berkman Klein Center Research Publication,* 2018–7: 1–20.

Freelon, Deen, Michael Bossetta, Chris Wells, Josephine Lukito, Yiping Xia, and Kirsten Adams. 2020. "Black Trolls Matter: Racial and Ideological Asymmetries in Social Media Disinformation." *Social Science Computer Review,* 40(3): 560–578.

Goffman, Erving. 1974. *Frame Analysis: An Essay on the Organization of Experience.* Cambridge, MA: Harvard University Press.

Goldmacher, Shane, and Rachel Shorey. 2021. "Trump's Sleight of Hand: Shouting Fraud, Pocketing Donors' Cash for Future." *New York Times*, February 1. https://www.nytimes.com/2021/02/01/us/politics/trump-cash.html.

Hacker, Jacob S, and Paul Pierson. 2020. *Let Them Eat Tweets: How the Right Rules in an Age of Extreme Inequality*. New York: Liveright Publishing.

Howard, Philip N., Aiden Duffy, Deen Freelon, Muzammil M. Hussain, Will Mari, and Marwa Maziad. 2011. "Opening Closed Regimes: What was the Role of Social Media during the Arab Spring?" Available at SSRN 2595096 (2011).

Jack, Caroline. 2017. "Lexicon of Lies: Terms for Problematic Information." *Data & Society* 3 (22): 1094–1096.

Kennedy, Ian, Andrew Beers, Kolina Koltai, Morgan Wack, Joey Schafer, Paul Lockaby, Michael Caulfield, Michael Grass, Emma Spiro, Kate Starbird, and Isabella Garcia-Camargo. 2020. "Emerging Narratives Around 'Mail Dumping' and Election Integrity." *Election Integrity Partnership*. September 19. https://www.eipartnership.net/rapid-response/mail-dumping.

Kennedy, Ian, Morgan Wack, Andrew Beers, Joey Schafer, Isabella Garcia Carmago, Emma S. Spiro, and Kate Starbird. 2022. "Repeat Spreaders and Election Delegitimization: A Comprehensive Dataset of Misinformation Tweets from the 2020 U.S. Election." *Journal of Quantitative Description: Digital Media* 2. https://journalqd.org/article/view/3137.

Klasfeld, Adam. 2020 "Trump Campaign Retreats from 'Sharpiegate' Lawsuit." *Law & Crime*, November 16. https://lawandcrime.com/2020-election/bye-bye-sharpiegate-trump-campaign-hastily-retreats-from-conspiracy-laden-lawsuit-after-brutal-hearing/.

Krafft, P. M., and Joan Donovan. 2020. "Disinformation by Design: The Use of Evidence Collages and Platform Filtering in a Media Manipulation Campaign." *Political Communication* 37 (2): 194–214.

Lukito, Josephine, Jiyoun Suk, Yini Zhang, Larissa Doroshenko, Sang Jung Kim, Min-Hsin Su, Yiping Xia, Deen Freelon, and Chris Wells. 2020. "The Wolves in Sheep's Clothing: How Russia's Internet Research Agency Tweets Appeared in US News as Vox Populi." *International Journal of Press/Politics*. 25 (2): 196–216.

Maddock, Jim, Kate Starbird, Haneen J. Al-Hassani, Daniel E. Sandoval, Mania Orand, and Robert M. Mason. 2015. "Characterizing Online Rumoring Behavior Using Multi-Dimensional Signatures." In *Proceedings of the 18th ACM Conference on Computer Supported Cooperative Work & Social Computing*: 228–241. https://dl.acm.org/doi/pdf/10.1145/2675133.2675280.

Mueller III, Robert S. 2019. "Report on the Investigation into Russian Interference in the 2016 Presidential Election. Mar. 2019." United States Department of Justice. https://www.justice.gov/storage/report.pdf.

Olson, Mancur. 1965. *The Logic of Collective Action: Public Goods and the Theory of Groups*, Cambridge, MA: Harvard University Press.

Ong, Jonathan Corpus, and Jason Vincent A. Cabanes. 2018. "Architects of Networked Disinformation: Behind the Scenes of Troll Accounts and Fake News Production in the Philippines." *Architects of Networked Disinformation: Behind the Scenes of Troll Accounts and Fake News Production in the Philippines* 74. https://doi.org/10.7275/2cq4-5396.

O'Sullivan, Donie, Naomi Thomas and Ali Zaslav. 2020. "Twitter Hits Trump for 'Misleading Health Claims' that could Dissuade People from Voting." CNN, August 23. https://www.cnn.com/2020/08/23/politics/trump-twitter-health-voting-claims-flagged/index.html.

Palen, Leysia, and Kenneth M. Anderson. 2016. "Crisis Informatics—New Data for Extraordinary Times." *Science* 353 (6296): 224–225.

Pomerantsev, Peter, and Michael Weiss. 2014. "The Menace of Unreality: How the Kremlin Weaponizes Information, Culture and Money." *The Interpreter*. Institute of Modern Russia. https://www.almendron.com/tribuna/wp-content/uploads/2015/08/The_Menace_of_Unreality_Final.pdf.

Rid, Thomas. 2020. *Active Measures: The Secret History of Disinformation and Political Warfare*. New York: Farrar, Straus and Giroux.

Roth, Zachary. 2016. "Donald Trump's 'Rigged Election' Claims Raise Historical Alarms." NBC News, October 17. https://www.nbcnews.com/politics/2016-election/donald-trumps-rigged-election-claims-raise-historical-alarms-n667831.

Snow, David A. 2007. "Framing and Social Movements." In G. Ritzer, ed., *The Blackwell Encyclopedia of Sociology*. https://doi.org/10.1002/9781405165518.wbeosf065

Soares, Felipe Bonow, Raquel Recuero, Taiane Volcan, Giane Fagundes, and Giéle Sodré. 2021. "Research Note: Bolsonaro's Firehose: How Covid-19 Disinformation on WhatsApp was Used to Fight a Government Political Crisis in Brazil." *Harvard Kennedy School Misinformation Review*, 2(1): 1–13. DOI: 10.37016/mr-2020-54

Starbird, Kate, Ahmer Arif, and Tom Wilson. 2019. "Disinformation as Collaborative Work: Surfacing the Participatory Nature of Strategic Information Operations." Proceedings of the ACM on Human-Computer Interaction 3, no. CSCW: 1–26. https://dl.acm.org/doi/pdf/10.1145/3359229

Starbird, Kate, Michael Caulfield, Renee DiResta, Jevin West, Emma Spiro, Nicole Buckley, Rachel Moran, and Morgan Wack. 2020. "Uncertainty and Misinformation: What to Expect on Election Night and Days After." *Election Integrity Partnership*, October 26. https://www.eipartnership.net/news/what-to-expect

Starbird, Kate, Jim Maddock, Mania Orand, Peg Achterman, and Robert M. Mason. 2014. "Rumors, False Flags, and Digital Vigilantes: Misinformation on Twitter after the 2013 Boston Marathon Bombing." *IConference 2014 Proceeding*: 654–662.

Starbird, Kate, and Leysia Palen. 2012. "(How) Will the Revolution be Retweeted? Information Diffusion and the 2011 Egyptian Uprising." In *Proceedings of the ACM 2012 Conference on Computer Supported Cooperative Work*: 7–16. https://dl.acm.org/doi/pdf/10.1145/2145204.2145212

Starbird, Kate, Emma Spiro, Isabelle Edwards, Kaitlyn Zhou, Jim Maddock, and Sindhuja Narasimhan. 2016. "Could this be True? I Think So! Expressed Uncertainty in Online Rumoring." In *Proceedings of the 2016 CHI Conference on Human Factors in Computing Systems*: 360–371. https://dl.acm.org/doi/pdf/10.1145/2858036.2858551

Stewart III, Charles. 2020. "How We Voted in 2020: A First Look at the Survey of the Performance of American Elections." *MIT Election Data and Science Lab*, December 15, 2020, http://electionlab.mit.edu/sites/default/files/2020-12/How-we-voted-in-2020-v01.pdf

Swisher, Kara. 2019. "A Journalist Trolled by Her Own Government." *New York Times*, February 22. https://www.nytimes.com/2019/02/22/opinion/maria-ressa-facebook-philippines-.html

U.S. House. 2022. Select Committee to Investigate the January 6th Attack on the United States Capitol. *Final Report*. https://january6th.house.gov/sites/democrats.january6th.house.gov/files/Report_FinalReport_Jan6SelectCommittee.pdf.

Vosoughi, Soroush, Deb Roy, and Sinan Aral. 2018. "The Spread of True and False News Online." *Science* 359 (6380): 1146–1151.

Wanless, Alicia, and Michael Berk. 2019. "The Audience is the Amplifier: Participatory Propaganda." In Paul Baines, Nicholas O'Shaugnessy, Nancy Snow, eds., *The Sage Handbook of Propaganda* (pp. 85–104). London: Sage.

Wardle, Claire, and Hossein Derakhshan. 2017. "Information Disorder: Toward an Interdisciplinary Framework for Research and Policymaking." Strasbourg: Council of Europe. http://tverezo.info/wp-content/uploads/2017/11/PREMS-162317-GBR-2018-Report-desinformation-A4-BAT.pdf.

Zhou, Kaitlyn, Tom Wilson, Kate Starbird, and Emma S. Spiro. 2023. "Spotlight Tweets: A Lens for Exploring Attention Dynamics within Online Sensemaking during Crisis Events." *Transactions on Social Computing* 6 (1–2): 1–33.

Chapter 3

How QAnon Developed from a Fringe Group to a Digital Surrogate for the GOP

Josephine Lukito, Yunkang Yang, and Sang Jung Kim

On October 17, 2021, QAnon celebrity Ron Watkins (also known by his 8kun alias "CodeMonkeyZ") submitted his paperwork to run for the US House of Representatives, representing Arizona's first congressional district (Cooper 2021). Five days later, Watkins and his father (Jim Watkins, owner of 8kun) were featured speakers at the QAnon-linked conference For God and Country: Patriot Double Down in Las Vegas, receiving a standing ovation following the announcement of his candidacy. How did Ron Watkins, a relatively unknown programmer, become a candidate for the US House of Representatives?

In this chapter, we apply Bennett and Livingston's connective action framework that explains how a digitally networked organization can bring scattered extremist factions into conservative parties, pushing them in illiberal directions. More precisely, we examine how an online fringe group developed into a digital surrogate with enough leverage to run political candidates within the Republican Party. In other words, our chapter explores how QAnon *became* a surrogate for the GOP.

Drawing from Ziblatt (2017) and Hacker and Pierson (2020), Bennett and Livingston conceptualize a digital surrogate as a virtually connected group that have a symbiotic relationship with political parties. Through this relationship, digital surrogates gain access to political institutional support, allowing them to advance their most important issues. In turn, parties are able to build multigroup coalitions that can mobilize citizens to vote.

While surrogate groups like churches, issue groups, and social organizations have existed long before the digital era (Ziblatt 2017), the internet has made it possible for nongeographically bounded groups and publics to emerge and organize, creating the opportunity for more and quite novel surrogate relationships. Surrogate groups, in the short term, may help parties

Josephine Lukito, Yunkang Yang, and Sang Jung Kim, *How QAnon Developed from a Fringe Group to a Digital Surrogate for the GOP*. In: *Connective Action and the Rise of the Far-Right*. Edited by: Steven Livingston and Michael Miller, Oxford University Press. © Oxford University Press (2025). DOI: 10.1093/oso/9780197794937.003.0003

electorally, but they also make the political parties vulnerable to extremism and anti-democratic beliefs (Hacker and Pierson 2020). The emergence of digital surrogates has only elevated that concern, as they thrive in an online environment that fuels political extremism and pro-violence discourse (Phadke and Mitra 2020; Rathje et al. 2021). As today's GOP relies increasingly on digital surrogates as part of its voting coalition, the involvement of digital surrogates, such as QAnon, may push the party toward more extreme policies and viewpoints.

Like other digital surrogates, QAnon began on digital platforms—specifically anonymous imageboards such as 4chan and 8kun—but matured to offline organizing as a result of bottom-up and top-down relationship-building between QAnon supporters and the Republican Party. While the comically outlandish narratives that QAnon employs make it unique relative to other right-wing movements, there are also important lessons from QAnon. More specifically, to develop into a digital surrogate for the GOP, an extremist online group must adapt its narratives, develop organizational capacities and resilience, and gain acknowledgment from the GOP. QAnon, therefore, makes for a useful case to study how online fringe groups develop into digital surrogates.

However, QAnon did not emerge as a fully formed digital surrogate: it took time and effort to build a relationship between QAnon and the GOP. This relationship-building process should be of particular concern to those who study democratic backsliding, as it reveals how political parties (in this case, the GOP) can lend legitimacy to extremist groups, choosing to "win" at the cost of democratic principles.

We analyze the rise of QAnon within the Republican Party along three dimensions: narrative shifts, organizational development, and institutional relationships. Narrative shifts refer to how QAnon adapted its discursive markers to align more closely with Republican issue agendas. Organizational development refers to the ways that QAnon coordinated themselves as a group and a public, both online and offline, and developed a resilience to de-platforming efforts. Finally, as the organizational structure of QAnon matured, QAnon began to develop institutional relationships with the Republican Party.

As QAnon blossomed into a full-fledged digital surrogate, the narrative, organizational, and institutional changes also became inextricable from one another. In other words, they mutually aided and influenced one another as QAnon became mainstream, exploited political opportunities, and responded to external shocks. In studying QAnon as a case of a fringe group turned digital surrogate, we highlight the importance of each dimension and explain how they work in tandem to strengthen the relationship between QAnon and the Republican Party.

Literature

In this section we provide a framework to analyze right-wing digital surrogates through their narratives, their organizational structure, and their relationship with political operatives and elected leaders. We refer to these as institutional relationships.

Evolving Narratives within QAnon

Narratives are discursive materials that build and sustain a group's identity. Traditional surrogates for the GOP, such as the National Rifle Association, evangelical churches, and anti-abortion groups, are all organized, first and foremost, around persistent narratives that manifest their respective worldviews and beliefs. Many of these narratives center on contentious, cleaving issues such as race, ethnicity, religion, and gender, which activate strong emotions and identities. One important feature distinguishing QAnon from other surrogates is its unique narratives.

QAnon is an outgrowth of the debunked Pizzagate conspiracy theory that extends and expands the role of then-President Trump as a savior against a global cabal of satanic pedophiles (Hannah 2021). QAnon's core belief of a cabal is not inherently linked to traditional Republican Party's issue agendas or far-right and hate group's ideologies (Zihiri et al. 2022). Yet QAnon has since expanded its belief system to incorporate other conspiracy theories driven by anti-elite and conspiratorial sentiments, aligning itself more closely with current events and the issue agendas of the MAGA movement, discussed elsewhere in this volume by Parker and Blum. For example, during the pandemic, a common QAnon narrative was that Bill Gates orchestrated the COVID-19 pandemic (Papasavva et al. 2021).

The narratives within QAnon have become so broad and encompassing that it is impossible to connect all of them to the core narrative about protecting children from sex trafficking. Yet as we will later explain, what may undergird these disparate narratives is deep-seated anti-elitism couched in the "do your own research" internet ethos. It evokes a sense of self-empowerment for the displaced and uprooted to look for meaning in a world of rapid changes that threaten to break down traditional cultural systems and moral values (Amarasingam and Argentino 2020).

We argue that narrative adaptation is essential for a fringe extremist group to grow into a digital surrogate. It is through its evolving narratives that QAnon gained political relevance outside its small community of fringe beliefs. Tracking how QAnon narratives evolved over time helps us understand how the group discursively aligned itself with right-wing issue agendas, becoming politically useful for certain elements within the GOP. For example, supporters of QAnon participated in Trump rallies in 2018 (Wilson 2018) and became one of the main instigators of the January 6th Capitol insurrection (Rubin et al. 2021). These incidents occurred largely because the evolving narratives of QAnon incorporated MAGA movements and pro-Trump sentiments aside from satanic pedophile conspiracy theory.

QAnon's Organizational Infrastructure and Institutional Linkages

A digital surrogate needs to develop organizational capacities to function effectively. Many studies have shown that digitally enabled social movements can leverage the affordances of digital technologies to effectively organize without the presence of traditional brick-and-mortar organizations. For example, the Occupy Wall Street movement crowd produced many organizational routines through the production, curation, and dynamic integration of various information resources in digital networks (Bennett et al. 2014). To paraphrase Bimber et al. (2012): collective action requires organizing but organizing can happen without an organization. Organizing involves "identifying interested people and their concerns, contacting them for purposes of developing common identity or trust or for purpose of sending appeals and requests, establishing agendas, and coordinating action or engagement" (Bimber et al. 2012, 79), which are all fundamentally informational and communicative, and can therefore be accomplished through communication routines which can "create patterned relationships among people that lend organization and structure" (Bennett and Segerberg 2013, 289).

In their book *The Logic of Connective Action*, Bennett and Segerberg (2013) outlined three ideal types of digital action networks: organizationally brokered collective action, crowd-enabled connective action, and organizationally enabled connective action. Organizationally brokered collective action is characterized by a strong presence of formal organizations that mobilize resources, manage digital technologies, and promote collection action frames; by contrast, crowd-enabled connective action leverages the affordances of commercial social media platforms and accomplishes organizational tasks through the sharing of personal action frames, often in the absence of recognizable leaders, formal organizations, or common goals. The hybrid of this is organizationally enabled connective action: formal organizations that operate in the background through loosely connected networks. Such organizations facilitate the spread of personal action frames and refrain from owning or controlling issue agendas (Bennett and Segerberg 2013).

Bennett and Segerberg (2013)'s typology offers a useful framework to examine the evolving organizational aspect of QAnon. Though QAnon started as a crowd-enabled fringe online conspiracy theory community, it morphed into a more structured, organizationally enabled action network with political goals like overturning the 2020 election results, thereby operating as a digital surrogate for certain elements within the GOP. The key to understanding the transformation of QAnon's organizational forms involves examining both bottom-up (QAnon-instigated) and top-down (Republican Party-instigated) efforts that aligned QAnon more closely with the agendas of the Trump administration/campaign while keeping the key tenets of QAnon (the concerns about children's safety) animated.

The transformation of a fringe group to a digital surrogate is as much the responsibility of the surrogate as it is of the political party. Notably, the organizational development of QAnon is accompanied by the strengthening of linkages to certain elements within the Republican Party. Relationships between a political party and its digital surrogates can be mutually beneficial: digital surrogates gain perceived legitimacy and greater access to power, while political parties garner more ground support, votes, and donations.

For example, as early as 2018, scatterings of QAnon signs could be seen at Trump rallies; a year later, some of the footage of these sign-holding QAnon believers were used in an advertising campaign for Trump's 2020 race. As conservative political operatives and the GOP politicians began to see the political value of QAnon, they wanted to utilize the group to achieve the party's aspirations—specifically, the goal of winning the 2020 national and local elections. Not only did more than two dozen GOP candidates who openly embraced QAnon run for office in the 2020 election cycle, but Trump's 2020 campaign explicitly gestured toward QAnon in its campaign ad and refused to publicly disavow QAnon. The building of institutional relationships, therefore, involved both bottom-up and top-down efforts that mutually aided one another.

We track the development of QAnon, attending to the narrative, organizational, and institutional aspects. It is important to reiterate that for digital surrogates, these three aspects—narrative, organization, and institutional— are interrelated and inseparable. However, these aspects are not born in harmony; rather, groups must develop all three to work in tandem.

Mixed-Method Approaches

Our analytical approach is informed by an expansive collection of QAnon content from a variety of online social media spaces. For this analysis, we leverage qualitative and quantitative data from the following social media spaces:

1. "Q Drops" from Q, the anonymous source of information from which QAnon believers construct narratives. All 4,953 4chan and kun posts from Q are available publicly on aggregators such as QAlert (http://qalerts.app/).
2. Reddit posts (n = 100,661) from /r/cbts_stream and /r/greatawaken ing, two popular QAnon subreddits.
3. Parler posts (n = 540,595) that used QAnon-related keywords.
4. The Patriot Voice Telegram channel posts (n = 63,012) (https://t.me/ThePatriotVoiceUS), which is organized by QAnon supporters and has amassed 39,235 followers.

These data are further synthesized with a trove of qualitative data about the For God and Country events. These events were organized by a QAnon couple, John Sabel (who goes by "QAnon John") and Amy Sabel (who goes by "Q Queen Amy"; see Sommer, Will@WillSommer 2021). As of February 2022 they have organized two such events: the Patriot RoundUp in Dallas, Texas and the Patriot Double Down in Las Vegas, Nevada. Recordings of this live-streamed conference provided important insights into how this conspiratorial digital surrogate has sought political legitimization through offline events that bring together grassroots organizers with political actors.

To bring these layers together, we take a chronological approach to our analysis of QAnon, breaking down their development into five phases. First, in the *start phase* (pre-2018), QAnon begins by building upon the Pizzagate conspiracy theory. Second, in the *growth phase* (January 1, 2018 to June 14, 2019), QAnon membership grew as the fringe group moved to the mainstream platform Reddit, creating a need for more organizational capacity and an opportunity to build relationships with certain elements of the GOP. Once Trump announced his re-election bid, QAnon moved into its third phase, taking advantage of the *political opportunity* (June 15, 2019 to November 3, 2020) to align its narrative and organizational structure more closely to that of the Trump campaign. Fourth, following the election, QAnon entered the fourth phase, responding to the *shock of the election loss*. Between November 2020 and January 2021, QAnon cemented their relationship with the Trump campaign by repeatedly expressing support for and organizing around the false election fraud narrative, to the point of using violence. The third and fourth phases created the path for a more closely aligned relationship between QAnon and parts of the Republican Party that can be seen in the ongoing fifth stage of QAnon, described as a *new beginning* for QAnon, post–January 6.

QAnon: A Case Study of a Conspiratorial Digital Surrogate

Narrative, Organizational, and Institutional Preconditions of QAnon

Before we analyze the surrogate development, let us briefly consider how the US societal system facilitated the conditions for QAnon, as a fringe group, to flourish. This is especially important because QAnon's development grew from the country's political, economic, and social circumstances.

The decades preceding the rise of QAnon were marked by substantial societal change. Economically, the US underwent rapid deindustrialization (an outcome of both technological developments and globalization; see Van Neuss 2018). Alongside this long-term change the economy also experienced significant volatility, exemplified by a succession of recessions.

These economic factors, among others (see Parker and Blum, this volume), contributed to growing support for populist political beliefs and movements (Rodrik 2021), including the Tea Party.

Shifts in the economic and political system occurred alongside changes in the lifeworld. Most notably, these changes were driven by the introduction of digital communication (Menke and Schwarzenegger 2019) and the rise of system-wide anomie—the breaking down of moral values that helped maintain solidarity within a society (Durkheim 1893; see also DeCook and Fujioka, this volume). Relatedly, traditional cultural systems, such as religiosity, have also been on the decline: church membership, for example, is at an all-time low (Lardieri 2021).

As a result of these substantial societal changes, political actors and citizens alike began to rely on new or revised "sensemaking" logic to explain the current state of US society and to address its issues. In other words, by the mid-2010s, there existed a vacuum of sensemaking logic—one that was vulnerable to misinformation and conspiracy theories.

The Start Phase: Explaining QAnon's Genesis (Pre-2018)

As we have noted, QAnon grew out of the 2016 Pizzagate conspiracy theory, which falsely claimed that Democrats (specifically, the Clintons) were running a pedophile ring out of Comet Ping Pong pizza, a restaurant in Washington, DC (Samuelson 2016). Emerging on the imageboard 4chan, which is known for politically incorrect humor, the Pizzagate conspiracy theory flourished among many Trump supporters in the lead up to the 2016 election (Doubek 2017).

During this time several anonymous accounts ("anons") in the 4chan boards gained popularity for building on this conspiracy; specifically, /pol/ (short for "politically incorrect"), a 4chan message board known for its abundance of hate speech, trolling, and online harassment tactics. These anon accounts, often claiming to have access to classified information, parroted the narrative of a pedophile trafficking ring and combined it with other conspiracy theories about historical events such as Princess Diana's death and the terrorist attacked of 9/11 (Zadrozny and Collins 2018a).

However, the popularity of other anons paled in comparison to "Q," which appeared first on 4chan as "Q Clearance Patriot" ("Q Clearance" refers to a US Department of Energy security clearance level that gives its holder

70 CONNECTIVE ACTION AND THE RISE OF THE FAR-RIGHT

access to top secret information) in an October 2017 post titled "Calm Before the Storm" (Martineau 2017). Like other anons, Q also promoted the false narrative of a pedophile ring. However, the claim advanced by Q involved a much larger, global conspiracy (a "cabal") and emphasized the role of Trump within the narrative, portraying him as the hero fighting against the global cannibalistic, pedophilic, sex trafficking cabal. Key within the narrative was the idea that Trump was conducting a sting operation, known as "the Storm," that would reveal all this information eventually.

Another factor that distinguished Q from other anons was how Q engaged its audiences. Posting vaguely and regularly, Q encouraged their followers to "do the research" by looking for clues in Q's posts. Referring to their posts as "crumbs," Q implied the necessity for users to work together to interpret the meaning of each post. This tactic effectively crowdsourced narratives, creating a community of Q supporters that worked together to interpret Q's posts and to amplify the false narrative of a pedophilic cabal, becoming what is now often referred to as "QAnon."

At this start phase QAnon narratives focused on child sex trafficking, building on the Pizzagate narrative and expanding its scope. Organizationally, the community existed most on message boards revolved around Q, with little evidence of offline organizing. To be sure, there were still individual offline activities, but they appeared to be individual actions.[1]

In this predevelopmental stage, QAnon's institutional linkage to the GOP was barely present. And yet one of Donald Trump's affiliates, Roger Stone, had begun to express support for the conspiracy theory (Goldberg 2018). This nascent endorsement would set the stage for a growing relationship between QAnon and the Republican Party.

The Growth Phase: QAnon Goes Mainstream (January 8, 2018–June 18, 2019)

As QAnon narratives became more popular, the QAnon community also began organizing aggregation websites such as "Q Alerts" (https://qalerts. app/). These websites compiled Q's 4chan and 8kun posts and updated their archive in near-real time. This organizational development made it possible

---

[1] In 2016, a man brought an assault rifle to Ping Pong pizza restaurant and fired several shots (Lopez 2016).

for more mainstream conservatives to access Q's posts directly without having to navigate the more controversial and niche image boards.

In addition, QAnon spaces[2] expanded from 4chan and 8kun to mainstream social media platforms in 2018. It experienced substantial growth on Reddit first: multiple QAnon subreddits such as /r/GreatAwakening and /r/cbts (cbts stands for "calm before the storm") grew from January 8, 2018, to September 12, 2018. During this phase, there were 73,342 posts made on /r/GreatAwakening and 27,319 posts made on /r/cbts (see Figure 3.1). Reddit was the first essential platform for disseminating Q drops to large audiences (Aliapoulios et al. 2021).

Other mainstream platforms witnessed the growth of QAnon in their networks much later. On Twitter, QAnon only started to gain traction in the summer of 2018: the number of QAnon related tweets had its first notable peak around 200,000 per day in early August of 2018 (Jackson et al. 2021). On Facebook, the number of QAnon related pages and public groups started

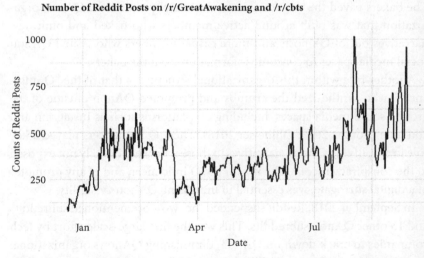

Figure 3.1 Daily count of Reddit posts on /r/GreatAwakening and /r/cbts, January 8, 2018 to September 18, 2018

---

[2] We define a social media space as a part of a social media platform that is used (sometimes loosely, in the case of networks) to facilitate a group or community's communication. Architecturally, social media spaces are a combination of the communicative needs and narratives of a group and the technological affordances of a platform.

to increase in late 2018, growing from fewer than 50 in November 2018 to more than 750 in June 2019 (Kim and Kim 2022).

The continued multiplatform proliferation of QAnon spaces benefited the community in two ways. First, it helped QAnon reach large audiences and build a following. Second, it made QAnon resilient to early de-platforming efforts. Despite account suspensions and deletions on Reddit in September 2018, QAnon persisted and grew in other social media spaces, continuing to promote its narratives and recruit supporters throughout 2018 and 2019.

As more users began to participate across multiple social media platforms, QAnon's organizational form also developed. During this time the QAnon community underwent what could be called a division of labor, with various participants taking on different roles within the group. One key role in the growth phase were "bakers," the most hardcore followers of QAnon who participated in the process of "baking"—taking the crumbs or clues in Q's posts and making sense of them. On Reddit, they concentrated on the subreddit /r/greatawakening, producing a majority of its content (Chang 2018). The bakers paved the way for a nascent hierarchy within the QAnon organization that was built around active members who baked and built new narratives out of Q's posts and more casual members who visited QAnon social media spaces to consume information from the bakers.

Another role within this organizational structure is that of the "Q influencer," who synthesized the crumbs and promoted QAnon outside of the group's social media spaces, including on platforms such as Instagram and YouTube (Lorenz 2019; Ohlheiser 2018). These Q influencers played a key role in amplifying QAnon narratives to those who were initially not exposed to the conspiracy theory. The role of the Q influencer, and of any promoter of a digital surrogate, was essential in increasing QAnon's visibility.

In September 2018, Reddit suspended the two aforementioned subreddits and 15 other QAnon subreddits. This was the first large-scale effort by tech companies to crack down on QAnon, diminishing QAnon's organizational capacity and the presence of QAnon narratives.

However, there were no coordinated efforts among tech companies to crackdown on QAnon at this stage. As a result, QAnon spaces flourished elsewhere, including mainstream platforms (e.g., Facebook), alternative platforms (e.g., Parler and Bitchute), and encrypted messaging applications (e.g., Telegram) that were more accepting of their narratives but not quite as seedy as the image boards. Twitter and Facebook saw notable jumps of

QAnon-related activities following the Reddit ban. Parler, the Twitter-style platform that launched in August 2018 with the brand of a "free speech platform"—a description often used by alternative platforms to justify the presence of hate speech and pro-violence content—also quickly became a space for a large QAnon constituency (Sipka et al. 2021).

Although Parler started in September 2018, the surge of QAnon activities on Parler came later—when news organizations like CBS (CBS News 2019) and Fox News (2019) covered Parler. Fox in particular invited the Parler CEO to their newscast on May 28, 2019, which was followed by a huge spike in Parler activity a day later (see Figure 3.2). Following the removal of QAnon subreddits, users on Parler attempted to build a QAnon community as an alternative to Facebook and Twitter. They aired grievances about the mainstream social media platforms—even though Facebook and Twitter did not enforce moderation policies against QAnon at this point. Parler posts ("parlays") about QAnon frequently mentioned platforms like Twitter (n = 37,335), often described as "Twatter," and Facebook (n = 25,898), often framed as "Fakebook" to express their displeasure with mainstream platforms for removing QAnon content. Reddit, already waning in popularity by this point, was only referenced 347 times. When Reddit was mentioned, it

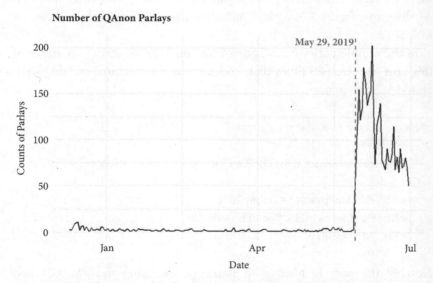

Figure 3.2 Daily count of Parler posts about QAnon, December 10, 2018 to June 30, 2019

was often about criticizing the platform in the context of QAnon narratives, such as in this July 2020 parlay: "Reddit is a source of pedophilic content. They ban 'hate' speech though."

On Parler, QAnon spread similar narratives previously seen on 4chan, 8kun, and Reddit, with a focus on child sex trafficking issues and other conspiracy theories. One of the most upvoted parlays in our Parler dataset reads, "Hillary Clinton ran a pedophile ring inside the State Department." Another reads, "BREAKING: Congressional sources confirm Adam Schiff used taxpayer money to payoff [sic] a sexual harrassment [sic] charge of a 19-year-old boy."

Nevertheless, compared to the previous phase, the growth phase witnessed an increasing number of references to hashtags such as #MAGA and #KAG—first on Reddit and then after Reddit's ban continued on Parler, a sign that QAnon started to integrate with the MAGA movement. Of the 100,661 Reddit posts on /r/GreatAwakening and /r/cbts, 14% (n = 14,326) referenced Trump or used the acronym KAG or MAGA (those that did not were more focused on discussing the cabal, Democrats, or mainstream news organizations). By comparison, of the 540,595 QAnon-referencing parlays in our dataset, roughly 30% (n = 132,864) made a reference to Trump or used the acronym KAG or MAGA (those that did not were more focused on discussing the cabal, Democrats, or mainstream news). As shown in Figure 3.3, parlays including these keywords skyrocketed in mid-2019.

In the sample parlay below, posted first on May 29, 2019 (variations of this post appeared 79 times that week), there is a combination of QAnon and MAGA references.

> Please Echo and follow me Patriots
>
> #WeAreTheNews #TrustThePlan #wwg1wga #SheepNoMore #GodOn OurSide
> #WakeUpAmerica #Q #Trump2020
> #BestPrezEvr #MAGA #VoteThoseFuckersOut
> #LoveMyCountry

Notably the post is filled with hashtags, including the #MAGA and #Trump2020 hashtags that were also popular on Twitter (Tran 2021) as well as QAnon hashtags, such as #wwg1wga (an acronym referring to the QAnon

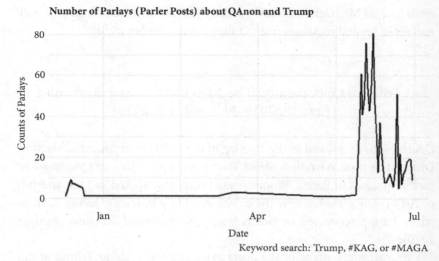

Figure 3.3 Daily count of Parler posts about QAnon and Trump, December 10, 2018 to June 30, 2019

slogan, "when we go one, we go all") and #Q. While the post itself focused on soliciting followership (using the term "patriots," a common reference to fellow Q supporters), the bulk of the post was actually comprised of the hashtags, all of which signaled a deliberate attempt to integrate collective support for QAnon with the support for the Trump administration (as well as a mutual hatred for Democrats), wrapped in a veneer of "patriotic" and religious zeal.

During this phase, the growing QAnon community was also establishing linkage to the Republican Party, as both groups shared a mutual interest to support then-President Trump. As we have noted, QAnon narratives at this phase had already begun to adopt Trump symbols and talking points, signaling bottom-up effort to build institutional relationships. Offline, signs and references to QAnon (including the letter "Q" and slogans such as WWG1WGA) began to show up in Trump rallies (Sommer and Suebsaeng 2019) alongside other Trump symbols such as MAGA and references to American patriotism, like the US flag (Brady 2018).

Meanwhile, elite endorsements of QAnon were beginning to take shape. For example, Lieutenant General Michael Flynn explicitly endorsed QAnon in 2018, going so far as to sign a copy of his memoir with "WWG1WGA" (Travis View@travis_view 2018). Beyond continued support from political elites such as Michael Flynn and celebrity lawyer Lin Wood, Trump himself retweeted several messages from Q supporters (Kaplan 2019).

A Political Opportunity: The 2020 Election as a Flashpoint (June 18, 2019–November 3, 2020)

QAnon activity peaked in the lead-up to the 2020 US presidential election. During this time, narratives about Trump were pervasive on QAnon social media spaces. On Parler, Trump-related discourse spiked in June and July of 2019 (see Figure 3.4; note the substantial jump in scale), during the time when Trump retweeted 14 tweets from QAnon-linked accounts (Nguyen 2020).

Unsurprisingly, many of the posts making a reference to Trump at this time were about the election, or election-related stories: of the 96,650 parlays about QAnon and Trump posted between January 1 and November 11, 2020, 45% of them (n = 44,228) used one of the following substrings: "elect," "vote," "ballot," "candidate," and "Biden." The increased discourse about QAnon, Trump, and the 2020 election demonstrates that Trump was

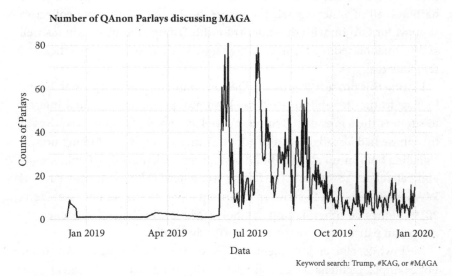

Figure 3.4 Daily count of Parler posts about QAnon and Trump, January 1, 2020 to December 31, 2020

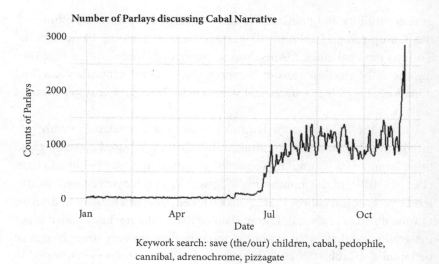

Figure 3.5 Daily count of Parler posts about the Cabal narrative, January 1, 2020 to November 11, 2020

at the heart of QAnon's conspiratorial narrative (not only that a pedophilic cabal exists, but that it will be taken down by the Trump administration). Tweets often made extreme claims about the consequences of a Biden administration; for example, one parlay posted in October 2020 claimed, "If Trump loses, white Americans will become the equivalents of Jews in Nazi Germany." Other tweets referencing Biden also referred to Hunter Biden, as many of the conspiracy theories being shared at this time focused on Hunter Biden's laptop.

It is worth noting, however, that parlays about Trump made up less than a third of the overall number of Parler posts (n = 315,593), whereas about a half of the parlays in this time (n = 152,236) were still referencing the conspiracy theory (see Figure 3.5). There was sustained attention given to this conspiracy theory, while parlays about Trump varied over the course of 2020. This shows that the core narrative—the idea of a pedophilic cabal—remained animated while discourse about Trump and the 2020 election grew in tandem.

The combined use of both the cabal narrative and the Trump narrative helped further the institutional relationship between the QAnon conspiracy theory group and President Trump. From the perspective of the QAnon community, the 2020 election represented an opportunity to gain

78 CONNECTIVE ACTION AND THE RISE OF THE FAR-RIGHT

greater visibility and political relevance through a closer relationship with the Trump campaign. From the perspective of the Trump campaign and Trump's political allies, QAnon was a strategically useful voting bloc during the 2020 election season: it represented ground support, votes, and donations, tangible resources that were needed to ensure Trump's electoral success.

During the 2020 election, Trump's presidential campaign explicitly gestured toward QAnon; for example, in July 2019, it released a campaign ad titled "women for Trump" that featured a Trump supporter holding Q signs (Derysh 2019). In the months that followed, Trump himself refused to criticize the conspiracy theory group. In October 2020, when asked to disavow QAnon during a town hall, Trump claimed that he did not know much about the group and that "what I do hear about it, they are very strongly against pedophilia" (Gabbatt 2020). The lack of denouncement was celebrated in QAnon social media spaces, as exemplified by this parlay posted after the town hall:

> At his town hall meeting, Trump refuses to condemn Qanon. Trump says that Qanon is against pedophilia, which he agrees with. Then asks why Biden hasn't condemned antifa.
>
> Qanon followers will be pleased. Whether you agree with the left's condemnation of Qanon, you got to admit it's getting coverage.

This subtle perceived endorsement also coincided with a growing effort to have QAnon-sympathetic individuals run for office, again displaying both a top-down and bottom-up synthesis of QAnon and the Republican Party. In the 2020 election cycle, there were more than two dozen GOP candidates who supported QAnon (Steck et al. 2020). Among its most prominent candidates was Marjorie Taylor Greene, who had begun promoting Pizzagate and QAnon conspiracy theories as early as 2017.[3] Greene, who announced her candidacy to represent Georgia's 14th congressional district in June of 2019, gained national attention due to her support for QAnon. On August 11, 2020, following Greene's primary victory, Trump endorsed Greene's campaign on Twitter, calling the QAnon candidate a "future Republican

---

[3] She distanced herself later in 2020 as her campaign gained momentum. See Juliegrace Brufke, "Controversial GOP Candidate Attempts to Distance from QAnon," *The Hill*, August 14, 2020, https://thehill.com/homenews/campaign/512143-controversial-gop-georgia-candidate-attempts-to-distance-from-qanon/.

Star" and "a real WINNER" (Cohen 2020). Again, this relationship was mutually beneficial: Trump's endorsement would give Greene legitimacy not only as a soon-to-be Representative, but also as a future star within the Republican Party. Greene would go on to be a vocal and voracious advocate for the Trump administration's policies and narratives in the House of Representatives.

At this point, the production of pro-Trump narratives that focused on the election, institutional efforts to integrate QAnon within the GOP, and organizational efforts to leverage QAnon narratives to run for office were beginning to work conjointly. During this political opportunity phase, we consider QAnon in this form to be a nascent and politically expedient digital surrogate, one with growing ties to the GOP due to its usefulness in the election cycle, but no long-term relationship yet.

The Transformation Point: Responding to the Election Loss (November 4, 2020–January 6, 2021)

After November 3, QAnon social media spaces were riddled with election fraud narratives. Among the 29,014 parlays posted the week after the election, 17,006 referenced Trump, Biden, the election, voting, fraud, or ballots (of the 8,753 posts referencing Biden, 7,231 used the substring "pedo" or "child"). Several posts called for a second Civil War and expressed complete rejection of the election results, including one that reads, "Your a fruckin pedophile Liar about everything. THERS NO WAY YOU WILL BE OUR NEXT PRESIDENT YOUR DILUSIONAL joey." These narratives aligned with the claims being made by Donald Trump and his campaign, and claims made by Trump were repeated frequently on Parler.

During this time parlays about the election were also rife with war metaphors, including hashtags like #fightback and #holdtheline. In messages posted the week after the election, 1,530 parlays referenced the Second Amendment, either in a hashtag or in the text, as part of the need for self-protection. A handful of posts also referenced the military as a cure-all to fix what they viewed as a rigged election. As one parlay post said three days after the election: "If they don't, we need to rise up and march on DC fully armed. This has to stop! The military should be on our side since they vow to protect against enemies both foreign and DOMESTIC!"

In this phase there were two significant shifts in QAnon discourse. First, it openly embraced election fraud disinformation in alignment with the position of the Trump campaign. In doing so, QAnon shifted from a fringe group with only tenuous relationships to the GOP to a digital surrogate that utilized its online platforms to mobilize Republicans and Trump supporters to advance the goals of the Trump administration, which (at that point) centered around election fraud. Second, and more worryingly, there was a palpable shift toward violent speech. Rather than denouncing QAnon, the Republican Party at best turned a blind eye to election conspiracy theories and pro-violence discourse, and at worst, encouraged it.

Narratives calling for violent mobilization materialized into action when QAnon followers, including the infamous QAnon Shaman Jake Angeli (Rabinowitz and Polantz 2021), stormed the Capitol Building on January 6. In the week leading up to the Capitol coup, there were 943 posts referencing January 6 and DC in Parler. Many of those parlays were about attending the Trump rally in DC, including two parlays posted on the morning of the rally. "Rented a Mini van drove to #washintondc for the #stopthesteal put the seats down and slept in the back," said one, alluding to the user's willingness to attend the event. Another user posted, "80% of all the weapons and ammo in this country is in DC right now! ! ! Look what our leaders have put us in!" While the statistic provided is likely untrue, it speaks to the prevalence of weapons and firearms at the January 6 Trump event. These messages suggest that some QAnon users were using Parler to organize offline rallies in DC that led to the Capitol coup. The repeated references to ammo and weaponry showed a willingness to use violence to overturn the outcome of the 2020 election.

At this point, it became apparent that QAnon functioned as a digital surrogate for the GOP to the detriment of American democracy. QAnon not only promoted conspiracy theories that sowed distrust in the electoral process, but also used violence to achieve anti-democratic goals on behalf and in support of the Trump campaign. QAnon was no longer a fringe group but an integral part of the Republican Party. The GOP's willingness to embrace of QAnon and harness its political energy shows its complete lack of distancing capacity that democracy theorist Nancy Bermeo deemed so pivotal for the viability of a liberal democracy (Bermeo 2020). As Bermeo (2020, 238) observed, to keep a democracy, a major political party must possess the ability to distance "its members from acts of violence and lawlessness." As of this writing, many Republican lawmakers still refuse to condemn the insurrection in unequivocal terms.

On January 28, 2022, the first January 6 trial began. Meanwhile, the House of Representative's January 6 Select Committee continues to gather news documents on "any direct role that Donald Trump and his top associates played in the January 6th assault on the U.S. Capitol" (Rhode 2021). Existing evidence points to political elites' involvement in the rallies on January 6: for example, far-right activist Ali Alexander, who was involved in the Capitol attack, testified that he was in touch with the White House and Republicans ahead of the time (Zurcher 2022).

The Maturation Phase: QAnon After January 6 (January 7, 2021 and Beyond)

Without warning, Q disappeared after their last post on 8kun on December 8, 2020. The combined events of the election loss, the end of Q's posts, the Capitol coup, and the subsequent mass de-platforming of QAnon by tech companies ushered in a new era for QAnon. QAnon had to adjust to this new political reality. Without posts from Q and with Trump out of office, the conspiracy theory group lacked both ideological and discursive leadership, creating a vacuum that would eventually be filled by others (specifically, Flynn and other Trump surrogates who had found a home in the conspiracy theory community).

During this time QAnon changed drastically, shifting their organizational structure, narratives, and institutional relationships to adjust to the post–Trump era. QAnon supporters were suspended from many mainstream platforms, including YouTube, Facebook, and Twitter (Bond 2021). Additionally, Parler's host Amazon Web Services decided to suspend the social network site in January of 2021 (Paczkowski and Mac 2021), though the platform has re-emerged on a Russian-owned host (Lanxon and Thomson 2021). These efforts to remove QAnon from mainstream social media spaces advanced a narrative of victimhood that is now at the core of QAnon's identity as a community and movement: deplatforming as a form of censorship and repression. Through this narrative, QAnon presents itself as a victim of "big tech," pointing toward their removal from mainstream platforms as evidence of censorship and a violation of the First Amendment.[4] This narrative runs alongside ongoing narratives about the pedophilic cabal and election fraud.

Importantly, as QAnon supporters have been largely removed from mainstream platforms, many have turned toward alternative platforms, though with not nearly the audience that they had on mainstream social media. Among the alternative platforms preferred by QAnon, Telegram has emerged as especially popular. Structured as a series of chat rooms, hundreds of QAnon groups, all varying in sizes, sprung up on Telegram. Among the largest is "QAnonOfficial" (https://t.me/qanonofficial), boasting 76,000 members at the time this chapter was written, and QAnon Fighters (https://t.me/qanonfighters), with over 53,000 followers.

Another organizational outcome of deplatforming was the rise of offline events that would not be moderated by big tech. This includes the Digital Soldiers Conference (Rondeaux 2021) and the For God and Country Patriot events, both of which featured associates of Trump like Sidney Powell, Lin Wood, and Michael Flynn. These offline events created new opportunities for QAnon to build on their relationship with Republican Party members and highlights the perseverance of digital surrogates, even when suspended from mainstream platforms.

Our recordings from two For God and Country Patriot events—the Patriot RoundUp in Dallas, May 2021 and the Patriot DoubleDown in Las Vegas, October 2021 (along with the affiliated "Patriot Voice" Telegram channel)—showed how QAnon had developed new organizational strategies and institutional relationships that resemble traditional surrogates. In addition to Trump associates, sitting congressman (such as Representative Louie Gohmert, R-TX) and political candidates were often panelists or guests (Gursky et al. 2021). Candidates attending these events talked to QAnon supporters as a voting constituency, rather than a fringe political conspiracy theory community. Notably, the candidates' talks focused on electoral fraud or traditionally conservative issues (e.g., Second Amendment rights, banning abortions), rather than QAnon narratives about pedophilia or a sex trafficking cabal, suggesting that narratives were "cherry-picked" by speakers to make the discourse more palatable and politically relevant. Nevertheless, candidates' talks and panels were scheduled alongside more conspiratorial QAnon panels, with deplatformed influencers who alluded

---

[4] Never mind that the First Amendment regulates Congress' ability to limit freedom of speech.

to more conspiratorial, extremist narratives. These offline events suggest that QAnon has matured into a fully fledged digital surrogate that bridges its fringe beliefs with Trump-aligned narratives, leveraging the organizing capacity of QAnon in support of GOP candidates.

At this stage of maturity, the relationship between QAnon and the GOP is very clear: Republicans attend QAnon events hoping to garner the support of QAnon-aligned voters, while QAnon, as a group, gain political legitimacy through its surrogate role. Narratives where they both align, such as con-spiratorial beliefs about election fraud or resentment toward big tech, are repeatedly mentioned, normalizing the narrative framework that also begets QAnon's more conspiracy beliefs. And organizationally, we see a transition-ing from online-only groups to a community that includes online spaces and offline places.

Conclusion

In this chapter we provided a chronological overview of QAnon, from its Pizzagate origins to its post-January 6, post-Q form. Though QAnon received little institutional support in the early phases, the mainstreaming of their narratives (particularly during the election) allowed them to gain more attention from conservative-leaning news organizations and members of the Republican Party. QAnon's loyalty to Trump in particular earned them praise throughout the election, paving the way for Trump-affiliated individuals to make a name for themselves within the conspiracy theory group.

In the start phase, QAnon was just getting off the ground: their narra-tives centered on outlandish conspiracy theories, building on its precursor, Pizzagate. During this time the organization of the group was almost exclu-sively online, with isolated offline activities and few institutional linkages. As QAnon grew in the growth phase, their narratives started to reach mass audiences through larger social media platforms. QAnon also started to organize more formally, with the emergence of different roles such as baker and Q influencer. Their growth persisted despite the early de-platforming efforts by Reddit, showing the organizational resilience of a multiplatform community. However, even in the growth phase, their nar-rative efforts, organizational capacity, and institutional relationships were disparate.

The 2020 US presidential election was a political opportunity for QAnon to develop into a digital surrogate. For QAnon believers, the election represented an opportunity to garner greater visibility; for the Trump campaign, QAnon provided political energy and votes. During this period, QAnon gained greater institutional support as it aligned its narratives more closely with the political goals of the Trump campaign. At the same time, the popularity of the movement among Republicans paved the way for QAnon-sympathetic candidates like Rep. Marjorie Taylor Greene to successfully run for office. These trends signal the development of a nascent digital surrogate that used more palatable narratives (alongside its fringe beliefs) and had achieved enough of an organizational capacity to attract institutional attention.

The outcome of the 2020 election was a transformation point for QAnon, and the group persisted in spite of Trump's loss and the disappearance of Q. Narratives in this phase contained a great deal of election fraud disinformation as well as calls for violence and mobilization. These developments show the organizational and narrative synthesis of QAnon and the Trump campaigns; however, it also highlights the grave risk of working with digital surrogates who are willing to resort to violence to achieve political goals. This was most evidently seen by QAnon's participation in the January 6 Capitol coup.

In the fifth and final stage of development, QAnon's perseverance—both as an organization and as a GOP surrogate—following the events of January 6, suggests that the group has reached a maturation phase. As a matured digital surrogate, QAnon's narratives, organizational capacity, and institutional relationship with the GOP persevered after the attack on the Capitol, despite the removal of QAnon groups from a variety of mainstream social media platforms. QAnon's resiliency as a community—including the rapid integration of the "victims of big tech" narrative and the relocation of QAnon to alternative social media spaces and offline events—suggests that matured digital surrogates may be more difficult to stop, even when these surrogates explicitly promote anti-democratic efforts.

By focusing on the integration of these three aspects—narrative, organizational, and institutional—over the lifespan of QAnon, our analysis reveals the essential factors of a fringe group's journey to digital surrogate status. First, while QAnon's fringe narratives persisted into their final phase, the integration of more mainstream narratives makes the movement more palatable to mainstream audiences and traditional institutional actors.

Second, as fringe groups get larger, it is necessary for them to develop an organizational structure that both facilitates online resilience and offline action. This offline activity can take place both within (e.g., running for office) and outside (e.g., storming the Capitol) of the democratic political process.

Finally, while groups may make concerted efforts to garner attention from political actors, institutional relationships are a two-way street: they require not only participation on the part of the digital surrogate but also attention on the part of the institutional actor. By partaking in such a relationship, the Republican Party effectively lent legitimacy to QAnon's more extreme actions and conspiratorial narratives. As a result, after January 6 (and despite their removal from many platforms), QAnon's status as a digital surrogate has not only persevered but flourished.

As we have noted, the ease by which QAnon developed these institutional relationships with the GOP should be of great concern to political communication scholars. By incorporating QAnon into its broader constituency, the GOP may have temporarily resolved their conservative dilemma, garnering support from some groups of the US population (groups that are otherwise quite anti-establishment). But the acceptance of QAnon comes at the cost of democracy: the legitimization of a fringe group as a digital surrogate effectively invites more conspiratorial thinking, extremist narratives, and potential violence. Already, we see some signs of the GOP being overrun by QAnon candidates, a possibility that Hacker and Pierson (2020) warned about with traditional surrogates. For example, in a 2020 Colorado primary, QAnon supporter Lauren Boebert beat out moderate incumbent Rep. Scott Tipton, and ultimately won the election.

It is unclear at this point what the next steps will be for QAnon, or whether they will be able to retain their digital surrogate role for the foreseeable future. What is clear, however, is the developmental path that QAnon has forged to become a digital surrogate for the GOP—a path that could (quite easily) be replicated by other extremist groups.

References

Aliapoulios, Max, Antonis Papasavva, Cameron Ballad, Emiliano De Cristofaro, Gianluca Stringhini, Savvas Zannettou, and Jeremy Blackburn. 2021. "The Gospel According to Q: Understanding the QAnon Conspiracy from the Perspective of Canonical Information." *AAAI International Conference on Web and Social Media*, 1–14.

Amarasingam, Amarnath, and Marc-André Argentino. 2020. "The QAnon Conspiracy Theory: A Security Threat in the Making." *CTC Sentinel* 13: 37–44.

Anwar, Ahmed, Ilyas, Haider, Yaqub, Ussama, and Salma Zaman. 2021. "Analyzing QAnon on Twitter in Context of US Elections 2020: Analysis of User Messages and Profiles Using VADER and BERT Topic Modeling." *The 22nd Annual International Conference on Digital Government Research*, 82–88.

Bank, Justin, Liam Stack, and Daniel Victor. 2018. "From 2018: Explaining QAnon, the Internet Conspiracy Theory That Showed Up at a Trump Rally." *New York Times*, August 1. https://www.nytimes.com/2018/08/01/us/politics/what-is-qanon.html.

Bennett, Lance W., and Alexandra Segerberg. 2013. *The Logic of Connective Action: Digital Media and the Personalization of Contentious Politics*. New York: Cambridge University Press.

Bennett, Lance W., Alexandra Segerberg, and Shawn Walker. 2014. "Organization in the Crowd: Peer Production in Large-Scale Networked Protests." *Information, Communication & Society* 17: 232–260.

Bimber, Bruce, Andrew, J. Flanagin, and Cynthia Stohl, Cynthia. 2012. *Collective Action in Organizations: Interaction and Engagement in an Era of Technological* Change. New York: Cambridge University Press.

Bermeo, Nancy. 2020. *Ordinary People in Extraordinary Times*. Princeton, NJ: Princeton University Press.

Bond, Shannon. 2021. "Unwelcome on Facebook and Twitter, QAnon Followers Flock to Fringe Sites." NPR, January 31. https://www.npr.org/2021/01/31/962104747/unwelcome-on-facebook-twitter-qanon-followers-flock-to-fringe-sites.

Brady, Jeff, 2018. "QAnon: The Conspiracy Theorist Group That Appears at Trump Rallies." NPR, August 3. https://www.npr.org/2018/08/03/635449555/qanon-the-conspiracy-theorist-group-that-appears-at-trump-rallies.

CBS News. 2019. "New Social Media App Parler a Haven for Users Kicked Off Traditional Platforms." YouTube, May 19. https://www.youtube.com/watch?v=q6hXgaJDuPE.

Chang, Alvin. 2018. "We Analyzed Every QAnon Post on Reddit." *Vox*, August 8. https://www.vox.com/2018/8/8/17657800/qanon-reddit-conspiracy-data.

Clark, Dartunorro. 2022. "Cyber Ninjas, Company that Led Arizona GOP Election 'Audit,' Is Shutting Down." CNBC, January 7. https://www.cnbc.com/2022/01/07/cyber-ninjas-company-that-led-arizona-gop-election-audit-is-shutting-down.html.

Cohen, Max. 2020. "Trump Calls Georgia GOP Candidate Who Embraces QAnon a 'Future Republican Star." *Político*, August 12. https://www.politico.com/news/2020/08/12/trump-georgia-qanon-taylor-greene-394204.

Cooper, Jonathan. 2021. "QAnon Figure Says He's Running for Congress to Fix Elections." Associated Press, October 18. https://apnews.com/article/donald-trump-elections-arizona-phoenix-house-elections-3c1c4cb13caaa168788418140d18bcd0.

De Zeeuw, Daniel, Sal Hagen, Stijn Peeters, and Emilija Jokubauskaite. 2020. "Tracing Normiefication: A Cross-Platform Analysis of the QAnon Conspiracy Theory." *First Monday*. https://firstmonday.org/ojs/index.php/fm/article/download/10643/9998.

Derysh, Igor. 2019. "Trump Campaign Ad Featured QAnon Signs Despite FBI Warning that Conspiracy Could Motivate Extremists." *Salon*, August 8. https://www.salon.com/2019/08/08/trump-campaign-ad-featured-qanon-signs-despite-fbi-warning-that-conspiracy-could-motivate-extremists/.

Doubek, James. 2017. "Conspiracy Theorist Alex Jones Apologizes for Promoting 'Pizzagate." NPR, March 26. https://www.npr.org/sections/thetwo-way/2017/03/26/521545788/conspiracy-thEorist-alex-jones-apologizes-for-promoting-pizzagate.

Durkheim, Emile. 1893. *The Division of Labour in Society*. New York: Simon & Schuster.

Fox News. 2019. "Parler CEO: Social Media is Supposed to be a Community Forum." YouTube, May 28. https://www.youtube.com/watch?v=j6iyAt1Ydpc.

HOW QANON DEVELOPED 87

Gabbatt, Adam. 2020. "Trump Refuses to Disavow QAnon Conspiracy Theory During Town Hall." *The Guardian*, October 15. https://www.theguardian.com/us-news/2020/oct/15/qanon-trump-refuses-disavow-conspiracy-theory-town-hall.

Goldberg, Michelle. 2018. "The Conspiracy Theory that Says Trump is a Genius." *New York Times*, April 4. https://www.nytimes.com/2018/04/06/opinion/qanon-trump-conspiracy-theory.html.

Gursky, Jacob, Katie Joseff, and Josephine Lukito. 2021. "QAnon Pivots its Exiled Online Movement to the Real World." *Wired*, July 8. https://www.wired.com/story/qanon-pivots-its-exiled-online-movement-to-the-real-world/.

Hacker, Jacob S., and Paul Pierson. 2020. *Let Them Eat Tweets: How the Right Rules in the Age of Extreme Inequalit*. New York: Liveright Publishing.

Hannah, Matthew N. 2021. "A Conspiracy of Data: QAnon, Social Media, and Information Visualization." *Social Media+Society* 7: 1–15.

Jackson, Sam, Brandon Gorman, and Mayuko Nakatsuka. 2021. " QAnon on Twitter: An overview." Institute for Data, Democracy and Politics, George Washington University, 1–54. chrome-extension://efaidnbmnnnibpcajpcglclefindmkaj/https://iddp.gwu.edu/sites/g/files/zaxdzs5791/files/downloads/QAnon%20on%20Twitter%3B%20Jackson.pdf.

Kaplan, Alex. 2019. "Trump has Repeatedly Amplified QAnon Twitter Accounts. The FBI has Linked the Conspiracy Theory to Domestic Terror." *MediaMatters*, August 1. https://www.mediamatters.org/twitter/fbi-calls-qanon-domestic-terror-threat-trump-has-amplified-qanon-supporters-twitter-more-20.

Kim, Soojong, and Kim Jisu. 2022. "Propagation of the QAnon Conspiracy Theory on Facebook." OSF Preprint. https://doi.org/10.31219/osf.io/wku5b.

Lanxon, Nate, and Amy Thomson. 2021. "Parler Moves to Hosting Service Owned by Russians after Ban." *Al Jazeera*, January 19. https://www.aljazeera.com/economy/2021/1/19/bb-parler-moves-to-hosting-service-owned-by-russians-after-ban.

Lardieri, Alexa. 2021. "Church Membership Hits All-Time Low in 2020, Gallup Finds." *USA Today*, March 21. https://www.usnews.com/news/national-news/articles/2021-03-29/church-membership-hits-all-time-low-in-2020-gallup-finds.

Lopez, German. 2016. "Pizzagate, the Fake News Conspiracy Theory that Led a Gunman to DC's Comet Ping Pong, explained." *Vox*, December 8. https://www.vox.com/policy-and-politics/2016/12/5/13842258/pizzagate-comet-ping-pong-fake-news.

Lorenz, Taylor. 2019. "Instagram Is the Internet's New Home for Hate." *The Atlantic*, March 21. https://www.theatlantic.com/technology/archive/2019/03/instagram-is-the-internets-new-home-for-hate/585382/.

Martineau, Paris. 2017. "The Storm Is the New Pizzagate—Only Worse." *New York Magazine*, December 19. https://nymag.com/intelligencer/2017/12/qanon-4chan-the-storm-conspiracy-explained.html.

Menke, Manuel, and Christian Schwarzenegger. 2019. "On the Relativity of Old and New Media: A Lifeworld Perspective." *Convergence* 25 (4): 657–672.

Ng, Lynnette Hui Xian, Iain Cruickshank, and Kathleen M. Carley. 2021. "Coordinating Narratives and the Capitol Riots on Parler." arXiv preprint, https://arxiv.org/abs/2109.00945.

Nguyen, Tina. 2020. "Trump Isn't Secretly Winking at QAnon. He's Retweeting its Followers." *Politico*, July 12. https://www.politico.com/news/2020/07/12/trump-tweeting-qanon-followers-357238.

Ohlheiser, Abby. 2018. "You'll Never Guess How the QAnon Conspiracy Theorists Feel About All This Media Coverage." *Washington Post*, August 3. https://www.washingtonpost.com/news/the-intersect/wp/2018/08/03/this-is-the-moment-how-a-wave-of-media-coverage-gave-qanon-conspiracy-theorists-their-best-week-ever/.

Paczkowski, John, and Ryan Mac. 2021. "Amazon Will Suspend Hosting for Pro-Trump Social Network Parler." *Buzzfeed News*, January 9. https://www.buzzfeednews.com/article/johnpaczkowski/amazon-parler-aws.

Papasavva, Antonis, Jeremy Blackburn, Gianluca Stringhini, Savvas Zannettou, and Emiliano de Cristofaro. 2021. "Is It a Qoincidence?: An Exploratory Study of QAnon on Voat." *Proceedings of the Web Conference 2021*, 460–471. https://discovery.ucl.ac.uk/id/eprint/10130483/1/papasavva_qoincidence_3442381.3450036.pdf.

Phadke, Shruti, and Tanushree Mitra. 2020. "Many Faced Hate: A Cross Platform Study of Content Framing and Information Sharing by Online Hate Groups." *Proceedings of the 2020 CHI Conference on Human Factors in Computing Systems*, 1–13.

Rabinowitz, Hannah, and Katelyn Polantz. 2021. "'QAnon Shaman' Jacob Chansley Sentenced to 41 Months in Prison for Role in US Capitol Riot." CNN, November 17. https://www.cnn.com/2021/11/17/politics/jacob-chansley-qanon-shaman-january-6-sentencing/index.html.

Rathje, Steve, Jay J. Van Bavel, and Sander Van Der Linden. 2021. "Out-Group Animosity Drives Engagement on Social Media." *Proceedings of the National Academy of Sciences* 118 (26): e2024292118.

Rhode, David. 2021. "The January 6th Investigation Gets Closer to Donald Trump." *The New Yorker*, November 11. https://www.newyorker.com/news/daily-comment/the-january-6th-investigation-gets-closer-to-donald-trump.

Rodrik, David. 2021. "Why Does Globalization Fuel Populism? Economics, Culture, and the Rise of Right-Wing Populism." *Annual Review of Economics* 13: 133–170.

Rondeaux, Candace. 2021. "The Digital General." *The Intercept*, June 27. https://theintercept.com/2021/06/27/qanon-michael-flynn-digital-soldiers/.

Rubin, Olivia, Lucien Bruggeman, and Will Steakin. 2021. "QAnon Emerges as Recurring Theme of Criminal Cases Ties to US Capitol Siege." ABC News, January 19. https://abcnews.go.com/US/qanon-emerges-recurring-theme-criminal-cases-tied-us/story?id=75347445.

Samuelson, Kate. 2016. "What to Know About Pizzagate, the Fake News Story with Real Consequences." *Time*, December 5. https://time.com/4590255/pizzagate-fake-news-what-to-know/.

Sipka, Andrea, Anikó Hannak, and Aleksandra Urman. 2021. "Comparing the Language of QAnon-related Content on Parler, Gab, and Twitter." *14th ACM Web Science Conference*, 411–421. https://dl.acm.org/doi/10.1145/3501247.3531550.

Skocpol, Theda, and Vanessa Williamson 2016. *The Tea Party and the Remaking of Republican Conservatism*. New York: Oxford University Press.

Sommer, Will@WillSommer. 2021. "In Another Example of QAnon Turning on Their Heroes." Twitter, July 13. https://twitter.com/willsommer/status/1415037773921325060.

Sommer, Will, and Asawin Suebsaeng. 2019. "Team Trump Wrestles with its QAnon Problem." *The Daily Beast*, September 12. https://www.thedailybeast.com/team-trump-wrestles-with-its-2020-qanon-problem.

Steck, Em, Nathan McDermott, and Christopher Hickey. 2020. "The Congressional Candidates who have Engaged with the QAnon Conspiracy Theory." CNN, October 30. https://www.cnn.com/interactive/2020/10/politics/qanon-cong-candidates/.

Tran, Huu Dat. 2021. "Studying the Community of Trump Supporters on Twitter during the 2020 US Presidential Election via Hashtags# maga and# trump2020." *Journalism and Media* 2 (4): 709–731.

Travis View@travis_view. 2018. "Gen. Flynn Likes to Play Footsie with the QAnon Community." Twitter, November 24. https://twitter.com/travis_view/status/1066134346342424576.

Van Neuss, Leif. 2018. "Globalization and Deindustrialization in Advanced Countries." *Structural Change and Economic Dynamics* 45: 49–63.

Wilson, Kirby. 2018. "Dozens of Trump Supporters Championed the 'QAnon' Conspiracy at His Tampa Rally. Here's What You Need to Know." *Tampa Bay Times*, August 1. https://www.tampabay.com/florida-politics/buzz/2018/08/01/dozens-of-trump-supporters-championed-the-qanon-conspiracy-at-his-tampa-rally-heres-what-you-need-to-know/.

Zadrozny, Brandy, and Ben Collins. 2018a. "How Three Conspiracy Theorists Took 'Q' and Sparked Qanon." NBC, August 14. https://www.nbcnews.com/tech/tech-news/how-three-conspiracy-theorists-took-q-sparked-qanon-n900531.

Zadrozny, Brandy, and Ben Collins. 2018b. "Reddit Bans Qanon Subreddits After Months of Violent Threats." NBC, September 12. https://www.nbcnews.com/tech/tech-news/reddit-bans-qanon-subreddits-after-months-violent-threats-n909061.

Ziblatt, Daniel. 2017. *Conservative Parties and the Birth of Democracy*. New York: Cambridge University Press.

Zihiri, Saifeldeen, Gabriel Lima, Jiyoung Han, Meeyoung Cha, and Wonjae Lee. 2022. "QAnon Shifts into the Mainstream, Remains a Far-Right Ally." *Heliyon*, e08764.

Zurcher, Anthony. 2022. "Five Big Questions About Trump and the Riot." BBC, January 6. https://www.bbc.com/news/world-us-canada-59703761.

Chapter 4

The Democratic Decay Within

The US Republican Party and QAnon as a Digital Surrogate

Daniel Kreiss and Aaron Sugarman

During the 2020 US electoral cycle, 26 candidates for state legislature and 107 candidates for Congress were identified by the left media watchdog group Media Matters as being QAnon supporters or using its symbols and narratives.[1] These candidates were overwhelmingly Republicans. Of the state legislature candidates, 23 were Republicans (one was an independent and the others were members of third parties; none were Democrats); of the congressional candidates, 98 were Republicans (two were Democrats, five were independents, and the rest were members of third parties). Of the winners, all were Republicans; six took office in states and three went to Congress. And Media Matters identified 73 congressional candidates who ran in the 2022 midterm elections, with two Republicans being reelected.[2]

QAnon is an increasingly global, digitally networked conspiracy movement (Lukito, Yang, and Kim this volume; Zihiri et al. 2022). As journalists and researchers have documented, its main narrative thread is a conspiracy theory that claims there is a US-based cabal of Democratic Party and other elites involved in the sexual trafficking of young children. Furthermore, adherents believe that there is a "deep state" (Skowronek et al. 2021) apparatus that is both complicit in its operation and undermines those looking to rectify it—such as former President Trump (Hannah 2021). QAnon has taken root and spread through a set of media platforms such as 4Chan and other, more widely used sites where its symbols and narratives have circulated, as well as news media that have amplified its claims (Aliapoulios et al., 2021; de Zeeuw et al. 2020). Central to the movement is a decentralized

---

[1] An updated running list from the 2020 election cycle on is found in Kaplan (2020).
[2] An updated running list from the 2022 election cycle is found in Kaplan (2021).

Daniel Kreiss and Aaron Sugarman, *The Democratic Decay Within*. In: *Connective Action and the Rise of the Far-Right*. Edited by: Steven Livingston and Michael Miller, Oxford University Press. © Oxford University Press (2025). DOI: 10.1093/oso/9780197794937.003.0004

THE DEMOCRATIC DECAY WITHIN   91

set of participatory, role-based interpretative practices among its adherents that resemble the exegesis of scripture (Marwick and Partin 2020; Tripodi 2022).

In the post–civil rights era (Mason 2018) the Republican Party's coalition is made up of a white economic elite (Skocpol and Hertel-Fernandez 2016), white small government, property-protecting ideological conservatives (Richardson 2014), white cultural evangelicals (Du Mez 2020), and white rural Americans (Cramer 2016). The party itself has—since the 1970s—been increasingly shaped by right-wing media including magazines and newspapers (Hemmer 2016), talk radio (Sobieraj and Berry 2011), Fox News (Peck 2019), Tea Party movement and media branding strategies (Costley White 2018), a network of right-wing websites (Benkler et al. 2018), and an increasingly prominent network of media sites and movements organized around anti-Black racism and nativism (Belew and Gutierrez 2021).

In his landmark *Conservative Parties and the Birth of Democracy,* political scientist Daniel Ziblatt (2017) details how democratic stability is premised on conservative, landed, economic interests deciding that they can better hold onto their incumbent power through electoral systems—even when their policy agendas conflict with the economic interests of the mass publics they need to remain competitive in fair and free elections. Conservative parties can secure and wield political power—including not only winning elections but also advancing and protecting economically conservative policies—in part by articulating and running on ideas (Adams and Kreiss 2021) of "religion, empire, and nationalism" (Ziblatt 2017, 44). These ideas are deep-rooted cultural and identity appeals that, crucially, are "cross-class"—but they always run the risk of pulling these parties "away from constitutional politics" (Ziblatt 2017, 44). They do so because these ideas potentially give rise to "a politics of ultimate ends" that do not allow for loss, compromise, a legitimate opposition, or moral ambiguity (Weber quoted in Ziblatt 2017, 40).

Central to the ability of conservative parties to hold onto power while engaging in competitive elections are the outside "interest groups and civil society organizations" that act as surrogates for weak or vulnerable party organizations (Ziblatt 2017, 174)—and even strong parties with potentially greater democratic consequences (see Hilton, this volume). Surrogates are central for their mobilization work, especially along the lines of propagating cultural ideas and identity appeals (Kreiss et al. 2020) that bridge class cleavages. As Ziblatt details, while weak parties rely on these surrogates to grow stronger, they are also potentially made vulnerable by them. Extreme activists who eschew pragmatic politics and constitutional democracy can gain access to electoral and policy machinery, and party institutions become vulnerable to potential capture by these interests. Ziblatt's case studies take shape mostly over the course of the nineteenth and early twentieth centuries, and as such he had in mind generally formally organized surrogates such as interest groups and civil society organizations (Kreiss et al. 2020, 174). That said, Ziblatt spends comparatively little time analyzing the nature of "surrogates" (there are only seven references to the concept in the volume), but the historical case studies make it clear that surrogates can also be "movements"—those comparatively less organized and more diffuse, yet networked, set of actors and organizations engaged in collective actions and sharing a set of identities and ideas.

This chapter draws on Ziblatt's framework to document and analyze the uptake of QAnon symbols and narratives by Republican Party candidates in the course of their 2020 electoral bids. As we argue, QAnon offers a set of symbolic resources to Republican candidates that center on fundamental(ist) ideas of religion, morality, and white, Christian, masculine, and heteronormative identity that accord with the party's main coalitions and are deeply mobilizational.

At the same time, this chapter argues that Ziblatt's framework needs a conceptualization of the unique role that "digital surrogate organizations" (Bennett and Livingston, this volume) play in conservative party politics and contemporary threats to constitutional democracy. While scholars such as Hacker and Pierson (2020) provide extensive discussion of surrogates, they generally do not consider the relationships between new digital movements or networks, such as QAnon, and institutional political parties. And yet since the 1990s, the increasing prevalence of digital networks has given rise to new repertoires of collective social and symbolic action including the ways that movements organize themselves internally and make claims on external actors (Caren et al. 2020). This includes "connective action," a concept that refers to the ways that self-expression and content sharing through "personal action frames" give rise to potentially global movements where communication itself constitutes the organizational form (Bennett and Segerberg 2013; Bennett and Livingston, this volume). It might be more accurate to speak of evolving or liminal surrogate networks that consist of an assemblage of traditional and digitally enabled organizational forms. As Bennett and Segerberg put it (2013, 44), "Expanding our perspective to include technologies helps shed light on the formation of fluid organizational assemblages in which agency becomes shared or distributed across individuals and organizations as networks reconfigure in response to changing issues and events." Knüpfer and Klinger in this volume also note the unique effects of digital surrogate networks on the far-right *Alternative für Deutschland* (AfD) party in Germany.

Media forms and mediated movements shape institutional party politics. Historians' accounts show us how the US Republican Party has long been shaped by dense networks of media that create and sustain conservative (and white) identity and wield important influence as the representation of public opinion for Republican legislators and elites, as well as serve as the creators of public opinion for Republicans in the electorate (e.g., Hemmer 2016; Peck 2019). Reading through Ziblatt's framework, in essence we can conceptualize talk radio and Fox News as "media surrogates" and movements such as QAnon as digital surrogates for the Republican Party. There is a lot of evidence that their influence is growing in Republican Party politics (see Lukito et al., this volume). For example, an Axios report (Swan and Markay 2022) based on interviews with 14 of the Republican Party's top consultants, spoke about a shift from the older surrogates of the sort that Ziblatt chronicles (the US Chamber of Commerce, NRA, Koch Network, and Tea Party) to comparatively newer media and digital surrogates (Tucker Carlson, Fox News, Breitbart, and online influencers including Candace Owens, Ben Shapiro, Dan Bongino, Joe Rogan, Jack Posobiec, Charlie Kirk, and Marjorie Taylor Greene) as the party's brokers in elections. Strikingly, congresswoman and apparent QAnon adherent Marjorie Taylor Greene is listed among these other right-wing luminaries—revealing the reach of the movement into the institution of the Republican Party. Also, these media and digital influencers are often known for their identity, and especially white identity, and cultural appeals.

Empirically, this paper analyzes the ways that Republican and independent candidates for office drew on QAnon symbols and narratives, those of a digital surrogate organization, in the course of their bids in 2020. We argue that QAnon has created a rich cultural field of ideas encoded in discourse (Adams and Kreiss 2021) that Republican candidates draw from in their attempts to mobilize their electorates. Through interpretative analysis of the social media content using QAnon references shared by these candidates, we show how the digital surrogate movement provides a set of narratives about morality, Christianity, anti-elite populism, race and ethnicity, "deviant" sexual and gender identities, and revolution and redemption to restore a true white, Christian order to America. The diversity of the elements here matter. QAnon offers an interrelated, yet flexible set of themes that people can identify with and take up on a personal basis in multiple ways—"personal action frames" that facilitate connective action (Bennett and Segerberg 2013). This, in turn, theoretically reveals how digital surrogate organizations can help create discursive orders that can be advantageous for parties. While for Republican Party candidates QAnon offers a set of mobilizational symbolic resources, for the movement its institutional uptake potentially offers validation, symbolic and stylistic outcomes (as opposed to policy outcomes), and access to broader audiences and institutional levers of power—all of which reveals how a conservative party with a policy agenda that protects wealth and existing distributions of property sits comfortably alongside the embrace of an existing racial and religious social order and an extremist, conspiracy oriented digital movement.

Our empirical analysis revealed that candidates used 45 discrete QAnon symbols during the 2020 cycle. By "symbol" we mean unique images or textual content associated with QAnon. Through inductive coding, we defined six central themes found within them: Christianity, opposition to elites, opposition to marginalized groups, nationalism, revolution, and a form of corrosive skepticism (as opposed to a healthy "civic skepticism"; see Kreiss 2016; Schudson 2022). We show how these symbols and themes map onto the Republican Party's coalition, offering clear mobilizing narratives for the party's base. Yet we also document potentially destabilizing elements for the party, such as a fealty to Trump as a political leader and the way QAnon espouses a rival form of nationalism to American patriotism.

Parties and Digital Surrogate Organizations

To date, much of the study of online conspiracy movements like QAnon, mis- and disinformation, and even propaganda is generally focused on their media and psychological dimensions. At the same time, there has been an explosion of work around the world on "democratic backsliding" (Haggard and Kaufman 2021) or "democratic decay" (Daly 2019) and the growth of right-wing parties, movements, or ideas within established democracies (Norris and Inglehart 2019). While each literature offers considerable insight into contemporary political dynamics, as generally separate domains of inquiry they often miss what they can learn from one another. Studies of online conspiracy movements, disinformation, and propaganda need to pay greater attention to politics, inequality, social power, and political institutions to understand the *form* that strategic appeals often take, or the *interests* they serve. This includes the affective, cross-class, and often white identarian appeals of the contemporary right in countries such as the US. Accounting for politics means understanding how things such as disinformation, propaganda, and conspiracy are embedded in larger social and political systems and social structures that provide the institutional contexts for political action and determine the stakes involved in contests for power. Studies of right-wing parties and democratic backsliding, meanwhile, need a better understanding of media and information environments as they shape the possibilities for social and symbolic action. This includes both the degree to which communication is organization (Bennett and Segerberg 2013) and disinformation is utilized asymmetrically as a right-wing tool to pursue political power (Freelon et al. 2020; Roudakova, 2017).

At the intersection of these two literatures would be the ways that shifts in forms of organization afforded by media and communications technologies impact the political institutions, such as political parties, that are central to democratic processes (see also Hilton, this volume). As Ziblatt (2017) argues, historically incumbent interests organized into well-institutionalized parties have provided for the stability of democracy in many countries. Ziblatt argues that it is conservative interests, and the comparative strength of their party organizations, that have kept democracy stable in countries such as Britain and Sweden or have unwound it as in Italy and Spain. The stability of democracies came from aristocracies becoming, and remaining, convinced that elections could be a path toward maintaining, or expanding, their power and therefore having a continued willingness to play the electoral game. That willingness relates, crucially, to the ability of their organizations to adapt and respond to democratization movements and contest elections effectively, especially through the development of professionals specialized in contesting elections who could lose with the confidence they would win in the future (Ziblatt 2017, 39). When conservative parties were weak, they struggled to make those effective cross-class appeals to things such as religion, national identity, and empire to keep themselves in power. In Ziblatt's account conservatives too organizationally weak to win elections turned to surrogates to enhance their mobilizational power.

96   CONNECTIVE ACTION AND THE RISE OF THE FAR-RIGHT

In Ziblatt's historical case studies, there is a clear risk with the turn to surrogates. As conservative parties lean on surrogates like interest groups and movements to increase their organizational strength, they also become vulnerable to anti-democratic radicals and extremists—who in turn are made all the more dangerous when a party is organizationally and institutionally weak.

The keys of Ziblatt's account are therefore two-fold: incumbent conservative interests only embrace democracy as long as they disproportionately gain from it, and in order to secure those gains, they need strong, coherent, political parties and organized interests to protect their wealth and status. While his cases center on Western Europe, we can adapt some of these insights to the US case and especially see the hallmarks of weak party organization in the contemporary US Republican Party.[3] Since the electoral reforms of the 1970s, which opened primaries to the wider electorate (Bawn et al. 2012), both main US political parties ceded some control over their nomination processes to the media (Carson and Williamson 2018; Sides et al. 2019), a problem especially pronounced on the political right given the extensive network of right-wing media around the party (Hemmer 2016). The financing of primary elections is decentralized in both parties, and on the right there is a network of ideological and business-backed interest groups that have clear motivations to protect incumbent interests against popular redistributive economic policies (Hacker and Pierson 2020). Perhaps most notably, however, is the technologically facilitated surge of loosely coordinated networks and sites—from incumbent media like Fox News and start up media like Breitbart and One America News to new social platforms like Telegraph and Parler—that have an increasingly forceful pull on Republican Party dynamics in elections (see, for example, Grossman and Hopkins 2018). Indeed, during the 2016 US presidential election then-candidate Trump outsourced much of the digital operations of his campaign to Facebook and a burgeoning racist "alt-right" (Daniels 2018) because of limited organizational capacity compared to his Democratic opponent (see Kreiss and McGregor 2018).

These media and digital surrogate organizations act strategically in loose coordination of interests with right-wing parties to contest elections by creating and exploiting social and cultural divisions in the service of political

---

[3] Features of weak parties include few or diminished mechanisms of accountability over candidates, interest groups that wield outsized power versus party elites, and weakened party coordination and control over nominating processes. See Rosenbluth and Shapiro (2018).

and economic power. The vast reach of technology platforms and social media and their transformation of many domains of social life (Van Dijck et al. 2018), the new forms of symbolic action, organizing, and organization made possible through digital media (Jackson et al. 2020) including its affective dimensions (Papacharissi 2015), and the broader attentional and temporal dynamics of "hybrid media systems" (Chadwick 2017) has meant that loose networks of affiliated and strategically aligned actors, at times formally coordinated and at others not, work in tandem to shape informational dynamics. In the process, on the right and left these networks can be aligned with and do mobilizational work in the service of the party in power, or in the opposition. When they serve the right in the US, they align with forms of ascriptive hierarchy along racial or other lines (Smith 1997). Numerous empirical studies, for instance, have documented the ways that online right-wing movements feature white identity appeals or express white nationalism (Belew 2018; Belew and Gutierrez 2021), which the "alt-right" advances in the form of memes and meme culture in the service of expanding the number of their adherents (Daniels 2018).

While Ziblatt generally only considers the economic interests of previous aristocracies, as these allied media and digital right-wing surrogates suggest, and a long body of literature argues, these are simultaneously racial interests (Brandon 2019; Hild and Merritt 2018; Mills 2004; Ralph and Singhal 2019; Robinson 2000 [1983]; Roediger 2017). Indeed, the Ziblatt framework lacks clear analysis of social difference beyond class and some detailing of the dynamics of empire. It is striking the degree to which a book that charts conservative parties and democratic fortunes in the mid-1800s through mid-1900s in countries such as Britain and Germany, along with discussion of other Western European countries, has little to say about colonization and the social distinctions (including and especially on racial, ethnic, and religious grounds) that underlay its economics and expansion (Jones 2023)—beyond how these things afforded the potential for "national," "religious," or "patriotic" appeals, generally seen as narrowly "cultural" and "non-class" cleavages (Ziblatt 2017, 83). Indeed, patriotic and national appeals are a fundamental part of a "white racial frame" that provides the cultural and ideological scaffolding for these things to make sense and be legitimate as appeals (Feagin 2020).

This matters because to understand the appeals of surrogate organizations requires analysis of the coalitions that parties seek to mobilize. As detailed above, in the United States for the Republican Party this means whites

CONNECTIVE ACTION AND THE RISE OF THE FAR-RIGHT

generally (Sides et al. 2019), and specifically white cultural evangelicals, rural-dwellers, and small government ideologues. This is reflected in the white identity appeals propagated by the party's elites, most visibly and effectively by the former president (Jardina 2019), but among elected officials and candidates for office at all levels.

For example, during the 2016 and 2020 US federal election cycles, scholars documented the Republican Party's various white identity appeals as they were textured with nationalism, religion, and geography. Scholarship, for instance, has documented how racial identity appeals to whites have grown as economic uncertainty in the country's manufacturing base has risen (Baccini and Weymouth 2021). Research on Fox News has demonstrated the degree to which populist appeals are constructed on the basis of the interpellation of an "authentic" white, working class, conservative identity, with the out party being "over educated elites" that "use government power to both expropriate the wealth of "producing" Americans and to impose non-traditional values on them" (Peck 2019, 4). Furthermore, the wave of anti–critical race theory bills that swept the country in advance of the 2021 midterm elections, espoused by candidates for office such as Virginia governor Glenn Youngkin and Florida governor Ron DeSantis, clearly establish strategic appeals to whites as victims at the center of Republican campaign communication (Kreiss et al. 2021).

QAnon

QAnon is a debunked conspiracy theory and movement that was created on the imageboard site 4Chan. It originated from a press conference by then-US President Donald Trump in 2017, wherein he referred to an impending storm (which many adherents believe to be a future military operation). The core belief of QAnon is that Trump, known as Q+, is leading a faction against the deep state—which includes prominent Democratic leaders, Hollywood and social elites, and the "mass media." QAnon adherents believe that these politicians and elites are corrupt satanic socialists who are trafficking children and extracting a life-sustaining drug known as "adrenochrome" from them. Adherents believe that messages to the QAnon community are sent by Q, a purported military insider with Q level (Top Secret) clearance. The community then deciphers these messages collaboratively but according to a defined set of roles and interpretative practices (Marwick and Partin 2020).

Q has declared that a military takeover is imminent to preserve America's "shining light"; this will involve martial law, extrajudicial arrests and trials, the detaining of dissenters, and a president who will crush all opposition. As the QAnon movement has gathered believers, the conspiracy has sprawled to encompass COVID-19 disinformation, claims of election fraud and white slavery, and more.

QAnon offers a case to analyze the potential power and de-stabilizing possibilities of digital surrogates. Indeed, while QAnon is likely a unique case in its scope, significant scale, and international reach, the very fact that it exists makes it a worthwhile empirical phenomenon in its own right as a potent digital surrogate. Beyond its significance as a movement, as a case it also offers up a number of elements that help us analyze the role of digital surrogates vis-à-vis institutional parties. And given that there is no necessary policy (or economic) reason that the groups within the Republican Party's coalition should be aligned, QAnon's work as a surrogate mobilizing adherents from across the party's constituent groups helps us clearly see the relationship between an institutional party and digitally enabled forms of connective action.

We focus here on the *content* of the appeals that Republican and independent candidates adopted during a particular moment in time (i.e., the 2020 election cycle). This contrasts with Lukito, Yang, and Kim's (this volume) excellent longitudinal approach to show how the conspiracy movement itself evolved from a fringe group into a digital surrogate for the GOP, including how QAnon "adapts its discursive markers to align more closely with Republican issue agendas." Our analysis of QAnon's role in politics—and QAnon's wider role in society—is grounded in the concepts of "adversarial narratives" and "identity propaganda." The nonprofit Global Disinformation Index refers to "adversarial narratives" as "intentionally distributed narratives without a required chronology or sequence of content ('artefacts'), and which seek to enrage and divide internet users'" (Decker 2019). The concept offers a framework for analyzing disinformation. Actors develop adversarial narratives to exploit underlying cleavages within a society. Adversarial narratives create, exploit, or maintain rifts between groups, and they disproportionately harm the most marginalized members of society. A complementary approach is the concept of "identity propaganda," which Reddi et al. (2021) define "as strategic narratives that target and exploit identity-based differences to maintain existing hegemonic social orders and/or undermine challenges to extant political power." As Reddi et al. show, actors on the right wielded identity propaganda during the 2020 presidential election to undermine the standing of Kamala Harris with Black voters by questioning her racial identity while "othering" her for white voters.

In the course of an election, the right deploys strategic narratives to mobilize and demobilize voters to build a winning electoral coalition around cleavages other than class. In this, adversarial narratives, like identity propaganda, are not synonymous with conspiracy theories. Although QAnon is often portrayed as a conspiracy theory in public discourse, we focus here on candidates' *strategic* use of QAnon symbols and narratives to *divide* and *mobilize*, including in highly adversarial ways that convey status threats to invoke rage and hatred among dominant groups to defend an existing class, racial, and religious order. The point is that this surely serves the political interests of these candidates, quite apart from whether they believe in the various conspiracy theories QAnon promotes.

Further, we see surrogate movements such as QAnon as being comparatively freer to develop adversarial narratives and identity propaganda that make explicit religious, racial, and gender appeals that threaten human rights and democracy, than politicians running for elected office. Once these narratives and symbols are encoded in discourse, however, candidates can strategically appropriate them for mobilizational and de-mobilizational purposes. In the process, these narratives have the potential to make dominant identities salient, convey status threat and victimhood, and drive bigotry against nondominant out-groups—made even more dangerous when it comes from candidates of a political party that will potentially be in a position to wield institutional power (Young-Bruehl 1998). For example, exposure to derogatory language has been found to increase political radicalization and undermine intergroup relations (Bilewicz and Soral 2020).

Platforms create opportunities for actors wielding adversarial narratives. The attention economy of platforms is driven by advertising dollars and reward engagement, often produced through negatively valenced affective content and social reputation processes (Munger 2020). This can be observed among news organizations, which have relied upon digital listening analytics to determine coverage by prioritizing stories that garner the most views—and as a result, in the 2016 Republican primary, the news media gave Donald Trump $1,898,000,000 in free media attention (Karpf, this volume).

Studying Digital Surrogates

Establishing whether a group, organization, or movement is a surrogate organization lends itself to empirical analysis. For a digital surrogate to function as a surrogate for a conservative political party it has to embrace the same cross-class cleavage issues—such as around race, ethnicity, nationalism, and religion, often with a strong affective dimension (Bennett and Livingston, this volume).

For this study, we analyze the use of QAnon symbols by predominantly Republican candidates for office. As detailed above, this is complementary to Lukito et al.'s (this volume) analysis of the changes in the narrative arc by QAnon itself, which revealed how the movement *became* a surrogate during the cycle. Here, we show the uptake of those symbols and narratives by candidates themselves in ways that dovetail with the Republican Party's coalition.

First, we document the wellspring of symbols and imagery that Republican candidates with affiliation to QAnon (or those just using its symbols) drew on and incorporated into their electoral campaigns. Second, we specifically analyze QAnon imagery in congressmembers' Lauren Boebert and Marjorie Taylor Greene bids for office. To do this, we compiled a glossary of QAnon symbols used by politicians in their public communications, including tweets, Facebook posts, town hall appearances, and television interviews during the 2020 US election cycle. We identified QAnon symbols drawing on journalistic work and chose the politicians for this study based on the 26 candidates for state legislature and 107 candidates for Congress identified by Media Matters as QAnon supporters in 2020 (Kaplan 2020) at the time we conducted this research in 2021. One candidate for the state legislature was independent, one was a member of the Conservative party, and one was a member of the Aloha Aina Party. Of the candidates for Congress, five were independents, two were Democrats, 98 were Republicans, and two were independents. Media Matters appears to have identified these candidates on the basis of their use of common QAnon iconography, such as variations of the catchphrase "Where We Go One, We Go All," typically abbreviated as "WWG1WGA."

We then categorized these symbols and narratives for whether they were direct, indirect, or contextual based on how explicitly they referenced QAnon theories or narratives. Through this approach we ended up with 45 discrete symbols in our glossary (as defined above). We provide a rationale for why these symbols are related to QAnon, as well as examples that reveal them being publicly used by political candidates. Using an inductive coding approach, we extracted the themes and prevailing narratives from this content. While this approach limited us to the candidates identified by Media Matters, given the extensive nature of the glossary, it is likely that any excluded politicians (i.e., not originally identified by Media Matters) used the same symbols as the candidates within the scope of this study. This method also limited us to the content posted by these candidates—we do not know whether they actually believe in the narratives QAnon sets forth, or simply are adopting its symbols strategically.

We readily acknowledge that by limiting ourselves to symbols used by candidates we are ignoring a vast array of QAnon iconography and discourse. Of course, there are a lot of themes in QAnon more broadly that do not necessarily map onto the Republican Party's coalition or politics more broadly. The widespread claims of child sex trafficking, for instance, which have led to things like the shuttering of the National Butterfly Center, do not neatly map onto party politics (although it does encapsulate longstanding white, right-wing concerns with sanctity, purity, and moral panics over sex). Meanwhile, QAnon's rituals, practices, and social organization cannot be easily mapped onto institutional party politics. Ultimately, this is why QAnon is a *digital surrogate*—not the Republican Party itself. We only seek to document how Party candidates draw on QAnon themes as a set of symbolic resources.

2020 Candidates and QAnon

On May 8, 2018, then-candidate Marjorie Taylor Greene explicitly endorsed QAnon in a tweet where she replied "truth trust the plan WWG1WGA" in reply to a QAnon member saying Q was not compromised (see Figure 4.1). "Where We Go One, We Go All," commonly abbreviated as "WWG1WGA," serves as a rallying symbol of unity for QAnon supporters. Greene, along with Lauren Boebert, is one of the most prominent Republican politicians who espoused far-right conspiratorial beliefs and used explicit QAnon symbols.

In all, we identified 45 discrete QAnon symbols used by politicians like Greene and many other less prominent ones that did not win their races. We present here six central themes found within these QAnon symbols

Figure 4.1 Tweet from Marjorie Taylor Greene, "truth trust the plan WWG1WGA."
Source: https://www.mediamatters.org/media/3885856.

and narratives in politics: Christianity, opposition to elites, opposition to marginalized groups, nationalism, revolution, and skepticism. The QAnon themes we found within the study are consistent with adversarial narratives and identity propaganda—clearly articulating and reinforcing strong in-group identities in defense of an existing racial and religious order and in opposition to nondominant, non-normative, and marginalized groups.

Following we provide examples of each theme.

Christianity

This theme includes references to the Christian canon and Bible (as shown in Figure 4.2). "The Great Awakening Worldwide" or #GreatAwakening refers to the moment when QAnon nonbelievers will finally awaken to "the truth." This QAnon theme resonates with Christian imagery; outside of the specific way QAnon adherents use it to refer to the opening of people's eyes as to the claims of the movement, it references a popular religious revival that impacted the English colonies in America during the 1730s and 1740s—and subsequently other Great Awakenings that emerged in later centuries (historians identify 3–4 in the US) (Lambert 1999).

They use ridicule as attack strategy. He's executing the plan to shut down their stranglehold over financial, energy, water, food systems that enrich themselves and impoverish the world. #GreatAwakening of the masses is feared. Don't buy owned #MSM hype. Think & be freed. @POTUS

Figure 4.2 Tweet showing QAnon and Christianity.
Source: https://twitter.com/Elled26/status/1210631828479963136.

Opposition to Elites

QAnon espouses a distrust of, and even hatred for, the perceived upper classes and those in elite social and political circles that are allegedly controlling and maintaining the current world order (as shown in Figure 4.3). To take an example, in QAnon mythology more broadly the deep state consists of those who adherents believe are part of the anti-Trump establishment: Barack Obama, Hillary Clinton, John Podesta, George Soros, and Joe Biden. They are typically high-level Democrats, Hollywood elites, and rich bankers, and QAnon perceives them as enforcing a secret "satanic cabal." QAnon believes that their ultimate plan is the destruction of America and the establishment of a "New Global World Order."

While the theme of opposition to elites might seem out of place for a Republican digital surrogate given the party's economic platform favors the wealthy, QAnon consistently fails to condemn those associated with and favored by Trump (ironically literally a member of the economic elite), instead typically targeting those associated with the Democratic Party.

THE DEMOCRATIC DECAY WITHIN   105

Figure 4.3 Tweet showing QAnon opposition to elites.
Source: https://twitter.com/AmericanRogue5/status/990231860495224833.

When QAnon symbols and narratives do invoke Republican elites, it is generally to signal that these candidates are identifying with a more radical, pro-Trump wing of the Republican Party (clearly captured in the use of the Republican In Name Only and MAGA hashtags). Fealty is offered to Trump as president, not the Republican Party more broadly (which reveals the potentially destabilizing aspects of the movement for the larger Republican Party).

Opposition to Nondominant, Non-Normative, and Marginalized Groups

This theme captures a broad opposition to people of nondominant races, ethnicities, religions, and sexual and gender identities (as shown in Figure 4.4). There are numerous examples of this theme. To take one,

Figure 4.4 Tweet showing QAnon opposition to nondominant, non-normative, and marginalized groups.
Source: https://twitter.com/Alison4Congress/status/1384300045730652165.

candidate references to the QAnon conspiracy of "Child Lives Matter/Save the Children" espouses the idea that elites are extracting life-extending chemicals from children's blood in underground lairs. This has deep roots in the antisemitic myth of blood libel, where Jews are falsely accused of murdering Christian children in order to use their blood for religious rituals (Kuo and Marwick 2021; Langer 2022). Save the Children also serves as an anti-LGBTQ dog whistle, with the conspiratorial suggestion of pedophilia historically being used to oppose the LGBTQ rights movement (Niedwiecki 2013). Indeed, anti-LGBTQIA themes abound in QAnon spaces (Miller 2021).

Nationalism

This theme captures the movement's aim to mold the US in QAnon's image, or the appeal to QAnon being the legitimate keeper of American identity (as shown in Figure 4.5). A common example is the QAnon flag, which represents the desire of QAnon believers to "reform" America and their commitment to creating a nation "saved" by QAnon. Again, we see here a potentially destabilizing element for the party in the embrace of rival understandings of American nationalism.

Figure 4.5 QAnon stylized American flag.
Source: https://www.mediamatters.org/media/3885856.

Revolution

This theme relates to the QAnon desire to incite an overthrow of the current system and social order to restore the "true" American legacy and order (as shown in Figure 4.6). On one level, it is a clear invocation of QAnon as the legitimate American tradition (the language of "restored")—on another, it is the idea of a necessary "revolution" to bring about this restoration. Phrases and hashtags such as "Qoldier" signal that a person is part of the Q movement and that they are willing to defend QAnon with violence like a soldier.

Corrosive Skepticism

This theme captures a generalized distrust in verified facts and mainstream media (as shown in Figure 4.7). This theme is threaded through almost

Figure 4.6 Tweet showing QAnon and revolution themes.
Source: https://twitter.com/AmericanRogue5/status/988196540014612480.

everything QAnon espouses, and broadly it refers to both a distrust of established elites and the concomitant belief in Q's plan to take down the "satanic" cabal—the ubiquitous phrase of "Trust the Plan."

There are often connections between these themes in posts. Broadly, the dominant story that candidate use of QAnon symbols tells about politics is that nondominant groups and elites are part of a secret cabal that is in charge of America and harming children, and a revolution is needed to restore a Christian America—and the skepticism of QAnon believers lets them see this perceived hidden reality.

At the same time, it is worth noting again that what was on display by these candidates was not the most extreme speech that is espoused on QAnon message boards. These social media posts by candidates were public communications by candidates for elected office, after all. Even still, the rhetoric used by these candidates, such as calls for revolution and arrests, references to 1776, and describing QAnon adherents as soldiers and political opponents as baby-blood drinkers (a dehumanizing trope), is clearly anti-democratic. Candidates referred to these things in both explicit and implicit ways—no doubt navigating a context of public scrutiny in pursuit of elected office. While there were explicit references to things such as a "Democrat child slavery ring," "child sacrifice," "organ harvesting," and "baby blood drinkers," more frequent were the use of comparatively discrete words derived from these narratives, such as "adrenochrome" (the chemical which is supposedly harvested from children by Democrats and elites) and "Save the Children" (the rallying cry by QAnon to stop the trafficking).

Figure 4.7 Tweet showing QAnon and corrosive skepticism.
Source: https://www.mediamatters.org/media/3847371.

This suggests that during online public communications, politicians might be incentivized to use the least extreme QAnon symbols they can while still referencing the overarching narrative. As we detail below, candidates can likely be more explicit in settings where they do not have to worry as much about content sanctions by platforms, having their speeches documented easily by journalists, or having comments become part of a public record that might turn off less extreme voters during a general election. For example, in a town hall, Marjorie Taylor Greene declared that Dr. Anthony Fauci created COVID-19 in a Wuhan lab using American tax dollars—all while more publicly disavowing the movement.

Candidate use of QAnon themes also complements issues in the Republican Party platform. Content under the themes of revolution and nationalism, such as "Qoldier," often emphasizes violence and the need for physical protection against outside oppressors, which draws parallels with the "pro Second Amendment" Republican platform of opposing firearm regulation and imagery espoused by other Republican surrogates such as the National Rifle Association (Steidley and Colen 2017). The Christian and Save the Children narratives, meanwhile, connect to the party's opposition to abortion, which are often justified by Christian religious values (also a movement surrogate issue and one that has transformed the party, see Lewis 2019). Another white Christian right issue has been opposition to equal protection and treatment for the LGBT community, which is also a product of the white Christian right movement being embedded in the Republican Party (Culicchia 2022) and broadly connects to opposition to nondominant groups. Given that there were overlaps between early QAnon and Trump supporters (Rothschild 2021), it is not surprising to find resonances between QAnon and Republican coalition themes, and QAnon themes even may have mutated from existing fringe Republican political narratives. The kinship of certain QAnon symbols and aspects of the Republican Party platform also makes QAnon symbols a more effective tool for Republican candidates, since their audience will likely already have a framework for understanding and interpreting these appeals (such as revolution, Save the Children, and anti-LGBTQ codes). This was particularly evident during the 2020 presidential election, when QAnon more explicitly embraced pro-Trump political narratives (Lukito et al., this volume).

Since the QAnon conspiracy movement is participatory in nature, with adherents able to create and understand evolving meanings within a community, the web of beliefs is interpretively flexible enough for participants to emphasize the themes that they find most personally compelling (the personal action frames Bennett and Segerberg (2013) referenced above). For example, symbols such as the Great Awakening are vague and expansive enough to have different uses among these candidates and interpretations among their audiences, and QAnon adherents more generally, and can be understood across multiple levels. This includes a manifest idea of awakening to a conspiracy theory and a deeper, latent meaning grounded in Christian theology (see Harding 2001 on the interpretative practices of Christians). This narrative and interpretative flexibility could explain the international spread of QAnon beyond American borders, and the survival of the conspiracy beyond the failure of the Trump reelection campaign. Indeed, following Trump's election loss, QAnon narratives did not distance themselves from Trump, but instead embraced election fraud disinformation and more violent rhetoric (Lukito et al., this volume).

Congressmembers Lauren Boebert and Marjorie Taylor Greene

It is worth briefly considering the campaigns of two elected Republican Congressional representatives, Lauren Boebert and Marjorie Taylor Greene, more closely for the ways that they drew on the symbols and narratives provided by QAnon.

Lauren Boebert ran as a Republican for Colorado's 3rd congressional district in 2020. Boebert defeated incumbent US Representative Scott Tipton in the primary election and the Democratic nominee, former state Representative Diane Mitsch Bush, in the general election. Her platform was pro-gun and pro-Trump, and she also incorporated extensive QAnon symbols and imagery into her campaign.

The earliest public usage of a QAnon symbol we found for Lauren Boebert was in May 2020, when she was interviewed on the *Steel Truth* podcast by QAnon supporter Ann Vandersteel (Kurtzleben 2020). During that interview Boebert stated, "Everything I've heard of Q, I hope that this is real because it only means America is getting stronger and better and people are returning to conservative values, and that's what I am for. So everything that I have heard of this movement is only motivating and encouraging and bringing people together stronger and if this is real then it could be really great for our country." Later that month she would go on to appear on Patriots' Soapbox, an important QAnon YouTube channel, prior to its being removed from the platform. In these two appearances, it is clear both that Boebert is connecting general calls for patriotism and conservatism to QAnon—broadening the meaning of QAnon for her Republican audiences—and making direct appeals to QAnon believers for electoral reasons.

Later that year, Boebert publicly rejected QAnon amid press scrutiny. In July 2020 she said to a reporter, "I do not follow QAnon." During two Fox News interviews (Harsha 2020) over the next few months before the election, she stated that she was not a follower of QAnon and that "I'm not into conspiracies. I'm into freedom and the Constitution of the United States of America. I'm not a follower." However, the congresswoman-elect also embraced themes of a deep state, tweeted that there is "no President elect" and that "Trump won the 2020 Presidential election," and hours before the attempted January 6, 2021 coup referred to it as "1776"—all QAnon narratives (if not exclusively so). Indeed, the congresswoman continued to use QAnon imagery in the days after 1/6/21, tweeting "Don't doubt in the dark what God told you in the light"—a "dark to light" reference that is common symbolism in the conspiracy and references broader Christian themes detailed above.

Marjorie Taylor Greene followed a similar pattern, but with a much longer connection to QAnon prior to running for office. After repeatedly changing which district she was running for in the election, she won Georgia's 14th district primary in a runoff, and eventually won the heavily Republican district in June 2020, during a special election. As early as 2017, Greene wrote favorably about the QAnon conspiracy movement, suggested that Hillary Clinton murdered her political enemies, and speculated about whether mass shootings were orchestrated to destroy the Second Amendment. In 2018, Greene discussed Q's posts and regularly endorsed QAnon on Facebook. In a now-deleted set of 2019 tweets, Greene even encouraged her followers to message her with questions regarding QAnon so she could "walk you through the whole thing." Soon after her primary runoff victory, in August 2020, Greene disavowed QAnon. Greene stated that her campaign was "never about QAnon" and that after learning more, she decided "I would choose another path." Not even a year later, in a June 2021 interview, Greene was repeating the QAnon conspiracy theory that Dr. Fauci made COVID-19 in a Wuhan lab (YouTube 2021).

Both politicians supported QAnon while campaigning, shortly before or after winning election disavowed the movement, and yet continued to use QAnon rhetoric and symbols in their public communications. This suggests that candidates might derive support from a widespread QAnon base by being direct about their support, and then when they disavow it to avoid more public backlash (just like racial dog whistles, see Thelen 2022), QAnon supporters might not view it as actually going against QAnon if they continue to use implicit symbols and rhetoric. Indeed, one of the QAnon narratives is "There is no QAnon"—the phenomenon where QAnon supporters hide their support in order to avoid public repercussions. Since this practice of hiding is already ingrained within the movement, a politician may be able to reject QAnon while actually keeping the support of QAnon believers. This might explain why Greene and Boebert have continued to use QAnon imagery, but with it being more indirect online, and more extreme offline.

Discussion

The case of candidates taking up QAnon themes offers a few insights into how these digital surrogate organizations might potentially work vis-à-vis political institutions such as parties. On one level, QAnon potentially offers tangible resources for adherents or endorsers among candidates to tap into: potentially money and votes, those staples of electoral campaigning. On another, the network of QAnon offers reach and exposure, where a candidate's words and deeds can extend far beyond the confines of a geographic district or even mass mediated broadcasts, especially through personal expressions of support. Even more, affiliation with or endorsement of QAnon means press coverage, as journalists seek novelty. Indeed, Boebert and Greene's national profiles as congressional candidates—and now as members—were likely directly related to media coverage of their embrace of QAnon, which in turn has implications for their role within the Republican Party broadly (i.e., they both have media status). Most broadly, QAnon created a field of discourse deeply complementary to the Republican Party's own rhetoric and policies that candidates could adopt strategically to shore up in-group identity appeals and define out-groups.

More speculatively, embracing QAnon might be tempting to a Republican politician because the conspiracy movement can work to undermine the ability of party leaders or the public to hold politicians accountable for their actions. For one, it is clear that QAnon attacked more moderate Republican candidates (opposition to "Republicans in Name Only" for instance). At the same time, the fierce loyalty of a conspiracy movement, and broader ways that it undermines epistemology and facts, also work to undercut political accountability. A digital surrogate like QAnon might also have other advantages for institutional party actors. Politicians may view QAnon believers as useful targets since they do not have specific policy preferences that need to be reflected through actual policymaking. Instead, QAnon seems to embrace a broad and diffuse set of conspiracies that seem more well suited to be addressed through a political style than a set of policies. A politician can use vague rhetoric, for instance, to suggest that their fight with the deep state is going strong, while actually not being forced to implement policy that might alienate other parts of their base.

At the same time, many of these characteristics likely also make the movement potentially destabilizing to an institutional political party. While we can only gesture to it here, we can read the destabilizing effects of a digital surrogate in terms of the degree to which it weakens a party's electoral prospects (especially during a general election); advances an agenda that weakens a political party's ability to achieve or fragments its own concerns; or, elevates adherents outside of established party structures—such as the media's outsized coverage of QAnon adherent Marjorie Taylor Greene that made her an important primary broker according to the *Axios* report (Swan and Markay 2022) discussed earlier. As in the case of Trump, a digital surrogate might offer a set of cultural and electoral resources that facilitate the rise of an authoritarian candidate aimed at party capture. On a less immediate level, a digital surrogate might create longer term destabilization strains for parties. For example, QAnon contributes broadly to the deeper institutionalization of conspiracy within the Republican Party and the power of outside media actors in shaping its electoral strengths and therefore the policy agendas of its candidates. QAnon has likely undermined the party's ability to set its own agenda, while also further associating it with the white nationalist movements that some of its party leaders have condemned (in 2022, for instance, Greene and Arizona Representative Paul Gosar spoke at a white nationalist event, prompting a rebuke from then Senator Mitt Romney). At the same time, while Ziblatt (2017) focuses on ways that surrogates change parties, it is likely that parties also change movements. In this case, candidates elevate certain narratives and themes and make them more visible in the movement, and they, in turn, might be selected over time, such as a steady drumbeat of explicit claims for election fraud.

All of these things are particularly troublesome from a democratic perspective given the dynamics of the online conspiracy movements. As Bennett and Segerberg (2013) argue, the nature of organization and collective action problems are significantly different in digital environments. Even though groups are large and therefore face traditional collective action problems, the collaborative, participatory, role-oriented, deeply symbolic, culturally multifaceted, and interpretively flexible QAnon movement creates strong bonds of collective identity but with many pathways of entry—ironically for a movement premised on anonymous adherents. Counterintuitively, even though there is "anon" in the name, the QAnon community tends to be personal due to its participatory culture. Research has highlighted that QAnon has a participatory culture where believers work together to create meaning from Q drops and contribute collectively to the theories and narratives it espouses (Marwick and Partin 2020). The personal and collaborative nature of deciphering "Q drops" helps create personal rapport between believers and invests individual contributions with collective meaning. This effect might be compounded in communities outside of 4chan that engage in deciphering drops, such as on Facebook or Gab (an alt-right social networking platform), since individuals might not necessarily be anonymous. Furthermore, regardless of platform, the fundamentally participatory structure of the movement would likely allow for an easier transition to political participation since there is already the expectation that QAnon believers should mobilize together around ideas that are *deeply* political by their nature.

From a media perspective, QAnon as a case of a digital surrogate reveals dynamics of communication as organization and collective, participatory media practices and identity work that forges and sustains digital-first movements. QAnon is a networked movement premised on a set of shared practices and identities, which reveals the degree to which changes in media provide opportunities for media practices such as collective, networked forms of "scriptural inference" that is "critical thinking" in the service of conspiracy (Tripodi 2018; 2022). QAnon is a digital surrogate organization premised on distributed interpretative practice grounded in identities that help in "the production and maintenance of knowledge that ensures the cohesion of a social or political community across space and time" (Marwick and Partin 2020). QAnon reveals the de-institutionalization of many aspects of contemporary public spheres, including political party communications, journalism, and partisan and identity media, facilitated and amplified by the rise of platforms.

From a political perspective, QAnon as a case reveals the capacity of digital surrogates to work in tandem with right-wing parties but not be beholden to them in the same ways as institutions such as conservative media. A key lesson of Fox News and other conservative media is the way that these media forms are embedded in political institutions and contexts, even as they work as a force upon them. As profit-earning enterprises, and often led by people with clear financial and political interests, media entities have comparatively more constraints within party networks. As a collective conspiracy, QAnon works institutionally as a tool of the right and simultaneously a destabilizing force to the Republican Party. Its seemingly independently constructed and circulated narratives, for instance, worked to bolster the president's stature during his time in office. The community quite literally helped elect its adherents to office—most notably GOP Congresswoman Marjorie Taylor Greene (Marcotte 2021). And the community served as a form of identity media for white evangelicals in particular (Rogers 2021)—a central part of the Republican Party's coalition. It did so, and continues to do so, by helping to construct a set of perceived threats—of an unaccountable deep state, immoral educated political elites, and non-white and non-Christian

116 CONNECTIVE ACTION AND THE RISE OF THE FAR-RIGHT

people—key, complementary appeals to the Republican Party's coalition as well. Reciprocally, QAnon also reveals the way that a networked online movement can be mobilized by the rhetoric of an authoritarian leader and undermine the epistemological aspects and norms of democracy in its embrace of conspiracy and disinformation—tactics that are also entirely consonant with a radicalized Republican Party. As such, it shows how digital surrogates can work alone, and in tandem with would be authoritarians, to destabilize the conservative parties that were built up historically out of a need to adapt to democratic electoral competition to preserve power.

Finally, this chapter analyzed and documented the QAnon symbols deployed by predominately Republican candidates in the context of the party's electoral coalition. The question of destabilization (or, more radically, capture) also lends itself to empirical analysis—and there is much to suggest that candidates who were QAnon adherents were generally unsuccessful in general elections and might have harmed other party candidates; that those candidates and adherents more broadly might have undermined the party's messaging and policy agenda; that media have elevated some of its adherents to the role of de facto party spokespeople; and yet that the presence of QAnon provided a base of support for Trump after he left office and helped further institutionalize conspiracy in the GOP—but the evidence here is too preliminary at this point in time to do more than gesture.

Conclusion

To conclude, the flexible organizational and cultural structure of QAnon makes it potentially more adept at mutation compared to other movements advancing adversarial narratives in defense of right-wing orders. Additionally, as a conspiracy movement grounded in skepticism, QAnon may help politicians draw support from previously disengaged voters whose distrust in institutions might otherwise have made them disinterested in voting. While QAnon offers a flexible set of narratives, its expansive core of a fight against an "evil cabal" is inherently adversarial and offers many potential subject positions within. And large numbers of disengaged voters suddenly turning out in elections has historically been destructive of democracy.

Disturbingly, the adversarial narratives of candidates may be artificially amplified, offering an added incentive to take them up. With media competing for limited attention and online platforms artificially amplifying content that maximizes strong emotions (hatred, envy, etc.) for commercial gain, divisive narratives garner greater attention. All the more so that these adversarial narratives are yoked to political and social interests in very real ways. Politicians may then be incentivized to use the adversarial narratives of movements such as QAnon and gain artificially large reach and influence during their competition for attention. Furthermore, the structure and debate occurring on online platforms is less governable by political party gatekeepers. It is difficult to censure a voice from joining an online debate, and fringe candidates that may otherwise have been minimized by gatekeepers are now given a platform. Party gatekeepers, seeing the disproportionate online attention a fringe candidate has amassed, may hesitate to punish or disassociate the politician from the party due to fears of outrage. This could help explain the political success of fringe extremist candidates like Marjorie Taylor Greene and Lauren Boebert, who embraced and trafficked QAnon symbols and won their congressional campaigns.

References

Adams, Kirsten, and Daniel Kreiss. 2021. *Power in Ideas: A Case-Based Argument for Taking Ideas Seriously in Political Communication*. Cambridge: Cambridge University Press.

Aliapoulios, Max, Antonis Papasavva, Cameron Ballard, Emiliano De Cristofaro, Gianluca Stringhini, Savvas Zannettou, and Jeremy Blackburn. 2021. "The Gospel According to Q: Understanding the QAnon Conspiracy from the Perspective of Canonical Information." arXiv preprint arXiv:2101.08750.

Baccini, Leonardo, and Stephen Weymouth. 2021. "Gone for Good: Deindustrialization, White Voter Backlash, and US Presidential Voting." *American Political Science Review* 115 (2): 550–567.

Bawn, Kathleen, Martin Cohen, David Karol, Seth Masket, Hans Noel., and John Zaller. 2012. "A Theory of Political Parties: Groups, Policy Demands and Nominations in American Politics." *Perspectives on Politics* 10 (3): 571–597.

Belew, Kathleen. 2018. *Bring the War Home: The White Power Movement and Paramilitary America*. Cambridge, MA: Harvard University Press.

Belew, Kathleen, and Ramón A. Gutiérrez (eds.). 2021. *A Field Guide to White Supremacy*. Oakland: University of California Press.

Benkler, Yochai, Robert Faris, and Hal Roberts. 2018. *Network Propaganda: Manipulation, Disinformation, and Radicalization in American Politics*. New York: Oxford University Press.

Bennett, Lance W., and Alexandra Segerberg. 2013. *The Logic of Connective Action: Digital Media and the Personalization of Contentious Politics*. New York: Cambridge University Press.

Bilewicz, Michał, and Wiktor Soral. 2020. "Hate Speech Epidemic: The Dynamic Effects of Derogatory Language on Intergroup Relations and Political Radicalization." *Political Psychology* 41 (1): 3–33.

Brandon, Pepijn. 2019. "Between the Plantation and the Port: Racialization and Social Control in Eighteenth-Century Paramaribo." *International Review of Social History* 64 (27): 95–124.

Caren, Neal, Kenneth T. Andrews, and Todd Lu. 2020. "Contemporary Social Movements in a Hybrid Media Environment." *Annual Review of Sociology* 46 (1): 443–465.

Carson, Jamie L., and Ryan D. Williamson. 2018. "Candidate Emergence in the Era of Direct Primaries." In Robert j. Boatright, ed., *Routledge Handbook of Primary Elections* (pp. 57–71). New York: Routledge.

Chadwick, Andrew. 2017. *The Hybrid Media System: Politics and Power.* 2nd ed. New York: Oxford University Press.

Costley White, Khadijah. 2018. *The Branding of Right-Wing Activism: The News Media and the Tea Party.* Oxford: Oxford University Press.

Cramer, Katherine J. 2016. *The Politics of Resentment: Rural Consciousness in Wisconsin and the Rise of Scott Walker.* Chicago: University of Chicago Press.

Culicchia, Catherine. 2022. "The Christian Right and State Legislatures: The New Battleground for 'Family Values.'" https://dspace.sewanee.edu/handle/11005/21802.

Daly, Tom Gerald. 2019. "Democratic Decay: Conceptualising an Emerging Research Field." *Hague Journal on the Rule of Law* 11 (1): 9–36.

Daniels, Jessie. 2018. "The Algorithmic Rise of the 'Alt-Right.'" *Contexts* 17 (1): 60–65.

de Zeeuw, Daniel, Sal Hagen, Stijn Peeters, and Emilija Jokubauskaite. 2020. "Tracing Normiefication: A Cross-Platform Analysis of the QAnon Conspiracy Theory." *First Monday* 25 (11). https://doi.org/10.5210/fm.v25i11.10643.

Decker, Ben. 2019. "Adversarial Narratives: A New Model for Disinformation." In Craig Fagan, ed., *Global Disinformation Index* (pp. 6–7). https://mediawell.ssrc.org/citations/adversarial-narratives-a-new-model-for-disinformation/.

Deen Freelon, Alice Marwick, and Daniel Kreiss. 2020. "False Equivalencies: Online Activism from Left to Right." *Science* 369 (6508): 1197–1201.

Du Mez, Kristin Kobes. 2020. *Jesus and John Wayne: How White Evangelicals Corrupted a Faith and Fractured a Nation.* New York: Liveright Publishing.

Feagin, Joe R. 2020. *The White Racial Frame: Centuries of Racial Framing and Counter-Framing.* New York: Routledge.

Grossmann, Matt, and David Allen Hopkins. 2018. "From Fox News to Viral Views: The Influence of Ideological Media in the 2018 Elections." *The Forum* 16 (4): 551–571.

Hacker, Jacob S., and Paul Pierson. 2020. *Let Them Eat Tweets: How the Right Rules in the Age of Extreme Inequality.* New York: Liveright Publishing.

Haggard, Stephan, and Robert Kaufman. 2021. *Backsliding: Democratic Regress in the Contemporary World.* Cambridge: Cambridge University Press.

Hannah, Matthew. 2021. "QAnon and the Information Dark Age." *First Monday* 26 (2). https://doi.org/10.5210/fm.v26i2.10868.

Harding, Susan Friend. 2001. *The Book of Jerry Falwell: Fundamentalist Language and Politics.* Princeton, NJ: Princeton University Press.

Harsha, Keagan. 2020. "Colorado Primary Winner Lauren Boebert Meets President Trump, Distances Herself from QAnon." Fox News. July 6. https://kdvr.com/news/politics/colorado-primary-winner-lauren-boebert-meets-president-trump-distances-herself-from-qanon/.

Hemmer, Nicole. 2016. *Messengers of the Right: Conservative Media and the Transformation of American Politics.* Philadelphia: University of Pennsylvania Press.

Hild, Matthew, and Keri Leigh Merritt (eds). 2018. *Reconsidering Southern Labor History: Race, Class, and Power.* Gainesville: University Press of Florida.

Jackson, Sarah J., Moya Bailey, and Brooke Foucault Welles. 2020. *# HashtagActivism: Networks of Race and Gender Justice*. Cambridge, MA: MIT Press.

Jardina, Ashley. 2019. *White Identity Politics*. Cambridge: Cambridge University Press.

Jones, R. P. 2023. *The Hidden Roots of White Supremacy: And the Path to a Shared American Future*. New York: Simon and Schuster.

Kaplan, Alex. 2020. "Here Are the QAnon Supporters Running for Congress in 2020." *Media Matters for America*, January 7. https://www.mediamatters.org/qanon-conspiracy-theory/here-are-qanon-supporters-running-congress-2020.

Kaplan, Alex. 2021. "Here Are the QAnon Supporters Running for Congress in 2022." *Media Matters for America*, June 6. https://www.mediamatters.org/qanon-conspiracy-theory/here-are-qanon-supporters-running-congress-2022.

Kreiss, Daniel. 2016. "Beyond Administrative Journalism: Civic Skepticism and the Crisis in Journalism." In Jeffrey C. Alexander, Elizabeth Butler Breese, and Maria Luengo, eds., *The Crisis of Journalism Reconsidered: Democratic Culture, Professional Codes, Digital Future* (pp. 59–76). New York: Cambridge University Press.

Kreiss, Daniel, Regina G. Lawrence, and Shannon C. McGregor. 2020. "Political Identity Ownership: Symbolic Contests to Represent Members of the Public." *Social Media+ Society* 6 (2). https://doi.org/10.1177/205630512092649

Kreiss, Daniel, Alice Marwick, and Francesca Bolla Tripodi. 2021. "The Anti–Critical Race Theory Movement Will Profoundly Affect Public Education." *Scientific American*. November 10. https://www.scientificamerican.com/article/the-anti-critical-race-theory-movement-will-profoundly-affect-public-education/.

Kreiss, Daniel, and Shannon C. McGregor. 2018. "Technology Firms Shape Political Communication: The Work of Microsoft, Facebook, Twitter, and Google with Campaigns During the 2016 US Presidential Cycle." *Political Communication* 35 (2): 155–177.

Kuo, Rachel, and Alice Marwick. 2021. "Critical Disinformation Studies: History, Power, and Politics." *Harvard Kennedy School Misinformation Review* 2 (4): 1–12.

Kurtzleben, Danielle. 2020. "GOP Candidates Open to QAnon Conspiracy Theory Advance in Congressional Races." NPR, July 1. https://www.npr.org/2020/07/01/885991730/gop-candidates-open-to-qanon-conspiracy-theory-advance-in-congressional-races.

Lambert, Frank. 1999. *Inventing the "Great Awakening."* Princeton, NJ: Princeton University Press.

Langer, Armin. 2022. "Deep State, Child Sacrifices, and the 'Plandemic': The Historical Background of Antisemitic Tropes within the QAnon Movement." In Monika Hübscher, and Sabine von Mering, eds., *Antisemitism on Social Media* (pp. 18–34). London: Routledge.

Lewis, Andrew R. 2019. "The Inclusion-Moderation Thesis: The US Republican Party and the Christian Right. In *Oxford Research Encyclopedia of Politics*. https://doi.org/10.1093/acrefore/9780190228637.013.665.

Marcotte, Amanda. 2021. "Don't Blame a Lack of Education—QAnon Proves Privileged White People are Losing their Minds too." *Salon*, February 4. https://www.salon.com/2021/02/04/dont-blame-a-lack-of-education—qanon-proves-privileged-white-people-are-losing-their-minds-too/.

Marwick, Alice, and William Clyde Partin. 2020. "The Construction of Alternative Facts: 'Qanon' Researchers as Scientist Selves." Paper presented at AoIR 2020: The 21th Annual Conference of the Association of Internet Researchers. October 2020. Virtual Event: AoIR. http://spir.aoir.org.

Mason, Lilliana. 2018. *Uncivil Agreement: How Politics Became our Identity*. Chicago: University of Chicago Press.

Miller, Daniel Taninecz. 2021. "Characterizing QAnon: Analysis of YouTube comments Presents New Conclusions about a Popular Conservative Conspiracy." *First Monday*. https://firstmonday.org/ojs/index.php/fm/article/view/10168.

Mills, Charles Wright. 2004. "Racial Exploitation and the Wages of Whiteness." In Maria Krysan and Amanda E. Lewis, eds., *The Changing Terrain of Race and Ethnicity* (pp. 235–262). Russell Sage Foundation. New York: Sage.

Munger, Kevin. 2020. "All the News that's Fit to Click: The Economics of Clickbait Media." *Political Communication* 37 (3): 376–397.

Niedwiecki, Anthony. 2013. "Save our Children: Overcoming the Narrative that Gays and Lesbians are Harmful to Children." *Duke Journal of Gender Law and Policy* 21: 125–175.

Norris, Pippa, and Ronald Inglehart. 2019. *Cultural Backlash: Trump, Brexit, and Authoritarian Populism.* Cambridge: Cambridge University Press.

Papacharissi, Zizi. 2015. *Affective Publics: Sentiment, Technology, and Politics.* Oxford: Oxford University Press.

Peck, Reece. 2019. *Fox Populism: Branding Conservatism as Working Class.* Cambridge: Cambridge University Press.

Ralph, Michael, and Maya Singhal. 2019. "Racial Capitalism." *Theory and Society* 48 (6): 851–881.

Reddi, Madhavi, Rachel Kuo, and Daniel Kreiss. 2021. "Identity Propaganda: Racial Narratives and Disinformation." *New Media and Society.* https://doi.org/10.1177/14614448211029293

Richardson, Heather Cox. 2014. *To Make Men Free: A History of the Republican Party.* New York: Basic Books.

Robinson, Cedric J. 2000 [1983]. *Black Marxism: The Making of the Black Radical Tradition.* Chapel Hill: University of North Carolina Press.

Roediger, David R. 2017. "The Wages of Whiteness: Race and the Making of the American Working Class." In Stanley Aronowitz, and Michael J. Roberts, eds., *Class: The Anthology* (pp. 41–55). Wiley Online Library. https://doi.org/10.1002/9781119395485.ch4.

Rogers, Kaleigh. 2021. "Why QAnon Has Attracted So Many White Evangelicals." *FiveThirtyEight*, March 4. https://fivethirtyeight.com/features/why-qanon-has-attracted-so-many-white-evangelicals/.

Rosenbluth, Frances McCall, and Ian Shapiro. 2018. *Responsible Parties: Saving Democracy from Itself.* New Haven, CT: Yale University Press.

Rothschild, Mike. 2021. *The Storm is Upon Us: How QAnon Became a Movement, Cult, and Conspiracy Theory of Everything.* London: Hachette.

Roudakova, Natalia. 2017. *Losing Pravda: Ethics and the Press in Post-Truth Russia.* Cambridge: Cambridge University Press.

Schudson, Michael. 2022. "What Does 'Trust in the Media' Mean?" *Daedalus* 151 (4): 144–160.

Sides, John, Michael Tesler, and Lynn Vavreck. 2019. *Identity Crisis.* Princeton, NJ: Princeton University Press.

Skocpol, Theda, and Alexander Hertel-Fernandez. 2016. "The Koch Network and Republican Party Extremism." *Perspectives on Politics* 14 (3): 681–699.

Skowronek, Stephen, John A. Dearborn, and Desmond King. 2021. *Phantoms of a Beleaguered Republic: The Deep State and the Unitary Executive.* Oxford: Oxford University Press.

Sobieraj, Sarah, and Jeffrey M. Berry. 2011. "From Incivility to Outrage: Political Discourse in Blogs, Talk Radio, and Cable News." *Political Communication* 28 (1): 19–41.

Smith, Rogers M. 1997. *Civic Ideals: Conflicting Visions of Citizenship in US History.* New Haven, CT: Yale University Press.

Steidley, Trent, and Cynthia G. Colen, 2017. "Framing the Gun Control Debate: Press Releases and Framing Strategies of the National Rifle Association and the Brady Campaign." *Social Science Quarterly* 98 (2): 608–627.

Swan, Jonathon, and Lachlan Markay. 2022. "The Making of a Modern Republican." *Axios*, February 5. https://www.axios.com/2022/02/04/modern-republican-party-primary-trump-gop.

Thelen, Sarah. 2022. "From Dog Whistles to Fog Horns: Richard Nixon, Donald Trump, and Their Silent Majorities." In Michael Harvey, ed., *Donald Trump in Historical Perspective* (pp. 111–122). New York: Routledge.

Tripodi, Francesca. 2018. "Searching for Alternative Facts." *Data and Society.* https://datasociety.net/library/searching-for-alternative-facts/.

Tripodi, Francesca. 2022. *The Propagandists' Playbook: How Conservative Elites Manipulate Search and Threaten Democracy.* New Haven, CT: Yale University Press.

Van Dijck, José, Thomas Poell, and Martijn De Waal. 2018. *The Platform Society: Public Values in a Connective World.* Oxford: Oxford University Press.

YouTube. 2021. "Marjorie Taylor Greene Slams Virus Research: I Don't Believe in Evolution, I Believe in God." https://www.youtube.com/watch?v=tcWytS3ThJk.

Young-Bruehl, Elisabeth. 1998. *The Anatomy of Prejudices.* Cambridge, MA: Harvard University Press.

Ziblatt, Daniel. 2017. *Conservative Parties and the Birth of Democracy.* New York: Cambridge University Press.

Zihiri, Saifeldeen, Gabriel Lima, Jiyoung Han, Meeyoung Cha, and Wonjae Lee. 2022. "QAnon Shifts into the Mainstream, Remains a Far-Right Ally." doi: 10.1016/j.heliyon.2022.e08764

Chapter 5
In-Groups and Outrage

How Narratives and Affect Shape Digital Surrogate Networks and Radicalize Right-Wing Parties

Curd Knüpfer and Ulrike Klinger

Introduction: Surrogate Organizations and Networked Radicalization

Surrogate organizations are ideologically connected with parties. Examples include social movements, associations, unions, or hyperpartisan news organizations (Hacker and Pierson 2020, 23). But in the age of digital connectivity governed by a new "logic of connective action" (Bennett and Segerberg 2012), they can also consist of online groups, loosely connected peripheral networks of ideologically like-minded communities, influencers, or online activists that push and amplify party messages. Digital media provide the affordances for such surrogate networks to take on quasi-organizational functions, with little to no need for brick-and-mortar headquarters or formalized membership (Bennett and Segerberg 2012). Our argument here is that such novel organization types can be based on communicative acts of connectivity, often facilitated by social media platforms and other digital technologies. They are flexible and fluid, spanning networks across national borders and social strata, and they can mobilize support around hashtags, memes, and other expressions of affective responses to specific events. In this volume, Bennett and Livingston apply this framework to explain democratic backsliding. In our chapter, we apply the connective action model to far-right political dynamics in Germany. In doing so, we help distinguish what might be more common to the United States and what might emerge elsewhere, despite legal, regulatory, and cultural differences. As a result, we can come to understand not only the German case, but the American case in a comparativist light.

Curd Knüpfer and Ulrike Klinger, *In-Groups and Outrage*. In: *Connective Action and the Rise of the Far-Right*. Edited by: Steven Livingston and Michael Miller, Oxford University Press. © Oxford University Press (2025). DOI: 10.1093/oso/9780197794937.003.0005

When political parties tap into digital networks, they do so to harness mobilization efforts, distill agenda items, or refine political narratives. This is how communicative networks essentially take on the role of surrogate organizations: they provide parties with a link to the attention capacities of potential supporters, and they enable mobilization efforts around hot-button issues that resonate across social cleavages. Moreover, surrogate organizations are not bound by party and electoral laws and regulations, as parties in most countries are, and they can be more radically oriented toward mobilizing specific supporters and resources. In short, harnessing such potentials and collaborating without having formal links and associations makes sense for established as well as emergent parties across the political spectrum.

In the case of right-wing populist parties, one benefit of such digital networks is to address what Daniel Ziblatt (2017) has called the conservative dilemma: the less these parties offer voters concrete social or welfare policies—addressing material conflicts in increasingly unequal societies—the more they must appeal to an electorate across class lines to gain majorities. But doing so comes at a price: while surrogate organizations may initially facilitate inclusion into a communicative network through shared affect and identity affirming narratives, they also potentially lock actors and institutions into the dynamics of cross-cutting cleavage issues from which it becomes difficult to deviate. Correspondingly, harnessing affect to mobilize followers and tying a party to surrogate organizations bears the danger of ideological lock-in and uncontrollable radicalization. We illustrate what this might look like by providing a specific case study, focused on Germany and the increasingly radicalized party Alternative für Deutschland (AfD).

We believe the argument we derive from this case could provide explanatory power in other contexts as well. While a cross-national comparison would exceed the limits of our chapter, we believe that a focus on other party systems might prove useful for case studies marked by similar dynamics. Examples might include the Vox party in Spain or the gradual transformation and rise of the Sweden Democrats over the past decade. In the US, the ongoing radicalization-spiral of the Republican Party (described by several other contributors to this volume) would certainly warrant further scrutiny in terms of the argument presented here. The contextual conditions provided by constitutional frameworks, historical trajectories, political constellations, media systems, and socioeconomic factors all differ greatly across these cases. Yet beyond the process of political radicalization, one other key commonality shared by all of them is the emergence of novel affordances for communicative relations by which they attempt to grow their base and mobilize supporters.

In essence, we present an argument concerning the role of digital platforms in the sort of democratic backsliding dynamics described by Daniel Ziblatt (2017)—a connective action framework, in other words, for describing the emergence of illiberal politics. We hope to fill in some of the gaps left by political scientists who have often neglected to account for the role of social media platforms and connective action in the rise of far-right extremism and the radicalization of erstwhile conventionally conservative political parties. At the same time, we hope to deepen the theoretical framing of communication scholars who sometimes fixate on democratic backsliding as solely a "media problem." How do these parties become radicalized and drawn into illiberal far-right politics? We hope to provide some of the answers to that question by highlighting the role of communicative networks emerging around *narratives*, which foster in-groups, and *affect*, which harnesses outrage for political purposes. We understand the communicative networks that are shaped by these dynamics as a form of digital surrogacy, which ultimately pulls political parties toward more radical positions.

The AfD as a Case Study of Radicalization

The still very young history of the Alternative für Deutschland is one of unexpected electoral success at unprecedented speed. In less than 10 years since its foundation, the party was able to establish itself as a fixture in Germany's political landscape on federal, state, and local levels. During this time, the party also underwent a transformation that saw its populist center-right platform morph into increasingly extreme, illiberal, and antidemocratic positions. These factors make it a case study in contemporary party radicalization processes while illustrating what has been referred to here as the conservative dilemma: a dynamic by which center-right political forces prime elections with nonmaterial issues (such as immigration or ethnic identity) that cut across class cleavages. In doing so, they align themselves with surrogate organizations and networks, many of which are ideologically positioned on the far right.

This development is certainly still ongoing. Yet due to its impact and novelty factor, the emergence and institutionalization of Germany's new far right and radical right has spawned a burgeoning academic literature, drawing on a wide variety of methodological approaches and data sources. Collectively, this has illustrated the party's transformation in terms of agendas and policy fields (Berg 2019; Sturm 2020; Wacker and Kieslich 2021; Ruhose 2021) along with its supporter networks and appeal to a specific demographic, which tends to be older, more male and affluent than the general population, while harboring xenophobic and illiberal sentiments (Schuler et al. 2020) as well as a fear of economic and social decline (Koller and Miglbauer 2019; Decker and Brähler 2020). Recent scholarship has also provided for a wide array of methodological approaches outlining and analyzing the party's communication strategies across various platforms and media formats (Haller 2020; Darius and Stephany 2019; Becker 2021; Rochnia et al. 2021; Maurer et al. 2022), which have collectively demonstrated the party's propensity to build and maintain highly engaged communicative networks using affordances provided by social media and alternative news sites.

Meanwhile, there is a broad consensus in the existing literature that the party's rapid rise was also accompanied by a continuous progression toward political radicalization (Heinze and Weisskircher 2021; Cohen 2021, 298; Heinze 2020, 137; Schuler et al. 2020). These observations often point to distinct phases, changes in leadership, and key events marking this development (cf. Arzheimer and Berning 2019; Özvatan and Forchtner 2019, 214; Decker and Brähler 2020, 150–151):

1. The initial phase, beginning in 2013, is generally seen as one marked by Euro-skepticism and (neo)liberal economic policy demands.
2. Between 2015 and 2017, under new leadership, the party pivoted toward an anti-immigration agenda, as it consolidated its electoral success in federal as well as state elections.
3. Since then, the party has been rocked by a series of intraparty conflicts, each of which appears to have ultimately been won by the more radical factions (most recently on display at the party convention in June 2022, when the extreme right within the party forced the "moderates" out of all levels of party leadership), pushing the party's platform ever farther toward ethnonationalism and illiberal, anti-democratic sentiment and culminating in currently being under surveillance by German state authorities for its political extremism.

What the existing literature is more ambiguous about, is the question of what may have caused these shifts. Arzheimer and Berning (2019) conclude that the AfD's transformation into a radical right party was fueled by an electoral demand for anti-immigration policies, implying a certain demand-side pull. Meanwhile, many of the empirical analyses of campaign materials or manifestos mentioned above, point to deliberately chosen communication strategies on the supply side. Yet so far, scholarship has not provided much on the basis of theoretical approaches that might outline some of the root causes for this observed process of radicalization.

Here, we believe that the conservative dilemma and digital surrogacy framework can provide more conclusive answers: in applying it, we might characterize the phases outlined above as first seeking to promote a (fairly unpopular) neoliberal economic agenda, followed by increasing appeals to "cross-cutting cleavage issues" around the topic of immigration to mobilize popular support. This also entailed tapping into the affordances of alternative media spheres and enlisting (digital) surrogate organizations. Tapping into these networks ultimately also meant that the party surrendered autonomy to more extreme actor types, which led to the increasing radicalization of its platform and leadership.

What Bennett and Livingston refer to as the institutional and connective action paradigms in this book's opening chapter, provides useful vantage points from which to analyze this ongoing development. Both perspectives provide important pieces of the puzzle and are equally important to consider. It is not a question of one or the other, but of how to incorporate both perspectives and the sets of factors they provide into a unitary analysis: to understand the AfD's radicalization, we need to first understand not only the party as an institution but as an integral part of a larger network, facilitated by digital media, along with the communicative and connective relations that this implies. Adding to this framework, we offer two core observations:

1) The more parties come to rely on communicative ties as part of their organizational structure, the more these ties will come to shape the parties' political positions.
2) Tapping into communicative networks connected via Manichean narratives and intense affective responses can lead parties to cater to narrower in-groups and radicalized positions.

We explore both of these dynamics in more detail below.

The AfD's Digital Surrogate Organizations

While intraorganizational interests should not be dismissed, it seems difficult to explain the rapid radicalization process of the AfD, without also taking its surrogate organizations and its dependence on digital platforms into account. In fact, one cannot disentangle the young history of the party from simultaneously occurring dynamics such as localized anti-immigrant mobilization via Facebook groups (Stier et al. 2017) or the proliferation of right-wing alternative new sites stylizing themselves as an alternative to mainstream or public service media formats (Heft et al. 2019; Rone 2021; Weisskircher 2020; Haller 2020, 167–169). The party is populist in the sense that it has relied heavily on catering to anti-establishment sentiments and harnessing an us-versus-them narrative, aimed at cutting across social cleavages and already circulating among its potential electorate (Breeze 2019; Haller 2020). To do so, it continuously gauges what topics and frames might resonate at a given moment. This, of course, leads to a certain degree of political opportunism, driving the party's agenda into whichever direction presently catering to the social anxieties it relies upon.

To understand the AfD's rapid rise as well as its radicalization, we might view it as a central node within a broader communicative network. As Weisskircher (2020, 488) points out, the quasi-institutional, digital surrogate organizations alluded to above, are not to be seen as a detached and isolated online sphere. Connective relations also exist in terms of interpersonal relationships and organizational capacities. Yet more than any other contemporary German party, most of which have a decades-spanning institutional genealogy, the AfD relies on novel forms of communication and digital media venues. Observers note that practically all party subchapters and elected officials actively engage on social media and across various platforms (Becker 2021, 156). On many of these platforms, the AfD maintains the largest and most engaged follower base compared to other German parties (Serrano et al. 2019) and has played a key role in facilitating and fanning online debates that have run outside of the scope of mainstream media discourse (Klinger et al. 2022).

Another key difference to other parties is that it has been more inclusive in terms of what types of surrogate organizations it has been willing to embrace. Elshehawy et al. (2021, 2) note, for example, how "Kremlin-sponsored media provided what AfD operatives may have found useful—a news forum publishing appropriately slanted migrant stories, to refer to in

128 CONNECTIVE ACTION AND THE RISE OF THE FAR-RIGHT

political discussions." More directly, the AfD has actively supported and boosted the profile of self-stylized alternative media, many of which only exist as blog-style websites or social media channels of individual influencers or political pundits, by organizing media conferences and inviting them into the German Bundestag (Weisskircher 2020, 479).

Besides hyperpartisan media, the party's network of surrogate organizations includes a variety of youth groups and fraternities, publishing houses, and foundations that function as a repository for ideas developed in direct opposition to a perceived mainstream and that would be unlikely to get traction in any other established party. This has included climate denialist (aka "skeptic") think tanks (Götze 2019; Kauhausen and Passeick 2021), conspiracy-driven anti–COVID-regulation protest movements (Ruhose 2021: 480), and neo-Nazi organizations (Berg 2019: 79). Importantly, the makeup of many of these surrogates often also seem highly dependent on novel affordances offered via modes of digital connectivity. A salient example is the neo-fascist Identitarian Movement, which as far as current research has been able to surmise, does not actually appear to be a broad social movement but rather an assemblage of highly tech-savvy media influencers (Virchow 2015). Analysis of political messaging via Twitter has demonstrated how the group's messaging often overlaps and converges with that employed by the AfD in their public communication (Ahmed and Pisoiu 2021, 251). In another prominent example, the party adopted—practically verbatim—a campaign initially launched via the Identitarian Movement's web presence, based on disinformation about the UN Global Compact on Migration. Top- and mid-level party accounts not only used much of the same rhetoric and tactics, such as promoting online petitions but also built a bridge to other, larger networks (Klinger et al. 2022).

Importantly, a core element of the joint communication is the propensity to define itself in active opposition to a perceived mainstream, while at the same time continuously seeking the attention of and entry into established deliberative arenas. Part of this communication strategy has been to actively instrumentalize "German news media by making deliberate provocations that journalists not only covered but also scandalized," as Maurer et al.'s (2022: 15) analysis of party messaging within the context of the larger media environment finds. Other scholarship has referred to digitally enabled strategies such as "hashjacking," whereby party accounts have tied their own agenda to prominent discussions on social media (Darius and Stephany

2019, 3). Ultimately, such forms of communicative action seek the normalization and mainstreaming of the AfD's preferred talking points—that is, radical right positions.

While the party has typically been careful to not coordinate too directly with extremist organizations or fringe movements, it has effectively facilitated a process of "informational laundering" (Becker 2021, 156) by adopting key agenda items and amplifying these via their own political platform or communication formats. In some measure, the process looks similar to what Starbird describes elsewhere in this volume in her tracking of the interaction between top-down and bottom-up personal action frames concerning the 2020 US presidential election. Key to this connective strategy has been the various actors' modes of mobilization as part of a networked public. This is aided via the affordances of social media that "help activate and sustain latent ties" (Papacharissi 2016, 310). In other words, direct institutional coordination may not be necessary, where a network of communicative relations makes the activities of each organization highly visible to the other.

Even more nebulous and difficult to define are assemblages of highly active social media accounts, many of which operate without clearly identifying as actually existing persons or institutions. We can collectively think of these "superspreaders" (Klinger et al. 2022) or "superusers" (Hindman et al. 2022), as technology-enabled communication networks running on the logic of connective action (Bennett and Segerberg 2012). In this capacity, they essentially function as digital surrogate organizations, active across various social media platforms where they are extremely prolific in amplifying the party's messages and connecting various nodes of the AfD's digital networks. Such activities go hand in hand with other modes of political mobilization, such as digital petitions which can be rapidly circulated among an online follower network, and which have traditionally been linked more to progressive forms of social protest (Rone 2021, 2).

Beyond this, Heinze and Weisskircher (2021, 263) find that in terms of organizational structures and collective decision-making practices, the party has relied on "'movement-party' strategy, collective leadership, and internal democracy—concepts that are usually associated with Green and left-wing parties." They further note that the party's transformation was accompanied by a rapid succession of actors in the top positions, which has (so far) failed to produce what they term the typical features of other radical right parties, namely "'charismatic' leadership and the centralization of power" (2021, 263). Rather than being guided by clear top-down directives, the party appears to have relied on practices akin to "analytic activism" (Karpf 2016), by which hybrid organizations utilize digital toolkits and heuristics (Schäfer 2021) to monitor and listen to their supporters, as well as provide them with input and informational infrastructures.

This orientation toward movement-party strategies and network growth took place at a time of imminent political success while entering all state parliaments and the Bundestag. Because of this rapid growth and success, stabilizing institutional hierarchies and shifting toward a formal membership base may not have been a priority: as of 2022, the AfD has by far the largest support base on social media compared to all other parties, but only very few formal, due-paying members. In numbers, while 554.000 people follow the party on Facebook (about twice as many as the conservative CDU), the AfD has under 30.000 registered members (CDU: 384.000).

Besides the elements by which the party actively ties in surrogate organizations and its base, the AfD has also retained features of what might be termed a "connective party," characterized by the "attempt to develop horizontal models potentially offer a response to voter demand for greater engagement at the electoral interface" (Bennett et al. 2018, 1670). Arguably, emphasizing horizontal modes of deliberation or fostering inclusive networks via active de-centralization efforts appear to be means rather than ends, and the party certainly retains a formalized structure and hierarchy, as is more typical of far-right political preferences and modes of organization. Nevertheless, around core issues, the AfD's leadership and its main institutional bodies do not control agenda-setting or framing processes independently. Instead, they draw on—and feed back into—a broader network of surrogate organizations, in which alternative right-wing media, online communities, political organizations, and ideological foundations collectively tap into more dispersed public sentiments, utilizing the affordances of digital media.

The advantage of these forms of connectivity, facilitated by digital technologies, has previously been described as permitting "people to express interest in or allegiance to issues without having to enter into complex negotiation of personal versus collective politics" (Papacharissi 2016, 314). This, in turn, raises the question of how sustainable such forms of organizations can prove to be over time. How can parties that draw momentum from such forms of connectivity meet the challenge of sharing "authority between the membership and the executive party leadership in a stable manner" (Bennett et al. 2018, 1671)—especially when this leadership is itself continuously destabilized? And by what mechanisms do such communicative relations unfold a logic of their own? We will provide two possible pathways into this line of thinking in the following sections, wherein we turn to the inclusive dynamic of tapping into unifying *narratives* and the mobilizing potential of *affect*. While both factors offer organizational advantages in terms of quickly building momentum, they ultimately also limit the capacities of institutional agency. We will exemplify what we mean by this below.

Narrative Networks as Cross-Cutting Issues: From In-Groups to Out-Groups

In a networked public, various forms of communication govern actors' and organizations' relationships with one another. In addition to the physical infrastructures and technological affordances necessary to maintain ideological networks, discursive infrastructures provide a framework in which communication occurs. A coherent and mutually shared *narrative* establishes and maintains a discursive network's architecture. Narratives shape a collective sense of meaning; wherein mediated information represents "a causal or associative 'chain' of real or fictional events . . . between which connections are made and which has a recognizable pattern" (Chandler and Munday 2011, 288). In the context of political communication, narratives create ties between political actors and their audiences. Here, "elite-produced stories simultaneously reflect and forge a political common sense" (Polletta and Callahan 2017, 392), while modes of dissemination and the practice of sharing stories serve "as a way of building collective identity" (2017, 392). Narratives might therefore provide a larger framework in which cross-cutting issues and surrogate organizations enable the mobilization of publics across class lines based on nonmaterial identity cues. What would this look like in the context we are describing here?

We argue that a key narrative framework on the contemporary (far-)right can be broken down into three consecutive dimensions:

1.) A global hegemony of progressive or leftist forces exists; and is
2.) actively involved in suppressing, excluding, and vilifying conservative[1] ideas or actors; . . .

---

[1] The term "conservative" is used here, as this is typically the self-ascribed ideological marker used by far- and radical right actors.

132 CONNECTIVE ACTION AND THE RISE OF THE FAR-RIGHT

3.) who are facing an existential threat to their personhood and way of life, legitimizing forms of active resistance against these perceived dynamics.

Crucially, this Manichean, us-versus-them narrative depends on the construct of a core in-group that defines itself primarily *ex-negativo* and in opposition to a perceived "Other." As such, it is continuously sustained and reinforced by cultivating a shared heuristic that exemplifies how these forces might operate. (Elsewhere in this volume, Parker and Blum, along with Bahador and Kerchner, explore Othering in greater depth.) Employing these heuristics entails naming and interpreting novel events by placing them within a causal framework. In other words, novel observations are communicated as part of a previously established and ongoing narrative structure, which spawns shared meaning-making, a sense of community (often in opposition to a perceived enemy Other), and thus further strengthens communicative bonds and future connectivity.

The far-right narrative thereby also generates the framework by which a focus on issues like immigration can cut across social cleavages. Such communicative processes may unfold productive power along the first dimension referred to above, in crafting qualifiers like "liberal" or "leftist" media, "woke" activists, "urban elites" or "globalists" that might be used to reductively describe entire arrays of various actors and institutions. Along the second dimension, concepts like "political correctness" or "cancel culture" function as signifiers pointing to a pervasive power of opposing forces, which are understood as structuring the order of social discourse and excluding or suppressing conservative viewpoints. Lastly, the third dimension would produce threat scenarios like those associated with a "new world order," "replacement," "*Überfremdung*" (foreign infiltration), or "*Umvolkung*" (repopulation) to communicate shared anxieties about changes in demographic or economic configurations and linking these to a perceived tyrannical administrative agenda that is actively pushing for such outcomes.

From Digital Connectivity to Radicalization

The existence of such narratives is far from new. Nor is it a recent phenomenon that right-wing or conservative forces rally around constant reaffirmations of a multifaceted threat of progressive forces. What is new, however, is the speed and scope at which the process of collective meaning-making might disseminate across communicative networks. Digital affordances have provided new modes of connectivity between elite actors and their respective audiences. They have also enhanced the ability of said audiences to recirculate and share narrative content as a marker of collective identity. Starbird, elsewhere in this volume, illustrates this dynamic with her analysis of "Sharpiegate." Another recent example is provided by Jambrina-Canseco (2023), who employs spatial econometrics to demonstrate how narratives circulating via local news and social media might explain support for the far-right Vox party in Spain.

As Polletta and Callahan have argued, the political effects of right-wing narratives "have been sharpened by two significant changes in the media landscape: the rise of right-wing media outlets and the profusion of user-shared digital news" (2017, 392). These increase the ability of entire networks to communicate a shared perception in response to novel events. Easily accessible narratives help broaden the reach of such forms of connectivity. Such findings illustrate how enticing such communicative dynamics might be for newly emerging political actors such as Vox or the AfD, seeking to broaden their reach while side-stepping discursive spaces already dominated by more established institutions and political competitors.

Narratives that draw initially disparate actor groups into communicative networks can thereby also come to function as the smallest common denominator. The more online communities and disparate actor types converge via the Manichean narrative described above, wherein they function as the corrective to an ideologically opposed Other, the larger the incentive not to be seen or portrayed as being part of said other side. More voices in a larger tent also mean that there are more eyes on key network nodes and leadership positions. Over time, this clearly limits the capacity to generate new frames and the spectrum for political stances. The role played by alternative media as an integral part of identity-based digital surrogates can be seen as an example of this. As Benkler's work on the news ecologies in the US has demonstrated, right-wing alternative media tend to "police each other for ideological purity, not factual accuracy" (Benkler 2020, 48). In an ideological environment primarily guided by the ordering force of an us-versus-them dynamic, the ultimate site of deviance is to be constructed as part of the oppositional Other. Being ostracized means being relegated back into the

134 CONNECTIVE ACTION AND THE RISE OF THE FAR-RIGHT

realm of the mainstream and to be marked as part of hegemonic power structures, rather than the side of the alternative. Simply put, tapping into the us-versus-them narrative also entails a certain commitment to remain on the "right" side.

The AfD's Main Narratives as Cross-Cutting Cleavage Issues

At first glance, the rapid transition of the AfD from a neoliberally oriented, center-right populist platform to a nationalist radical right one might seem somewhat contradictory. Yet the narrative devices laid in place in the early phase, in many ways foreshadowed what was to come: The party's early opposition to EU responses to the financial crisis drew centrally on the idea of a specifically German *Volk*—a core in-group whose values were under threat by an external set of elite institutions. At the same time, the party presented itself as the only alternative to the hegemonic consensus of mainstream media and established parties. With this, the devices of the core narrative are laid in place. At first, the productive work these devices provide is marked by the inclusion of all those voices and perspectives feeling alienated from a perceived mainstream and who are in search of an alternative political platform or perspective. Crucially, the party's populist impetus of rhetorically pitting elites versus the will of the true people (Kranert 2019; Donovan 2020) already provides "a discursive, if not a logical, justification for taking positions that are (potentially) racist or at least, non-PC" (Breeze 2019, 101). This, in other words, helps the AfD shape cross-cutting issues among surrogates and supporters likely to see themselves as part of the (nonelite) in-group.

Consequently, the second phase, marked by a shift toward anti-immigrant sentiment, presents a first narrowing of the narrative scope and its ability to provide the basis for an inclusive in-group. Key to this communication strategy was the depiction of (mainly Muslim) immigrants and Syrian refugees as an external threat, which serves as "a projection to legitimize the AfD's self-image as a 'we' group of rebel heroes" (Doerr 2021, 12), and courageous truth-tellers. In the overall narrative structure, the very act of publicly assuming these positions goes against the will of the perceived mainstream hegemony and thus constitutes an act of self-assertion and defiance in its refusal to be silenced.

At the same time, however, the out-group has now expanded to not only include a corrupt elite, but also immigrants as the constructed Other.

As Özvatan and Forchtner (2019) point out, this represents a coherent progression in the AfD's narrative, wherein "the 'evil' opponent is not simply the African or Muslim non-white immigrant, but, in 'good' populist fashion, the political establishment, which is responsible for allowing ethnocultural pollution to happen" (2019, 218). This does not constitute a break from previous narrative structures, but rather a narrower continuation, which at the same time expands the definition of the Othered out-group and positions establishment institutions such as other political parties "on the side of the perpetrators" (Berg 2019, 85).

Building on this type of messaging, the next phase of the AfD's radicalization process thereby increasingly shifted its focus from the externalized Other and onto an ethno-nationalist notion of a German people (*Volk*) in danger of being replaced, affectively mobilizing potential voters from all social strata. This too, draws centrally on narrative devices previously laid in place, such as those popularized in 2010 by a best-selling book by a former social-democratic (i.e., cross-cutting) politician under the title of "Germany Is Doing Away with Itself" (cf. Kranert 2019, 272). Here, the populist concept of the "the people" (*das Volk*) morphs into the threat scenario of ethno-cultural replacement (Özvatan and Forchtner 2019, 201). In doing so, the AfD's messaging latches onto previously mainstreamed narratives long espoused by far-right and radical right extremist groups, which "create an apparently logical and consistent (conspiratorial) story of how the left is set to 'destroy' Germany through migration" (Ahmed and Pisoiu 2021, 249–250).

Transitioning from a rigid focus on migration, the party has since also adopted similar contrarian stances when it comes to climate policy and stylizes itself as the key antagonist to the German Green party (Knüpfer and Hoffmann 2024). Götze (2019) points out how similar the party's stances on climate change are to those on migration, wherein the potential political response to both issue fields is seen as the actual threat, capable of upending an existing economic and cultural order and ushering in a decline in the social status of its constituents (Götze 2019, 101). Along similar lines, Berg finds that the party's positions on women's rights and gender politics "consists largely of anti-gender politics" and this, in turn, is defined "in opposition to an imagined gender ideology" (2019, 82). The party's public position on public health policy during the COVID-19 pandemic has shown similar markings, pitting the imagined interest of a corrupt scientific and political elite against those of the "true" people (Wacker and Kieslich 2021, 5).

Here too the core narrative is evoked in order to make sense of complex developments and communicate a position linking the party to surrogate organizations that already mobilize supporters who share this perception. This way the AfD profits from hot-button controversies and successfully claimed ownership of issues around identity, immigration, and crime that cut across class cleavages, deflecting from the fact that the party had little to promise or deliver on the part of actual solutions to the larger socioeconomic disparities. Yet to maintain these cross-cutting communicative connection points, the party increasingly becomes locked into the us-versus-them dynamics that initially fostered these ties. The continued need to foster an anti-hegemonic narrative comes at the cost of adopting increasingly radical positions outside the scope of mainstream debate. While digital connectivity initially provides the means to form such connections, it now also becomes the tool by which the party is monitored by a growing roster of surrogates seeking to maintain closed ranks.

Affective Publics as Digital Surrogates: From Input to Outrage

While the previous section looked at forms of messaging via narratives that resonate within the party and its surrogate organizations, we now turn our attention to forms of organizational analysis and mobilization of supporter networks. This constitutes a second dynamic by which parties might seek to broaden their reach. It describes how digital networks of communicative *affect* can be seen as surrogate organizations. Facilitated via the affordances of digital communication, these connective ties require a continuous stoking of communal affective responses, lest they become invisible and disappear.

By *affect* we mean "the subjective or evaluative dimension in human experience," and hence the processes of meaning-making that might be "aroused in audiences" (Chandler and Munday 2011, 8). We are thereby referring to the concept not in the individual and psychological sense, but in its communicative and mediated capacities, by which it gives rise to mutually shared experiences and hence, in its potential to elicit forms of (mass) mobilization. Zizi Papacharissi's concept of "affective publics" (2016) is grounded in this understanding. It too is closely tied to the dynamics of "connective action" (Bennett and Segerberg 2012), which gives rise to networks that "are mobilized and connected, identified, and potentially disconnected through expressions of sentiment" (Papacharissi 2016, 311). Social media facilitate the connective relations that function both as a canvas for expression as well as a lens through which audiences may monitor and gauge the reactions of others.

While social movements and election campaigns have always included emotional appeals (e.g., Derks et al. 2008; Russmann 2018), the increasing importance and immediacy of social media, user-generated content, mobilization through personal networks, and algorithmic curation further catalyze this development. In the wake of the 2016 US election and the increasing visibility of far-right movements, both online and offline, recent scholarship has argued that the dynamics by which affective communities spawn political mobilization appear to be especially pronounced on the radical right (Karpf 2017; Boler and Davis 2018). The concept has therefore also described emergent forms of digital networks in their propensity to actively "deploy public emotions like outrage, disgust, and fury to build solidarity based on xenophobic exclusion' (Lünenborg 2020, 31)—thus essentially taking on the function of digital surrogates.

From Digital Listening to Radicalization

Studies have shown that political actors monitor the success of their social media messages—they adopt communication strategies that increase user engagement, especially emotional messages, photos, writing in the first person, and addressing users directly (Jost 2022). Recent empirical studies of far-right digital networks point to this potential, in terms of the speed and reach with which collective reactions to events might be disseminated among them and the cross-cutting potential this holds for mobilizing communities that might otherwise be spatially far removed from one another. Adlung et al. (2021, 21) focus on affective publics that form in the context of gender politics and demonstrate how far-right extremists may "exploit network structures and their logics deliberately to absorb women's rights into anti-migration propaganda and thereby enlist more followers to their cause." Knüpfer et al. (2020) show how this online campaign instantaneously carried across borders and into other national contexts, where key nodes in far-right networks were employed to undermine the Me Too movement.

For political organizations seeking to utilize social media to find, monitor, and listen (Karpf 2016 and elsewhere in this volume) to their respective audience, the sudden visibility of such affective communicative relations provides the ability to essentially "ping" entire networks of potential supporters that share a specific reaction to key events. Yet the core challenge for political actors seeking to harness their potential for mobilization lies in being able to discern between sustainable and more ephemeral forms of affective connectivity.

Analytically monitoring affective networks increases the risk of mis- or overinterpreting particularly loud and visible reactions. This entails that an affective public's visibility might be driven by most vocal and digitally visible actors within the network (Schäfer 2021). In digital spaces, this often also means that these highly engaged voices are those of actor nodes with extreme views and particularly zealous immediate followers. Catering to these actors might prove to be highly effective in boosting the visibility of particular narratives or issues. At the same time, this can be highly off-putting for less-engaged actors and more moderate spectators. Second, the type of information that these forms of connective communication are conducive of, also appears to be somewhat limited: as Corbu and Negrea Busuioc (2020, 191) note, "the magnetism of affective content makes people more receptive to false content, which they accept uncritically." This may lead to a convergence of "populist communication and various types of fake news that use sensational features are subject to viralization and emotional persuasive appeals" (Corbu and Negrea Busuioc 2020, 190).

Over time, relying on these forms of highly attention-grabbing connectivity and the fast connective relations they invoke, will therefore likely come at the cost of increasingly alienating other communities and will disseminate informational content that is highly emotionally engaging—but not necessarily true or politically productive. At the same time, the more effective such tactics prove in generating audiences and mobilizing communities, the more they are likely to create incentives to stoke further cross-cutting affective reactions for political gain, creating a potential spiraling effect. Maintaining affective publics in order to harness their propensity to fulfill surrogate functions requires a constant stream of issues likely to generate affective responses. Over time, this has tied the AfD to a political platform of cultivating outrage rather than pragmatic solutions or coalition-building.

The AfD's Outrage-Based Affective Surrogates

The AfD has clearly benefited from algorithmic systems optimized for strategically stoking outrage around core cleavage issues in exchange for more user engagement in their in-group, activating support networks and surrogates. Yet these dynamics are not driven, but merely amplified by digital affordances: in characterizing the AfD's electoral base, survey-based research has shown that it is primarily a *felt* sense of deprivation and cultural threat, along with emotions of ethnocentrism and distrust against the establishment that mobilizes them to vote for the far-right populist party (Pickel 2019, 145; Decker and Brähler 2020). While early explanations for the rising popularity of the AfD often centered on economic disparities, research has since indicated that it is not so much the actual social or economic status of this demographic that might justify their relative sense of decline, but rather it is the *perception* thereof along with the *feelings* of anger and resentment this evokes. Put differently, the AfD's relationship with its electorate is primarily driven by forms of "mobilizing emotions in a 'politics of passion'" (Ahmed and Pisoiu 2021, 250).

Heinze and Weisskircher (2021, 267) point to the AfD candidates' propensity to actively seek out particularly vocal protest groups that might mobilize against such disparate topics as the construction of wind turbines or COVID-19 policies, while their crusade against a renaturalization of wolf populations in rural areas is another illustrative case (Clemm von Hohenberg and Hager 2022). Such alliances between protest movements and the party are rhetorically accompanied by the narrative devices laid out above, wherein, as Breeze (2019, 101) writes, "the projected double threat—from 'above' *and* from 'outside'—is calculated to trigger powerful reactions, in particular, resentment and rage." Core tropes of the AfD's messaging therefore emerge around reactions to key events, oftentimes involving violent crimes by (ostensibly) foreign perpetrators.

Yet beyond these factors that might generally tie voters or movements to a particular party, the AfD's rise also coincided with a rapid transformation of the digital network infrastructures provided via social media. As we have noted above, the party came to quickly rely on these affordances, and much more so than other parties. At the same time, platforms like Facebook, where the party has been especially active in connecting its membership to affect-driven protest movements (Stier et al. 2017), made it much easier for communities to share their affective reactions and embed these forms of engagements into connective relations via a platform structure geared toward immediate reactions. Meanwhile, content-based platforms like YouTube increasingly morphed into social media sites, where core communities and niche audiences form around particular forms of emotionally engaging content. The ability for digitally networked users to respond with memes, emojis, and gifs has arguably also added to the collective ability to quickly form communicative relations around shared affective responses. Lastly, the demographics using these communicative tools expanded greatly, over the course of the past decade alone—with many older German citizens becoming much more active via social media.

All of this has created a wealth of new potential for identifying affective communities and subsequently viewing these as digital surrogates. As the party has come to rely on these tools, these tools have in turn also shaped the party's output: multiplatform analysis across social media accounts has shown a discrepancy between the party's official manifestos and what it catered to in an online environment, for example, wherein "as part of its social media strategy, the AfD avoided discussion of its economic proposals and instead focused on pushing its anti-immigration agenda to gain popularity" (Serrano et al. 2019, 1). Other case studies have demonstrated how the party has come to adopt messaging from the extremist fringe of its digital networks, fueled by affective responses to a deliberate disinformation campaign (Klinger et al. 2022). Yet while these networks might provide for a momentary flurry of online activity, the agenda items this eventually resulted in, arguably led nowhere in terms of political outcomes. Instead, they merely further cemented the party's propensity to be driven by protest fads and what Julia Rone (2021) has succinctly dubbed "far-right indignation mobilization mechanisms."

Conclusion: The Logic of Connective Radicalization

What caused the sudden rise of the radical right as an institutional actor in Germany? Ultimately this is a complex question, perhaps better left to institutionalists and political theorists. Yet as scholars of political communication, we hope to contribute to the question of why the rapid radicalization process outlined above may have occurred. We see the concepts of surrogate organizations formed through narrative networks and affective publics as two of many possible, overlapping drivers behind this process. Both are, at their core, communication phenomena. In and of themselves, they say little to nothing about material interests or ideological preferences. And yet in an increasingly complex media environment, where the shape and nature of political parties has shifted toward more hybrid forms of organizational mobilization, it is communicative relations that come to codetermine a party's political orientation—especially in cases where these parties rely heavily on connectivity and decentralized modes of decision-making and the mobilization of supporters.

Before all else, the transition to digital and hybridized media environments has facilitated and accelerated such forms of connectivity and information exchange. Remaining mindful of the pitfalls of a purely technocentric argument, we also see the AfD's institutional agency in making deliberate choices guided partly by political opportunism as well as ideological fervor: party leadership undoubtedly sought to utilize anti-elite and xenophobic sentiments, while harnessing the technological affordances at their disposal. These were deliberate choices by the party's elites as well as its rank-and-file membership. Yet viewing the radicalization process solely through the lens of an institutionalist paradigm fails to consider the limitations and path dependencies that specific forms of communicative network dynamics and connective action might entail. Simply put: the more parties come to rely on communicative relations to grow and mobilize their base and spectrum of surrogate organizations, the more such relations are likely to unfold a logic of their own.

The case presented here illustrates novel ways in which populist rightwing actors and organizations communicate via digital platforms and public forums. While they engage with wider audiences and ultimately seek to harness political power, it is also important to understand that certain forms of communication take place parallel to, and for the most part isolated from, the political mainstream. We have argued that this creates a somewhat isolated in-group dynamic, wherein cleavage issues and narratives are circulated among party members and surrogates, which run parallel to and outside of more traditional sites of public deliberation.

At the same time, however, the case study reveals dynamics wherein the party appears to be utilizing social media affordances in order to monitor its base and employ these digital tools in order to better listen to their supporters and mobilize these across social cleavages. This process ultimately seeks to selectively amplify messages that emerge from lower organizational levels. Here, outrage is strategically fostered around key issues, which fulfill the function of providing central focal points for disparate actor types and across various media formats. Outrage unites the in-group: it serves as a base for community-building and places anger at the heart of (online) practices geared toward collective meaning-making. In addition, outrage is rewarded by algorithmic systems of platforms that have been optimized for business models around increasing user engagement. Thus, fanning outrage makes sense for the AfD from both an institutional as well as a technological perspective. Yet it also puts the party platform on a road toward ever more radical positions.

If we were to predict the future of the AfD's political platform, based on these observations, it seems reasonable to assume that this will increasingly be driven by something other than institutional agency and strategic interests, in the classic sense of how political organizations operate. What seems likely, instead, is that to the degree that the party retains its dependence on forms of digital connectivity, it will increasingly come to define itself *ex-negativo*, that is, in reaction to a perceived mainstream. This will limit the party's capacity to define new fields of interest or proactive agenda items. Instead, core in-group dynamics born out of a shared sense of opposition will structure a coherent line between party leadership and the various forms of surrogate organizations shaping its periphery.

It is likely that these communicative ties will be fed by intermittent bouts of collective outrage in reaction to specific events or political decisions that are activated by a collective narrative framework. While these can serve to grow the party's base and appeal to wider audiences disaffected by the existing political landscape, they are also likely to rely on reductive readings of mediated events. And while such simplistic narratives might draw a crowd, continuously fostering outrage provides little basis for proactive policy proposals, deliberative processes, or compromise—that is, the core tenets of governance in a parliamentary democracy. Yet ultimately the most relevant question might not be whether parties like the AfD and their surrogate organizations are going to continue down their path toward radicalization—they most likely will. Instead, the important question currently faced by many democratic societies is how successful the emerging far-right networks will be in advocating for their preferred narratives and affective responses within the political mainstream.

References

Adlung, Shari, Margreth Lünenborg, and Christoph Raetzsch. 2021. "Pitching Gender in a Racist Tune: The Affective Publics of the #120decibel Campaign." *Media and Communication* 9 (2): 16–26.

Ahmed, Reem, and Daniela Pisoiu. 2021 "Uniting the Far Right: How the Far-Right Extremist, New Right, and Populist Frames Overlap on Twitter—a German Case Study." *European Societies.* March 15. 23 (2): 232–254.

Arzheimer, Kai, and Carl Berning. 2019. "How the Alternative for Germany (AfD) and Their Voters Veered to the Radical Right, 2013–2017." *Electoral Studies*. https://doi.org/10.1016/j.electstud.2019.04.004.

Becker, Andrea. 2021. "Die wollen nicht reden: Über die digitale Manipulierbarkeit von Diskursen." In Farrokhzad von Schahrzad, Thomas Kunz, Saloua Mohammed Oulad M´Hand, and Markus Ottersbach, eds., *Migrations- and Fluchtdiskurse im Zeichen des erstarkenden Rechtspopulismus* (pp. 143–162). Wiesbaden: Springer Fachmedien.

Benkler, Yochai. 2020. "A Political Economy of the Origins of Asymmetric Propaganda in American Media." In Steven Livingston and W. Lance Bennett, eds., *The Disinformation Age* (pp. 43–66). Cambridge: Cambridge University Press.

Bennett, W. Lance, and Alexandra Segerberg. 2012. "The Logic of Connective Action: Digital Media and the Personalization of Contentious Politics." *Information, Communication & Society* 15 (5): 739–768.

Bennett, W. Lance, Alexandra Segerberg, and Curd B. Knüpfer. 2018. "The Democratic Interface: Technology, Political Organization, and Diverging Patterns of Electoral Representation." *Information, Communication and Society* 21 (11): 1655–1680.

Berg, Lynn. 2019. "Between Anti-Feminism and Ethnicized Sexism. Far-Right Gender Politics in Germany." In Maik Fielitz and Nick Thurston, eds., *Post-Digital Cultures of the Far Right: Online Actions and Offline Consequences in Europe and the US* (pp. 79–92). Bielefeld: transcript Verlag. https://doi.org/10.1515/9783839446706

Boler, Megan, and Elizabeth Davis. 2018. "The Affective Politics of the 'Post-Truth' Era: Feeling Rules and Networked Subjectivity." *Emotion, Space and Society* May 27: 75–85.

Breeze, Ruth. 2019. "Positioning 'the People' and its Enemies: Populism and Nationalism in AfD and UKIP." *Javnost: The Public* 26 (1): 89–104.

Chandler, Daniel, and Rod Manday. 2011. *A Dictionary of Media and Communication*. New York: Oxford University Press.

Clemm von Hohenberg, Bernhard, and Anselm Hager. 2022. "Wolf Attacks Predict Far-Right Voting." *Proceedings of the National Academy of Sciences of the United States of America* 119 (30): e2202224119. https://doi.org/10.1073/pnas.2202224119.

Cohen, Denis. 2021. "Ökonomisches Risiko and die elektorale Anziehungskraft der AfD." In Weßels von Bernhard and Harald Schoen, eds., *Wahlen and Wähler* (pp. 297–320). Wiesbaden: Springer Fachmedien.

Corbu, Nicoleta, and Elena Negrea-Busuioc. 2020. "Populism Meets Fake News: Social Media, Stereotypes and Emotions." In Benjamin Krämer and Christina Holtz-Bacha, eds., *Perspectives on Populism and the Media: Avenues for Research* (pp. 181–200). Baden-Baden: Nomos Verlagsgesellschaft mbH and Co. KG.

Darius, Philipp, and Fabian Stephany. 2019. "Twitter 'Hashjacked': Online Polarisation Strategies of Germany's Political Far-Right." Preprint. SocArXiv, 10. October 2019. https://doi.org/10.31235/osf.io/6gbc9.

Decker, Oliver, and Elmar Brähler, eds. 2020. *Autoritäre Dynamiken*. Gießen: Psychosozial-Verlag.

Derks, Daantje, Agneta H. Fischer, and Arjan E. R. Bos. 2008. "The Role of Emotion in Computer-Mediated Communication: A Review 'Instructional Support for Enhancing Students' Information Problem Solving Ability." *Computers in Human Behavior* 24 (3): 766–785.

Doerr, Nicole. 2021. "The Visual Politics of the Alternative for Germany (AfD): Anti-Islam, Ethno-Nationalism, and Gendered Images." *Social Sciences* 10 (1). https://doi.org/10.3390/socsci10010020.

Donovan, Barbara. 2020. "Populist Rhetoric and Nativist Alarmism: The AfD in Comparative Perspective." *German Politics and Society* 38 (1): 55–76.

Elshehawy, Ashrakat, Konstantin Gavras, Nikolay Marinov, Federico Nanni, and Harald Schoen. 2021. "Illiberal Communication and Election Intervention during the Refugee Crisis in Germany." *Perspectives on Politics* November 18: 1–19.

Götze, Susanne. 2019. "Heimat, Boden and Natur: Warum die AfD für den Tierschutz, aber gegen die Energiewende ist." In Eva Walther and Simon D. Isemann, eds., *Die AfD–psychologisch betrachtet* (pp. 81–103). Wiesbaden: Springer Fachmedien Wiesbaden.

Hacker, Jacob S., and Paul Pierson. 2020. *Let Them Eat Tweets: How the Right Rules in the Age of Extreme Inequality.* New York: Liveright Publishing.

Haller, André. 2020. "Populist Online Communication." In Benjamin Krämer, and Christina Holtz-Bacha, eds., *Perspectives on Populism and the Media* (pp. 161–180). Baden-Baden: Nomos.

Heft, Annett, Eva Mayerhöffer, Susanne Reinhardt, and Curd Knüpfer. 2019. "Beyond Breitbart: Comparing Right-Wing Digital News Infrastructures in Six Western Democracies." *Policy and Internet.* https://onlinelibrary.wiley.com/doi/abs/10.1002/poi3.219.

Heinze, Anna-Sophie. 2020. "Streit um demokratischen Konsens–Herausforderungen und Grenzen beim parlamentarischen Umgang mit der AfD." In Cathleen Bochmann, and Helge Döring, eds., *Gesellschaftlichen Zusammenhalt gestalten* (pp. 121–135). Wiesbaden: Springer Fachmedien Wiesbaden.

Heinze, Anna-Sophie, and Manès Weisskircher. 2021. "No Strong Leaders Needed? AfD Party Organisation between Collective Leadership, Internal Democracy, and 'Movement-Party' Strategy." *Politics and Governance* 9 (4): 263–274.

Heyen, S. 2020. Die AfD in den Medien: Eine Analyse des medialen Framings der Partei "Alternative für Deutschland" am Beispiel politischer Talkshows. Edited by G. Hoofacker and M. Liesching. Vol. 2. Carl Grossmann. https://doi.org/10.24921/2020.94115952.

Hindman, M., Lubin, N. and Davis, T. (2022) 'Facebook Has a Superuser-Supremacy Problem', *The Atlantic*, 10 February. Available at: https://www.theatlantic.com/technology/archive/2022/02/facebook-hate-speech-misinformation-superusers/621617/ (Accessed: 21 January 2025).

Jambrina-Canseco, Beatriz. 2023. "The Stories We Tell Ourselves: Local Newspaper Reporting and Support for the Radical Right." *Political Geography* 100 (January): 102778. https://doi.org/10.1016/j.polgeo.2022.102778.

Jost, Pablo. 2022. "How Politicians Adapt to New Media Logic: A Longitudinal Perspective on Accommodation to User-Engagement on Facebook." *Journal of Information Technology and Politics*: 1–14.

Karpf, David. 2016. *Analytic Activism.* New York: Oxford University Press.

Karpf, David. 2017. "Digital Politics After Trump." *Annals of the International Communication Association.* 41 (2): 198–207.

Kauhausen, Klara, and Yannick Passeick. 2021. "Völkischer Klimaschutz?! Strategien zum Umgang mit der Besetzung ökologischer Themen durch rechte Ideologien." *POLIS.* 25 (2): 20–23.

Klinger, Ulrike, W. Lance Bennett, Curd Knüpfer, Franziska Martini, and Xixuan Zhang. 2022. "From the Fringes into Mainstream Politics: Intermediary Networks and Movement-Party Coordination of a Global Anti-immigration Campaign in Germany." *Information, Communication and Society* 26 (9): 1890–1907.

Knüpfer, Curd, and Matthias Hoffmann. 2024. "Countering the 'Climate Cult'"—Framing Cascades in Far-right Digital Networks." *Political Communication* 42: 85–107.

Knüpfer, Curd, Matthias Hoffmann, and Vadim Voskresenskii. 2020. "Hijacking MeToo: Transnational Dynamics and Networked Frame Contestation on the Far Right in the Case of the '120 decibels' Campaign." *Information, Communication and Society* 25 (7): 1010–1028.

Koller, Veronika, and Marlene Miglbauer. 2019. "What Drives the Right-Wing Populist Vote? Topics, Motivations and Representations in an Online Vox Pop with Voters for the Alternative Für Deutschland." *Zeitschrift Für Anglistik and Amerikanistik* 67 (3): 283–306.

Kranert, Michael. 2019. "Populist Elements in the Election Manifestoes of AfD and UKIP." *Zeitschrift Für Anglistik and Amerikanistik* 67 (3): 265–282.

Lünenborg, Margreth. 2020. "Affective Publics: Understanding the Dynamic Formation of Public Articulations Beyond the Public Sphere." In Anne Fleig, and Christian von Scheve, eds., *Public Spheres of Resonance Constellations of Affect and Language* (pp. 30–48). London: Routledge.

Maurer, Marcus, Pablo Jost, Marlene Schaaf, Michael Sülflow, and Simon Kruschinski. 2022. "How Right-Wing Populists Instrumentalize News Media: Deliberate Provocations, Scandalizing Media Coverage, and Public Awareness for the Alternative for Germany (AfD)." *International Journal of Press/Politics.* https://doi.org/10.1177/19401612211072692.

Özvatan, Özgür, and Bernhard Forchtner. 2019. "The Far-Right Alternative Für Deutschland in Germany: Towards a 'Happy Ending'?" *The New Authoritarianism* 2: 199–226.

Papacharissi, Zizi, 2016. "Affective Publics and Structures of Storytelling: Sentiment, Events and Mediality." *Information, Communication and Society* 19 (3): 307–324.

Pichler, Siegrid, Luisa Wilczek, Masha Taric, and Verena Krömer. 2019. "Die AfD and ihr Wahlkampf auf Facebook Eine Analyse der Facebook-Posts and des User Engagements während der Landtagswahlen in Bayern and Sachsen-Anhalt." *kommunikation.medien. Open-Access-Journal für den wissenschaftlichen Nachwuchs*. Universität Salzburg, Nr. 10.

Pickel, Susanne. 2019. "Die Wahl der AfD. Frustration, Deprivation, Angst oder Wertekonflikt?" In Korte von Karl-rudolf and Jan Schoofs, eds., *Die Bundestagswahl 2017* (pp. 145–175). Wiesbaden: Springer Fachmedien.

Polletta, Francesca, and Jessica Callahan. 2017. "Deep Stories, Nostalgia Narratives, and Fake News: Storytelling in the Trump Era." *American Journal of Cultural Sociology* 5 (3): 392–408.

Rochnia, Michael, Hannah Kleen, Cornelia Gräsel, Sonja Ulm, and Fabian Soermann. 2021. "Die Argumentation der AfD in sozialen Medien zum Thema Flucht and Migration." *Bildungsforschung*: 1–19.

Rone, Julia. 2021. "Far Right Alternative News Media as 'Indignation Mobilization Mechanisms': How the Far Right Opposed the Global Compact for Migration." *Information, Communication and Society* 7: 1–18.

Ruhose, Fedor. 2021. "Die AfD vor der Bundestagswahl 2021." *Forschungsjournal Soziale Bewegungen* 34 (3): 479–489.

Russmann, Uta. 2018. "Going Negative on Facebook: Negative User Expressions and Political Parties' Reactions in the 2013 Austrian National Elections." *International Journal of Communication* 12: 2578–2598.

Schäfer, Andreas. 2021. "Digital Heuristics: How Parties Strategize Political Communication in Hybrid Media Environments." *New Media and Society* 25 (3). https://doi.org/10.1177/14614448211012101.

Schuler, Julia, Johannes Kiess, Oliver Decker, and Elmar Brähler. 2020. " Rechtsextremismus, Gewaltbereitschaft, Antisemitismus and Verschwörungsmentalität: AfD-Wähler_innen weisen die höchste Zustimmung zu anti-demokratischen Aussagen auf." Leipziger Autoritarismus-Studien. Leipzig: Universität Leipzig.

Serrano, Juan Carlos Medina, Morteza Shahrezaye, Orestis Papakyriakopoulos, and Simon Hegelich. 2019. "The Rise of Germany's AfD: A Social Media Analysis." *Proceedings of the 10th International Conference on Social Media and Society*: 214–223. Toronto: ACM. https://doi.org/10.1145/3328529.3328562.

Stier, Sebastian, Lisa Posch, Arnim Bleier, and Markus Strohmaier. 2017. "When Populists Become Popular: Comparing Facebook Use by the Right-Wing Movement Pegida and German Political Parties." *Information, Communication and Society* 20 (9): 1365–1388.

Sturm, Georg. 2020. "Populismus and Klimaschutz. Der AfD-Klimadiskurs." *Soziologiemagazin* 13 (2–2020): 69–82.

Virchow, Fabian. 2015. "The 'Identitarian Movement': What Kind of Identity? Is it Really a Movement?" In Patricia Anne Simpson and Helga Druxes, eds., *Digital Media Strategies of the Far Right in Europe and the United State*s (pp. 177–190). Lanham, MD: Lexington Books.

Wacker, Philipp, and Katharina Kieslich. 2021. "The Alternative for Germany (AfD) and Health Policy: Normalization or Containment of Populist Radical Right Tendencies?" In Michelle Falkenbach, and Scott L. Greer, eds., *The Populist Radical Right and Health* (pp. 47–57). Cham: Springer International Publishing.

Weisskircher, Manès. 2020. "The Strength of Far-Right AfD in Eastern Germany: The East-West Divide and the Multiple Causes behind 'Populism'." *Political Quarterly* 91 (3): 614–622.

Ziblatt, Daniel. 2017. *Conservative Parties and the Birth of Democracy*. New York: Cambridge University Press.

Chapter 6
Japan's *Netto Uyoku* and the Crisis of Transnational Digital Surrogate Organizations

Julia R. DeCook and Brett J. Fujioka

Introduction

The increase and visibility of far-right extremism in the United States and much of the Western world has become a point of major concern for these nations. Along with this, increasing right-wing terrorist attacks in the past 10 years—including the January 6 US Capitol Insurrection—fuel discomfort and fear in much of the citizenry of these countries about the state and strength of democracy. Certainly, right-wing authoritarianism is nothing new and once was the ruling political ideology in many Western countries, but this "democratic backsliding" and erosion of what many view as the fabric of Western democracy has created a maelstrom of debates over who—or what—is to blame. Many point to economic anxiety but note that this is an insufficient lens to understand the sociopolitical conditions that create the larger metahistorical context in which these movements gain traction (Mudde 2019; Parker and Barreto 2013, and Parker and Blum, this volume). In the US and Western Europe in particular, many of these movements have rejected traditional brick-and-mortar organizations and parties, and the platformized internet has played a significant role in the prominence of these kinds of surrogate organizations and independent groups who reject traditional party politics (Daniels 2009; Miller-Idriss 2022; Stern 2019).

Constituted mainly in digital space (e.g., QAnon) with spillovers into the offline world (e.g., #StoptheSteal), these communities either remain mostly on the internet or become a sort of hybrid; oftentimes being bankrolled by existing organizations like in the case of the DeVos backed "Michigan Freedom Fund" state capitol protests that occurred early on in the COVID-19

Julia R. DeCook and Brett J. Fujioka, *Japan's Netto Uyoku and the Crisis of Transnational Digital Surrogate Organizations*. In: *Connective Action and the Rise of the Far-Right*. Edited by: Steven Livingston and Michael Miller, Oxford University Press. © Oxford University Press (2025). DOI: 10.1093/oso/9780197794937.003.0006

pandemic (Gabbatt 2020). But for scholars, policymakers, journalists, and concerned citizens alike, it's not enough to only examine online hate speech and extremist organizing as it occurs on these platforms, but to take a more panoramic view of what is occurring in the larger social context in which these kinds of groups materialize. Ultimately, the COVID-19 pandemic made abundantly clear to laypersons what many activists, scholars, and journalists had been ringing the alarm bell about for years: that the rising tide of "post truth" and "fake news" would create fertile ground for radicalization, worsening an already fragile social fabric. The underlying social conditions that gave rise to these platforms, the whitelash and malcontent, and outbursts of violence (ranging from mass shootings to insurrections), are all intertwined.

An attempt to make sense of the factors that support the emergence of democratic parties were introduced by Ziblatt in the conservative dilemma framework (Ziblatt 2017). As others have outlined in other chapters in this volume, the conservative dilemma fails to consider the role that the internet and digital platforms play in the formation of political and social realities, which of course makes sense for Ziblatt, given his historical cases. Hacker and Pierson (2020) apply Ziblatt's model to explain democratic backsliding in the contemporary United States but fail to consider the possible role of social media in their analysis. We mean to fill this gap, though with a focus on Japan, rather than the United States. Focusing on the US context misses some critical history about the nature of online spaces in the formation of meaning and construction of political realities. Although many discussions occurring in the West about right-wing populism tend to ignore countries like Japan, South Korea, Singapore, Indonesia, the Philippines, and others, we believe that an analysis of the conditions and growth of right-wing populist movements in these countries are important to consider in any analysis of the global far right and in extending the conservative dilemma framework—not just in internationalizing it, but in considering the role of the digital in the formation of surrogate organizations and in particular, the explosion of online-to-offline hate groups that often function without an alignment with a political party or leader.

Japan is neither a cautionary tale nor the precursor to online extremist cultures in the West (Fujioka and DeCook 2021), but an important case study for understanding how and why external social and cultural change affects connective action (Bennett and Segerberg 2012). We argue that the crisis of social cohesion and the postmodern collapse of "grand narratives"

148 CONNECTIVE ACTION AND THE RISE OF THE FAR-RIGHT

help to explain the emergence of these alternative political groups, including surrogate organizations, but we believe it specifically helps to provide explanation of the growth and spread of divergent political movements that often do not have discernible political leaders. Although blame for the rise in conspiracy theory and other online hate groups is often pointed at algorithmically curated social media feeds and platforms' reluctance to moderate hate speech (Daniels 2018; Bauerlein and Jeffery 2020; Cox 2021; Mak 2020), there are external social and cultural factors that influence these types of behavior and political action as well. This chapter examines the phenomenon of online hate and right-wing political activities of the *netto uyoku* (Japanese online right-wingers) to understand the current situation we are facing in the US, particularly regarding right-wing radicalization that foments and evolves in online communities.

Moreover, our chapter introduces readers to perspectives of East Asian theorists (particularly the concept of the database model as theorized by Azuma Hiroki (Azuma 2009) observing similar phenomena in their own countries to provide a parallel to make sense of the democratic backsliding occurring in the West. We use this chapter as an opportunity to engage in a cultural analysis of similar political issues, spaced decades apart, and attempt to discern what we can learn from these seemingly disparate examples. Although the *netto uyoku* do not neatly align with or even meet the definition of a true surrogate organization per Ziblatt, the way that they navigated early online spaces to create some semblance of a cohesive social movement that had mainstream effects, warrants examination of how these kinds of peripheral social movements can affect party politics and, more importantly, mainstream beliefs and attitudes.

Although Japanese politicians tried to court the *netto uyoku* to gain votes, they failed to do so, and attempting to manage these groups' activities and political ideologies have proven to be futile. We understand the *netto uyoku* not as a hallmark example of a surrogate organization but as a leaderless social movement and believe that it's critical to analyze these movements that then influence surrogate organizations, and eventually political parties. However, it's important to note that the relationships between these groups are not linear, and they are constantly informing one another in a more cyclical fashion. Foregrounding our analysis of the *netto uyoku* against theories of postmodernity and the collapse of the grand narrative, is our contribution to this volume to understand the complex relationship between sociopolitical milieu, political parties, surrogate organizations, and online social movements that do not neatly align with any parties or even their surrogates.

Crisis of Postmodernity

To underscore the importance of social context in understanding surrogate organizations, we begin with a short analysis of the crisis of postmodernity, which has become a hallmark affect experienced and felt by people all over the world. We use affect here according to Ahmed's articulation of the term; namely that *affect* is in reference to the relationship between emotions, language, and bodies; producing social relationships in communities that determines the rhetoric of the nation (Ahmed 2013). Affect is not a psychological state but a cultural practice, and cultural politics via affect create the Other by aligning some bodies and identities within a community while marginalizing others. More simply, emotions aren't just psychological states of being, but gateways into social and material worlds that can create identities, and Ahmed's work asks us to consider the political implications and power of emotion. Johnson (2018) has previously used this framework to make sense of the affective networks that drive conspiracy theory communities and affect is a critical function of understanding the relationship between political ideology, identity, and social contexts.

The erosion of social cohesion and the dismantling of what drove people's understandings of the social and political sphere, in particular the collapse of the grand narratives that held society together, is a critical aspect of the postmodern condition as it exists today. In the West, the grand narratives that held society together came from the Enlightenment, democracy, capitalism, Christianity, Liberalism, Marxism, and modernism (Lyotard 1984).

For the Japanese, the postmodern period was defined by the collapse of high-economic growth, the oil shocks, the waning of the Season of Politics (the student protest movement), and a succession of domestic terrorist attacks beginning with the Asamo-Sanso incident by the United Red Army (Azuma 2009). But the examination of postmodernity was extended by Japanese theorists—namely, that grand narratives were focused specifically on the narratives and worldviews themselves and the influence they had on the process of narrative consumption to give meaning to and make sense of the world. Influenced by Japanese critic Ōtsuka Eiji, Japanese philosopher and theorist Azuma Hiroki (2009) proposes that rather than consuming narratives in a way that creates meaning and purpose in one's life that connects one to a greater whole or community, such as the importance of mythology in the creation of a national identity (Anderson 2006), people consume narratives via a *database model* that privileges *content* over *cohesive narratives*. Similar to Walter Benjamin's argument and lament in the 1930s that stories

150 CONNECTIVE ACTION AND THE RISE OF THE FAR-RIGHT

were being replaced by merely information (Benjamin 1968), Ōtsuka and Azuma extended their analysis of the postmodern condition in Japan by not just looking at the ideological fissures that postmodernity left in its wake but the fundamental changes to how people seek out and consume narratives.

Azuma argued that in an online and connected world, people are no longer seeking out narratives for creating a greater sense of meaning or connecting them to a community, but rather to fulfill an animalistic need to collect, procure, and store away content without any critical engagement (2009). Grand narratives are replaced with thousands, if not millions, of smaller narratives or variations, leaving people constantly grasping and searching for more. Azuma's work focuses specifically on the *otaku* subculture[1] that emerged during Japanese postmodernity, and he argues that otaku consumers, driven by a similar kind of cynicism for institutions as the *netto uyoku*, fixate on manga, anime, and other consumer goods that replaced these grand narratives with the database (2009). Embracing hyperreality[2] and only seeking out meaning through consumption of these massive databases made up of websites, forums, and digital images and videos, the consumption of these objects is animalistic and impulsive.

The database model of consumption is perhaps the most applicable for an unfamiliar audience to critiques of mass consumption under capitalism that burgeoned particularly during the mid-twentieth century and is continuing well into the twenty-first century with fast fashion, breakneck speeds of social media trends, and algorithmically driven mass advertising. To draw a parallel, people are driven to purchase and buy more goods not for the sake of necessity but to fit in with the latest trends, to signal a certain social status, and to communicate their participation within capitalism itself as a method of sensemaking, much how the database model of narrative consumption is focused on content and not the cohesive narrative as a whole. The social and political dynamics that occurred in the 1980s, 1990s, and 2000s (natural disasters, worldwide financial crises, terrorist attacks, to name a few) led to an erosion of trust in institutions, accelerated by the speed at which information can now be exchanged and communities formed, that have never felt

---

[1] "Otaku" is a term used—sometimes derogatorily by outsiders or even by members of the subculture itself—to refer to someone who is an avid consumer of manga (Japanese comic books) and anime series; its Western counterpart would be "nerd" or "geek," but these terms do not capture the social phenomena of *otaku* in the same way.

[2] According to Baudrillard, hyperreality is the inability to distinguish between "the real" from its signifier, essentially a blending of fiction and reality that is so seamless that there appears to be no separation or clear distinction where one begins and ends (Baudrillard 1994).

the constraint of borders or time. In Japan specifically, in the 1990s, the bubble of economic and social progress that the Japanese had flourished under burst, and similar crises occurred all over East Asia in the 1990s and 2000s. These shocks to the seemingly stable system came at the country from all angles—and had significant cultural and societal consequences as a result, which we explicate more in detail in the following sections.

The digitization of the world did not cause, but perhaps accelerated, the search for a new sense of meaning and purpose in life as other seemingly steadfast narratives dissipated. Lyotard wrote in the 1970s (Lyotard 1984) that due to technological innovation, particularly in the areas of communication and mass media, grand narratives that were heralded during the Enlightenment and within Marxist thought would become less relevant as humanity hurtled toward the creation of communities constituted by smaller narratives to make sense of and give meaning to the world (Lyotard 1984). We can certainly see how these predictions played out not just in the West, but how it affected Japanese net culture as well via Azuma's application of the idea of smaller narratives in the formation of the database model. Increasing digitization was followed by significant shifts in how people connected with and used technology (Steinberg 2019). Arguably, Japan and its adoption of the internet paved the way for the platformed internet in the first place, and Japanese net culture—at both a software and hardware level—had a significant role in the creation and formation of the platform internet that we know today (Steinberg 2019).

But what does this have to do with the growth of far-right extremist groups? In considering the role of surrogate organizations in the conservative dilemma framework, we must look to the work of Azuma to make sense of what we see in much of the world in terms of the memes, symbols, and other forms of digital communication that circulate within these surrogate communities and other online social movements, particularly among the far right. Memes, like other kinds of digital images, can be collected, created, and shared by members of these forums, and carry with them a certain level of cultural capital (Nissenbaum and Shifman 2017), much like the *otaku*'s database of *anime* and *manga* characters in digital form. Consumption, then, becomes mostly about collection as a means of achieving some higher sense of meaning, but meaning is never achieved and is instead replaced by endlessly consuming, collecting, and creating more content to contribute to the database—animalistic pleasure replaces that of anything deeper or more stable, and instant gratification with little regard for consequences is the goal (Azuma 2009). Memes, trolling, and swarming are all influenced by this logic, afforded and exacerbated by online forums and in the case of platforms, their algorithmically driven feeds.

But the postmodern society is not only defined by these new consumer logics informed and maintained by databases, but also by its transformation of control. As people go through cyberspace, their personal data are collected simultaneously by multiple sources, and they experience surveillance from their peer networks as well as from corporations (Han 2017). Any deviance from the structural controls that create these rigid environments is punished, either by other users or by the system itself, guaranteeing the homogeneity of users, creating more intolerance of the Other. In the case of the *netto uyoku*, they were fixated on the media coverage of the 2002 World Cup and the growing popularity of the *Hallyu* (Korean Wave, the mass cultural export of Korean music, television series, and films), meshing their hatred for the institution of media with existing xenophobia that already permeated Japanese society in its laws and culture.

Members of these forums who identified as being a part of the *netto uyoku* belonged to a generation of Japanese citizens who had seen significant technological and economic progress in their youth only to have the economy fall apart when they were coming of age, much like how Millennials in the United States have been affected by the 2008 financial crisis. In Japan, the period of economic stagnation that occurred in the early 1990s, and has continued since, is referred to as the *lost decades* (Kim et al. 2010; Takahashi 2013). In early 1992, Japan's bubble economy burst following a period in the late 1980s through 1991 where real estate and stock market prices were greatly inflated. The aftermath of this bubble bursting has continued to have effects today—nearly 30 years later—and despite mild recovery in the 2000s, consumption levels by regular citizens never returned to that of the 1990s (Kim et al. 2010). Along with stagnating wages, the loss of secure jobs with benefits that became the hallmark of the Japanese "salaryman" (stable wages at a good company for life) also eroded alongside growing trends in temp work and the day laborer phenomenon. The corporation as a replacement for a family, in this sense, failed to live up to its promises, and permanent employment has suffered since. As a result of its economic collapse, Japan's power in sectors such as technology and the automotive industry are under threat and have been overtaken by the growth of these industries in other countries, particularly the US, South Korea, and China. Japan's economy, as a result, never fully recovered and is still struggling to this day.

Along with this, Japan experienced a series of cultural and natural disasters that took aim at the already fragile psyche of a nation. In January 1995, the Great Hanshin earthquake (measuring 6.9 on the magnitude scale) struck, killing over 6,000 people in Hyōgo prefecture, concentrated mostly in Kobe. Only a few short months after that, members of the Aum cult unleashed sarin gas on the Tokyo subway in an act of domestic terrorism. In five attacks, the perpetrators released sarin gas (which is an extremely toxic nerve agent used as a chemical weapon), targeting three lines of the Tokyo metro that connected the Japanese parliament in Tokyo during rush hour (Reader 2013). These attacks, along with an attack nine months earlier in the Matsumoto area in 1994, cumulatively harmed around 1,500 people, severely injured many, and killed around 20 or more people (those previously injured at the time of the attack later died). Along with these larger scale disasters, the Kobe child murders in 1997 further created a social crisis, where many Japanese lost faith in institutions, especially their faith in the power of the Japanese economy and Japan as a nation-state as a whole.

It is unsurprising then that in response to these conditions, social phenomena like *hikikomori*,[3] the *netto uyoku*, and *otaku* subcultures started to proliferate, further exacerbated by the internet revolution in Japan and the country's consumer technology industries in the 1990s. Although these are seemingly disparate communities, they're all connected by a similar erosion of trust (and the subsequent postmodern crisis) in institutions and the grand narratives that had long defined Japanese society. To reiterate, the grand narratives in the West were primarily the Enlightenment, Christianity, liberalism, and Marxism. In Japan it's a bit more complicated, mostly because historical transitions in Japan can be better understood from a synchronic standpoint rather than a diachronic one (e.g., premodern, modern, postmodern) (Sawai 2013). Instead, Sawai argues, we should understand Japanese postmodernity to be more of a hybrid-modern, distinguishing itself from the Western postmodern condition (2013).

Although beyond the scope of this chapter, Munesuke Mita introduced labels that defined the social condition of Japanese society: the period of

---

[3] "Hikikomori" is the term used to describe people (mostly men, although women are also afflicted) who suffer from a form of severe social withdrawal, mostly adolescents and young adults who become recluses, not leaving their homes or even bedrooms for months or even years. Observed and named in Japan, cases of hikikomori have increased, with estimates as high as a million currently afflicted with the condition.

154   CONNECTIVE ACTION AND THE RISE OF THE FAR-RIGHT

"Fiction" (mid-1970s to 1990s); the period of the "Ideal" (1945–1960); and the period of the "Dream" (1960 to early 1970s) (Mita 1992). Mita argued that in earlier periods people had little to no doubts about the nature of reality, but the Fiction period was defined by consumerism and hyperinformationalization and the postmodern system of capitalism "that promoted the creation of artificial demand through information" (Sawai 2013, 205). As a result, the communication patterns of young people in the 1990s is characterized by the small "island-universes" they inhabit ("Shimauchu-ka" or nebularization) (Miyadai 1993, 1994, 1995, cited in Sawai 2013). For the Japanese, the grand narrative was focused on the traditional family, the company (as mentioned earlier), Japanese traditional society, and the nation state (Sawai 2013). To put it simply, the age of mass consumerism and identity, being predicated on the acquisition of material goods rather than being formulated by communities, led to a state of hyperindividualism that left people feeling aimless, empty, and wandering, searching for a sense of meaning that would disrupt the "endless everyday" monotony of life (Miyadai 1995).

Miyadai (1995) argued that it was this escape from the endless everyday that the Aum cult offered that attracted so many of its members to participate in the community. Searching for a "true" sense of life, members of the cult were well-educated and had successful careers; joining the cult was an escape. In this same period, the rise of the hikikomori can be understood as being a part of the same social condition that drove people to join the Aum cult—it's not only a loss of trust in these institutions but a rejection of them completely, a mutiny against the expectations of life and withdrawing from it altogether (Saito and Angles 2013). For the *otaku* communities that at their core are defined by consumption, the loss of trust manifests in a constant search for instant gratification rather than a search for a higher meaning and a grounded sense of identity (Azuma 2009). For the *netto uyoku*, a rejection of traditional politics and government, and its affiliated institutions like the media, are some of their defining features. Like the US and Western European far right, it's simultaneously simpler but also more difficult to assess and discern their visible ideologies as they exchange memes, posts, and videos on their forums; but at the core of this networked participation is a shared lack of trust and the constant grasping for meaning, by rejecting a previous sense of reality by embracing a new community.

Japan's Internet Right-Wingers: The *Netto Uyoku*

Long before seedy forums like 4chan and leaderless social movements that defined much of the 2010s and the emergence of QAnon, Japan's cyber nationalists, the *netto uyoku*, were loosely organizing in Japanese internet forums. They have a long and turgid history similar to that of the cyber white supremacists who started gathering online in the mid to late 1990s (Daniels 2009; Fujioka and DeCook 2021). In Japan, however, the roots of a visibly organized *netto uyoku* can be traced back to the 2002 World Cup, jointly hosted by Japan and South Korea (Tsunehira 2016). Although Japanese netizens had previously expressed xenophobic views and hate speech on internet forums, it wasn't until 2002 that there was any cohesion to the views expressed. The 2002 World Cup provided the perfect target for a reactionary ideology comprised of nationalism, mistrust in media, and sense of betrayal and collapse felt by Japanese citizens following the economic, social, and natural disasters in the 1990s as described above. In the case of the *netto uyoku*, the exchange of symbolic resources and connective action that was fostered in early bulletin boards, such as 2Channel,[4] were an essential component for their engagement in surrogate, or to be more concise, alternative politics. These exchanges, and the cultural communities they formed, were the main source of their strength—the forums provided them with the necessary infrastructure to gather anonymously, gain validation for taboo views, and create new identities premised on new symbols and communicative actions (Sakamoto 2011; Kavedžija 2016). Anonymity, a critical component of these forums, allowed the subcultures that formed in them to flourish.

But what's important to note about the *netto uyoku* is that they are mainly an online movement, comprised mostly of men in their forties who live in large urban areas (Tsunehira 2016). Most are also university graduates and have a higher than average median income, negating the stereotypical image

---

[4] It's critical to note that 4chan, the notorious American bulletin board, took its source code from 2Channel. Christopher Poole, 4chan's founder, relied on the early web translator BabelFish to make sense of the code (Fujioka and DeCook 2021). Despite Poole (whose username was "moot" on the forum) including anonymity as a key feature of the 4chan board, he seemingly never quite grasped the significance of why anonymity was important for 2channel and other Japanese forums (Dibbell 2010). Namelessness and anonymity are key features of Japan's internet and part of the allure of these communities for Japanese users, who navigate strict cultural distinctions between public and private life and a separation of selves depending on the sphere and context where interaction occurs; it is notable that Facebook, with its "real name" policy, struggled to succeed in the Japanese market as a result (Dibbell 2010; SoraNews24 2021).

156 CONNECTIVE ACTION AND THE RISE OF THE FAR-RIGHT

of economically dispossessed youth who are seduced into these movements due to frustrations about their economic status who, in turn, blame immigrants for their lack of success (Tsunehira 2016; see also Parker and Blum, this volume). Although similar claims were made in Japan to try and uncover *who* would participate in such a movement, actual demographic data proved the opposite. Similarly, a majority of the participants in the January 6 US Capitol Insurrection were upper-middle-class white Americans who had never been formally associated with any white supremacist group (Pape and Ruby 2021), and the theory that economically disadvantaged people were at higher risk of being drawn into these movements has time and again been proven to be false. This same point is made by Parker and Blum in this volume in their assessment of the motives behind the MAGA movement. This then necessitates us to look toward cultural issues, not just material ones, to understand these movements and organizations.

The creation of 2channel and its founder, Nishimura Hiroyuki, and its Western counterparts 4chan and 8kun (formerly 8chan) are all deeply intertwined, beyond just being the inspiration for these non-Japanese forums that have become synonymous with the "seedy underbelly" of the internet (Fujioka and DeCook 2021). Notably, Nishimura bought 4chan in 2015, and Jim Watkins of the infamous 8kun also owns 2channel. 2channel was founded in 1999 by Nishimura in his dorm room at the University of Arkansas and continues to be particularly popular among the *netto uyoku*, though it has a controversial reputation in Japan. Despite its reputation, the site has a level of influence comparable to that of traditional mass media (particularly in the early to mid-2000s) and continues to attract millions of posts per day. However, despite the forum's popularity among the *netto uyoku*, the ideologies and political imaginings shared by its users never quite translated into offline traditional politics. Although there were a series of marches organized on the forum—targeting the mainstream media corporations that they all loved to hate—the forum has largely failed to materialize actual political candidates embraced and supported by the group.

Two far-right political candidates emerged in the 2000s that attempted to pander to the *netto uyoku* and their growing discontent with the state of Japan and its institutions—but the *netto uyoku*, to put it bluntly, hated them, albeit for different reasons. One of them, Hashimoto Tōru, was a media darling and frequently made appearances on television shows and was generally regarded to be a charismatic leader, propelling him to victory in 2008 as the governor of Osaka Prefecture (Weathers 2014). In 2012, he attempted to enter national politics, establishing a new party, the *Nippon Ishin no Kai* (the Japan Innovation Party), which quickly became Japan's third largest. Despite these gains and his initial popularity, Hashimoto's brand of neoliberal populism quickly fell out of favor in 2013, and 2channel users overwhelmingly rejected Hashimoto despite his populist rhetoric. Namely, they were critical and suspicious of Hashimoto's positive relationship with the mainstream mass media, an institution that the *netto uyoku* held in particularly low regard (Fujioka 2019). Another candidate that seemingly should have been embraced by the *netto uyoku*, Ishihara Shintaro (former governor of Tokyo and a former novelist), was rejected because of his attempts to censor and ban anime and manga (Walker 2011).

But the cyberactivism of the *netto uyoku* doesn't neatly or coherently align with what actually happens in Japanese politics, and the group has not been successful in finding a suitable figurehead or face of the movement that holds actual political power. Despite Ishihara's nationalist views that were used to court the *netto uyoku*, he ultimately supported pro-immigration policies during his time in office that were at odds with the beliefs he espoused previously. Similarly, in 2014, Hashimoto nearly got into an altercation during a televised debate with the leader of the *Zaitokukai*, an ultranationalist and far-right extremist political organization that specifically calls for an end to the alleged privileges extended to Zainichi Koreans (Kaigo 2013).[5] The *Zaiotokukai* and the *netto uyoku*'s ideologies, however, clearly align—they are both racist and xenophobic toward Koreans, particularly Zainichi Koreans, and 2channel was the home of a deeply racist, anti-Korean manga *kenkanryu* ("hating the Korean wave"), which is rife with revisionist history and seeped with the same conspiracy theories that animate the *netto uyoku* (Shibuichi 2015; Fujioka and DeCook 2021). As ideological entrepreneurs (Fujioka and DeCook 2021), the *Zaitokukai* engage in the discourse that delegitimizes more left-leaning news outlets and other media sources through smear campaigns. Similar to their Western counterparts, the *Zaitokukai* and *netto uyoku* want to liberate ordinary Japanese citizens from the mainstream media, believing that the internet would help reveal the truths hidden from the general public. And even though the *netto uyoku* never quite materialized as an offline movement like the movements we see emerging in the West, they and the *Zaitokukai* have had some success: anti-Korean sentiment in Japan has continued to grow and become more

[5] Ethnic Koreans who were born and live in Japan.

158 CONNECTIVE ACTION AND THE RISE OF THE FAR-RIGHT

mainstream in the past 10 years, gaining significant traction very recently (Yoon and Asahina 2021).

Unlike the *netto uyoku*, since 2012 the *Zaitokukai* started moving off online forums where they shared conspiracy theories like Koreans being the cause of economic stagnation in the country, calling them cockroaches and other dehumanizing language, and started engaging in public demonstrations and street protests, including verbally harassing and intimidating Zainichi North Korean children at their schools (Yoon and Asahina 2021). Similar to far-right movements in the West, the *Zaitokukai* have also spread anti-Korean sentiment more broadly in the mainstream through circulating manga like *Kenkanryu* online and through the popular book industry to target older generations who may not be participating in online forums (Yoon and Asahina 2021). The *Asahi* had long been seen as an anti-Japanese newspaper, one that was actively contributing to the decay of traditional Japanese society and culture.

The *Zaitokukai* also took advantage of the worsening trust in Japan's once highly regarded and trusted liberal newspaper, the *Asahi Shimbun*, which was under fire for their coverage of "comfort women" (women and girls forced into sexual slavery by Imperial Japan) (Yoshida 2014). Specifically, the *Asahi Shimbun* retracted all of their articles on comfort women going back decades due to the discovery that a key source used in their articles had lied extensively, ultimately being found to have totally fabricated his accounts (Yoshida 2014). The *Asahi* had previously been targeted by a right-wing group in the 1980s, the *Sakihoutai*, who forced their way into the newspaper's Osaka office and killed one staff writer and severely injured another with a shotgun (Yoon and Asahina 2021). Holding public demonstrations at the *Asahi* office on the same date 30 years later calling for the death of the *Asahi*, the *Zaitokukai* also made it their mission to destroy the life of a journalist who had written on the comfort women issue extensively. Uemera Takashi, as a result of the constant harassment from *Zaitokukai* members, was fired from his position as a lecturer at Hokusei Gakuen University due to constant threats, even circulating a photo of his daughter online with calls to harass her to commit suicide (Yoon and Asahina 2021). He has since left Japan to live in South Korea, according to sources (Yoon and Asahina 2021).

This online to offline trolling behavior that has been introduced as a form of protest movement repertoire is telling. Although there is not enough space in this chapter to give a thorough overview of the long history of anti-Korean sentiment in Japan and the continued political and social dynamics of the two countries, the growing popularity of anti-Korean sentiment since 2012 that fuels the *netto uyoku* and *Zaitokukai*, is indicative of how the far right globally takes advantage of a number of social and technological factors. Alarmingly, some ethnographic accounts suggest that young protestors within these movements did not identify as anti-Korean or even illiberal (Furuichi 2017). Instead, what connected them to those harboring explicit anti-Korean sentiments was that they also hated the mainstream mass media and were attracted to the festival-like atmosphere and collective effervescence of the *Zaitokukai* protests themselves (Furuichi 2017).

As others have noted, the *netto uyoku* created a *matsuri* (festival)-like atmosphere through what outsiders would view as toxic online behavior (Kaigo and Watanabe 2007), giving support to the old cliché that nothing brings people together faster than mutual dislike or hatred. As DeCook (2020) has argued, trolling itself has become a political aesthetic and form of connective action for the far right. Similarly, in Japan these protestors weren't necessarily there for the ideology, but rather to participate in symbolic exchange that coincided with the connective action occurring within online forums (Sakamoto 2011; Furuichi 2017). This raises questions about whether one can engage in practice or action without belief and isn't meant to excuse the presence of these "nonbelievers," but to complicate assumptions about these surrogate organizations and the participants' level of agency.

Although members of these groups and online communities are certainly being driven by the platformized internet, to try and place blame on the internet itself as a main driver of these ideologies removes the agency of those who participate within these communities. The people in these groups are still actively making choices to engage in and be a part of these communities, and mainstream attempts to blame social media alone for the growth in far-right extremism infantilizes the people who participate in these movements. Although surrogate organizations are a useful framework in understanding how parties can appeal to these organizations and how parties can motivate them, the relationship between these surrogate organizations and their respective political parties are becoming more fraught and parties are struggling to control them. Attempts by parties to appeal to online social movements—who explicitly do not align with any specific party—may gain them an advantage in the short term but in the long term can lead to deleterious consequences, as we've seen in the case of the embrace of QAnon by the Republican Party.

160 CONNECTIVE ACTION AND THE RISE OF THE FAR-RIGHT

Into the Storm: What the *Netto Uyoku* Teaches Us About QAnon

Readers of this chapter will quickly make connections between 2channel's culture above to that of 4chan and its related ecosystem. But to blame 2channel for the reactionary movements borne in and outside of 4chan would be to underestimate its influence and significance. This is not the point of this chapter. We are not arguing that views espoused by white supremacists and the *netto uyoku* on these boards are not racist, xenophobic, and dangerous. But to declare that these forums are racist as a whole is too simple—though many of these users certainly are racists. Rather, viewing these platforms through the lens of what the Hong Kong philosopher Hui Yuk (Hui 2017) refers to as the "unhappy consciousness of neoreactionaries," reveals that something larger is occurring—the political and social fatigue of the West manifests in a rejection of the grand narratives (particularly those of the Enlightenment) that for so long created meaning for much of the Western modern world. For the West, the Enlightenment ideals of modernity, progress, liberalism, and French Republican ideals of equality, democracy, and liberty (and their universalization) have failed to live up to their promise (Hui 2017). The postmodern crisis in the West is mirrored by similar crises in the East, with neoliberal globalization connecting them transnationally. Similar themes are common to Western political philosophical discourse (Deneen 2019; Douthat 2020; Vermeule 2020).

As sociologist Kitada Akihiro noted about 2channel, the communicative actions of these cyber nationalists highlight the potential of the medium itself (Kitada 2012). Despite its reputation, the forum provided connection to people who did not ascribe to these ideologies and had a positive impact and even produced a wildly successful television series (Trainman) that was based on a series of posts. Similarly, despite 4chan's reputation, it is the source and home of much of what we know as digital culture—its memes, symbolic forms, and other practices inform much of what constitutes online logics, toxic and otherwise (Nissenbaum and Shifman 2017; Phillips 2019; Simcoe 2012). Thus, the same questions about practice without belief or the strength of these beliefs arise—in the case of Japan, they are longing to be connected with others, and turn to nationalism as their romantic object of fixation (Fujioka 2019; Kitada 2012). The emergence of this mode of cynical romanticism that permeates the psyche of the *netto uyoku* can be tied not just to the decline of the grand narratives that gave society some sense of cohesion (Deneen 2019; Fujioka and DeCook 2021), but the growth of the information and surveillance society itself (Sawai 2013). As disaster abounded around them, Japanese citizens also found themselves navigating a new age of information networks—in just a few short years, internet users went from 9.2% of the population in 1997 to 46.3% in 2001, and the penetration rate for mobile phone usage similarly increased (Sawai 2013; Steinberg 2019).

But it's important to note that the social phenomena being observed by Japanese sociologists and theorists mentioned in this chapter were occurring in the late 1990s and in the early 2000s, including the database model mentioned earlier, long before the introduction of an algorithmically curated social media feed and even before the existence of Facebook, Twitter, and other major social media platforms themselves. In a pessimistic view of the potential of algorithmically curated online space in creating meaningful social change, Korean-German philosopher Han Byung- Chul views communicative action not as a mass or a crowd, but as a swarm (Han 2017). This swarm is fragmented, incapable of forming a conception of "we," and is incapable of formulating a future (i.e., some form of a grand narrative) because of its obsession with the affective present. It reacts solely to affective stimuli, and algorithms create crowds of individuals, "alienated, digital *hikikomori* who do not participate in discourse or constitute a public sphere" (Han 2017, 65). We see this logic manifesting in online movements today, which spillover into offline politics in the West in the form of QAnon-supporting members of Congress, attempts to overthrow the government, and mass murders.

It is easy to dismiss QAnon believers, January 6 insurrectionists, white supremacists, and other far-right groups as "crazy," as being detached from reality. But taking a step back from their espoused ideology and connecting them to larger macrohistorical structures reveals something deeper and more insidious, and platforms are just one piece of a larger, fragmented puzzle in explaining their rise. As others have argued previously, these current movements are driven by whitelash, and the Tea Party that emerged in 2008 was a warning of how politics would shift in the twenty-first century (Parker and Barreto 2013; Carstarphen et al. 2017; Anderson 2017; see also Parker and Blum, this volume). The US and much of Western Europe are ravaged by similar economic, cultural, and natural crises as Japan was rocked by in the 1990s—in the US alone, these events include the terrorist attacks of 9/11, hurricanes, massive wildfires, the 2008 recession, the war in Afghanistan and Iraq, rising student debt and youth unemployment, increasing numbers of mass murders carried out by white supremacists, and a pandemic that has resulted in one million deaths (and counting).

Along with this, there is a continued erosion of trust in institutions from people all along the political spectrum, and the COVID-19 pandemic has fully exposed all the gaping cracks that were barely hidden under the surface of American society. QAnon started off as a 4chan conspiracy in 2017 and spread to reddit but was relegated mostly within the walls of these internet forums and seemed to have died off—but reemerged with a vengeance, spreading to every single corner of the internet, and driving physical violence as well as participation and connection with other extremist movements (Amarasingam and Argentino 2020). Like the *netto uyoku*, QAnon believers fixate on the mainstream media and create their own media in response to their lack of trust in these institutions, using YouTube and other social media platforms to spread their beliefs and attract new members. Their creation and exchange of symbolic resources, ranging from YouTube videos to ephemeral media like Instagram Stories and live-streaming feeds, and massive maps explaining the conspiracy itself, help to solidify a group identity and are forms of connective action (Bleakley 2021; Hannah 2021). The impulse to log on, to gain followers and likes, to witness events live, and to constantly be in the know about what is occurring in these online spaces are emblematic of the database mode of consumption and has reached its logical conclusion.

The vast amounts of data being produced by the world's netizens have created a moderation nightmare, and the extension of the database model of consumption to every corner of the internet has accelerated the ways that capitalism and the platform economy increasingly control every aspect of our lives. The symbols created within these spaces—their constant evolution, co-optation, and remixing included—are placed into their own kind of database and requires a significant level of embeddedness within these communities to navigate. But rather than having dedicated fora to them, in the age of algorithms, algorithms create the databases that these symbols circulate in. And it's because of this massive repertoire of symbolic resources that they are able to sustain and continue their movements even despite attempts by platforms to ban and deplatform them (Frenkel 2020; DeCook 2019).

Although it feels natural to blame the platforms—who are certainly implicated—for failing to control the movement, doing so strips users of their own subjective agency in participating in these communities and in the creation of these resources. They create these databases using and exploiting the platforms' affordances, and actively seek out meaning through them and through their consumption, creating new identities in a society where they no longer see themselves—and these actions are driven by both affect and logic, informed by the crises that have always haunted society. The database consumption model is one way of understanding the process of meaning-making necessary for social life—but is not the only path forward.

Conclusion: The Decaying Fabric

Certainly, in many ways, the *netto uyoku* and the *Zaitokukai* can inform us much about extremist online cultures and are not so much formal precursors to the growing online extremism in the West but are connected by their similar responses to crises, evolving technology, and the influence of an increasingly anomic society informed by the logic of (consumer capitalist) surveillance. Despite a tendency for Western media and academia to point to and blame the East for many of its own ills, an inward look at why and how these movements come about in the West requires a deeper level of introspection. Namely, much of the research on the decay of the American political fabric and American democracy focuses primarily on these issues as they affect, and are affected by, white Americans, to the point that white Americans are even infantilized and turned into sympathetic figures despite their participation in hate movements (Anderson 2017; Baker, Perry, and Whitehead 2020; Embrick et al. 2020; Klein 2017). Although scholars like Putnam lamented the decline of community and social cohesion in works like *Bowling Alone* (2001), arguably the United States has never had social cohesion and has violently shut down civil rights movements, and what we are witnessing today is influenced by decades of strategic political organizing by the right.

This coincides with the overly optimistic claims that the election of Barack Obama indicated a shift into a "post-racial society," but the Black Lives Matter (BLM) movement sprang up during his presidency (Taylor 2016). BLM protests have often been used as fuel for right-wing movements, with many on the right using the protests to fuel their conspiracy theories about a New World Order that is attempting to replace Western civilization and whites as a whole. These conspiracies drove a man to open fire on a racial justice protest in Portland, Oregon, in February 2022 (Reinstein 2022). Despite increasing white supremacist violence, many Americans seem to be in denial about the lack of progress the US has made socially and culturally. As psychologist Michael Kraus (2022) noted, "Many Americans have a hard time recognizing the magnitude and persistence of racial inequality because, psychologically, we resist these truths."

164 CONNECTIVE ACTION AND THE RISE OF THE FAR-RIGHT

Thus, the crisis of (and the longstanding lack of) social cohesion in the US is not anything new—but the white American psyche is deeply affected by larger socioeconomic and political crises that are major contributors to growing extremism, and in turn, these actors lash out at those they deem responsible for the decline of their dominance in a search for power. As Parker and Blum note in this volume, the emergence of the far right is as much about status anxiety as it is anything else. This is not to say that a bad economy is solely responsible for extremism, and that these reactionary movements are desperately trying to maintain their dominance in times of change and cultural transition (Carstarphen et al. 2017; Baker, Perry, and Whitehead 2020). The *netto uyoku* and the more extreme *Zaitokukai* express similar desires to maintain a racially and culturally homogenous Japan, and this desire to hold on to this sense of nationalist identity occurred in tandem with a desire to create a new identity unfettered by the constraints of traditional Japanese culture and institutions.

Although on the surface these simultaneous desires to maintain (racially pure) Japanese identity while resisting the power and control of institutions seem to be at odds with one another, we see a similar duality with these movements in the US and Western Europe. In some way, these contradictions are the point—and more importantly, demonstrate how institutions are no longer a source of identity nor representative of "the people." Rather, consumption and surveillance are the source of subjectivity, online networks provide roads into new identities that promise freedom and liberation from institutions, and in our increasingly digital world, trust is replaced with control (Han 2017). With trust eroded, desire to control these institutions, as well as society and reality in general, becomes a primary driver of political ideology, fueled by the logics of surveillance capitalism that gives the illusion of control over people's consumptive habits (Zuboff 2018). Moreover, online communication that is unconstrained by borders, times, or physical space helps to inform and inspire global right-wing movements that share ideas, resources, and playbooks in usurping traditional politics and institutions (Miller-Idriss 2022; Yoon and Asahina 2021). Paranoia is the natural state of being, conspiracy is the logic that undergirds connection, and figures like Q and Trump become romantic objects, with conspiracy theories like QAnon taking on characteristics typical of mystery games with the deciphering of codes and riddles that participants pore over, taking on qualities typical to that of fandoms (Reinhard et al. 2022).

These affective networks that gamify and encourage the animalistic consumption of information (e.g., the database model) result in rage-fueled outbursts, as we've seen with the increasing number of white supremacist mass shootings in the past 10 years and other forms of political violence (Miller-Idriss 2022). Although in Japan the *netto uyoku* never quite materialized, the *Zaitokukai* have grown in prominence (Yoon and Asahina 2021), and have been deemed a threat to law and order by the Japanese police due to their extreme hate speech. Although members of the *Zaitokukai* have not been implicated in acts of physical violence, they do engage in verbal abuse, intimidation, and harassment, using psychological terror, and encouraging discrimination against Zainichi Koreans (Yoon and Asahina 2021). The *Zaitokukai*, like the *netto uyoku*, are opportunistic, and despite not having success in terms of political party politics, they've influenced mainstream perceptions of Zainichi and other ethnic minorities in Japan. Their influence is not necessarily targeting traditional party politics, but is ideological in nature, and Japanese citizens' views toward Koreans have grown increasingly hostile over the past 10 years (Yoon and Asahina 2021). All over the world, surrogate organizations and digitally constituted movements are no longer informing politics from the periphery and are now a dominant mode of political participation.

To address these ills—and since they are global social problems—there will need to be a collective effort on part of the world's citizens, governments, and stronger regulation of the ever-ballooning tech industry and its oligarchs. The growth of the far right is not a local crisis but a transnational one, and cybernationalists that feel betrayed by their governments and institutions are attempting to forge new sources of meaning, politics, and mechanisms of cultural and political control. But they are attempting to draw legions of similarly disaffected citizens into their ranks and are succeeding in doing so using the bevy of resources made available to them by the platform economy. To extend the conservative dilemma framework and to firmly grasp the role of connective action in the formation of digital surrogate organizations and leaderless social movements as they exist in our current sociotechnical time, we must look to the past and internationally to places like Japan. With its significant role in the formation of the platform economy and the database mode of consumption, it can help us make sense of our current political and social situation while simultaneously paying heed to the external conditions and period of constant global disaster wrought by late-stage capitalism.

References

Ahmed, Sara. 2013. *The Cultural Politics of Emotion*. London: Routledge.
Amarasingam, Amarnath, and Marc-André Argentino. 2020. "The QAnon Conspiracy Theory: A Security Threat in the Making?" Combating Terrorism Center at West Point.

July 31. https://www.ctc.usma.edu/the-qanon-conspiracy-theory-a-security-threat-in-the-making/.

Anderson, Benedict. 2006. *Imagined Communities: Reflections on the Origin and Spread of Nationalism.* 3rd ed. London: Verso Books.

Anderson, Carol. 2017. *White Rage.* Reprint edition. New York: Bloomsbury.

Azuma, Hiroki. 2009. *Otaku: Japan's Database Animals.* Minneapolis: University of Minnesota Press.

Baker, Joseph O., Samuel L. Perry, and Andrew L. Whitehead. 2020. "Keep America Christian (and White): Christian Nationalism, Fear of Ethnoracial Outsiders, and Intention to Vote for Donald Trump in the 2020 Presidential Election." *Sociology of Religion* 81 (3): 272–293.

Baudrillard, Jean. 1994. *Simulacra and Simulation.* Translated by Sheila Faria Glaser. Ann Arbor: University of Michigan Press.

Bauerlein, Monika, and Clara Jeffery. 2020. "Facebook Manipulated the News You See to Appease Republicans, Insiders Say." *Mother Jones* (blog), October 21. https://www.motherjones.com/media/2020/10/facebook-mother-jones/.

Benjamin, Walter. 1968. "The Storyteller: Reflections on the Works of Nikolai Leskov." In Hannah Arendt, ed. *Illuminations*, translated by Harry Zorn (pp. 83–107). New York: Harvard University Press and Harcourt.

Bennett, W. Lance, and Alexandra Segerberg. 2012. "The Logic of Connective Action: Digital Media and the Personalization of Contentious Politics." *Information, Communication & Society.* 15 (5): 739–768.

Bleakley, Paul. 2021. "Panic, Pizza and Mainstreaming the Alt-Right: A Social Media Analysis of Pizzagate and the Rise of the QAnon Conspiracy." *Current Sociology* 71 (3). https://doi.org/10.1177/00113921211034896.

Carstarphen, Meta G., Kathleen E. Welch, Wendy K. Z. Anderson, Davis W. Houck, Mark L. McPhail, David A. Frank, Rachel C. Jackson, et al. 2017. "Rhetoric, Race, and Resentment: Whiteness and the New Days of Rage." *Rhetoric Review* 36 (4): 255–347.

Cox, Kate. 2021. "70% of Top 'Civic' Facebook Groups Are Toxic or Violent, Report Finds." *Ars Technica*, February 1. https://arstechnica.com/tech-policy/2021/02/70-of-top-civic-facebook-groups-are-toxic-or-violent-report-finds/.

Daniels, Jessie. 2009. *Cyber Racism: White Supremacy Online and the New Attack on Civil Rights.* Lanham, MD: Rowman & Littlefield Publishers.

Daniels, Jessie. 2018. "The Algorithmic Rise of the 'Alt-Right.'" *Contexts* 17 (1): 60–65.

DeCook, Julia Rose. 2019. "Curating the Future: The Sustainability Practices of Online Hate Groups." PhD dissertation, Michigan State University.

DeCook, Julia Rose. 2020. "Trust Me, I'm Trolling: Irony and the Alt-Right's Political Aesthetic." *M/C Journal* 23 (3). https://doi.org/10.5204/mcj.1655.

Deneen, Patrick. 2019. *Why Liberalism Failed.* Politics and Culture series. New Haven, CT: Yale University Press.

Dibbell, Julian. 2010. "Radical Opacity." *MIT Technology Review.* https://www.technologyreview.com/2010/08/23/200890/radical-opacity/.

Douthat, Ross. 2020. *The Decadent Society: How We Became the Victims of Our Own Success.* New York: Avid Reader Press/Simon & Schuster.

Embrick, David G., J. Scott Carter, Cameron Lippard, and Bhoomi K. Thakore. 2020. "Capitalism, Racism, and Trumpism: Whitelash and the Politics of Oppression." *Fast Capitalism* 17 (1). https://doi.org/10.32855/fcapital.202001.012.

Frenkel, Sheera. 2020. "QAnon Is Still Spreading on Facebook, Despite a Ban." *New York Times*, December 18. sec. Technology. https://www.nytimes.com/2020/12/18/technology/qanon-is-still-spreading-on-facebook-despite-a-ban.html.

Fujioka, Brett. 2019. "Japan's Cynical Romantics, Precursors to the Alt-Right." *Tablet Magazine*, August 8. https://www.tabletmag.com/sections/news/articles/japans-cynical-romantics.

Fujioka, Brett J., and Julia R. DeCook. 2021. "Digital Cynical Romanticism: Japan's 2channel and the Precursors to Online Extremist Cultures." *Internet Histories* 5 (3–4): 287–303.

Furuichi, Noritoshi. 2017. *The Happy Youth of a Desperate Country.* Chiyoda-ku, Tokyo: Japan Publishing Industry Foundation for Culture.

Gabbatt, Adam. 2020. "Why the DeVos Family's Backing of the Michigan Protests is No Surprise." *The Guardian*, April 26. https://www.theguardian.com/us-news/2020/apr/26/devos-family-michigan-protest-rightwing-donors.

Hacker, Jacob S., and Paul Pierson. 2020. *Let Them Eat Tweets: How the Right Rules in the Age of Extreme Inequality*. New York: Liveright Publishing.

Han, Byung-Chul. 2017. *In the Swarm: Digital Prospects*. Translated by Erik Butler. Cambridge, MA: The MIT Press.

Hannah, Matthew. 2021. "QAnon and the Information Dark Age." *First Monday* 26 (2). https://doi.org/10.5210/fm.v26i2.10868.

Hui, Yuk. 2017. "On the Unhappy Consciousness of Neoreactionaries—Journal #81 April 2017—e-Flux." *E-Flux* 81. https://www.e-flux.com/journal/81/125815/on-the-unhappy-consciousness-of-neoreactionaries/.

Johnson, Jessica. 2018. "The Self-Radicalization of White Men: 'Fake News' and the Affective Networking of Paranoia." *Communication, Culture and Critique* 11 (1): 100–115.

Kaigo, Muneo. 2013. "Internet Aggregators Constructing the Political Right Wing in Japan." *JeDEM: EJournal of EDemocracy and Open Government* 5 (1): 59–79.

Kaigo, Muneo, and Isao Watanabe. 2007. "Ethos in Chaos? Reaction to Video Files Depicting Socially Harmful Images in the Channel 2 Japanese Internet Forum." *Journal of Computer-Mediated Communication* 12 (4): 1248–1268.

Kavedžija, Iza. 2016. "Introduction: Reorienting Hopes." *Contemporary Japan* 28 (1): 1–11.

Kim, YoungGak, Kyoji Fukao, and Tatsuji Makino. 2010. "The Structural Causes of Japan's Two Lost Decades." (Japanese) Research Institute of Economy, Trade and Industry (RIETI).

Kitada, Akihiro. 2012. "Japan's Cynical Nationalism." In Mizuko Ito, Daisuke Okabe, and Izumi Tsuji, eds., *Fandom Unbound: Otaku Culture in a Connected World* (pp. 68–84). New Haven, CT: Yale University Press.

Klein, Ezra. 2017. "Where the New York Times Article on an American Nazi Went Wrong." *Vox*, November 27. https://www.vox.com/policy-and-politics/2017/11/27/16701780/nyt-nazis-trump.

Kraus, Michael. 2022. "Deep Racial Inequality Persists in the U.S.—but Many Americans Don't Want to Believe It." *Los Angeles Times*, February 28. https://www.latimes.com/opinion/story/2022-02-28/american-perception-racial-inequality-u-s.

Lyotard, Jean-Francois. 1984. *The Postmodern Condition: A Report on Knowledge*. Translated by Geoff Bennington, and Brian Massumi. Minneapolis: University of Minnesota Press.

Mak, Aaron. 2020. "How 'Stop the Steal' Exploded on Facebook and Twitter." *Slate*, November 5. https://slate.com/technology/2020/11/how-stop-the-steal-exploded-on-facebook-and-twitter.html.

Miller-Idriss, Cynthia. 2022. *Hate in the Homeland: The New Global Far Right*. Princeton, NJ: Princeton University Press.

Mita, Munesuke. 1992. "Reality, Dream and Fiction—Japan, 1945–90." In xxx, ed., *Social Psychology of Modern Japan*, translated by Stephen Suloway (pp. 515–528). London: Routledge.

Miyadai, Shinji. [1993] 2007. *Sabukarucha Shinwa Kaitai* [The Dissolution of the Myth Sub-Culture]. expanded edn. Tokyo: Chikuma-shobo.

Miyadai, Shinji. [1994] 2006. *Seifuku Shojotachi no Sentaku* [The Choice of the School Uniform Girls]. expanded edn. Tokyo: Asahishinbun-sha.

Miyadai, Shinji. 1995. *Owarinaki Nichijo o Ikiro* [Live the Endless Everyday]. Tokyo: Chikuma-shobo.

Mudde, Cas. 2019. *The Far Right Today*. Cambridge: Polity.

Nissenbaum, Asaf, and Limor Shifman. 2017. "Internet Memes as Contested Cultural Capital: The Case of 4chan's /b/ Board." *New Media & Society* 19 (4): 483–501.

Pape, Robert A., and Kevin Ruby. 2021. "The Capitol Rioters Aren't Like Other Extremists." *The Atlantic*, February 2. https://www.theatlantic.com/ideas/archive/2021/02/the-capitol-rioters-arent-like-other-extremists/617895/.

Parker, Christopher S., and Matt A. Barreto. 2013. *Change they Can't Believe in: The Tea Party and Reactionary Politics in America*. Illustrated edition. Princeton, NJ: Princeton University Press.

Phillips, Whitney. 2019. "It Wasn't Just the Trolls: Early Internet Culture, 'Fun,' and the Fires of Exclusionary Laughter." *Social Media+ Society* 5 (3): 2056305119849493.

Putnam, Robert D. 2001. *Bowling Alone: The Collapse and Revival of American Community*. London: Touchstone Books.

Reader, Ian. 2013. *Religious Violence in Contemporary Japan: The Case of Aum Shinrikyo*. London: Routledge.

Reinhard, CarrieLynn D., David Stanley, and Linda Howell. 2022. "Fans of Q: The Stakes of QAnon's Functioning as Political Fandom." *American Behavioral Scientist* 66 (8): 1152–1172.

Reinstein, Julia. 2022. "A 60-Year-Old Woman Was Killed After A Man Who Reportedly Had Radical Right-Wing Views Shot At Anti-Racist Protesters." *BuzzFeed*, February 22. https://www.buzzfeednews.com/article/juliareinstein/portland-protest-shooter-radical-victim.

Saito, Tamaki, and Jeffrey Angles. 2013. *Hikikomori: Adolescence without End*. Chicago: University of Minnesota Press.

Sakamoto, Rumi. 2011. "'Koreans, Go Home!' Internet Nationalism in Contemporary Japan as a Digitally Mediated Subculture." *Asia-Pacific Journal* 9 (10): 1–21.

Sawai, Atsushi. 2013. "Postmodernity." In Anthony Elliott, Masataka Katagiri, and Atsushi Sawai, eds., *Routledge Companion to Contemporary Japanese Social Theory: From Individualization to Globalization in Japan Today* (pp. 200–220). London: Routledge.

Shibuichi, Daiki. 2015. "Zaitokukai and the Problem with Hate Groups in Japan." *Asian Survey* 5 (4): 715–738.

Simcoe, Luke. 2012. "The Internet Is Serious Business: 4chan's/b/Board and the Lulz as Alternative Political Discourse on the Internet." PhD dissertation, Ryerson University.

SoraNews24. 2021. "Japan One of Only Two Countries Where Twitter Beats Facebook in Social Media Market Share." *Japan Today*, January 10. https://japantoday.com/category/tech/japan-one-of-only-two-countries-where-twitter-beats-facebook-in-social-media-market-share-1.

Steinberg, Marc. 2019. *The Platform Economy: How Japan Transformed the Consumer Internet*. Minneapolis: University of Minnesota Press.

Stern, Alexandra Minna. 2019. *Proud Boys and the White Ethnostate: How the Alt-Right Is Warping the American Imagination*. Boston: Beacon Press.

Takahashi, Wataru. 2013. "Japanese Monetary Policy: Experience from the Lost Decades." *International Journal of Business* 18 (4): 287.

Taylor, Keeanga-Yamahtta. 2016. "Why Is the Black Lives Matter Movement Happening Now?" *Los Angeles Times*, July 28. https://www.latimes.com/opinion/op-ed/la-oe-taylor-blm-obama-20160726-snap-story.html.

Tsunehira, Furuya. 2016. "The Roots and Realities of Japan's Cyber-Nationalism." *Nippon*, January 21. https://www.nippon.com/en/currents/d00208/.

Vermeule, Adrian. 2020. "Beyond Originalism." *The Atlantic*, March 31. https://www.theatlantic.com/ideas/archive/2020/03/common-good-constitutionalism/609037/.

Walker, Lee Jay. 2011. "Ishihara Adamant on Manga Censorship Ordinance." *Japan Today*, June 20. https://japantoday.com/category/features/opinions/ishihara-adamant-on-manga-censorship-ordinance.

Weathers, Charles. 2014. "Reformer or Destroyer? Hashimoto Tōru and Populist Neoliberal Politics in Japan." *Social Science Japan Journal* 17 (1): 77–96.

Yoon, Sharon J., and Yuki Asahina. 2021. "The Rise and Fall of Japan's New Far Right: How Anti-Korean Discourses Went Mainstream." *Politics & Society* 49 (3): 363–402.

Yoshida, Reiji. 2014. "Asahi Shimbun Admits Errors in Past 'comfort Women' Stories." *Japan Times*, August 5. https://www.japantimes.co.jp/news/2014/08/05/national/politics-diplomacy/asahi-shimbun-admits-errors-in-past-comfort-women-stories/.

Ziblatt, Daniel. 2017. *Conservative Parties and the Birth of Democracy*. New York: Cambridge University Press.

Zuboff, Shoshana. 2018. *The Age of Surveillance Capitalism: The Fight for a Human Future at the New Frontier of Power*. New York: PublicAffairs.

Chapter 7

Advocates and Authoritarians

Surrogate Management and Asymmetric Party Development in American Politics

Adam Hilton

Introduction

Political parties, it is often claimed, play a critical role in supporting the development, consolidation, and stability of modern democracy. Schattschneider's (1942) famous claim that parties created democracy, and that democracy is unthinkable without parties continues to receive routine endorsement today. But while parties may help to make democracy, they can evidently help break it too. In his study of early European democratization, Daniel Ziblatt (2017) argues that the emergence and consolidation of modern democracy hinged on how conservative parties negotiated the transition of mass enfranchisement and institutional change while also continuing to defend the wealth, power, and privilege of old-regime elites. Those that negotiated this shifting terrain well, as in Britain, democratized. Those that did not or could not, like Germany, ended up rejecting democracy. The difference, Ziblatt holds, depended on *the kinds of parties* that conservatives built. In countries where they mobilized ahead of mass suffrage and the rise of competitor socialist parties, conservatives built strong parties— geographically dispersed and highly professionalized branch organizations. In countries where they were late to the game, conservatives built weak parties that lacked clear and professionalized lines of authority or a local presence in civil society, and came to depend on outside interest groups to perform party functions, such as electoral mobilization (Ziblatt 2017, 37). The latter "contracting out" model compromised party leaders' autonomy and their ability to control the agenda, ceding authority to party surrogates, who in some cases came to dominate and push conservatives away from

Adam Hilton, *Advocates and Authoritarians*. In: *Connective Action and the Rise of the Far-Right*. Edited by: Steven Livingston and Michael Miller, Oxford University Press. © Oxford University Press (2025).
DOI: 10.1093/oso/9780197794937.003.0007

any pragmatic accommodation with modern democratizing pressures and toward far-right reaction instead.

Jacob Hacker and Paul Pierson (2020) have usefully applied this conservative dilemma framework to make sense of modern Republicans' plutocratic populism. In a Faustian bargain to remain competitive in democratic elections, GOP leaders have allied their party with reactionary social conservatives, right-wing media organizations, and wealthy business elites. These surrogates have promoted a public-facing agenda centered on crosscutting cultural and social issues while relentlessly pursuing a policy agenda to deregulate business and cut taxes for the wealthy—essentially using "white identity to defend wealth inequality" (Hacker and Pierson 2020, 4). Like the weak conservative parties of nineteenth- and early twentieth-century Europe, Republicans have become subjugated by their own surrogates, effectively having lost control of their party to the illiberal, far-right forces they have helped conjure up.

While the conservative dilemma framework orients us toward new ways of thinking about large-scale processes like democratization and serves to alert us to the ominous signs of democratic backsliding in the present (Bermeo 2016; Levitsky and Ziblatt 2018), this stream of research also has the potential to help us rethink existing ideas about political parties as such. Specifically, if the relationship between parties and surrogates can make or break democracy, how should we understand the nature and dynamics of this relationship? What is the proper place of party surrogates in party theory? What strategies are available to parties to manage this relationship, and what historical-institutional factors condition the viability of those strategies?

The absence of clear answers to these questions is perhaps most evident in the puzzle of modern polarization. The literature on American party politics widely recognizes the asymmetrical character of the modern era: Republicans have shifted dramatically to the right while Democrats have moved only modestly to the left (Grossmann and Hopkins 2016; Mann and Ornstein 2016; McCarty et al. 2016). Yet researchers have also documented that both Republicans and Democrats possess extensive connections with organized party surrogates at the grassroots and netroots levels, most of which strongly advocate off-median preferences (Karpf 2012; Kreiss 2012; Layman et al. 2010; Rosenfeld 2018). If this is the case, why does the pressure exerted by the surrogacy universe affect the Republicans and Democrats so differently?

In this chapter I argue that the asymmetry of surrogate influence on the Democrats and Republicans—pushing the former slightly to the left while pushing the latter far to the right—is the result of the unique and divergent developmental paths the parties have travelled for decades, specifically regarding their relationships with social movement organizations and interest group networks as surrogate organizations of the predigital age. Democrats' long-standing associations with social movement and interest group advocates, stretching back to the 1930s, entrenched an early pattern of "contracting out," which in turn disincentivized party leaders from making sustained investments in the formal party organization, hollowing out its institutional capacities (Schlozman and Rosenfeld 2019; see also Mair 2013). When labor unions were strong, reliable surrogates, Democrats refashioned their agenda and identity to curry their electoral support (Farhang and Katznelson 2005). Later, when civil rights groups, women's organizations, LGBTQ advocates, and megadonor consortia came on the scene (and unions declined), Democrats shifted to cater to these groups and access their resources, networks, and activists to help them win elections. The outcome of this historical process is a configuration of party authority I have called an *advocacy party order* (Hilton 2021), in which party leaders manage the competing demands of the surrogates on which they depend for electoral assistance and popular legitimacy while attempting to keep them at arm's length, ceding as little agenda control as possible.

By contrast, Republicans' relatively belated linkage with mass-mobilizing surrogates in the 1980s and their consequent investments in party-building as an alternative strategy laid the groundwork for a potent and potentially dangerous mixture: an *authoritarian party order* that combines robust party organization and presidential domination on the one hand with mass-mobilized surrogate pressure on the other. In this configuration, surrogates not only bombard the party leadership with their demands; they have penetrated deeply into the party apparatus itself, making boundary maintenance a pernicious problem for the GOP but not for the Democrats.

To be clear, this is not to suggest that Republicans had *no* significant surrogates before the 1980s. On the contrary, the GOP had longstanding ties to the business community stretching back to the late nineteenth century. In the postwar period, Republicans found additional surrogates among college campus activists in Young Americans for Freedom, highbrow intellectuals at the *National Review*, social traditionalists in the nascent Christian right, and grassroots anticommunists in suburban communities across the

US—all of whom played major roles in shaping the identity and the trajectory of the GOP over time (Andrew 1997; McGirr 2001; Nash 1976; Williams 2010). However, if the disastrous 1964 presidential candidacy of the New Right's adopted champion Barry Goldwater proved anything, it was that though these surrogates could muster a successful insurgent campaign, they were not yet close to delivering the majorities necessary to challenge the Democrats' nearly continuous control of Congress and moderate Republicans' success at winning the presidency (Perlstein 2001). That goal would continue to elude the GOP until the late twentieth century, when Republican surrogates—old and new—became more adept at effectively mobilizing masses of voters to bring the party into electoral parity with the Democrats.

Thus, while digital and traditional brick-and-mortar surrogates apply their polarizing pressure on both parties today, their relative receptivity to such pressure is an outcome that has been decades in the making. However, unlike Ziblatt's attribution of surrogate containment to party strength (2017, 38), I find an association between Republican organizational strength and surrogate dominance. Ironically, while the hollowness of the Democrats' organization is often a point of criticism, it may prove to be an asset in resisting surrogate control, if not their influence.

The rest of the chapter elaborates these claims. First, in a brief review of the literature, I show that despite recent advances, existing party research has not sufficiently theorized party-surrogate relations, even though the former has become ubiquitous in modern democracies. I then elaborate an alternative framework that places the contentious relations between politicians and surrogate groups at the center of party politics. Using this "contentious orders" framework, I then trace the developmental paths of the Republicans' and Democrats' distinctive party orders, showing how their variable relations with outside surrogates affected their institutional development. Finally, to conclude, I take a step back to briefly consider the extent to which parties' inexorable relations with surrogates should prompt us to rethink our assumptions about what makes a strong party and whether parties should be positively associated with democratic stability.

The Place of Party Surrogates in Party Research

Among its illuminating insights, the conservative dilemma exposes a lacuna in the subfield of American party politics; namely, the place and role of party surrogates. The traditional school of party research, stemming from the work of Anthony Downs (1957), conceives of parties as teams of ambitious officeholders (Aldrich 2011; Schlesinger 1994). While some scholars leave space for party activists or surrogate groups to play a role in shaping partisan strategy (Aldrich 2011; Carmines and Stimson 1989), it is officeholders who are clearly in the driver's seat. More recently, the political scientists collectively known as the UCLA School have bent the stick far in the opposite direction. For them, parties are long coalitions of intense policy-demanding groups who coordinate around nominations to install a loyal friend in office (Bawn et al. 2012; Cohen et al. 2008). From their perspective, it is surrogates that constitute the core of the party; politicians are merely their agents (but see Karol 2009).

Neither of these approaches is entirely satisfactory in helping to think systematically about the place of party surrogates in party theory, nor in explaining the apparent asymmetrical character of surrogate influence on the two American parties today. The traditional, politician-centered school nearly excludes surrogates from the picture (except insofar as they enter into party elites' strategic considerations), while the group-centered alternative obscures any meaningful distinction between surrogates and parties altogether. The problem stems in part from the functionalist assumptions underpinning both approaches, each of which conceive of parties as solutions to collective action problems faced by their principals, whether they are politicians in government or groups in society (see Galvin 2016). Functionalism of this kind obscures the power dynamics inherent in political institutions (Moe 2005) and unduly circumscribes analysis of how party politicians manage the demands placed on them by the party surrogates they depend on. Although these politician- and group-centered approaches differ in obvious ways, both understand parties as instruments that serve the purposes of their creators, obscuring the reality that parties are durable institutions which distribute power in unequal ways across a range of stakeholders, problematizing the assumption that either politicians or groups exercise functional control over them (see Schlozman and Rosenfeld 2017).

Parties and Surrogates in a Contentious Orders Framework

To better understand the relationship between parties and surrogates, a new approach is needed. Drawing on previous work (Hejny and Hilton 2021, 2025; Hilton 2019, 2021), this chapter uses an alternative theoretical framework that places the contentious relations between politicians and surrogate groups at the center of the analysis.

174 CONNECTIVE ACTION AND THE RISE OF THE FAR-RIGHT

In the modern democratic polity, parties are mediating institutions, meaning they straddle the line separating the state from civil society. This gives parties a Janus-like quality. On the one hand, in civil society, parties are mobilizational vehicles that articulate, aggregate, and integrate public preferences during electoral contestation. On the other hand, they are agents of governance and administration and make the machinery of state work. This fundamentally two-faced character is what makes representative democracy work, of course: parties are the collective actors necessary to translate public preferences into coherent public policy and hold officeholders accountable for their performance in office. Yet it also helps illuminate the inadequacy of defining parties as *either* teams of politicians or coalitions of policy-demanding groups, as most of the literature tends to do. Depending on which way you look at them, parties can legitimately appear as both.

But in bridging the state-society divide and bringing politicians and groups together, parties also create a host of principal-agent problems (Schlozman and Rosenfeld 2017). Long recognized as the tension between trustee and delegate forms of representation (Pitkin 1967), parties are subject to rival claims of authority by groups and politicians.[1] On the one hand, society-based actors such as interest groups, advocacy networks, donor consortia, movement activists, and intellectuals can and do lay claim to rightfully "steer the party ship" (Fishkin and Gerken 2014, 199). It is their work in turning out voters, channeling resources, and granting the party legitimacy that ultimately powers the party, helps it win elections, and gives it the authority to govern. On the other hand, politicians in government also lay claim to govern parties. For them, the party is a "service provider" to help coordinate the law-making process and assist them in their bid for reelection by defining a distinctive party brand and facilitating legislative logrolls (Aldrich 2011; Cox and McCubbins 2005, 2007). Parties are thus host to rival and discordant claims of authority from politicians in government and surrogate groups in society, each of which bring to party politics a distinct set of interests, expectations, and temporal horizons, locking them into relations of

---

[1] The politician–group binary may be disaggregated to include important intermediaries found between and adjacent to these two sets of actors. A more elaborate theoretical account could include the specific but differentiated party roles occupied by party officials (Heersink 2018), public intellectuals (Noel 2013), media outlets (Hemmer 2016; Peck 2019), political consultants (Sheingate 2016), primary voters, and others still. However, while this would add greater sophistication and nuance to the model, most of these finer gradations would still fall on one side or the other of the politician-group binary. Thus, for the purposes of this chapter, the simple, barebones model serves as a sufficient heuristic.

contention with one another (Heaney and Rojas 2015; McAdam and Kloos 2014; McAdam and Tarrow 2010).

Although these dynamics of contention are inscribed in the logic of what parties are as intermediary institutions, they do not render successful coalitions impossible. On the contrary, officeholders and groups need each other and regularly ally as means to their respective ends (Krimmel 2017; Milkis and Tichenor 2019; Schlozman 2015; Tarrow 2021). Without access to politicians and policymakers, groups seeking major political change are unlikely to be able to achieve their goals. Politicians, in turn, need the resources that party surrogates are well positioned to supply: namely votes, money, information, networks, audiences, endorsements, legitimacy, and volunteer labor (Skinner 2007). While electoral success remains the modus operandi of parties, managing these endemic relations of intraparty contention is the unavoidable means to that end.

The need to manage this endemic contentiousness presents an opportunity for political entrepreneurs to construct and maintain *party orders*—durable institutional and ideational arrangements that can contain intraparty contention, win elections, and govern. These entrepreneurs—whether formal or informal party leaders, factional operators, surrogate group spokespersons, or movement intellectuals—seek to manipulate and maintain favorable institutional arrangements, adopt or articulate coherent public philosophies, develop a shared issue agenda, and define a distinctive party identity, all with the purpose of facilitating an operational degree of cohesion and constraint across the party (see Hejny and Hilton 2022). While *order* has been a term used in the past to describe a historically specific configuration of interests and ideology at the regime level (Fraser and Gerstle 1989; Gerstle 2022; Plotke 1996; Polsky 2012; Skowronek 1997), it must be recognized that parties are themselves temporally ordered, hierarchically differentiated coalitions that cut across institutional venues and generate and disseminate distinctive public philosophies (Lewis 2019). Party orders structure intraparty politics by defining the site and character of party authority, conveying expectations of how individuals and factions ought to behave, and promoting particular types of candidates and campaigns while discouraging or dismissing others (see Klinghard 2010).

The construction of order by entrepreneurial party actors is an ongoing, open-ended project aimed at restraining the inherent forces of intraparty contention and steering the institutional agency of the party as a cohesive coalition. But the term should not be construed as necessarily implying

176 CONNECTIVE ACTION AND THE RISE OF THE FAR-RIGHT

top-down or centralized forms of party authority. On the contrary, decentralization or localized authority is itself a distinctive type of party order, as when the leaders of the mid- to late-nineteenth century "party period" lodged institutional authority at the state and local levels to inhibit the potential for nationalized parties and presidential leadership (Klinghard 2010; Schattschneider 1942). Party orders should also not be interpreted to imply the imposition of an ideal model or preconceived blueprint on a party coalition. Rather, orders are mostly pragmatic constructions patched together by an ensemble of entrepreneurial leaders and a much larger group of followers, all of whom possess a mix of motives for going along on the path of least resistance to access the benefits of office, patronage, or policy influence.

Still, party orders are unlikely to be harmonious coalitions (cf. Cohen et al. 2008). As distinct arrangements of political power, party orders always advantage some individuals and groups more than others. These "junior members" of the coalition may find their ideological preferences frustrated, their signature issues marginalized, or their demands addressed with lip service. Given the constraints of the American party system, however, aggrieved interests have few realistic options of exit (Hirschman 1970). A party order, then, while beneficial to many, also provides incentives for continual intraparty agitation. Indeed, while party orders are constructed and maintained to contain contention by defining a shared "idea of party" (Klinghard 2010), they are likely to inspire efforts to *reorder* the party should the opportunity present itself.

In sum, a contentious orders framework presents an alternative to the two prevailing views of parties. Rather than seeing parties as *either* creatures of politicians or groups, parties necessarily encompass both, neither of which should be assumed to be subordinate to the other. On the contrary, parties' intermediary role between state and society creates an inescapable ambiguity about the precise location of party authority, setting both society-based surrogates and state-based politicians in contention with one another. From this perspective, the construction of a durable partisan order must be seen as a contingent political outcome, one that depends partly on the ability of party leaders, factions, and their allied surrogates to construct and maintain a workable coalition, and partly on the dynamics of the larger party and political system in which they are embedded.

While this framework offers a new way of thinking about parties and surrogates in the United States, its real value lies in its ability to explain what other frameworks overlook or obscure. Though many scholars have noted the asymmetric character of American polarization, few have offered compelling explanations that resist overemphasizing the contingency of proximate causes or the retreat into timeless generalities of partisan differences (e.g., Grossmann and Hopkins 2016; Mann and Ornstein 2016). The following two sections provide brief historical sketches that trace the asymmetric patterns of party development since the New Deal period, shaped in large part by the Democrats' and Republicans' variable relations with surrogate groups.

The Republicans' Authoritarian Party Order and the Problem of Boundary Maintenance

In contrast to the relative continuity of the Democrats' advocacy party order over recent decades (see below), the Republican side of the story offers a more perplexing mix of continuity and change, unfolding in multiple phases, each of which did not inexorably lead to the next nor was anticipated by its central architects. Republicans have gradually constructed, and recently consolidated, a new *authoritarian party order*: an organizationally robust party apparatus that has married a long tradition of presidential domination to an ideologically reactionary and increasingly illiberal coalition of surrogates. Having for decades nurtured populist distrust of political elites (Fried and Harris 2021), employed dog-whistle forms of race-baiting (López 2014), and honed an increasingly sophisticated grievance-based media empire as a counterestablishment to the New Deal state (Hemmer 2016, 2022), the conservative party order consolidated under Ronald Reagan and, lasting until the end of George W. Bush's presidency, incubated within itself the authoritarian order that almost irresistibly supplanted it with the rise of Donald Trump. As such, though cognizant of the role that more recent events and novel actors have played in this story, a contentious orders perspective contextualizes these factors within the long-run trajectory of Republican Party change. Such a perspective helps to account for the outsized importance some of these events, groups, and individuals have assumed, while avoiding the allure of myopic or idiosyncratic explanations.

The GOP travelled to the present on a fundamentally different and divergent developmental path than did the Democrats. While the latter benefited early on from the support of mass-mobilizing surrogates and large, durable majorities in the electorate, the Republican path was marked by the relative absence of any comparable mass-level surrogates prior to the reemergence of the Christian right in the late 1970s. Republican presidents and party leaders spent the postwar period convinced of the party's seemingly intractable minority status, even during periods when they controlled the White House (Galvin 2010). In response, while drawing on the largesse of their deep-pocketed surrogates in the business community, Republican presidents and national committee chairs routinely made forward-looking institutional investments in the nuts-and-bolts of party-building activity, beginning under Dwight Eisenhower in the early 1950s and persisting through the Trump era. Unlike the Democrats, who felt self-assured of their status as the natural majority party and made no similar investments in party-building, the GOP expanded its organizational reach into state and local politics, especially in the South, where the party had been looking to revive its fortunes for decades (Heersink and Jenkins 2020). Across the country, the party invested in campaign service provisioning to help recruit high-quality candidates, deepen the Republican bench, and enhance the technical skills of their operations in raising campaign finance and mobilizing voters (Galvin 2010; Klinkner 1994).

While those investments were initially aimed at broadening the appeal of moderate Republicanism in the Eisenhower mold, the party-building project eventually intersected with the growing power and scope of the Christian right, especially in the Sunbelt, during the post–civil rights phase of America's racial realignment (Conley 2013; Lowndes 2008; Schickler 2016). While the Christian right was itself nothing new in American politics (see Williams 2010), its reemergence as a mass-mobilized social movement in the late 1970s held out the potential to deliver to the GOP precisely the form of mass-level surrogate support the party had so severely lacked in earlier years (Baylor 2018; Schlozman 2015). This coincided with the New Right's takeover of the mass-membership National Rifle Association in 1977 (Lacombe 2021) and the subsequent expansion of the conservative media ecosystem from its traditional talk radio and newsprint outlets to cable news and, later, the internet (Hemmer 2016, 2022).

By the Reagan presidency, a new and distinct configuration of party authority had taken shape. As the Democrats' New Deal party order collapsed (see below), a conservative coalition centered around the fusion of free markets, traditional, religious values, and an aggressive foreign policy displaced the moderate Republicans from the party leadership. They were flanked by policymaking think tanks such as the American Enterprise Institute and neoconservative outlets like the *Weekly Standard*. At the grassroots level, the coalition peeled off disaffected white working-class Democrats and combined them with evangelical voters, especially in the South, motivated to vote Republican by their pastors and favorite tele-vangelists who disseminated crosscutting culture-war talking points. After decades spent agitating from the sidelines, a new "conservative establish-ment" had come together and over the next generation recreated the GOP in its image (Continetti 2022).

However, as was the case with the nascent New Right and the moderate GOP old guard during the postwar years, contention continued to simmer between politicians and surrogate groups inside the conservative party order across the turn of the millennium. Foreign policy hawks, initially hailed as the West triumphed over the Soviet Union, discredited themselves by vastly overreaching in their imperial bid to remake the Middle East in an unending War on Terror. Advocates of laisse-faire economics suffered a lasting ideo-logical wound in the financial crisis that led to the Great Recession. And the social and religious conservatives who felt they had found a righteous ally in the "compassionate conservative," born-again president of George W. Bush failed to see their surrogacy rewarded with tangible policy break-throughs, such as constitutional amendments banning abortion or same-sex marriage. In fact, throughout the long Reagan era (1980–2008), Republi-can Party leaders faced vocal hostility from their right flank, which became increasingly angry, impatient, and distrustful—sentiments that swelled the audiences for populist voices on talk radio, cable news, and eventually social media (Hemmer 2022).

The Tea Party mobilization in response to the Obama presidency marked a clear turning point in the Republican Party order. For all its vitriol directed at the nation's first Black president, the populist uprising focused its tactics and strategy around disciplining Republican officeholders deemed insuffi-ciently conservative. In many states, with the help of the libertarian billion-aire Koch brothers, Tea Party activists took control of local party organiza-tions (as their evangelical counterparts had in places such as Iowa and South Carolina years earlier), or, where this proved impossible, they constructed rival "shadow party organizations" to outflank recalcitrant GOP officials (Blum 2020). Tea Partiers eventually displaced many Republican incum-bents from office at the state and national levels, while those that remained altered their behavior and rhetoric to preempt a primary challenge, swelling the overall influence of the new Tea Party faction (Gervais and Morris 2018; Skocpol and Williamson 2012).

This combination of robust party organization and an army of populist party surrogates has also been coupled to an immensely strong pattern of presidential domination, stretching back to the Eisenhower years. As Galvin

(2020) argues, this paved the way for the domineering party leadership of Donald Trump, who deviated from this tradition in degree only: his personalization of the party and demand for total loyalty reached new heights and took a public form rare in the annals of Republican Party politics. Indeed, the Republican National Committee's remarkable decision to not issue a party platform ahead of the 2020 election—itself a novel departure in modern American political history—spoke to the nearly complete concentration of party authority in the figure of the party leader himself.

This unique configuration—robust party organization, mass-level surrogate mobilization, and presidential domination—constitutes a party order fundamentally different from that of the Democrats. Where Democratic Party hollowness was a result of and limit on surrogate influence, Republican Party robustness has provided surrogates with a greater opportunity to exert leverage over officeholders. This fundamental distinction has been most evident in the aftermath of the dramatic events surrounding the January 6, 2021 insurrection at the US Capitol. Despite Trump's unprecedented effort to disrupt the peaceful transfer of power, perhaps the most impressive feature of the fallout was the near total degree of constraint on Republican partisans to challenge and discredit his authority. In the days and weeks following the attack, the few high-profile repudiations issued from the congressional leadership were quickly walked back. The 10 House Republicans who crossed the aisle to vote for Trump's second impeachment were met with swift punishment: stripped of their leadership responsibilities and subject to formal censures and official condemnations from state and national party organizations and threatened by the promise of primary challenges in 2022 (Fandos and Martin 2021). Indeed, at the same time as congressional Republicans were briefly flirting with the idea of "moving beyond Trump" in the wake of the deadly attack (Martin and Burns 2021), national, state, and local party officials continued to openly declare their "almost-religious" level commitment to the former president (Lerer and Epstein 2021; Martin 2021).

Although this level of devotion to the party leader is an amplification of past trends, the new Republican Party order is authoritarian in nature for reasons beyond the personal influence of Trump; namely, the political goals motivating surrogates themselves and the tactics they are willing to employ to achieve them. In recent years, as these surrogates have assisted Republicans in dominating most state governments, achieving near-parity with Democrats at the national level and gaining supermajority control of the Supreme Court, their demands for policy, ideological patronage, and identity recognition have escalated dramatically. Not only have some long-shot policy victories (e.g., overturning *Roe*) now been achieved, but demographic, cultural, and electoral trends portend a limited window of opportunity for success (at least within the parameters of majoritarian democracy). This reinforces an increasingly desperate—often apocalyptic—politics of "white protectionism" in the face of perceived status threats that fuel conspiratorial and racist fears behind a looming "great replacement" (Blake 2021; Mutz 2018; Parker and Blum, this volume; Smith and King 2021; Thompson, this volume). This has manifested itself in the increasing prominence of "menace" and violent rhetoric in Republican discourse (Lerer and Herndon 2021), typically directed at Democrats—especially Democratic women of color (Arora 2021; Wu and Caygle 2021)—but also GOP copartisans deemed to be "traitors" to the party or "RINOS" (Republicans In Name Only) (Alemany et al. 2021).

This impressive capacity to keep intraparty contention contained, despite the turbulence of the Trump and early post-Trump years, belies a stream of journalistic and academic commentary that characterizes the contemporary GOP as mired in an ongoing "identity crisis" (Sides et al. 2018), in the midst of a "civil war" (Alberta 2019), or on the verge of a full-scale "crackup" (Popkin 2021). From a contentious orders perspective, the Republicans' authoritarian party order has proven remarkably (and disturbingly) resilient. While Trump's personal future status in the party is uncertain at this moment, his potential successors appear to be casting themselves in his mold (Mazzei 2021), and nearly 200 victorious GOP candidates in the 2022 midterm elections endorsed his Big Lie that the 2020 election was stolen (Yourish et al. 2022). Rather than being in doubt, the future of the Republican Party is all too clear. That the party is *not* mired in crisis is precisely the reason that it poses such a threat to American democracy.

The Democrats' Advocacy Party Order and the Limits of Surrogate Influence

Over the past several decades, the Democrats have consolidated and maintained a party order centered around a constellation of social movement and interest group advocates (Hilton 2019, 2021). On the one hand, the party compensates for its institutional hollowness through an alliance with a broad and interconnected network of surrogates, who not only contribute their considerable electoral support in exchange for policy demands and ideological patronage, but have come to define the very identity of the party itself, lending the Democrats a greater degree of legitimacy than US public opinion general reserves for parties (see Rosenblum 2008). On the other hand, politicians and party leaders manage surrogate demands through the practice of advocacy politics—an inherently ambiguous form of representation that lacks formal mechanisms of authorization and accountability. As a distinctive political style, advocacy enables Democratic politicians to attempt to reconcile the inevitable disjuncture between their promissory commitments to their surrogates and their inability or unwillingness to deliver on those expectations.

This advocacy party order gradually took shape in fits and starts following the breakdown of the New Deal party order in the late 1960s. This prior configuration had managed to reproduce its strange-bedfellow coalition of southern conservatives, labor-liberals, and urban machines since the Great Depression. During that long era, Democratic leaders carefully contained intraparty contention through a decentralized party structure and congressional committee system that typically prevented liberals from overcoming the obstructionist tactics of their Southern copartisans. Meanwhile, in contrast to the Republican Party, large, durable majorities in Congress, the states, and in the electorate disincentivized national party leaders, especially Democratic presidents, from making party-building investments at the national, state, and local levels (Galvin 2010; Klinkner 1994), while a robust alliance with the trade union movement provided the party with a compensatory electoral machine (Dark 1999; Greenstone 1977).

By the late 1960s, however, tectonic stresses between racial liberals and conservatives on the one hand, foreign policy hawks and doves on the other, overwhelmed the party leadership's ability to continue to broker interest group and ideological cohesion around a shared policy agenda and partisan identity. The delegitimization of the party leadership in the tumultuous 1968 national convention in Chicago, and its aftermath, implicated the institutions of leadership selection, providing a short-lived window of opportunity for party entrepreneurs in the McGovern-Fraser Commission to engineer extensive changes to the presidential nomination system and propose even farther-reaching (but ultimately defeated) reforms to reconstruct the national party organization (Hilton 2021; Shafer 1983).

The upshot of this contentious struggle between reformers and their opponents was an institution more open to surrogate influence, ideologically inclined toward the causes championed by newly mobilized identity groups, and yet due to its hollowness, dependent on presidential discretion, initiative, and leadership for programmatic coherence and direction. Some early leaders of the post–New Deal era, like Jimmy Carter and Bill Clinton, actively sought to counter the logic of the advocacy order they inherited by distancing themselves from its key constituencies, shunning their signature causes, and asserting their independence as technocratic managers or pragmatic Third Way triangulators. Others, like Barack Obama and Joe Biden, embraced the advocacy order as their own and sought to harness its potential in service of their own presidential ambitions. In recent decades, the issue agenda has slowly but steadily expanded to encompass the demands of many progressive movements, interest groups, and donors. After a major retreat from its historical commitment to equality in the 1990s (Gerstle 2022; Geismer 2022), the Democratic Party has been more unified around a pluralistic progressive platform than perhaps at any point in its recent past (Malpas and Hilton 2021). Moreover, the identity of the party has diversified significantly, striking a closer resemblance to the demographic characteristics projected to be the future of the United States, especially in contrast to the predominately white and male GOP.

Yet while the Democrats' increasingly dense linkages with outside surrogates has partially compensated for its institutional deficiencies and its persistent failure to make organizational investments in in-house capacities to recruit and train candidates for office, expand voter databases, innovate new communications technologies, or build state and local party organizations, it is precisely this hollowness that poses some significant limits to surrogate groups' leverage over elected officeholders and party leaders. In comparison to the GOP, the constellation of advocates in the Democratic Party orbit have often practiced an insider-outsider strategy premised on their expectation that party elites will repay their electoral debts with something more than lip service. While this expectation often results in disappointment and frustration, due in part to minority party obstruction, the basic pattern is clear: Democratic surrogates tend to substitute party victory for policy victory and demobilize in the wake of electoral success (Heaney and Rojas 2015). While partly because of the continuing legacy of "sixties civics" (Heclo 2005), which expects more from political institutions while trusting them less, as well as the hard reality of being "electorally captured" by a party that takes their support for granted (Frymer 1999), Democratic surrogates also face an institutional venue that has been hollowed out by years of neglect. As a result, Democratic surrogates have not colonized the party apparatus in a comparable way to their Republican counterparts.

184   CONNECTIVE ACTION AND THE RISE OF THE FAR-RIGHT

In the absence of robust formal organization, party leaders have stepped into the vacuum and manage surrogate demands with a relatively free hand. In a novel departure, Obama, who described himself as a "fierce advocate" for progressive constituencies, spun off his 2008 campaign organization into a permanently active personal advocacy vehicle—known as Organizing for America (OFA)—that sought to harness the potential ferment at the grassroots level in support of his agenda (Milkis and York 2017). When Republican opposition to his legislative initiatives proved insurmountable, OFA helped to rally advocates behind the president's "We Can't Wait" campaign, which sought to build popular support for circumventing Congress with a barrage of unilateral executive actions. Thus, while surrogates could see their demands registered at the highest levels of the party leadership (OFA merchandise displayed the slogan "Climate Change & Economic Opportunity & Gun Violence Prevention & Health Care & Immigration Reform & Marriage Equality & Women's Rights"), Obama's party governance was top-down in nature, building no institutional mechanisms for surrogate groups to play a role in agenda-setting nor providing any means for leadership accountability.

This historical pattern of Democratic Party development helps clarify why, despite very similar surrogate pressures visible on both sides of the aisle today, we do not see a mirror image of two parties rushing toward polar extremes of the political spectrum. The advocacy party order that the Democrats have operated in recent decades has indeed moved to the left, not only in terms of its recognition of equal citizenship for historically marginalized groups but also, more recently, in its most serious (though ill-fated) attempt to reconstruct the American welfare state since the 1960s. But that form of party change, significant though it is, has been the result of the contentious but arm's length relationship Democrats have sometimes struggled to manage with the surrogates on which they depend. The institutional hollowness of the Democratic Party has made this relationship necessary and often mutually beneficial. But it has also limited surrogates' ability to subjugate the party leadership to its demands.

Party Strength, Surrogate Influence, and the Future of Liberal Democracy

The Democratic and Republican parties differ significantly in how they have managed the contentious politician-surrogate relations at their core and sought to maintain a semblance of order in their coalitions. Since at least the New Deal, Democrats have developed and maintained durable relationships with social movement and interest group surrogates. However, their long-running reliance on "outsourcing" so many party functions to their surrogate allies carried the opportunity cost of investing in the party organization, leaving it institutionally hollowed out. After the intraparty battles of the late 1960s and early 1970s, the evolving advocacy party order has been defined by the politics of surrogate management, as groups agitate to hold Democratic officeholders accountable for their campaign promises and party leaders cede as little agenda control as possible. By contrast, postwar Republicans had no surrogates with comparable mass-mobilizing capacity on the scale of the labor movement in the early postwar period and, instead, invested heavily in party-building to better contest elections. This pattern produced a well-oiled party machine that when paired with mass-level surrogates, such as the Christian right, the NRA, and the Fox News-centered conservative media ecosystem, it proved a potent combination. The Republican Party's shift to the right over the past generation is the result of a combination of robust party organization, mobilized surrogate demands, and their fusion in the figure of the party leader. Those demands—driven increasingly by a feeling of becoming "strangers in their own land" (Hochschild 2016)—are illiberal in nature. But when interwoven with the organization of the official party apparatus, they become a decisive influence on party behavior and, as Never Trump Republicans discovered to their chagrin, nearly impossible to resist (Saldin and Teles 2020).

The analysis set out here—brief though it is—speaks to a broader discussion regarding the role of parties in liberal democracy. As stated at the outset of this chapter, it is commonplace to assert that democracies need parties. But as we are increasingly coming to understand, parties don't necessarily need democracy. And as the conservative dilemma reminds us, the conditions under which parties may reject democracy are determined by the institutional strength of party organizations and the consequent influence of party surrogates.

Prescriptive analyses of our present discontents echo Ziblatt's (2017) historical findings: weak parties fail to resist the polarizing pressures of their surrogates, so we should therefore make our parties stronger (Jacobs 2022; Rosenbluth and Shapiro 2018; Schlozman and Rosenfeld 2019). There is little to find at fault with these "pro-party" solutions. They resist the naïve temptation of anti-partyism that has been the frequent refrain of political reformers across the centuries (Rosenblum 2008) and approach "the party question" as one that needs to be managed and lived with rather than solved permanently (Muirhead 2014). Yet the findings of this chapter problematize these prescriptions in several ways. First, as I have argued, surrogate influence and party strength are highly interdependent factors in the processes of party development. In modern democratic polities, which are host to densely populated interest group universes, the evolution of party strength— understood here as institutional capacity to raise resources and mobilize voters in order to win elections—has been shaped significantly by parties' relationships with outside groups, social movement organizations, and advocacy networks capable of stepping into a surrogate role. For Democrats and Republicans, the respective presence or absence of high-capacity party surrogates in the New Deal era was a key factor conditioning the different paths they took regarding party-building activity. Party strength or weakness is therefore an outcome that cannot be analytically divorced from the influence of party surrogates. It is not that strong parties weaken surrogates; it is that strong surrogates sustain weak parties.

Second, and relatedly, rather than strong parties necessarily diminishing surrogate influence, strong parties may well enhance it. A robust party apparatus, with well-resourced state and local organizations and a wide range of official positions open to talent, provides plentiful opportunities for surrogate-linked activists to make a career in politics by exercising "small power," which in the aggregate shapes the party's interests, ideology, and identity (Doherty et al. 2022). Weak or hollow parties, by contrast, with only a skeletal organizational structure, provide fewer opportunities for surrogates to infiltrate, staff, and colonize the formal party apparatus, leaving the line separating surrogates from the party relatively distinct.

Perhaps most fundamentally, if parties are contentious orders along the lines I have argued, and party surrogates' contentious relations with politicians are placed at the center of party theory, then the assertions we often make about parties safeguarding liberal democracy must be rethought. Parties are likely no more committed to democracy than are their surrogates. But the determinants of surrogate influence are more complex than a simple inverse relationship to party strength. It is a matter of the distinctive party order built and maintained over time.

References

Alberta, Tim. 2019. *American Carnage: On the Front Lines of the Republican Civil War and the Rise of President Trump.* New York: HarperCollins.

Aldrich, John H. 2011. *Why Parties? A Second Look.* Chicago: University of Chicago Press.

Alemany, Jacqueline, Marianna Sotomayor, and Josh Dawsey. 2021. "A MAGA squad of Trump Loyalists Sees its Influence Grow Amid Demands for Political Purity among Republicans." *Washington Post*, November 21, 2021.

Andrew, John A. 1997. *The Other Side of the Sixties: Young Americans for Freedom and the Rise of Conservative Politics*. New Brunswick, NJ: Rutgers University Press.

Arora, Maneesh. 2021. "Rep. Boebert Labels Rep. Omar a Jihadist. Why don't GOP Leaders Condemn the Slur?" *Washington Post*, December 6, 2021.

Bawn, Kathleen, Martin Cohen, David Karol, Seth Masket, Hans Noel, and John Zaller. 2012. "A Theory of Political Parties: Groups, Policy Demands and Nominations in American Politics." *Perspectives on Politics* 10 (3): 571–597.

Baylor, Christopher. 2018. *First to the Party: The Group Origins of Political Transformation*. Philadelphia: University of Pennsylvania Press.

Bermeo, Nancy. 2016. "On Democratic Backsliding." *Journal of Democracy* 27 (1): 5–19.

Blake, Aaron. 2021. "The GOP's Gradual Descent into 'Replacement Theory' and 'Nativist Dog Whistles.'" *Washington Post*, April 17.

Blum, Rachel M. 2020. *How the Tea Party Captured the GOP: Insurgent Factions in American Politics*. Chicago: University of Chicago Press.

Carmines, Edward G., and James A. Stimson. 1989. *Issue Evolution: Race and the Transformation of American Politics*. Princeton, NJ: Princeton University Press.

Cohen, Marty, David Karol, Hans Noel, and John Zaller. 2008. *The Party Decides: Presidential Nominations Before and After Reform*. Chicago: University of Chicago Press.

Conley, Brian M. 2013. "The Politics of Party Renewal: The 'Service Party' and the Origins of the Post-Goldwater Republican Right." *Studies in American Political Development* 27 (April): 51–67.

Continetti, Matthew. 2022. *The Right: The Hundred Year War for American Conservativism*. New York: Basic Books.

Cox, Gary W., and Mathew D. McCubbins. 2005. *Setting the Agenda: Responsible Party Government in the U.S. House of Representatives*. New York: Cambridge University Press.

Cox, Gary W., and Mathew D. McCubbins. 2007. *Legislative Leviathan: Party Government in the House*. New York: Cambridge University Press.

Dark, Taylor E. 1999. *The Unions and the Democrats: An Enduring Alliance*. Ithaca, NY: Cornell University Press.

Doherty, David, Conor M. Dowling, and Michael A. Miller. 2022. *Small Power: How Local Parties Shape Elections*. New York: Oxford University Press.

Downs, Anthony. 1957. *An Economic Theory of Democracy*. New York: Harper & Row.

Fandos, Nicholas, and Jonathan Martin. 2021. "McConnell Was Done with Trump. His Part Said Not So Fast." *New York Times*, January 27.

Farhang, Sean, and Ira Katznelson. 2005. "The Southern Imposition: Congress and Labor in the New Deal and Fair Deal." *Studies in American Political Development* 19: 1–30.

Fishkin, Joseph, and Heather K. Gerken. 2014. "The Party's Over: McCutcheon, Shadow Parties, and the Future of the Party System." *Supreme Court Review*: 175–214.

Fraser, Steve, and Gary Gerstle. 1989. *The Rise and Fall of the New Deal Order, 1930–1980*. Princeton, NJ: Princeton University Press.

Fried, Amy, and Douglas B. Harris. 2021. *At War with Government: How Conservatives Weaponized Distrust from Goldwater to Trump*. New York: Columbia University Press.

Frymer, Paul. 1999. *Uneasy Alliances: Race and Party Competition in America*. Princeton, NJ: Princeton University Press.

Galvin, Daniel J. 2010. *Presidential Party Building: Dwight D. Eisenhower to George W. Bush*. Princeton, NJ: Princeton University Press.

Galvin, Daniel J. 2016. "Political Parties in American Politics." In Orfeo Fioretos, Tulia A. Falleti, and Adam Sheingate, eds., *The Oxford Handbook of Historical Institutionalism* (pp. 310–324). Oxford: Oxford University Press.

Galvin, Daniel J. 2020. "Party Domination and Base Mobilization: Donald Trump and Republican Party Building in a Polarized Era." *The Forum* 18 (September): 135–168.

Geismer, Lily. 2022. *Left Behind: The Democrats' Failed Attempt to Solve Inequality*. New York: Public Affairs.

Gerstle, Gary. 2022. *The Rise and Fall of the Neoliberal Order: America and the World in the Free Market Era*. New York: Oxford University Press.

Gervais, Bryan, and Irwin L. Morris. 2018. *Reactionary Republicanism: How the Tea Party in the House Paved the Way for Trump's Victory*. New York: Oxford University Press.

Greenstone, J. David. 1977. *Labor in American Politics*. Chicago: University of Chicago Press.

Grossmann, Matt, and David A. Hopkins. 2016. *Asymmetric Politics: Ideological Republicans and Group Interest Democrats*. New York: Oxford University Press.

Hacker, Jacob S., and Paul Pierson. 2020. *Let Them Eat Tweets: How the Right Rules in an Age of Extreme Inequality*. New York: Liveright Publishing.

Heaney, Michael T., and Fabio Rojas. 2015. *Party in the Street: The Antiwar Movement and the Democratic Party after 9/11*. New York: Cambridge University Press.

Heclo, Hugh. 2005. "Sixties Civics." In Sidney M. Milkis and Jerome M. Mileur, eds., *The Great Society and the High Tide of Liberalism* (pp. 53–82). Amherst: University of Massachusetts Press.

Heersink, Boris. 2018. "Party Brands and the Democratic and Republican National Committees, 1952–1976." *Studies in American Political Development* 32 (April): 79–102.

Heersink, Boris, and Jeffrey A. Jenkins. 2020. *Republican Party Politics and the American South, 1865–1968*. Princeton, NJ: Princeton University Press.

Hejny, Jessica, and Adam Hilton. 2021. "Bringing Contention In: A Critical Perspective on Political Parties as Institutions." *Studies in Political Economy* 102 (2): 161–181.

Hejny, Jessica, and Adam Hilton. 2025. "Explaining the Durability and Dynamism of American Party Politics." In Jessica Hejny and Adam Hilton, eds., *Parties, Power, and Change: Developmental Approaches to American Party Politics* (pp. 1–22). Philadelpha: University of Pennsylvania Press.

Hemmer, Nicole. 2016. *Messengers of the Right: Conservative Media and the Transformation of American Politics*. Philadelphia: University of Pennsylvania Press.

Hemmer, Nicole. 2022. *Partisans: The Conservative Revolutionaries Who Remade American Politics in the 1990s*. New York: Basic Books.

Hilton, Adam. 2019. "The Path to Polarization: McGovern-Fraser, Counter-Reformers, and the Rise of the Advocacy Party." *Studies in American Political Development* 33 (1): 87–109.

Hilton, Adam. 2021. *True Blues: The Contentious Transformation of the Democratic Party*. Philadelphia: University of Pennsylvania Press.

Hirschman, Albert O. 1970. *Exit, Voice, and Loyalty: Responses to Decline in Firms, Organizations, and States*. Cambridge, MA: Harvard University Press.

Hochschild, Arlie Russell. 2016. *Strangers in their Own Land: Anger and Mourning on the American Right*. New York: The New Press.

Jacobs, Lawrence R. 2022. *Democracy Under Fire: Donald trump and the Breaking of American History*. New York: Oxford University Press.

Karol, David. 2009. *Party Position Change in American Politics: Coalition Management*. New York: Cambridge University Press.

Karpf, David. 2012. *The MoveOn Effect: The Unexpected Transformation of American Political Advocacy*. New York: Oxford University Press.

Klinghard, Daniel. 2010. *The Nationalization of American Political Parties, 1880–1896*. New York: Cambridge University Press.

Klinkner, Philip A. 1994. *The Losing Parties: Out-Party National Committees, 1956–1993*. New Haven, CT: Yale University Press.

Kreiss, Daniel. 2012. *Taking Our Country Back: The Crafting of Networked Politics from Howard Dean to Barack Obama*. New York: Oxford University Press.

Krimmel, Katherine. 2017. "The Efficiencies and Pathologies of Special Interest Partisanship." *Studies in American Political Development* 31 (2): 149–169.

Lacombe, Matthew J. 2021. *Firepower: How the NRA Turned Gun Owners into a Political Force*. Princeton, NJ: Princeton University Press.

Layman, Geoffrey C., Thomas M. Carsey, John C. Green, Richard Herrera, and Rosalyn Cooperman. 2010. "Activists and Conflict Extension in American Party Politics." *American Political Science Review* 104 (2): 324–346.

Lerer, Lisa, and Reid J. Epstein. 2021. "Abandon Trump? Deep in the GOP Ranks, the MAGA Mind-Set Prevails." *New York Times*, January 14.

Lerer, Lisa, and Astead W. Herndon. 2021. "Menace Enters the Republican Mainstream." *New York Times*, November 12.

Levitsky, Steven, and Daniel Ziblatt. 2018. *How Democracies Die*. New York: Crown.

Lewis, Verlan. 2019. *Ideas of Power: The Politics of American Party Ideology Development*. New York: Cambridge University Press.

López, Ian Haney. 2014. *Dog Whistle Politics: How Coded Racial Appeals Have Reinvented Racism and Wrecked the Middle Class*. Oxford: Oxford University Press.

Lowndes, Joseph E. 2008. *From the New Deal to the New Right: Race and the Southern Origins of Modern Conservatism*. New Haven, CT: Yale University Press.

Mair, Peter. 2013. *Ruling the Void: The Hollowing of Western Democracy*. London: Verso.

Malpas, Amelia, and Adam Hilton. 2021. "Retreating from Redistribution? Trends in Democratic Party Fidelity to Economic Equality, 1984–2020." *The Forum* 19 (2): 283–316.

Mann, Thomas E., and Norman J. Ornstein. 2016. *It's Even Worse Than It Looks: How the American Constitutional System Collided with the New Politics of Extremism*. New York: Basic Books.

Martin, Jonathan. 2021. "In Capital, a GOP Crisis. At the RNC Meeting, a Trump Celebration." *New York Times*, January 8.

Martin, Jonathan, and Alexander Burns. 2021. "Republicans Splinter Over Whether to Make a Full Break From Trump." *New York Times*, January 7.

Mazzei, Patricia. 2021. "Could Ron DeSantis Be Trump's GOP Heir? He's Certainly Trying." *New York Times*, April 10.

McAdam, Doug, and Karina Kloos. 2014. *Deeply Divided: Racial Politics and Social Movements in Postwar America*. New York: Oxford University Press.

McAdam, Douglas, and Sidney Tarrow. 2010. "Ballots and Barricades: On the Reciprocal Relationship between Elections and Social Movements." *Perspectives on Politics* 8 (June): 529–542.

McCarty, Nolan, Keith T. Poole, and Howard Rosenthal. 2016. *Polarized America: The Dance of Ideology and Unequal Riches*. Cambridge, MA: MIT Press.

McGirr, Lisa. 2001. *Suburban Warriors: The Origins of the New American Right*. Princeton, NJ: Princeton University Press.

Milkis, Sidney M., and Daniel J. Tichenor. 2019. *Rivalry and Reform: Presidents, Social Movements, and the Transformation of American Politics*. Chicago: University of Chicago Press.

Milkis, Sidney M., and John Warren York. 2017. "Barack Obama, Organizing for Action, and Executive-Centered Partisanship." *Studies in American Political Development* 31 (April): 1–23.

Moe, Terry M. 2005. "Power and Political Institutions." *Perspectives on Politics* 3 (June): 215–233.

Muirhead, Russell. 2014. *The Promise of Party in a Polarized Age*. Cambridge, MA: Harvard University Press.

Mutz, Diana C. 2018. "Status Threat, Not Economic Hardship, Explains the 2016 Presidential Vote." *Proceedings of the National Academy of Sciences* 115 (19): E4330–4339.

Nash, George H. 1976. *The Conservative Intellectual Movement in American Since 1945*. Wilmington, DE: ISI Books.

Noel, Hans. 2013. *Political Ideologies and Political Parties in America*. New York: Cambridge University Press.

Peck, Reece. 2019. *Fox Populism: Branding Conservatism as Working Class*. New York: Cambridge University Press.

Perlstein, Rick. 2001. *Before the Storm: Barry Goldwater and the Unmaking of the American Consensus*. New York: Hill and Wang.

Pitkin, Hanna. 1967. *The Concept of Representation*. Berkeley: University of California Press.

Plotke, David. 1996. *Building a Democratic Political Order: Reshaping American Liberalism in the 1930s and 1940s*. New York: Cambridge University Press.

Polsky, Andrew J. 2012. "Partisan Regimes in American Politics." *Polity* 44 (January): 51–80.

Popkin, Samuel L. 2021. *Crackup: The Republican Implosion and the Future of Presidential Politics*. New York: Oxford University Press.

Rosenblum, Nancy L. 2008. *On the Side of the Angels: An Appreciation of Parties and Partisanship*. Princeton, NJ: Princeton University Press.

Rosenbluth, Frances, and Ian Shapiro. 2018. *Responsible Parties: Saving Democracy from Itself*. New Haven, CT: Yale University Press.

Rosenfeld, Sam. 2018. *The Polarizers: Postwar Architects of Our Partisan Era*. Chicago: University of Chicago Press.

Saldin, Robert P., and Steven Teles. 2020. *Never Trump: The Revolt of the Conservative Elites*. New York: Oxford University Press.

Schattschneider, E. E. 1942. *Party Government*. New York: Reinhart.

Schickler, Eric. 2016. *Racial Realignment: The Transformation of American Liberalism, 1932–1965*. Princeton, NJ: Princeton University Press.

Schlesinger, Joseph A. 1994. *Political Parties and the Winning of Office*. Ann Arbor: University of Michigan Press.

Schlozman, Daniel. 2015. *When Movements Anchor Parties: Electoral Alignments in American History*. Princeton, NJ: Princeton University Press.

Schlozman, Daniel, and Sam Rosenfeld. 2017. "Prophets of Party in American Political History." *The Forum* 15 (4): 685–709.

Schlozman, Daniel, and Sam Rosenfeld. 2019. "The Hollow Parties." In Frances E. Lee and Nolan McCarty, eds., *Can America Govern Itself?* (pp. 120–150). New York: Cambridge University Press.

Shafer, Byron E. 1983. *Quiet Revolution: The Struggle for the Democratic Party and the Shaping of Post-Reform Politics*. New York: Russell Sage.

Sheingate, Adam. 2016. *Building a Business of Politics: The Rise of Political Consulting and the Transformation of American Democracy*. New York: Oxford University Press.

Sides, John, Michael Tesler, and Lynn Vavreck. 2018. *Identity Crisis: The 2016 Presidential Campaign and the Battle for the Meaning of America*. Princeton, NJ: Princeton University Press.

Skinner, Richard. 2007. *More Than Money: Interest Group Action in Congressional Elections*. Lanham, MD: Rowman & Littlefield.

Skocpol, Theda, and Vanessa Williamson. 2012. *The Tea Party and the Remaking of Republican Conservatism*. New York: Oxford University Press.

Skowronek, Stephen. 1997. *The Politics Presidents Make: Leadership from John Adams to Bill Clinton*. Cambridge, MA: Harvard University Press.

Smith, Rogers M., and Desmond King. 2021. "White Protectionism in America." *Perspectives on Politics* 19 (2): 460–478.

Tarrow, Sidney. 2021. *Movements and Parties: Critical Connections in American Political Development*. New York: Oxford University Press.

Williams, Daniel K. 2010. *God's Own Party: The Making of the Christian Right*. New York: Oxford University Press.

Wu, Nicholas, and Heather Caygle. 2021. "House Votes to Punish Gosar for Video Depicting Killing of AOC." *Politico*. November 17.

Yourish, Karen, Danielle Ivory, and Weiyi Cai. 2022. "Election Skeptics are Winning Races Across the Country." *New York Times*, November 9.

Ziblatt, Daniel. 2017. *Conservative Parties and the Birth of Democracy*. New York: Cambridge University Press.

Chapter 8
Exploring the Motivations of the MAGA Movement

Christopher Sebastian Parker and Rachel M. Blum

Exploring the Motivations of the MAGA Movement

The MAGA movement crashed onto the American political scene in 2016 with the candidacy of the erstwhile business mogul Donald Trump. The MAGA wing of the GOP, at roughly 50% of the GOP faithful,[1] practically runs the party. They are the base to whom Trump played, as well as much of the current GOP. To illustrate, in the aftermath of the Charlottesville racial upheaval in 2017, Trump commented that "there are good people on *both* sides" [emphasis ours]. While one set of protagonists included people with racially progressive views, the *other* side was represented by a cadre of white nationalists. Trump preferred migrants from Norway to those from "shithole" countries, such as Haiti and African nations. He thought Mexico sent rapists and thugs to America. The sitting president also claimed that the coronavirus was the "Asian flu." Prior to the emergence of MAGA, the GOP was known as the "party of white people." Now, with MAGA in charge, who can deny that the Republican Party has tripled down on this assessment?

The implications for democracy are at least as ominous. Trump challenged democratic institutions and norms by interrogating the rule of law, a free press, and the legitimacy of the political opposition. One might argue that compromising any *one* of these would result in the irrevocable decline of American democracy. Ultimately, Trump took a swipe at two of these pillars: free and fair elections, and the peaceful transfer of power. He undermined the former by challenging the latter. Not to put too fine a point on it: Trump

---

[1] We equate the MAGA wing of the GOP with the Trump wing since this is the base to whom he played. For an assessment of the Trump (MAGA) wing of the Republican Party, see Barber and Pope (2019).

Christopher Sebastian Parker and Rachel M. Blum, *Exploring the Motivations of the MAGA Movement*. In: *Connective Action and the Rise of the Far-Right*. Edited by: Steven Livingston and Michael Miller, Oxford University Press. © Oxford University Press (2025). DOI: 10.1093/oso/9780197794937.003.0008

tried to undermine a free and fair election because he had the support of MAGA, and he did—they ransacked the Capitol as a means of keeping him in office.

Many think the MAGA movement is something new; that we've never seen this in the annals of American politics prior to the current moment. This isn't true. The emergence of a *president* like Trump is new, one so brazenly self-centered, ignorant, and cares not one wit about democratic institutions. But nothing is more American—and constant—than the appearance of reactionary movements during times of social change (Parker and Barreto 2014). As we detail below, reactionary movements like MAGA have always been around, dating as far back as the nineteenth century. As a general proposition, movements have the capacity to manipulate parties, pulling them ever more toward their more extreme wings (McAdam and Kloos 2014). Reactionary social movements such as the Tea Party and MAGA can be thought of in terms of the organizing conceptual framework used in this volume. They function as surrogate organizations for the GOP, ones that rely on "cross-cutting cleavage issues" to mobilize publics. They do so by marshalling racial resentments and status anxiety to form cross-class coalitions, much in the way that Bahador and Kerchner illustrate elsewhere in this volume. More recently, reactionary movements like the Tea Party have proven adept at pulling the Republican Party further and further to the right.[2] MAGA, we argue, is no different.

This chapter is driven by a single question: what are the sources of support for MAGA? If we classify MAGA as a reactionary movement—and we do—then it's connected to similar movements of the past. (We elaborate in the next section.) Generally, there are at least two factors that are believed to propel right-wing movements. Perhaps the most widely accepted resides in economics: the working-class whites thesis.[3] The dominant narrative is that economic anxiety, driven by an economy that leaves them behind, pushes working-class whites to join right-wing movements. Another popular explanation for the emergence of these kinds of movements is embedded in identity. To wit: right-wing movements are borne of threats to the dominant culture, where the members of this group feel as though their way of life is becoming eclipsed. Thus, these people turn to these movements because they (right-wing movements) are about maintaining the social and cultural

---

[2] For more on this, see Blum (2020) and Gervais and Morris (2018).

[3] Carnes and Lupu (2020), among others, also see this as the dominant narrative before debunking it.

status quo. A third approach, one made relevant by Trump's presidency, is tethered to authoritarianism. Trump's occupation of the White House comforted those for whom social conformity is a priority. It stands to reason, therefore, that threats to social conformity will push authoritarians toward MAGA.

Drawing on original data, we explore these competing hypotheses. The data offers two ways of expressing support for the MAGA movement. One requires the respondent to simply report the extent to which they approve of MAGA. The other gauges involvement with the movement, where response options range from antipathy to attending rallies. Roughly speaking, the first item identifies simple MAGA-related sentiments, where the latter ultimately taps into commitment to the movements. As it turns out, these are meaningful distinctions (Oegema and Klandermans 1994). In the end, we find no support for the working-class white hypothesis. More to the point, differences in class, proxied with educational attainment and income, have no bearing on whether people in the mass public are attached to the movement. This result supports the organizing theme for this volume that working and middle-class voters' material self-interest is undone by symbolic politics.[4] Further, while we do find robust support for the hypotheses associated with identity-based claims, authoritarianism offers no leverage whatsoever on the connection between individuals and MAGA. In what follows, we furnish the reader with a brief introduction to the major reactionary movements of roughly the last 100 years. We then use this to inform our hypotheses.

Background and Theory

We argue that identity-based explanations ultimately drive affinity toward MAGA. Similar to the way in which the Tea Party movement represented a reaction to threat stimulated by social change and the election of a Black president, we argue that MAGA serves a similar purpose: that is, as a vessel for reactionary sentiment. Put another way, it is the sort of cross-class coalition one would expect with our organizing framework. In fact, much of what we have to say about MAGA supporters, references existing work on the Tea Party (Arceneaux and Nicholson 2012; Parker and Barreto 2014; Skocpol

---

[4] For the classic, social-psychological statement on symbolic politics, as distinguished from "material" politics, see Sears and Kinder (1981).

and Williamson 2011). After all, the demographic composition of the former and latter are quite similar. According to data we collected recently,[5] MAGA supporters are more likely to be male, older, white, strong conservatives, relatively well-off economically, and Christian. This is the same demographic that supported the Tea Party movement. Notwithstanding the time period during which each appeared, we argue that little, if any, daylight separates MAGA from its forebears: the Know Nothing Party, the Ku Klux Klan (KKK) of the 1920s, the John Birch Society (JBS), and the Tea Party. What is more, there is strong suggestive evidence pointing to a far-reaching overlap between MAGA and white Christian nationalism. Without exception, these groups felt threatened by the social change happening around them: they were losing "their" country.[6]

There are a range of possible explanations for why people are attracted to reactionary movements. Generally, one is driven to embrace right-wing movements as a means of forestalling loss of some kind, a response to a threat to one's economic or social standing. We begin with the former. A recent spate of work on the reactionary impulse in the United States claims that support for right-wing movements is, to a large extent, driven by economic concerns. For instance, the Tea Party was said to be motivated largely by its concerns about taxes and fiscal responsibility. However, the tax piece is typically tied to undeserving Others, generally racial minorities (Skocpol and Williamson 2011; Cramer 2016). There's another side of the economic coin and its association with right-wing movements, what some call the politics of (white) precarity (Hosang and Lowndes 2019). According to this argument, working-class whites feel left behind as global capitalism and other shifts in the economy eliminates their livelihood (Cramer 2016; Hochschild 2016). This argument is of a piece with studies on the KKK in which scholars make the case that working-class whites, underbid by immigrants, lost jobs in the 1920s (McVeigh 2009; MacLean 1994). Of course the Klan had the answer: remove immigrants from the labor pool.

---

[5] Rachel M. Blum and Christopher Sebastian, "Panel Study of the MAGA Movement," https://sites.uw.edu/magastudy/ (accessed December 18, 2024).

[6] Right-wing movements generally emerge to preserve the status, interests, or cultural preferences of dominant groups. Theoretically, this is called the "status politics" model, ultimately made famous by Gusfield (1963), in which an attempt is made to either preserve or restore the power and privilege, or cultural preference of a dominant social group thought to be in decline or completely without influence. Political action, moreover, was seen as an attempt to project their anxiety onto public objects. Bell (2002), Hofstadter (1965), and Lipset (Lipset and Raab 1970) were the most visible supporters of this approach, which rose to prominence from the late 1950s through the mid-1960s.

We now turn from a more materialist perspective on right-wing movements, to ones that are more symbolic. We believe that authoritarianism, a preference for social conformity, may also motivate people to support MAGA. Theodor Adorno and colleagues' landmark study on authoritarianism, *The Authoritarian Personality*, was published more than 60 years ago (Adorno et al. 1950). Originally conceived to better understand anti-Semitism, it eventually morphed into a study of what's commonly known as ethnocentrism, a form of generalized prejudice (something we will discuss below) (Feldman 2003). Authoritarianism, as a psychological theory, was believed to be a product of upbringing by strict, even punitive, parents during childhood. The internal conflict generated by a childhood fraught with such stress, scholars believe, results in social, political, and moral "outsiders" serving as scapegoats for repressed hostility (Stenner 2005, ch.1).[7] Recent work conducted by political psychologist Stanley Feldman (2003) and Karen Stenner (2005) has refined this approach to authoritarianism. Theoretically, for them, it's a matter of autonomy versus social cohesion. In the end they argue that authoritarianism is about a desire for social conformity, that any threat to upset the social order is worthy of punishment. Among authoritarians, coercion is favored as a means of regulating what is thought to be deviant behavior of any kind. Intolerance, therefore, is triggered by the failure of people to conform to what are believed to be widespread social norms: in the present case, any deviation from a white-dominated society. Thus, those who prefer social conformity may well prefer MAGA.

Other symbolic, identity-based explanations for attachment to the right wing exist, one of which is white consciousness. Making sense of this requires that we must first elaborate on the social psychology of consciousness. Group consciousness, according to Gurin and colleagues (1980, 30), is a cognition "about a stratum's (group's) position in society." More to the point, group consciousness is a function of shared interests, (dis)satisfaction with the group's relative position on society compared to out-groups, whether or not this position is legitimate, and a commitment to work toward change if the group's position is deemed unjust, or a commitment to maintain the status quo if it's all good (Miller et al. 1981). Ashley Jardina (2019) builds on this framework, applying it to white people. She finds that consistent with theory, white consciousness predisposes whites to prefer the

---

[7] For an alternative approach based on social learning theory, see Altemeyer (1996).

preservation of whites' group position. As such, white consciousness should encourage attachment to MAGA.

Racism may also contribute to support for the Tea Party. Consider our examples from other right-wing, reactionary movements: the Ku Klux Klan and the JBS. Of course, preservation of white supremacy was one of the reasons for the Klan's existence. The JBS avoided aligning itself with racism directly. Still, the position it adopted on civil rights, as a Trojan horse for communism, is difficult to square with anything but racism. Since "old-fashioned" racism is no longer, well, fashionable (but see Huddy and Feldman 2009), a new type of Black antipathy has replaced it. Instead of saying that African Americans are biologically inferior, some whites' hostility toward Blacks is now a matter of joining prejudice with the perception that Blacks are in violation of the Protestant work ethic. In fact, recent research by psychologist Cheryl Kaiser and colleagues suggests that the election of Barack Obama may even sharpen the resentment directed at African Americans. Kaiser argues that for many whites, Obama's election signals that racial injustice is overwith, that it's a thing of the past. Now, with a little effort, Blacks could achieve success (see Kaiser et al. 2009), and are securing "special favors" from the government that they scarcely deserve. Whites, then, become "racially resentful." This, scholars believe, explains the manifold reactions to race and race policy held by whites (Kinder and Sanders 1996).

Since we're on the subject of racism, it's appropriate that we now mention how Christianity may well predispose some to become attached to MAGA. Christianity, according to some, is part of the edifice of white supremacy (Jones 2020). For instance, by associating Black people as descendants of Cain, what they were thought to inherit is less-than-stellar morality, making the descendants of Abel (whites) morally superior: if the Bible says it, it must be true. With the relationship between Christianity and white supremacy setting the stage, it's but a short leap to Christian nationalism. As it turns out, Christian nationalism is a belief system in which adherents believe Christians are a nation onto themselves, complete with the belief that "real" American Christians are generally white, male, native born, and heterosexual. This, according to Christian nationalists, is the group on which American national identity should rest. Christian nationalists, therefore, are committed to restoring the Christian culture to its past glory as part of American national identity.[8]

---

[8] References to Christian nationalism are drawn from the work of Whitfield and Perry (2020).

Another factor we think contributes to support for right-wing, reactionary movements, but is never mentioned in the literature, is the tendency of societies to become divided into dominant and subordinate groups. Psychologist Jim Sidanius and colleagues explain the persistence of this arrangement, in part by arguing that near universal agreement exists on ideologies responsible for maintaining social hierarchy. In the American context, racism, sexism, and the Protestant work ethic, among others, are all ideologies that serve to enhance social hierarchy, legitimating discrimination as a means of maintaining a social order in which a group of dominants presides over subordinates. Another set of ideologies, such as egalitarianism, in the American context, helps to attenuate inequality. Social dominance orientation (SDO), part of a larger theory of intergroup relations (social dominance theory, SDT hereafter), is a psychological predisposition that describes the extent to which individuals subscribe to these ideologies. In short, SDO is a reflection of one's "preference for inequality among social groups" (Pratto et al. 1994, 741).[9] Someone who has high levels of SDO is likely to buy into the hierarchy-enhancing ideologies, ones that result in the perpetuation of inequality. People who are low on SDO are more likely to promote equality.[10] We contend that people high in SDO, people who are intent on keeping subordinate groups down as a means of maintaining group-based prestige, are likely to support right-wing movements and, therefore, MAGA.[11]

We close with a discussion of status threat, a concept some believe is at the core of reactionary movements (Parker 2021). It is a response by members of in-groups to periods of great social change that they fear will threaten their place in society. The threatened response is not simply a reaction to change: it is a way of understanding and coping with threatening and disturbing

[9] For more on the psychological properties of social dominance orientation, see Pratto et al. (1994).

[10] The larger theory to which SDO belongs is social dominance theory. Social dominance theory synthesizes individual-level factors (SDO), institutional, and structural explanations to explain the persistence of inequality. For the most complete explanation of the theory, see Sidanius and Pratto (1999). For an explanation of the evolutionary roots of social dominance theory, see Sidanius (1993).

[11] An allied model of intergroup relations, one fairly close to the social dominance model, is group position theory. Sociologist Lawrence Bobo uses it to great effect as an explanation of prejudice toward Blacks and American Indians. Among other things, as Bobo argues, group position theory stresses intergroup competition and threat; social dominance theory is really more about maintaining social stability, about maintaining group dominance. We sought to go with the social dominance model instead of group position model because we think right-wing movements are really about maintaining the prestige associated with their constituencies. We also sought to draw on a model whose reach exceeds race-based prejudice. For more on group position theory, see Bobo and Tuan (2006). For a comparison between the social dominance model and the group position model, see Bobo (1999).

social environments, ones rooted in paranoia. For people who respond in this way to change, the process of figuring out their place in their new surroundings is fraught with anxiety. This makes them so sensitive to their position relative to their shifting status that they spend too much time processing information on what may (or may not) come next. Often, this causes them to contemplate their circumstances even more. In the context of this volume, one would say that political parties such as the GOP weaponize status anxieties to attract working-class voters, with a goal of creating a sense of anxiety, anger, paranoia.

Paranoid-like social misperception is the belief, according to social psychologist Roderick Kramer suggests, that one is the target of persecution. Put differently, other members of the system are in cahoots, conspiring against the persecuted party (Kramer 1998, 254). Status threat has proven a powerful source of motivation for the Tea Party (Parker and Barreto 2014). We think it should work at least as well when it comes to MAGA. In the present context, it appears that MAGA believes itself under threat from change. Arguably more importantly, the group that MAGA represents, considers itself superior: its values and way of life are the highest expressions of human achievement. As a means of explaining its suddenly changing circumstances, MAGA often suggests an organized conspiracy of some kind is responsible.

Hypotheses

We test two sets of hypotheses. The first consider factors that might predict *support* for MAGA. The second considers factors that might predict active *involvement* in the MAGA movement. We do this for theoretical reasons. For instance, scholars have often found differences between those willing to support a given sentiment and those who are truly committed, so much so that they're willing to take some kind of action based on said sentiment or belief. (See, for example, Schuman et al. 1997; and also Parker 2009.) We now arrange our hypotheses in accordance with this theme.

Hypotheses: Predicting MAGA Support

H1(a): Among members of the voting public, those who identify as supporters of past reactionary movements (e.g., the Tea Party), those who are racists, race-conscious whites, those who are social dominants, and avowed Christian nationalists will be more likely to support MAGA than others.

H2(a): Among members of the voting public, those with lower class status, as defined by education and income, will be more likely to support MAGA than those with higher economic status.

H3(a): Among members of the voting public, those with more authoritarian attitudes will be more likely to support MAGA than those with less authoritarian attitudes.

Hypotheses: Predicting Active Involvement in MAGA Movement

H1(b): Among members of the voting public, those who identify as supporters of past reactionary movements (e.g., the Tea Party), those who are racists, race-conscious whites, those who are social dominants, and avowed Christian nationalists will be more actively involved than others.

H2(b): Among members of the voting public, those with lower class status, as defined by education and income, will be more likely to become actively engaged in MAGA than others.

H3(b): Among members of the voting public, those with more authoritarian attitudes are more likely to be actively involved in the MAGA movement than those with less authoritarian attitudes.

Data, Measures, and Results

We test these propositions with original data collected by YouGov. The data was collected from late December 2021 to early January 2022. It's a nationally representative sample of adults, with 2,432 interviews were completed. The survey was approximately 22 minutes in length. The dependent variables are fairly straightforward. The first one is a simple question that asks the extent to which the respondent supports the MAGA movement, from "strongly approve" to "strongly disapprove." The other dependent measure, the one we use to assess one's level of commitment to the MAGA movement, asks respondents to describe their relationship to the MAGA movement:

"I'm an active opponent of this movement," "I'm unsympathetic toward the movement, but I don't actively oppose it," "I'm neutral toward this movement," "I'm sympathetic toward the movement, but not active in it," and "I'm an active participant in the movement." To test our working-class whites hypotheses, we rely on objective class indicators such as income and education. For our test of authoritarianism, we rely on the index developed by Feldman (2003). White consciousness and racism, respectively, are tapped using indices developed by Jardina (2019), and Kinder and Sanders (1996). Likewise, we use a well-developed scale to represent Christian nationalism, as well as SDO (Whitfield and Perry 2020). For status threat, we use Tea Party approval as a proxy, something validated by Parker and Barreto (2014).

In Table 8.1, left to right, the models are nested such that the base model is confined to correlates related to basic demographics and political orientation (i.e., PID and ideology). However, since our working-class indicators are included in the demographics (education and income), the base model permits a preliminary peek at hypotheses 2A and 2B. Columns 2 and 3 examine hypotheses 1A and B, as well as 3A and B, relating to identity-based explanations, and one rooted in authoritarianism respectively. Column 4 provides a robustness check. Here, the point is to make sure that whatever we find, it isn't all about Trump. To foreshadow the results, all identity-based explanations remain valid explanations for MAGA approval, save for white consciousness. When it comes to explaining one's commitment MAGA a similar pattern emerges: all identity-based explanations survive except white consciousness. Class and preference for social conformity provide nothing in the way of analytical leverage in these models.

First, we explore results for what drives simple approval of the MAGA movement (Maga Approval). In the first specification, the one in which the working-class hypothesis is tested, it's clear that a distinction exists between the college-educated and others. For the moment, it seems that those completing a four-year degree harbor less-than-favorable sentiment toward MAGA than their less educated brethren. However, there's no such distinction when it comes to income. Even so, the two controls designed to capture political orientation work as one might think: conservatives and Republicans are more sympathetic to MAGA than progressives and Democrats. In column 2 where we include preference for social conformity, that is, authoritarianism, it performs as anticipated: preference for conformity paves the way for the approval of MAGA, all else equal. From

Table 8.1 MAGA Approval

	(1)	(2)	(3)	(4)
Strong Republican	.0283*** (t=13)	.280*** (t=13)	.182*** (t=9)	.0509** (t=3)
Strong Conservative	0.381*** (t=15)	.352*** (t=13)	00659* (t=2)	.0390 (t=1.6)
Age (5)	.0995 (t=.47)	−.00332 (t=.15)	−.00207 (t=0.10)	−0.00357 (t=.20)
College=1	−0.259*** (t=4)	−.214*** (t=4)	−.0553 (t=−1)	−.00790 (t=.16)
Income	.00379 (t=.60)	.00291 (t=.46)	−.0742 (t=.13)	−.000556 (t=−0.1)
Female	0.0360 (t=.61)	.0282 (t=.48)	.0848 (t=1.6)	.0450 (t=.95)
South=1	.0527 (t=.85)	0.0404 (0.65)	−.0896 (t=−1.62)	−.0885 (t=1.79)
Authoritarianism		.388*** (t=4)	−.0386 (t=.44)	.00695 (t=.09)
Tea Party			.452*** (t=16)	.298*** (t=12)
Christian nationalism			.243*** (t=7)	.130*** (t=4)
Social dominance orientation			.0709* (t=2)	.0525* (t=2)
Racism			.171*** (t=5)	.0994** (t=3)
White consciousness			−.0496 (t=.58)	−.0618 (t=.81)
Trump approval				.461*** (t=18)
Constant	0.0996 (t=0.85)	0.0802 (t=0.69)	−0.650*** (t=−5.01)	−.340** (t=−2.91)
N	1416	1416	1284	1284

t statistics in parentheses
* $p < 0.05$, ** $p < 0.01$, *** $p < 0.001$

here, however, things change drastically. Again, with the exception of white consciousness, all of the identity-related measures encourage support for MAGA. In short, the racists, nonbelievers in social equality (SDO), Christian nationalists, and the status-threatened are all onboard with MAGA.

202 CONNECTIVE ACTION AND THE RISE OF THE FAR-RIGHT

Yet on the inclusion of this new set of explanations, the analytical leverage furnished by authoritarianism declines—significantly, as does education. Yet again, political orientation, that is, PID and ideology, survives.

Shifting to the models in which we examine *commitment* to the MAGA movement (Table 8.2), the results are almost identical (no huge surprise: r=.80 between the DVs), with the same patterns. That is, authoritarianism is an important predictor—until it isn't, when identity-related explanations are introduced. Likewise, class completely drops out when these factors are taken into account, and political orientation survives. All of this suggests that identity explains the relationship between class and preference for social conformity on all things MAGA, indicating that identity, not class, is crucial to the formation of cross-class alliances on the right. Put another way, if cross-cutting cleavage issues are intended to mobilize non–materially based coalitions, MAGA represents a stellar example of such a coalition.

How robust are these findings? One way to find out is to account for the proverbial (orange) elephant in the room: Trump. After all, he birthed the MAGA movement, and before that the racist Birther movement. He's also renowned for invoking all the identity-based explanations we've modeled. Thus, it's quite possible that the relationship between identity—however defined, and MAGA is explained by Trump. Fortunately, this is something for which we are prepared. This is why we included a fourth column to our results in both tables. However, for both MAGA sentiment, and commitment to MAGA, nothing changes from model 3. In other words, Trump-related sentiments cannot account for symbolic, identity-based explanations when it comes to commitment to the latest insurgent right-wing movement.

Overall, it appears that symbolic, identity-related explanations carry the day when it comes to understanding attachment to the MAGA movement, in both word and deed. The failure of class to offer anything in the way of explanatory leverage when it comes to the reactionary right is far from something new. In terms of the model here, MAGA is a cross-class coalition, just as would be expected. Extensive research has found that Tea Party supporters were fueled more by cultural anxiety, not concerns over government spending (Blum 2020; Parker and Barreto 2014). Likewise, extant research finds that anti-Obama sentiment among conservatives was mostly explained by racial attitudes, not the price tag of his healthcare bill (Tesler 2012). While Trump movement supporters may well have been anxious, it was not about

EXPLORING THE MOTIVATIONS OF THE MAGA MOVEMENT   203

Table 8.2 MAGA Views

	(1)	(2)	(3)	(4)
Strong Republican	.184*** (t=12)	.183*** (t=11)	.106*** (t=7)	.0274 (t=1.7)
Strong Conservative	.321*** (t=17.12)	.304*** (t=15.24)	.128*** (t=5.80)	.111*** (t=5.3)
Age (5)	−.00175 (t=−0.11)	−.00987 (t=−0.61)	−.00127 (t=−.08)	−.000908 (t=−.06)
College	−0.169*** (t=−3.66)	−.141** (t=−3.01)	−.0415 (t=−0.93)	−.0143 (t=−.34)
Income	−.000690 (t=−0.14)	−.00111 (t=−0.23)	−.00159 (t=−0.35)	−.00139 (t=−.33)
Female	−.0412 (t=−0.92)	−.0469 (t=−1.05)	.00827 (t=0.19)	−.0131 (t=−.32)
South	.0770 (t=1.63)	.0702 (t=1.49)	.00532 (t=0.12)	0.0107 (t=.25)
Authoritarianism		.232*** (t=3.32)	−.118 (t=−1.68)	−.0858 (t=−1.29)
Tea Party			.298*** (t=13.46)	.208*** (t=9.40)
Christian nationalism			.156*** (t=5.43)	.0885** (t=3.20)
Social dominance orientation			.0638* (t=2.43)	.0530* (t=2.14)
Racism			.139*** (t=5.10)	.0962*** (t=3.70)
White consciousness			−.0234 (t=−0.34)	−.0245 (t=−.38)
Trump approval				.275*** (t=12.64)
Constant	.681*** (t=7.63)	.666*** (t=7.48)	.0431 (t=0.41)	.224* (t=2.23)
N	1473	1473	1303	1303

t statistics in parentheses
* $p < 0.05$, ** $p < 0.01$, *** $p < 0.001$

their economic condition, but about their declining status in a changing America (Mutz 2018; Green and McElwee 2019; Sides et al. 2018). Even when movement supporters explicitly stated economic concerns, a deeper look suggests this was nothing more than a proxy for their cultural anxiety amid changing demographics.[12]

All of this is to say that only the first hypotheses (H1a and H1b), ones related to symbolic politics, are the more reliable predictors of MAGA-related sentiment. The balance of the hypothesized relationships (H2a, H2b, H3a, and H3b) aren't at all associated with the aforementioned perceptions of MAGA. It bears mentioning that white consciousness is the sole symbolic identity that fails in its association with MAGA. While an empirical question, we think it is quite likely that the effect of white consciousness is mediated by status threat, that is, support for the Tea Party. After all, when Jardina (2019) describes white consciousness and white identity, it bears a strong resemblance to our description of status threat. In the end, support for MAGA and its activities, aren't rooted in white identity politics, though it is related to intergroup conflict. Nor, it seems, is it related to class.

References

Adorno, Theodor W., Else Frenkel-Brunswik, Daniel Levinson, and Nevitt Sanford. 1950. *The Authoritarian Personality*. New York: Harper and Row.

Altemeyer, Bob. 1996. *The Authoritarian Spectre*. Cambridge, MA: Harvard University Press.

Arceneaux, Kevin, and Stephen P. Nicholson. 2012. "Who Wants to Have a Tea Party? The Who, What, and Why of the Tea Party Movement," *PS: Political Science and Politics* 45 (4): 700–710.

Barber, Michael, and Jeremy C. Pope. 2019. "Conservatism in the Era of Trump," *Perspectives on Politics* 17 (3): 719–736.

Bell, Daniel. 2002. "The Dispossessed." In Daniel Bell, ed., *The Radical Right*, 3rd ed. (pp. 1–46). New York: Routledge.

Blum, Rachel M. 2020. *How the Tea Party Captured the GOP: Insurgent Factions in American Politics*. Chicago: University of Chicago Press.

Bobo, Lawrence D. 1999. "Prejudice as Group Position: Microfoundations of a Sociological Approach to Racism and Race Relations." *Journal of Social Issues* 55 (3): 445–472.

Bobo, Lawrence D., and Mia Tuan. 2006. *Prejudice and Politics: Group Position, Public Opinion, and the Wisconsin Treaty Rights Dispute*. Cambridge, MA: Harvard University Press.

Carnes, Nicholas, and Noam Lupu. 2020. "The Working Class and the 2016 Election." *Perspectives on Politics* 19 (1): 55–72.

Cramer, Katherine J. 2016. *The Politics of Resentment: Rural Consciousness in Wisconsin the Rise of Scott Walker*. Chicago: University of Chicago Press.

Feldman, Stanley. 2003. "Enforcing Social Conformity: A Theory of Authoritarianism." *Political Psychology* 24 (1): 41–72.

---

[12] Others arrive at a similar conclusion, in a different context, in which perceived symbolic threat pushed those in the cultural majority to adopt less tolerant positions far more so than more material concerns, such as one's economic circumstance; see Sniderman et al. (2004).

Gervais, Bryan T., and Irwin L. Morris. 2018. *Reactionary Republicanism: How the Tea Party in the House Paved the Way for Trump's Victory*. New York: Oxford University Press.

Green, Jon, and Sean McElwee. 2019. "The Differential Effects of Economic Conditions and Racial Attitudes in the Election of Donald Trump." *Perspectives on Politics* 17 (2): 358–379.

Gurin, Patricia, Arthur H. Miller, and Gerald Gurin. 1980. "Stratum Identification and Consciousness." *Social Psychology Quarterly* 43 (1): 30–47.

Gusfield, Joseph R. 1963. *Symbolic Crusade: Status Politics and the American Temperance Movement*. Urbana: University of Illinois Press.

Hochschild, Arlie Russell. 2016. *Strangers in their Own Land: Anger and Mourning on the American Right*. New York: The New Press.

Hofstadter, Richard. 1965. *The Paranoid Style in American Politics*. New York: Vintage Books.

Hosang, Daniel Martinez, and Joseph E. Lowndes. 2019. *Producers, Parasites, and Patriots: Race and the New Right-Wing Politics of Precarity*. Minneapolis: University of Minnesota Press.

Huddy, Leonie, and Stanley Feldman, 2009. "On Assessing the Political Effects of Racial Prejudice." *Annual Review of Political Science* 12 (2009): 423–447.

Jardina, Ashley E. 2019. *White Identity Politics*. New York: Cambridge University Press.

Jones, Robert P. 2020. *White Too Long: The Legacy of White Supremacy in American Christianity*. New York: Simon & Schuster.

Kaiser, Cheryl R., Benjamin J. Drury, Kerry E. Spalding, Sapna Cheryan, and Laurie T. O'Brien. 2009. "The Ironic Consequences of Obama's Election: Decreased Support for Social Justice." *Journal of Experimental Social Psychology* 45 (2009): 556–559.

Kinder, Donald R., and Lynn M. Sanders 1996. *Divided by Color: Racial Politics and Democratic Ideals*. Chicago: University of Chicago Press.

Kramer, Roderick M. 1998. "Paranoid Cognition in Social Systems: Thinking and Acting in the Shadow of Doubt." *Personality and Social Psychology Review* 2 (4): 251–275.

Lipset, Seymour Martin, and Earl Raab. 1970. *The Politics of Unreason: Right-Wing Extremism in American Politics, 1790–1977*. New York: Harper and Row.

MacLean, Nancy. 1994. *Behind the Mask of Chivalry: The Making of the Second Ku Klux Klan*. New York: Oxford University Press.

McAdam, Douglas, and Karina Kloos. 2014. *Deeply Divided: Racial Politics and Social Movements in Postwar America*. New York: Oxford University Press.

McVeigh, Rory. 2009. *The Rise of the Ku Klux Klan: Right-Wing Movements and National Politics*. Minneapolis: University of Minnesota Press.

Miller, Arthur H., Patricia Gurin, Gerald Guring, and Oksana Malanchuk, 1981. "Group Consciousness and Political Participation." *American Journal of Political Science* 25 (3): 494–511.

Mutz, Diana. 2018. "Status Threat, not Economic Hardship, Explains the 2016 Presidential Vote." *Proceedings of the National Academy of Science* 115 (19) E4330–E4339. https://doi.org/10.1073/pnas.1718155115/.

Oegema, Dirk, and Bert Klandermans. 1994. "Why Social Movement Sympathizers Don't Participate: Erosion and Non-conversion of Support." *American Sociological Review* 59 (5): 703–722.

Parker, Christopher S. 2009. *Fighting for Democracy: Black Veterans and the Struggle Against White Supremacy in the Postwar South*. Princeton, NJ: Princeton University Press.

Parker, Christopher Sebastian. 2021. "Status Threat: Moving the Right Further to the Right," *Daedalus* 150 (2): 56–75.

Parker, Christopher S., and Matt A. Barreto. 2014. *Change They Can't Believe In: The Tea Party and Reactionary Politics in America*. Princeton, NJ: Princeton University Press.

Pratto, Felicia, Jim Sidanius, Lisa M. Stallworth, and Bertram F. Malle. 1994. "Social Dominance Orientation: A Personality Variable Predicting Social and Political Attitudes." *Journal of Personality and Social Psychology* 67 (4): 741–763.

Schuman, Howard, Charlotte Steeh, Lawrence D. Bobo, and Maria Krysan. 1997. *Racial Attitudes in America: Trends and Interpretations*. Revised edition. Cambridge, MA: Harvard University Press.

Sears, David O., and Donald R. Kinder. 1981. "Prejudice and Politics: Symbolic Racism versus Racial Threats to the Good Life." *Journal of Personality and Social Psychology* 40 (3): 414–431.

Sidanius, Jim. 1993. "The Psychology of Group Conflict and the Dynamics of Oppression: A Social Dominance Perspective." In Shanto Iyengar and William J. McGuire, eds., *Explorations in Political Psychology* (pp. 183–224). Durham, NC: Duke University Press.

Sidanius, Jim, and Felicia Pratto. 1999. *Social Dominance*. New York: Cambridge University Press.

Sides, John, Michael Tesler, and Lynn Vavreck. 2018. *Identity Crisis: The 2016 Presidential the Campaign and the Battle for the Meaning of America*. Princeton, NJ: Princeton University Press.

Skocpol, Theda, and Vanessa Williamson. 2011. *The Tea Party and the Remaking of Republican Conservatism*. Oxford: Oxford University Press.

Sniderman, Paul M., Louk Hagendorn, and Markus Prior. 2004. "Predisposing Factors and Situational Triggers: Exclusionary Reactions to Immigrant Minorities." *American Political Science Review* 98 (1): 35–39.

Stenner, Karen. 2005. *The Authoritarian Dynamic*. New York: Cambridge University Press.

Tesler, Michael. 2012. "The Spillover of Racialization into Health Care: How President Obama Polarized Public Opinion by Racial Attitudes and Race." *American Journal of Political Science* 56 (3): 690–704.

Whitfield, Andrew L., and Samuel L. Perry. 2020. *Taking America Back for God: Christian Nationalism in the United States*. New York: Oxford University Press.

Chapter 9
The Rise of Conservative Illiberalism and the Parallel Ascendance of Right-Wing Surrogates

Steven Feldstein

Following the January 6 insurrection, many hoped that the shocking political violence witnessed in Washington would finally break Donald Trump's hold on the Republican Party and restore more civil politics. Indeed, President Joe Biden fanned these expectations, underscoring in his inauguration speech that "politics need not be a raging fire destroying everything in its path. Every disagreement doesn't have to be a cause for total war. And, we must reject a culture in which facts themselves are manipulated and even manufactured" (Biden 2021). And yet several years after the insurrection, conservative polarization, stoked by propaganda and disinformation, remains at alarming levels. In his remarks commemorating the January 6 events a year later, Biden was less sanguine about politics returning to normal. Instead, he warned: "We must decide, what kind of nation are we going to be? Are we going to be a nation that accepts political violence as a norm? Are we going to be a nation where we allow partisan election officials to overturn the legally expressed will of the people?" (Biden 2022). Biden's admonition was borne from the fact that not only did Republicans fail to extinguish Trump's Big Lie but the opposite came to pass—a majority of conservatives openly question the legitimacy of the 2020 election, refer to the insurrectionists as patriots or tourists, and describe COVID vaccination efforts as "woke propaganda" (Kaufman 2021; Parker et al. 2022; *Kansas City Star* 2021). A January 2022 NPR/Ipsos poll, for instance, found that two-thirds of GOP respondents believed that "voter fraud helped Joe Biden win the 2020 election" (Ipsos 2022). Less than half of surveyed Republicans were willing to accept the results of the 2020 election and nearly one-third

---

Steven Feldstein, *The Rise of Conservative Illiberalism and the Parallel Ascendance of Right-Wing Surrogates.*
In: *Connective Action and the Rise of the Far-Right.* Edited by: Steven Livingston and Michael Miller,
Oxford University Press. © Oxford University Press (2025). DOI: 10.1093/oso/9780197794937.003.0009

agreed that the January 6 insurrection was a staged event carried out by Antifa and government agents.

How did American conservatives reach a point where their main political messages are either blatantly anti-democratic or outright falsehoods? Which messengers are responsible for seeding these narratives? And what role have digital technology and social media played in advancing these ideas in the Republican Party?

Many researchers rely on "technocentric" explanations, with a particular focus on the internet and social media, to describe the growth of conservative disinformation. Cass Sunstein (2017), for example, argues that internet "filter bubbles" have created segregated classes of individuals who are prone to follow fringe perspectives. As individuals self-sort online, it becomes more effective for politicians to mobilize base support through hardline rhetoric rather than adopt conciliatory positions to sway moderate voters. The outcome of this process, writes Pablo Barberá (2020, 34), "is a society that is increasingly segregated along partisan lines and where compromise becomes unlikely due to rising mistrust of public officials, media outlets, and ordinary citizens on the other side of the ideological spectrum." Shoshana Zuboff (2021) focuses on the economic incentives of internet platforms to deploy micro-targeted algorithms that keep users addicted to their social media feeds through the deliberate peddling of conspiracies and falsehoods: "America and most other liberal democracies have, so far, ceded the ownership and operation of all things digital to the political economics of private surveillance capital, which now vies with democracy over the fundamental rights and principles that will define our social order in this century." She argues that neoliberal revenue incentives have initiated a destructive information spiral that threatens the core of democracy.

And yet faulting the internet for facilitating the mainstreaming of far-right viewpoints and driving polarization doesn't fully satisfy. For one, this does not account for what Yochai Benkler, Robert Faris, and Hal Roberts describe in *Network Propaganda* as an "asymmetric polarization" between the conservative information ecosystem—which is rife with disinformation and extreme viewpoints—and the liberal ecosystem, where "traditional professional media" predominates (Benkler et al. 2018, 60). If social media is principally responsible for exacerbating fringe viewpoints, then the asymmetry between conservative and liberal information ecosystems should be less stark. But the differences between the right-wing information ecosystem and its liberal counterpart are profound, meaning that something more than algorithms are leading conservatives to embrace extremist ideology. This illustrates the limits of technocentric approaches to explaining political polarization; they frequently fail to take into account relevant political, social, or economic explanations regarding the radicalization of the political right in America.

This chapter seeks to go beyond technological explanations regarding the causes of conservative propaganda and disinformation. Instead, it argues that two elements are most relevant to understanding conservatives' extreme turn: First, the synergies and connections between the mass media ecosystem and internet platforms have provided fertile ground for right-wing conservative entrepreneurs, acting as political surrogates, to seed narratives on talk radio or Fox News and to then exploit the virality of social media to disseminate disinformation on an industrial scale. Second, this propaganda feedback loop would not be possible without an underlying illiberal drift by the Republican Party, which accelerated in the early 2000s, that moved the GOP considerably farther to the right than comparable center-right parties in other democracies.

These dynamics have laid the groundwork for a new class of right-wing elite surrogates, peddling false and conspiratorial narratives, to wrest control of the Republican Party from traditional party gatekeepers (Benkler et al. 2018, 78). This has allowed multiple political factions comprising the MAGA movement—from the Boogaloo Bois and Oath Keepers to the Proud Boys and Christian white nationalist organizations—to emerge as GOP surrogates, leveraging mass media outlets alongside social media platforms to advance their ideas and solidify their influence. This model contrasts with Daniel Ziblatt's (2017) historical analysis of party surrogates, as well as Jacob Hacker and Paul Pierson's treatment of surrogate organizations, which they largely define in traditional terms—comprising formal groupings of individuals working toward shared purposes—similar to "conventional bureaucratic organizations" (Hacker and Pierson 2020). This chapter instead hews more closely to Lance Bennett and Alexandra Segerberg's description of "organizationally enabled" networks, which reside in between conventional organizations and full technologically enabled networks (2013).

The chapter proceeds as follows. First, it describes how the elevation of far-right narratives and the creation of the modern conservative "propaganda feedback loop" dates back over three decades, undercutting arguments that social media is primarily responsible for driving contemporary polarization and dysfunction. Next, it examines the rise of a new class of right-wing surrogates, who leverage television appearances, radio shows, podcasts, social media platforms, and other media outlets to drive their narratives—upending traditional notions of what constitutes a party surrogate. Finally, the chapter looks at the context of conservatism in America, probing the underlying factors which have allowed a new class of right-wing surrogates to ascend and dominate the GOP.

A note on terminology: this chapter uses terms such as "illiberalism," "polarization," "political dysfunction," "extreme content," "disinformation," "falsehood," and "conspiracy" to describe the manner in which right-wing surrogates operate and the type of messaging they are disseminating to the conservative electorate. These terms have distinct meanings and are not intended to be used interchangeably. However, they do represent a closely related set of anti-democratic behavior leveraged by conservative surrogates to advance their political agenda; these terms are therefore interspersed throughout the chapter.

How Mass Media Interacts with Social Media to Drive Conservative Disinformation

In an influential article in *The Atlantic*, social psychologist Jonathan Haidt wrote about political dysfunction and injustice in America and pinpointed social media as primarily responsible for its rise: "We can date the fall of the tower to the years between 2011 . . . and 2015, a year marked by the 'great awokening' on the left and the ascendancy of Donald Trump on the right" (Haidt 2022). But what Haidt and others fail to appreciate is that the elevation of right-wing disinformation narratives and the creation of the modern conservative "propaganda feedback loop" date back over three decades. Many experts consider the repeal of the Fairness Doctrine in 1987 as the precipitating factor that ushered in modern conservative talk radio and vaulted broadcasters like Rush Limbaugh into prominence (Jamieson and Cappella 2008). The Fairness Doctrine, a policy implemented by the Federal Communications Commission (FCC) between 1949 and 1987, held that broadcasters had an affirmative duty to "determine what the appropriate opposing viewpoints were on these controversial issues, and who was best suited to present them" (Ruane 2011)· Barely one year after its repeal, Rush Limbaugh's three-hour right-wing talk radio program was nationally

THE RISE OF CONSERVATIVE ILLIBERALISM   211

syndicated, eventually attracting an estimated weekly audience of 14 to 20 million listeners (Benkler et al. 2018, 321).[1] Limbaugh openly fomented mistrust and grievances against those who didn't share his viewpoints and pushed baseless rumors "long before Twitter and Reddit became havens for such disinformation" (McFadden and Grynbaum 2021). Recognizing the strength of Limbaugh's model, Roger Ailes and Rupert Murdoch founded Fox News in 1996, which used an audience segmentation strategy to cultivate a loyal following that could tune in at any point in a 24-hour period to sustained right-wing partisan content. Benkler, Faris, and Roberts write, "by the 2016 election cycle American right-leaning audiences had been exposed for two decades on television (and nearly three on radio) to a propagandist mass media outlet built on feeding its viewers with news that fit and reinforced their world view while constantly pointing fingers at all other media sources as biased" (2018, 324). The right-wing media stars who emerged in the late 1980s and 1990s served as GOP surrogates and laid the groundwork for the cadre of right-wing surrogates who now dominate the conservative ecosystem and Republican Party. While the public fixated on Russian election interference in social media, the overlooked story was the 28 years of conservative mass media priming and surrogate formation that Donald Trump adeptly exploited for an electoral victory.

Elsewhere in this volume, Bahador and Kerchner describe the hateful speech transmitted by far-right broadcast channels. Their findings are aligned with the broader conclusions of research that confirms mass media's role in disseminating false hate-filled narratives and disinformation. A 2020 study carried out by researchers from Harvard's Berkman Klein Center found that voter mail fraud allegations tied to the election were principally driven by media and political elites who used agenda setting and framing strategies to spread false narratives: "This disinformation campaign is carried out primarily by means of mass media, with social media playing a secondary role. It is supported by a right-wing media ecosystem that has long been subject to a propaganda feedback loop that marginalizes or suppresses dissenting views within the conservative sphere" (Benkler et al. 2020). Agenda-setting interventions by Trump, closely aligned with the Republican Party, and parroted by right-wing media outlets such as Fox News, Breitbart, Infowars, and Newsmax, served as progenitors of false content. These

---

[1] The antecedent to Limbaugh's talk radio show can be traced back even further to Father Coughlin's incendiary radio broadcasts of the 1930s.

findings seem aligned with those reported by Starbird elsewhere in this volume.

Several studies examining the dissemination of false content on YouTube, conclude similarly that the means by which viewers encountered far-right videos is diverse and that platform algorithms steer only a small percentage of users toward extreme content. In a 2020 study by Homa Hosseinmardi et al. (2020), they found that the prevalence and appeal of inflammatory content on YouTube should be considered "as part of a larger information ecosystem in which extreme and misleading content is widely available, easily discovered, and both increasingly and actively sought out." They posit that focusing on platform algorithms as drivers of disinformation misses the bigger picture when it comes to understanding how false conservative narratives are consumed and produced. Likewise, Annie Chen et al. (2022) found that the watching of extremist videos is concentrated among a few "superconsumers" who frequently encountered them through external links or prior subscriptions rather than through algorithmic recommendations.

In the digital era, a more accurate model in which to understand the interaction between mass media and digital platforms is media hybridity. Researchers such as Andrew Chadwick (2013), W. Lance Bennett and Alexandra Segerberg (2013), and Daniel Kreiss and Shannon McGregor (2018) describe the evolution of organizations that are not strictly confined to offline or online ecosystems. Instead, these organizations exist in a hybrid system that is "digitally fluid, liminal, sometimes virtual and with connections to other organizations that are equally fluid" (Bennett and Livingston, this volume).

A conservative exemplar of media hybridity is right-wing commentator Dan Bongino.[2] Bongino is one of the most popular conservative pundits in the country. He has a major presence on multiple platforms: he occupies Rush Limbaugh's old radio slot, drawing an estimated weekly listenership of 8.5 million. He hosts his own Fox News show on Saturday nights. He also runs a podcast that has ranked No. 1 on iTunes. His Facebook page generates a huge audience as well, attracting more engagement in 2021 than Facebook pages operated by the *New York Times*, *Washington Post*, and *Wall Street Journal* (Osnos 2021). Bongino specializes in peddling fear that preys upon and amplifies the sort of white grievance and anxieties highlighted

---

[2] Bongino was appointed by Trump to be the second-in-command at the FBI in March 2025; his podcast and radio show ended production on March 14, 2025.

THE RISE OF CONSERVATIVE ILLIBERALISM   213

by Parker and Blum in this volume. A typical Bongino monologue will rachet up the anxiety level of his audience while denigrating his opponents. In a *New Yorker* profile, Evan Osnos (2021) describes an April podcast from Bongino:

> Bongino had elevated it to a larger showdown with opponents whom he called "pieces of human filth." "There are people now openly silencing and attacking conservatives, trying to have them jailed, trying to have them sanctioned, bankrupted financially, fired from their jobs. This is all happening right now! And it's all happening because of the Democrat Party and the liberals." He was shouting now, waving a hand in front of the lens. "They are fascists! That's not in dispute!"

Bongino is acutely aware that he is peddling a product designed to appeal to right-wing audiences across different platforms and listening/viewing patterns. To that end, he has assembled a small staff to pick and choose soundbites, memes, and video clips to amplify user engagement. He has even created a news aggregator site, the Bongino Report (similar in scope and intent to the Drudge Report) to serve as an "engagement machine" that will boost his audience numbers (Osnos 2021). As Osnos relates, "I think fundamentally, this is about what he [Bongino] once called on a video stream the product. And the product is a podcast, a radio show and a set of political ideas that are determined to challenge the consensus view on masks, vaccines and the integrity of American elections" (Kelly and Osnos 2021).[3]

Thus, it is not that mass media matters more than social media—or vice-versa—when it comes to peddling conservative disinformation. What is more relevant are the synergies and connections between the mass media ecosystem and internet platforms. In this regard, extreme conservative entrepreneurs acting as political surrogates seed narratives on talk radio or Fox News, and then exploit the virality of social media to disseminate disinformation on an industrial scale. This process involves what Karpf elsewhere in this volume calls listening, in which conservative actors continuously assess narratives for their capacity to mobilize publics. As studies show, this model closely tracks the strategy used by far-right groups following Biden's electoral victory in November 2020. Research from the Carter Center found that "repeat offenders" in right-leaning Facebook groups posted

---

[3] Another conservative pundit who has garnered a similarly large following using the politics of fear and grievances to power his ratings is Fox News host Tucker Carlson (see Confessore 2022).

264,709 links to outside media sources, over 50% of which were rated as "not trustworthy." The top linked news sites were Breitbart, Fox News, The Gateway Pundit, The Epoch Times, and Daily Wire (Baldassaro et al. 2021). The Gateway Pundit, for example, brought a long record of spreading false and misleading content. One week before the 2016 election, the site disseminated disinformation originating from Russian IRA operatives regarding false voter fraud allegations linked to Democrats in Florida. During the 2020 election, the Gateway Pundit was an early adopter of #StopTheSteal.[4] In sum, users posted over 650,000 messages on Facebook groups attacking the legitimacy of Biden's victory through the January 6 insurrection, averaging over 10,000 posts a day (Silverman et al. 2022).

It is also worth noting that digital platforms are not monolithic—different platforms and online services play distinctive roles when it comes to disseminating false content and disinformation narratives. As researchers from the Election Integrity Project note, most social media users are not confined to a single platform, but "turn to different platforms for different reasons" (Center for an Informed Public 2021, 150). Particularly, political operators and those who intend to shape public opinion "employ multiplatform strategies, leveraging different platforms for different parts of their information strategies, and often intentionally moving content from one platform to another" (Center for an Informed Public 2021, 150). A conservative influencer seeking to promote an election stealing narrative would peddle the hashtag #stopthesteal on multiple platforms. They would post inflammatory content on Reddit (which has much looser guidelines about what content users can post), post a link on X or Facebook to the Reddit thread, and then promote #stopthesteal on a WhatsApp or Signal group or even on a Fox News or Newsmax segment to amplify user engagement. This not only illustrates the cross-platform nature of information sharing, but also the fluidity between sharing fraudulent information through mass media outlets as well as via social media.

The Ascendance of a New Class of Right-Wing Surrogates

These dynamics have laid the groundwork for a new class of elite right-wing surrogates, peddling conspiratorial and illiberal messages to conservative

---

[4] In 2021, Twitter (now called X) permanently suspended *The Gateway Pundit*'s editor-in-chief, Jim Hoft, for repeatedly manipulating or interfering in elections.

THE RISE OF CONSERVATIVE ILLIBERALISM   215

audiences prone to "partisan-confirming news over truth," to wrest control of the Republican Party from traditional party leaders (Benkler et al. 2018, 78). In a 2020 article published in *Science*, researchers identified "elite ideological polarization" as a major driver of political division in America (Finkel et al. 2020). They noted that in contrast to polarization trends among the general public, "politicians and other political elites have unambiguously polarized recently on ideological grounds, with Republican politicians moving further to the right than Democratic politicians have moved to the left" (2020, 534). They observed that this ideological divergence has resulted in "political sectarianism," as elites increasingly rely upon disciplined messaging to discuss and disseminate their preferred topics in their preferred manner (Finkel et al. 2020). Analyses of the conservative information ecosystem support this conclusion, revealing that a small heterogeneous group of elite actors—politicians, media pundits, social medial influencers, political operatives, and behind-the-scenes funders—are offering explicit normative cues to fellow conservatives. They are driving the GOP's agenda and serving as a surrogate organization of networks.

Taking a look back at the 2020 election is instructive. Researchers from the Election Integrity Project identified "repeat spreaders" as key perpetrators of false election narratives and propaganda. Not only were they individually responsible for aggressively amplifying deceptive narratives across multiple platforms, but they frequently "promoted and spread each other's content" (Center for an Informed Public 2021, 188). A look at the repeat spreader list in Table 9.1 shows many familiar elite faces. Most of these accounts operate as conservative political surrogates.

Trump and his two sons feature prominently. They are joined by former Trump administration officials (Rich Grenell) and political operatives (Charlie Kirk of Turning Point USA; James O'Keefe, founder of Project Veritas). Far-right media outlets are also major disseminators of disinformation (Breibart News, Gateway Pundit), along with two Fox News hosts (Sean Hannity, Mark Levin). These are not unknown figures. The bulk of them are directly tied to Trump's political machinery, right-wing political outlets, or conservative media organizations.

Another disinformation analysis carried out by *Politico* and the Institute for Strategic Dialogue came to a similar conclusion (Gatewood and O'Connor 2020). Researchers analyzed online discussions around the Black Lives Matter (BLM) movement and electoral voter fraud concerns. They also found that a small cluster of elite conservative activists and right-wing

216 CONNECTIVE ACTION AND THE RISE OF THE FAR-RIGHT

Table 9.1 Top Repeat Spreader Twitter Accounts During the 2020 Election

Account	Affiliation	Followers
DonaldJ TrumpJr	Trump family	6,392,929
Seanhannity	Fox News host	5,599,939
Eric Trump	Trump family	4,580,170
Marklevinshow	Fox News host	2,790,699
RealJamesWoods	Conservative celebrity and actor	2,738,431
Charliekirk11	Turning Point USA	1,915,729
BreibartNews	Far-right media outlet	1,647,070
Tom Fitton	President of Judicial watch	1,328,746
Jack Posobiec	Alt-right political activist	1,211,549
James OKeefeIII	Founder, Project Veritas	1,021,505
Richard Grenell	Former Trump White House official	691,441
The right Melissa	Conservative activist	497,635
Prayingmedic	Qanon "interpreter"	437,976
Catturd2	Pro-Trump comic account	436,601
Gatewaypundit	Far-right media outlet	424,431
ChuckCallesto	Conservative political activist	311,517
citruth		256,201

Source: Center for an Informed Public (2021, 188).

media figures were primarily responsible for propagating disinformation narratives, whether portraying BLM as a violent protest movement or claiming rampant voter fraud ahead of the 2020 elections ("You see the same people popping up all the time," notes Ciaran O'Connor with the Institute for Strategic Dialogue) (Scott 2020).

A 2021 report from the Aspen Institute's Commission on Information Disorder also hones in on the "repeat offender" concept. Researchers conclude that a small number of accounts with an outsized impact are responsible for spreading a range of false narratives, from election fraud disinformation to anti-vaccine propaganda. "These influential and often 'verified' accounts function as both content producers and amplifiers. These include elected officials, hyperpartisan media outlets and pundits, and other social media influencers, driven by political objectives as well as financial incentives (relevant to Karpf's argument in Chapter 12 that economic opportunism is a potential motivating factor for surrogate organizations). Taken together, it is a group of actors who are uniquely identifiable and uniquely necessary to hold to a high standard of scrutiny" (Couric et al. 2021). More recently, initial research from Matthew Hindman, Nathaniel Lubin, and Trevor Davis, published in *The Atlantic*, found a heavy skew on Facebook toward a handful of far-right voices: "Top pages such as those of Ben Shapiro, Fox News, and Occupy Democrats generated tens of millions of interactions a month in our data, while all U.S. pages ranked 300 or lower in terms of engagement received less than 1 million interactions each" (Hindman et al. 2022). They observed a steep drop-off beyond the top 500 US Facebook pages, estimating that the top pages "accounted for about half of the public U.S. page engagement on the platform" (Hindman et al. 2022).

As a result, figures such as Steve Bannon, Michael Flynn, Matt Gaetz, Marjorie Taylor Greene, Candace Owens, Ben Shapiro, and Peter Thiel have risen to the forefront. They have been joined by a slew of GOP politicians and media operatives who were former members of the party's gatekeeping class who subsequently moved into Trump's wing (e.g., Elise Stefanik, Ted Cruz, J.D. Vance).[5] They have replaced traditional Republican gatekeepers at the front of the party—the party's Reagan wing, such as the Bushes, Liz Cheney, Bill Kristol, George Will, Mitt Romney, and others—who have declined to take part in peddling extreme narratives and conspiracy theories. After Trump won his electoral victory in 2016, conservative outlets quickly jumped on his bandwagon and turned on traditional party gatekeepers. Benkler, Faris, and Roberts (2018, 7) write, "Our data show, in 2017 Fox News joined the victors in launching sustained attacks on core pillars of the Party of Reagan—free trade and a relatively open immigration policy, and, most directly, the national security establishment and law enforcement when these threatened President Trump himself." Bongino, Owens, Shapiro, Bannon, and others are not part of formal political organizations, but each plays a critical role in generating and disseminating messages that move the GOP into increasingly extreme and anti-democratic directions, supplanting the gatekeepers of the recent past. In these shifts we can see the drift of the GOP as a conventional conservative party, one centering on free market economics and internationalism to a nationalist party centering

[5] In early 2022, for example, the publication *Axios* polled senior operatives about the changing elite power balance among US conservatives. Respondents agreed that traditional power brokers and information outlets, such as the US Chamber of Commerce, Koch network, National Review, FreedomWorks, and the Drudge Report, had been supplanted by Donald Trump, Tucker Carlson, Fox News, Breitbart, Steve Bannon, and a slew of online influencers including Ben Shapiro, Dan Bongino, Joe Rogan, and Charlie Kirk. See Swan and Markay (2022). See also Mac and Lerer (2022).

on identity politics. In the end, the risk associated with conservative party reliance on surrogates pushing highly emotive issues is that the party will lose its moorings and drift into illiberalism.

The change in fortune experienced by Liz Cheney epitomizes this shift. Cheney developed a well-earned reputation as a conservative stalwart—for the 117th session of Congress, the conservative think-tank Heritage gave her a 96% conservative score (out of 100) (Heritage Action for America 2022). She describes herself as anti-abortion and pro-gun rights, voted to repeal Obamacare, and supports waterboarding terrorist suspects (characterizing the constitutional right to due process as an "inconvenience") (Stahl 2021; Serwer 2021). And yet Cheney's conservative bona fides ended up mattering little. Along with a small minority of her colleagues, she voted to impeach Trump from office and joined the House Select Committee investigating the January 6 insurrection. Her presence was so polarizing for conservatives that the Wyoming GOP voted to stop recognizing her as a member of the party (NPR 2021). During the Republican National Committee's (RNC) 2022 winter meeting, party leaders declared the January 6 attacks to be "legitimate political discourse," and censured Cheney and Illinois representative Adam Kinzinger for participating in a House investigation of those events (Weisman and Epstein 2022). Unsurprisingly, she lost her 2022 primary election bid to a rival candidate backed by Donald Trump (Allen and Gomez 2022). The defenestration of Cheney illustrates the ascendence of the Trump wing and the substitution of a new set of elites. Historian Rebecca Solnit writes:

> It's often said that the joiners of cults and subscribers to delusions are driven by their hatred of elites. But in the present situation, the snake oil salesmen are not just Alex Jones, QAnon's master manipulators and evangelical hucksters. They are senators, powerful white Christian men, prominent media figures, billionaires and their foundations, even a former president. (Maybe the belief that these figures are not an elite is itself a noteworthy delusion.) (Solnit 2022)

Some researchers maintain that the Republican Party's turn has been driven less by partisan elites and is instead a reflection of grassroots pressure. In a 2022 piece in *Foreign Affairs*, Steven Levitsky and Lucan Way contend that although Trump "catalyzed" the authoritarian turn of the Republican Party, its core white Christian constituency is exerting "powerful pressure from below" due to relative declines in their social and economic status (Levitsky and Way 2022). (Again, this top-down/bottom-up dynamic is captured in Starbird's contribution to this volume.) They cite surveys showing that nearly 60% of Republicans "feel like a stranger in their own country" and that the "traditional American way of life is disappearing so fast that we may have to use force to stop it" (Levitsky and Way 2022). Levitsky and Way are correct in pointing out the significance of underlying conservative disaffection, but it is important to bear in mind that stoking such disaffection has been a cornerstone of conservative political strategy for decades, cultivated by the likes of Gingrich, Limbaugh and others. They foresaw how social conservative issues could be potent instruments for assembling an enduring voting bloc and deliberately exploited these issues for political gain. Narratives of polarization, grievance, and loss primarily flow in a top-down direction, manipulated by elites for their political benefit. There is a distinction between populations which harbor generalized resentments against liberals and big government versus elite-driven narratives designed to mobilize populations for specific political purposes. It is the difference between an individual who is generally distrustful of the government versus an individual—activated by extreme conservative rhetoric—who comes to Washington to fix a "rigged" election and participate in an armed insurrection.

The Rise of Conservative Illiberalism: Strong Partisanship, Weak Parties

The dynamics above raise a basic question—what factors have paved the way for the new class of right-wing surrogates to dominate the GOP? The United States has a long history of extreme speech and polarized rhetoric, replete with political violence and targeted hostility toward minorities— what Richard Hofstadter described as a "paranoid style in American politics" comprised of "heated exaggeration, suspiciousness, and conspiratorial fantasy" (Hofstadter 1964). In some respects, the heightened level of polarization occurring in the country is not especially unique. But one aspect bears special notice—much of the current polarization is driven by the Republican Party's rightward turn. Data reveals that since 2000, the GOP has moved considerably farther to the right than comparable center-right parties in other democracies. In a V-Dem dataset and accompanying paper measuring political party illiberalism, researchers found that across a range of anti-pluralist factors, from disrespecting opponents and espousing cultural superiority, to violating minority rights and encouraging violence, the GOP is experiencing substantial erosions in its commitment to upholding democratic norms. Their conclusion (see Figure 9.1): the Republican Party is "now more similar to autocratic ruling parties such as the Turkish AKP, and Fidesz in Hungary than to typical center-right governing parties in democracies such as the Conservatives in the UK or CDU in Germany" (Lührmann et al. 2020).[6]

Research analyzing sub-national trends illuminates the GOP's anti-democratic effect. In his 2022 book, *Laboratories Against Democracy*, political scientist Jacob M. Grumbach (2022) presents a "State Democracy Index," comprised of 61 state indicators of democratic performance, from voter registration policies to legislative districting. Looking at measurements from 2000 to 2018, Grumbach finds that Republican control of state government resulted in across-the-board reductions in democratic performance, such as voter suppression, gerrymandering, and the repression of protest.

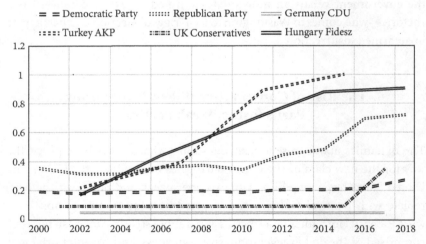

Figure 9.1 Comparative levels of political party illiberalism, 2000–2018.
Source: Lindberg et al. (2022).

---

[6] Data from the Manifesto Project, which reviews and categorizes political party documents laying out goals and policy ideas, found that the Republican Party occupied similar ideological ground to far-right parties like the Alternative for Deutschland and sat farther to the extreme than populist parties such as France's National Rally or the UK's Independence Party. In contrast, the Democratic Party fell "closer to mainstream left and center-left parties in other countries, like the Social Democratic Party in Germany and Britain's Labour Party" (see Chinoy 2019).

He concludes that the nationalization of American politics is a key driver of the GOP's anti-democratic behavior, noting that regardless of circumstance or geography, state governments are engaged in comparable activities once they take power, from Alabama and Ohio to North Carolina: "The results of this analysis point to the Republican Party as the anti-democracy coalition in American politics and state governments as a key venue in which they are pursuing their goals" (Grumbach 2022, 194). These same themes are described by Hilton in this volume.

In a similar vein, researchers from the Institute for Research and Education on Human Rights (IREHR) carried out a comprehensive analysis of US state legislators in the 2021–2022 legislative period. The group identified at least 875 legislators (872 of whom are registered Republicans) who had joined one of 789 far-right Facebook groups. In total, 11.9% of all state legislators in the United States, or 21.7% of all Republican legislators, had joined far-right Facebook groups falling into 13 distinct categories, including "militia and sovereign citizen groups, antisemitic conspiracy groups, militant COVID Denial groups, Stop the Steal groups, and more" (IREHR 2022). Of note, the IREHR excluded membership in traditionally mainstream conservative organizations from its list—such as the NRA or pro-Trump and MAGA groups—instead focusing on more extreme groups defined by white nationalist or anti-democratic attributes.

All of this adds up to a phenomenon Julia Azari (2016) describes as "strong partisanship, weak parties." She observes: "What we've known about party organizations has long indicated that they are weak, with little to hold over candidates or officeholders . . . but while parties as organizations are weak, parties as ideas—partisanship—is strong" (Azari 2016). She notes that the rise in obstructionist politics, polarized presidential approval ratings, and increasing gaps between Republican and Democratic votes indicate the extent to which partisanship has eclipsed party organization as a defining feature of American politics. This sort of weak party condition is, according to Ziblatt's conservative dilemma model, a principal feature of democratic decay (Ziblatt 2017, Ch. 9). What does extreme conservative partisanship look like in practice? In 2021, Barton Gellman carried out extensive investigative reporting to better understand the psychology of conservative Trump voters. He writes in one passage:

> Tens of millions of Americans perceive their world through black clouds of his [Trump's] smoke. His deepest source of strength is the bitter grievance

of Republican voters that they lost the White House, and are losing their country, to alien forces with no legitimate claim to power. This is not some transient or loosely committed population. Trump has built the first American mass political movement in the past century that is ready to fight by any means necessary, including bloodshed, for its cause. (Gellman 2021)

Azari and Gellman's findings echo research carried out by Finkel et al. They find that while Democrats and Republicans have "grown more contemptuous of opposing partisans for decades," only recently has their mutual aversion exceeded their affection for copartisans (Finkel et al. 2020). Using a "feeling thermometer" scale, their analysis shows that affect toward copartisans has stayed in the 70° to 75° range, but that affect toward opposing partisans has plummeted from 48° in the 1970s to 20° today (Finkel et al. 2020). In the present environment, out-party hate has become a more powerful predictor of voting patterns and may even exceed long-standing preferences around race or religion.

Self-identified conservatives have adopted increasingly hardened political perspectives. A 2019 Pew Research Center survey, for example, indicated that nearly two-thirds of Republicans viewed the other side as unpatriotic, while less than a quarter of Democrats felt that way. Republicans evinced a strong reluctance to compromise with Democrats. Just 39% mentioned that it was important to make political compromises even if it meant achieving some of their political goals. In contrast, almost six in 10 Democrats emphasized that it was important to find common ground with Republicans and were willing to give up certain priorities to do so (Pew Research Center 2019).

These studies suggest that America is increasingly beset by "affective partisan polarization," a political science concept describing when citizens evince more negative sentiments toward opposing political parties than positive feelings toward their own (Feaver 2021). There is some debate about whether affective polarization directly leads to the undermining of democratic norms, or whether it is a symptom of larger anti-democratic forces at work (some researchers argue that even if affective polarization diminished, threats to democracy would still persist) (see, for example, Broockman et al. 2020). While there is room for argument when it comes to questions of causality, what is manifestly clear is that the overall political climate in the United States is sharply divided and partisan—with little room in the middle for compromise—thus laying the foundation for distrust and acrimony.

THE RISE OF CONSERVATIVE ILLIBERALISM   223

It remains plausible that center-right positions could regain currency in the future. However, what remains concerning is the self-reinforcement taking place in the conservative electorate. Even basic national security issues have been polluted by illiberal narratives. For example, in the initial days of Russia's invasion of Ukraine, despite mainstream news outlets broadcasting catastrophic images of Russian missile strikes targeting Ukrainian civilians, a Yahoo News-YouGov poll of Trump voters revealed higher unfavorability for Biden (95%) than for Putin (78%). Moreover, nearly half of Trump voters (47%) indicated they thought Putin was doing a better job than Biden, notwithstanding crippling sanctions decimating Russia's economy—or Russia's descent to a pariah state (Romano 2022). Combatting such anchored sentiments is not just a matter of tamping down false narratives disseminated on social media or minimizing Trump from the political scene. It belies a deeper conservative discontent, cultivated assiduously for three decades and rooted in polarization, that will take a concerted effort to change.

Conclusion

As this chapter has laid out, mass media and social media amplification of extreme right-wing narratives, combined with underlying conservative polarization, have elevated a new class of right-wing surrogates, not formally bound to party or organization, who are reshaping the GOP. These trends are of course subject to fluctuation due to demographic, social, or technological factors. One aspect that will continue to shift is the interaction between mass media and social media, and the roles each currently play in shaping conservative narratives. Fox News has maintained its position as a kingmaker for conservatives—ideas that are disseminated on its nightly opinion shows play a direct role in setting the national conversation and creating a "searing narrative" for conservative viewers about how to interpret and understand what is happening in the world (Koblin and Corasaniti 2017). But demographics are working against Fox News and other conservative television outlets. Younger generations of viewers—both conservative and liberal—are rapidly abandoning traditionally programmed television. The past 20 years witnessed the emergence of social media as an influential pillar in America's information ecosystem; the next 20 years will see digital media solidify as mediators of America's politics over cable television. These trends will be even more pronounced when it comes to conservative talk radio—a medium under increasing strain from digital on-demand products like podcasts. As social media eclipses the mass media ecosystem, how will this affect conservative politics? Will filter bubbles, self-sorting, and audience fragmentation become even more acute? Given the extensive transformations that have already remade America's information ecosystem, big shifts are inevitable. Their political effect is harder to gauge.

Another issue that researchers should continue to monitor is the extent to which asymmetric polarization persists between conservative and liberal communities. As prior studies have found, liberal communities have not mirrored the rightward shift reflected by domestic conservative groups. But that also doesn't mean that liberals haven't undergone swings as well, or that the current dynamic is static. For example, the Democracy Fund's Voter Study Group released a report examining political attitudes on identity-related topics between 2011 and 2020. The researchers found that most of the divergence between liberal and conservative communities on issues such as racial equality, law enforcement, Black Lives Matter movement, immigration, and Muslims involved changes among Democrats, who "have grown much more liberal over this period" (Griffin et al. 2021). While the authors found that Trump had contributed to this divergence, they note that these changes predate Trump's presidency; they pinpoint 2011 as the onset of a profound attitudinal shift among liberals, particularly on racial inequality issues.

When it comes to diagnosing political dysfunction, researchers should also be careful not to overstate the impact of information communications on human behavior. Scholars such as sociologist Aliza Luft (2019) observe that there is limited evidence to suggest that "dehumanizing propaganda" convinces ordinary individuals to change their minds and commit political violence. Instead, Luft finds that in-group norms, peer pressure, obedience to authority, or related hierarchical pressures play much more important roles in driving these acts, and that propaganda is "more often an outcome of participation in violence rather than a precursor" (Luft 2019.

This calls into question whether the "paranoid" tradition of American conservative media, from Father Coughlin to Rush Limbaugh and Tucker Carlson, really is the driving force behind societal polarization in America, or whether other factors, such as economic inequality and dislocation, bear more responsibility. As Benkler asks in a 2019 essay, rather than look to "intentional, discrete propagandist interventions" as drivers of illiberalism in the United States, perhaps a better explanation should consider "the more basic dynamic of the past decade: the collapse of neoliberalism in the Great Recession and the struggle to define what the new settlement that replaces it must become" (Benkler 2019). There is much to reflect upon when it comes to explaining the influence of information and media on political violence and polarization, let alone understanding the specific impact of social media on democracy.

References

Allen, Jonathan, and Henry J. Gomez. 2022. "Rep. Liz Cheney Loses her Primary in Wyoming to Trump-backed Challenger." NBC News, August 16. https://www.nbcnews.com/politics/2022-election/rep-liz-cheney-loses-primary-wyoming-trump-backed-challenger-rcna43379.

Azari, Julia. 2016. "Weak Parties and Strong Partisanship are a Bad Combination." Vox, November 3. https://www.vox.com/mischiefs-of-faction/2016/11/3/13512362/weak-parties-strong-partisanship-bad-combination.

Baldassaro, Michael, Katie Harbath, and Michael Scholtens. 2021. "The Big Lie and Big Tech: Misinformation Repeat Offenders and Social Media in the 2020 U.S. Election." The Carter Center. August 2021. https://www.cartercenter.org/resources/pdfs/news/peace_publications/democracy/the-big-lie-and-big-tech.pdf.

Barberá, Pablo. 2020. "Social Media, Echo Chambers, and Political Polarization." In Nathaniel Persily and Joshua A. Tucker, eds., Social Media and Democracy: The State of the Field, Prospects for Reform (pp. 34–55). New York: Cambridge University Press.

Benkler, Yochai. 2019. "Cautionary Notes on Disinformation and the Origins of Distrust." MediaWell. Social Science Research Council. https://mediawell.ssrc.org/expert-reflections/cautionary-notes-on-disinformation-benkler/.

Benkler, Yochai, Robert Faris, and Hal Roberts. 2018. Network Propaganda: Manipulation, Disinformation, and Radicalization in American Politics. New York: Oxford University Press, 2018), 60.

Benkler, Yochai, Casey Tilton, Bruce Etling, Hal Roberts, Justin Clark, Robert Faris, Jonas Keiser, and Carolyn Schmitt. 2020. "Mail-In Voter Fraud: Anatomy of a Disinformation Campaign." Berkman Klein Center for Internet and Society, Harvard University, October 1, 2020, https://cyber.harvard.edu/publication/2020/Mail-in-Voter-Fraud-Disinformation-2020.

Bennett, W. Lance, and Alexandra Segerberg. 2013. The Logic of Connective Action. New York: Cambridge University Press.

Biden, Joseph R. 2021. "Inaugural Address by President Joseph R. Biden, Jr." Speech, Washington, DC, January 20. The White House. https://www.whitehouse.gov/briefing-room/speeches-remarks/2021/01/20/inaugural-address-by-president-joseph-r-biden-jr/.

Biden, Joseph R. 2022. "Speech on the Anniversary of the January 6 Insurrection." Speech, Washington, DC, January 6. NPR. https://www.npr.org/2022/01/06/1070931178/jan-6-anniversary-biden-speech-transcript.

Broockman, David, Joshua Kalla, and Sean Westwood. 2020. "Does Affective Polarization Undermine Democratic Norms or Accountability? Maybe Not." OSF Preprints. December 22. https://doi.org/10.31219/osf.io/9btsq.

Center for an Informed Public, Digital Forensic Research Lab, Graphika, and Stanford Internet Observatory. 2021. *The Long Fuse: Misinformation and the 2020 Election*, v1.2.0. Stanford Digital Repository: Election Integrity Partnership. https://purl.stanford.edu/tr171zs0069.

Chadwick, Andrew. 2013. *The Hybrid Media System: Politics and Power*. New York: Oxford University Press.

Chen, Annie Y., Brendan Nyhan, Jason Reifler, Ronald E. Robertson, and Christo Wilson. 2022. "Subscriptions and External Links Help Drive Resentful Users to Alternative and Extremist YouTube Videos." arXiv preprint arXiv:2204.10921.

Chinoy, Sahil. 2019. "What happened to America's political center of gravity?" *New York Times*, June 26. https://www.nytimes.com/interactive/2019/06/26/opinion/sunday/republican-platform-far-right.html.

Confessore, Nicholas. 2022. "What to Know about Tucker Carlson's Rise." *New York Times*. April 30. https://www.nytimes.com/2022/04/30/business/media/tucker-carlson-fox-news-takeaways.html.

Couric, Katie, Chris Krebs, and Rashad Robinson. 2021. *Commission on Information Disorder Final Report*. Washington, DC: Aspen Digital. https://www.aspeninstitute.org/wp-content/uploads/2021/11/Aspen-Institute_Commission-on-Information-Disorder_Final-Report.pdf.

Feaver, Peter D. 2021. "The Future of Democracy: National Security Begins at Home." In "Democracy's Future: Abroad and at Home." Special issue. *Democracy*, 62. https://democracyjournal.org/magazine/62-special-issue/the-future-of-democracy-national-security-begins-at-home/.

Finkel, Eli J., Christopher A. Bail, Mina Cikara, Peter H. Ditto, Shanto Iyengar, Samara Klar, Lilliama Mason, Mary C. McGrath, Brendan Nyhan, David G. Rand, Linda J. Skitka, Joshua A. Tucker, Jay J. Van Bavel, Cynthia S. Wang, and James N. Druckman. 2020. "Political Sectarianism in America." *Science* 370 (6516): 533–536.

Gatewood, Cooper, and Ciarán O'Connor. 2020. *Disinformation Briefing: Narratives around Black Lives Matter and Voter Fraud*. Institute for Strategic Dialogue and Politico. October. https://www.isdglobal.org/wp-content/uploads/2020/10/Disinfo-Briefing-BLM-and-Voter-Fraud.pdf.

Gellman, Barton. 2021. "Trump's Next Coup has Already Begun." *The Atlantic*, December 6. https://www.theatlantic.com/magazine/archive/2022/01/january-6-insurrection-trump-coup-2024-election/620843/.

Griffin, Robert, Mayesha Quasem, John Sides, and Michael Tesler. 2021. "Partisan Shifts on Racial Attitudes over the Last Decade." Democracy Fund–Voter Study Group. October. https://www.voterstudygroup.org/publication/racing-apart#emerging-racial-liberalism-in-the-democratic-party.

Grumbach, Jacob M. 2022. *Laboratories Against Democracy: How National Parties Transformed State Politics*. Princeton, NJ: Princeton University Press.

Hacker, Jacob S., and Paul Pierson. 2020. *Let Them Eat Tweets*. New York: Liveright Publishing Corporation.

Haidt, Jonathan. 2022. "Why the Past 10 years of American Life have been Uniquely Stupid." *The Atlantic*, April 11. https://www.theatlantic.com/magazine/archive/2022/05/social-media-democracy-trust-babel/629369/.

Heritage Action for America. 2022. "Rep. Liz Cheney." https://heritageaction.com/scorecard/members/C001109/117.

Hindman, Matthew, Nathaniel Lubin, and Trevor Davis. 2022. "Facebook Has a Superuser-Supremacy Problem." *The Atlantic*, February 10. https://www.theatlantic.com/technology/archive/2022/02/facebook-hate-speech-misinformation-superusers/621617/.

Hofstadter, Richard. 1964. "The Paranoid Style in American Politics." *Harper's Magazine*. https://harpers.org/archive/1964/11/the-paranoid-style-in-american-politics/.

Hosseinmardi, Homa, Amir Ghasemian, Aaron Clauset, Markus Mobius, David M. Rothschild, and Duncan J. Watts. 2020. "Evaluating the Scale, Growth, and Origins of Right-Wing Echo Chambers on YouTube." November 25. arXiv preprint arXiv:2011.12843.

Ipsos. 2022. "Seven in Ten Americans Say the Country is in Crisis, at Risk of Failing." January 3. https://www.ipsos.com/en-us/seven-ten-americans-say-country-crisis-risk-failing.

IREHR. 2022. "Breaching the Mainstream: A National Survey of Far-Right Membership in State Legislatures." Institute for Research and Education on Human Rights. https://www.irehr.org/reports/breaching-the-mainstream/#.

Jamieson, Kathleen Hall, and Joseph N. Cappella. 2008. *Echo Chamber: Rush Limbaugh and the Conservative Media Establishment*. New York: Oxford University Press.

Kansas City Star. 2021. Editorial Board, "Now Josh Hawley Says Trying to Protect Americans From COVID-19 Is 'Woke Propaganda'," October 21. https://www.kansascity.com/opinion/editorials/article255148487.html.

Kaufman, Amanda. 2021. "'Peaceful Patriots': Months after Jan. 6 Insurrection, GOP Members of Congress Attempt to Recast Events of Deadly Attack." *Boston Globe*, May 12. https://www.bostonglobe.com/2021/05/12/nation/peaceful-patriots-months-after-jan-6-insurrection-gop-members-congress-attempt-revise-events-deadly-attack/.

Kelly, Mary L., and Evan Osnos. 2021. "How Dan Bongino Is Building a Right-Wing Media Empire on His Own Terms." *All Things Considered*, December 30. NPR. https://www.npr.org/2021/12/30/1069273204/how-dan-bongino-is-building-a-right-wing-media-empire-on-his-own-terms.

Koblin, John, and Nick Corasaniti. 2017. "One Nation, Under Fox: 18 Hours with a Network That Shapes America" *New York Times*, March 25. https://www.nytimes.com/2017/03/25/business/media/fox-news.html.

Kreiss, Daniel, and Shannon C. McGregor. 2018. "Technology Firms Shape Political Communication: The Work of Microsoft, Facebook, Twitter, and Google with Campaigns during the 2016 US Presidential Cycle." *Political Communication* 35 (2): 155–177.

Levitsky, Steven, and Lucan Way. 2022. "America's Coming Age of Instability: Why Constitutional Crises and Political Violence Could Soon Be the Norm." *Foreign Affairs*, January 20. https://www.foreignaffairs.com/articles/united-states/2022-01-20/americas-coming-age-instability.

Lindberg, Staffan, Nils Düpont, Masaaki Higashijima, Yaman Berker Kavasoglu, Kyle L. Marquardt, Michael Bernhard, Holger Döring, Allen Hicken, Melis Laebens, Juraj Medzihorsky, Anja Neundorf, Ora John Reuter, Saskia Ruth–Lovell, Keith R. Weghorst, Nina Wiesehomeier, Joseph Wright, Nazifa Alizada, Paul Bederke, Lisa Gastaldi, Sandra Grahn, Garry Hindle, Nina Ilchenko, Johannes von Römer, Steven Wilson, Daniel Pemstein, and Brigitte Seim. 2022. "Codebook Varieties of Party Identity and Organization (V–Party) V2." Varieties of Democracy (V–Dem) Project. https://doi.org/10.23696/vpartydsv2.

Luft, Aliza. 2019. "Dehumanization and the Normalization of Violence: It's Not what you Think." Social Science Research Council. May 21. https://items.ssrc.org/insights/dehumanization-and-the-normalization-of-violence-its-not-what-you-think/

Lührmann, Anna, Juraj Medzihorsky, Garry Hindle, and Staffan I. Lindberg. 2020. *New Global Data on Political Parties: V-Party*. Gothenburg, Sweden: V-Dem Institute. https://www.v-dem.net/static/website/img/refs/vparty_briefing.pdf.

228   CONNECTIVE ACTION AND THE RISE OF THE FAR-RIGHT

Mac, Ryan, and Lisa Lerer. 2022. "The Right's Would-Be Kingmaker." *New York Times*, February 14. https://www.nytimes.com/2022/02/14/technology/republican-trump-peter-thiel.html.

McFadden, Robert D., and Michael M. Grynbaum. 2021. "Rush Limbaugh Dies at 70; Turned Talk Radio into a Right-Wing Attack Machine." *New York Times*, February 17. https://www.nytimes.com/2021/02/17/business/media/rush-limbaugh-dead.html.

NPR. 2021. "Wyoming GOP votes to stop recognizing Cheney as a Republican." November 15. https://www.npr.org/2021/11/15/1056025589/wyoming-gop-votes-to-stop-recognizing-cheney-as-a-republican.

Osnos, Evan. 2021. "Dan Bongino and the Big Business of Returning Trump to Power." *The New Yorker*, December 27. https://www.newyorker.com/magazine/2022/01/03/dan-bongino-and-the-big-business-of-returning-trump-to-power.

Parker, Ashley, Amy Gardner, and Josh Dawsey. 2022. "How Republicans Became the Party of Trump's Election Lie after Jan. 6." *Washington Post*, January 5. https://www.washingtonpost.com/politics/republicans-jan-6-election-lie/2022/01/05/82f4cad4-6cb6-11ec-974b-d1c6de8b26b0_story.html.

Pew Research Center. 2019. "Partisan Antipathy: More Intense, More Personal." October 10. https://www.pewresearch.org/politics/2019/10/10/the-partisan-landscape-and-views-of-the-parties/.

Puyosa, Iria, and Esteban Ponce de Leon. 2022. "Understanding Telegram's Ecosystem of Far-Right Channels in the US." Atlantic Council DFRLab. March 23. https://medium.com/dfrlab/understanding-telegrams-ecosystem-of-far-right-channels-in-the-us-22e963c09234

Romano, Andrew. 2022. "Poll: 74% of Americans Call Russia's Ukraine Invasion Unjustified." *Yahoo News*, February 28. https://news.yahoo.com/poll-74-percent-of-americans-call-russias-ukraine-invasion-unjustified-142128676.html?guccounter=1.

Ruane, Kathleen A. 2011. *Fairness Doctrine: History and Constitutional Issues*. Washington, DC: Congressional Research Service. https://sgp.fas.org/crs/misc/R40009.pdf.

Scott, Mark. 2020. "Despite Cries of Censorship, Conservatives Dominate Social Media," *Politico*, October 26, 2020. https://www.politico.com/news/2020/10/26/censorship-conservatives-social-media-432643.

Serwer, Adam. 2021. "Liz Cheney has only herself to Blame." *The Atlantic*, May 6. https://www.theatlantic.com/ideas/archive/2021/05/liz-cheney-trump-fraud/618820/.

Silverman, Craig, Craig Timberg, Jeff Kao, and Jeremy B. Merrill. 2022. "Facebook Groups Topped 10,000 Daily Attacks on Election Before Jan. 6, Analysis Shows." *Washington Post*, January 4. https://www.washingtonpost.com/technology/2022/01/04/facebook-election-misinformation-capitol-riot/.

Solnit, Rebecca. 2022. "Why Republicans Keep Falling for Trump's Lies." *New York Times*, January 5. https://www.nytimes.com/2022/01/05/opinion/republicans-trump-lies.html.

Stahl, Lesley. 2021. "Liz Cheney on being a Republican while Opposing Donald Trump." *60 Minutes*, September 26. https://www.cbsnews.com/news/liz-cheney-donald-trump-wyoming-60-minutes-2021-09-26/.

Sunstein, Cass R. 2017. "#Republic: Divided Democracy in the Age of Social Media." Princeton, NJ: Princeton University Press.

Swan, Jonathan, and Lachlan Markay. 2022. "The Making of a Modern Republican." *Axios*, February 5. https://www.axios.com/modern-republican-party-primary-trump-gop-d445dd51-adfc-469e-b1dd-5d6b25118bc7.html.

Weisman, Jonathan, and Reid J. Epstein. 2022. "G.O.P. Declares Jan. 6 Attack 'Legitimate Political Discourse.'" *New York Times*, February 4. https://www.nytimes.com/2022/02/04/us/politics/republicans-jan-6-cheney-censure.html.

Ziblatt, Daniel. 2017. *Conservative Parties and the Birth of Democracy*. New York: Cambridge University Press.

Zuboff, Shoshana. 2021. "The Coup we are Not Talking About." *New York Times*, January 29. https://www.nytimes.com/2021/01/29/opinion/sunday/facebook-surveillance-society-technology.html.

Chapter 10
Hating the Other as a Cross-Cutting Issue

Assessing the Role of Media Surrogate Organizations

Babak Bahador and Daniel Kerchner

How do center-right parties promote the policy preferences of economic elites, yet form cross-class coalitions needed to remain competitive in fair elections? Daniel Ziblatt (2017) calls this the conservative dilemma and describes how this quandary is especially prevalent during times of demographic change, socioeconomic inequality, and social justice activism. Hacker and Pierson (2020) consider a similar predicament, by asking "How [are conservative parties] to side with the elites ... yet attract the support of voters losing out?" One way in which this is addressed is through the promotion of cross-cutting cleavage issues, defined as compelling social issues and narratives that cut across class divides by drawing attention to emotional issues characterized by prejudice and fear. According to Ziblatt's model, such issues are promoted by the party and by surrogate organizations— groups aligned with the party that are often better suited to generating outrage. As Hacker and Pierson put it, "These organizations can focus on building strong emotional bonds with citizens and tapping shared identities. Crucially, these organizations may feel much less need to moderate and equivocate" (Hacker and Pierson 2020, 23). What started out as a winning strategy for building a cross-class coalition runs the risk of pulling a conventional party into an illiberal morass. Often, the cross-cutting issues rely on creating hateful distinctions between "us" and "them." Again, to quote Hacker and Pierson,

> In modern societies, the list of such "cleavages" is short, and their history unpleasant. There are racial, ethnic, and religious divisions. There is the call of nationalism or foreign military adventures. There are sectional loyalties. There is opposition to immigration. In short, there is a set

---

Babak Bahador and Daniel Kerchner, *Hating the Other as a Cross-Cutting Issue*. In: *Connective Action and the Rise of the Far-Right*. Edited by: Steven Livingston and Michael Miller, Oxford University Press. © Oxford University Press (2025). DOI: 10.1093/oso/9780197794937.003.0010

of noneconomic issues—many racially tinged, all involving strong identities and strong emotions—that draw a sharp line between "us" and "them." (Hacker and Pierson 2020, 22)

Outrage narratives blaming "other" minority identity-based groups for various real and imagined social problems are not new. The use of divisive and hateful rhetoric by political leaders to rile up the majority or in-group against various, often marginalized, out-groups is a well-established tactic used throughout history by populists and political opportunists to gain and consolidate power. In such scenarios, the news media have often followed the political elite to set their agenda and framing on political issues. However, in recent decades, even before the internet and social media, conservative media organizations and personalities in the United States appeared to play an increasingly leading role in moving the conservative public and center-right politicians to more extreme positions. Using brash, partisan, and polarizing language, personalities like Rush Limbaugh on the radio and various Fox News hosts on cable news, increasingly blamed groups associated with their political opposition's coalition as the source of society's problems.

This chapter aims to better understand the role of conservative media as surrogate organizations, using the period surrounding the 2020 election as a case study. Specifically, it attempts to examine which marginalized groups were targeted for negative and hateful outrage narratives, the intensity of such attacks and the themes of their attacks. To this end, the daily shows of the top 10 conservative media personalities (by audience size) in the United States are analyzed from one week before the 2020 presidential election on November 3, 2020, to one week after the January 20, 2021, inauguration—a period of heightened political drama, highlighted by the January 6, 2021, insurrection. The aim is to illustrate how even conventional media can serve as surrogate organizations, and by extension, as elements of what other chapters in this volume refer to as digital surrogate networks. Rather than stand-alone surrogate organizations as Ziblatt (2017) saw in operation in his analysis of late nineteenth- and early twentieth-century politics, the internet means that "digital surrogate networks" contain diverse elements, including social media accounts, television and radio networks, and personalities such as Tucker Carlson. This chapter illustrates the role of conventional right-wing media in feeding hateful cross-cutting issues into conservative parties' attempts to resolve the conservative dilemma.

Conservative Media and Outrage Narratives

Today's conservative media traces its roots to two key events: the syndication of Rush Limbaugh's talk radio show in 1988 and the launch of Fox News in 1996. Both found commercial success by promoting a particular type of messaging—both in content and style—that would encourage other right-wing media personalities and organizations (on television and online) to follow suit, leading to the creation of a conservative media ecosystem that would shift both conservative voters and politicians toward extremism and tribalism (Hacker and Pierson 2020). Of course, as Hemmer has pointed out, the trajectory of conservative media was set decades before (Hemmer 2016). But it is the emergence of right-wing talk radio, followed by television, and then the internet, that has super-charged the creation of a digital surrogate network, with conventional media playing a crucial role in addressing the challenges of the conservative dilemma. According to Hacker and Pierson (2020), the right-wing media's approach to audiences has three pillars: isolation, loyalty, and emotion. Isolation involves the delegitimization of other sources of hitherto credible information, such as experts and mainstream media through relentless attacks on them. For conservatives, experts such as university professors and cultural elites, like entertainers and liberal politicians, are "out of touch" elites who are responsible for various social ills (Bahador et al. 2019). Elites are, therefore, key targets of outrage and ridicule by conservative media personalities, who position themselves as common folk and defenders of the working class (even though they are themselves members of the economic elite). According to Knüpfer and Klinger, right-wing media often presents itself under "liberal democratic values such as pluralism and inclusion" (Knüpfer and Klinger, this volume). No slogan, of course, is more obvious in this regard than Fox News' claim to be "Fair and Balanced."

Once traditional sources of credible information are delegitimized, trust in them significantly diminishes, opening the way for a loyal and insular audience. As a result, conservatives in the United States hold large trust gaps, consisting of the difference between their loyalty to right-wing media and distrust in mainstream media (Hacker and Pierson 2020, 102). Once isolation and loyalty are established, the void is then filled with emotive outrage narratives that target different nonmajority groups with hateful rhetoric, often based on exaggerated and false claims about threats posed against them by the majority in-group. In this regard, the emphasis transitions from one of inclusion to one of exclusion, demarcation, and "othering" (Knüpfer and Klinger, this volume).

Outrage narratives against minority groups involve the use of hate speech. While hate speech is legally permitted with few exceptions in the United States, it nonetheless poses a danger to the groups targeted by such speech. The following section defines hate speech, presents a model to measure its intensity, and then uses this model to examine the nature of the cross-cutting issues used to target groups by conservative media within the context of the 2020 election and January 6th Capitol insurrection.

Hate Speech

Hate speech is communication that discriminates, dehumanizes, demonizes, or incites violence against groups that hold immutable qualities (or protected status) such as a particular ethnicity, nationality, religion, gender, age bracket, or sexual orientation. While hate speech technically refers to the expression of thoughts in spoken words, it can be over any form of communication, including text, images, videos, and even gestures. However, at its core, hate speech is based on a causal claim that postulates that exposure to a particular type of message is likely to evoke the emotion of hate, and lead to changes in opinion and behavior against those targeted by it. Hate has been defined as an emotion that leads to an enduring dislike, loss of empathy, and potential desire to harm those against whom the emotion is directed (Waltman and Mattheis 2017). In relation to the focus of this book, hate speech is central to outrage narratives that often constitute a cross-cutting cleavage issue.

Of course, it should be noted that there are concerns with ambiguities over tying an emotion such as hate to an effect, as different individuals, even in the same in-group, are likely to have different predispositions and react differently to the same message (Gagliardone et. al. 2015; Howard 2019). As such, some thinkers prefer more precise concepts such as fear speech (Buyse 2014), which emphasizes the use of fear of particular groups to stoke reactions; ignorant speech (Lepoutre 2019), which highlights the underlying falsehood behind such speech; and dangerous speech (Benesch 2013; Brown 2016), which focuses on speech that is likely to lead to violence.

While hate speech is largely permitted in the United States due to the First Amendment of its Constitution, it would be subject to more legal scrutiny internationally, and any media personality with large audiences that would use it in many other countries would be much more likely to face legal sanctions. In terms of international law, the UN's International Covenant on Civil and Political Rights, Article 20, states that "Any advocacy of national, racial or religious hatred that constitutes incitement to discrimination, hostility or violence shall be prohibited by law" (United Nations 1966). In the United States, however, prosecution of speech is limited to cases in which "lawless action" is incited and such cases must be both imminent and likely (Tucker 2015).

This study focuses on hate speech targeted at groups, which is more likely to lead to more harm than speech targeting individuals. This is because when a group is associated with extremely negative actions or characteristics, all members of the group become guilty by association and targets for collective punishment. Of course, history is replete with examples in which groups have been targeted for hate, both domestically and internationally, to justify and prepare society for state violence against them (Bahador 2015; Carruthers 2011; Dower 1986; Keen 1991). According to Sam Keen, "We think others to death and then invent the battle-axe or the ballistic missiles with which to actually kill them" (1991, 10). While hate speech by popular media personalities in the United States may seem distant from the mass atrocities of history, it is important to monitor such activity, as history also shows that political conditions can sometimes change rapidly, with demonized groups losing their former protections and becoming targets of real-world harm and violence.

Furthermore, while the research on hate speech largely focuses on groups that have protected status or immutable qualities, there are other groups that are targeted for hate that are important to include in hate speech monitoring research, as these groups are also often targeted for various forms of harm. A leading group in this regard is composed of journalists and members of the media industry, who are often targets of outrage narratives by the conservative media.

Hate Speech Intensity Scale

While much of the literature on hate speech views hate speech as a single category, a more detailed examination shows important distinctions. It is also important to note that hate speech typologies such as demonization, dehumanization, and incitement to violence do not sporadically emerge,

HATING THE OTHER AS A CROSS-CUTTING ISSUE 235

and that other types of less intense negative speech against groups can be an early warning before more traditional categories of hate speech emerge. To this end, this chapter utilizes a six-point hate speech intensity scale for analysis. This scale was developed following an extensive content analysis of US news and political talk media, and a review of the academic literature on hate speech. Table 10.1 presents the scale and shows a color, number, title, description, and examples for each point on the scale.

The six categories from least intense to most intense are 1) disagreement, 2) negative action, 3) negative character, 4) demonizing/dehumanizing, 5) incitement to violence, and 6) incitement to death. Importantly, a distinction is made between "rhetorical language," negative words/phrases ascribed to the group (in the past, present or future), and "responses," which describe

Table 10.1 Hate Speech Intensity Scale

Color	Title	Description	Examples
	6. Death	Rhetoric implies literal killing by group. Responses include the literal death/elimination of a group.	Kill, annihilate, destroy
	5. Violence	**Rhetoric implies infliction of physical harm or metaphoric/aspirational physical harm or death.** Responses include literal violence or metaphoric/aspirational physical harm or death.	Hurt, rape, starve, torturing, mugging
	4. Demonizing/ Dehumanizing	Rhetoric includes sub-human and superhuman characteristics. There are no responses for #4.	Alien, demon, monkey, Nazi, cancer, monster, germ
	3. Negative character	Rhetoric includes nonviolent characterizations and insults. There are no responses for #3.	Stupid, aggressor, fake, crazy
	2. Negative actions	Rhetoric includes negative nonviolent actions associated with the group. Responses include nonviolent actions including metaphors.	Threaten, stop, outrageous behavior, poor treatment, alienate, hope for their defeat
	1. Disagreement	Rhetoric includes disagreeing at the idea/mental level. Responses include challenging the group's claims, ideas, beliefs, or trying to change them.	False, incorrect, wrong, challenge, persuade, change minds

what the in-group has done, is doing or should do against the out-group. This response can either be a reaction by the in-group to the alleged actions of the out-group or an independent action that is not directly tied to the out-group's actions or character.

At the least intense level (#1) are statements of disagreement, such as indications that the out-group is wrong, that what they claim is false or that what they believe is incorrect. In general, this is the mildest form of negative speech against groups, as it addresses their ideas rather than their actions or character. Responses are also at the ideational level and deal with rejecting the idea or trying to persuade against the group's alleged views. Level 1 is generally not considered hate speech (and thus designated with the color green), but rather an early sign that sets the parameters for future possible hate speech. At its core, it involves identifying an out-group and othering them, in which a group is distinguished as separate from the in-group and is alleged to be incorrect in their ideas and beliefs. While this is not hateful, it conditions the in-group to begin seeing the other group as having clear differences in thoughts and values that are presented as being wrong or false. This creates a clear us versus them divide and can fester over time to permit an atmosphere of even more extreme rhetoric involving greater disdain.

Statements at the next level (#2) identify negative nonviolent actions in association with the target groups. Words/phrases that are ambiguous on violence (e.g., defeat/stop) are included in #2 and only moved to #5/6 (violence and death categories) if their context clearly refers to violence. As with rhetoric, this category includes only nonviolent responses or independent actions by the in-group toward the out-group. Responses/independent actions that are ambiguous on violence are included in #2 and only moved to # 5/6 if their context clearly refers to violence. This category also includes nonviolent negative metaphors.

The next level (#3) refers to negative characterizations or insults. This is worse than #2 (negative nonviolent actions), as it suggests that the negativity is intrinsic to the group and less likely to change, whereas actions, being episodic, could be an anomaly not central to the group's core nature. There are no responses in this category as it is not action oriented.

The next level (#4) refers to extreme negative characterizations that are either dehumanizing or demonizing. Dehumanization refers to despised sub-human entities that are considered inferior such as pigs, rats, monkeys or even germs and dirt/filth. Demonization involves portraying an enemy as superhuman, such as a monster, robot or even equating an enemy with fatal diseases like cancer, to depict them as a mortal threat to the in-group's survival. When presented this way, the destruction of the adversary is not only acceptable, but even desirable and beneficial for the in-group and its survival (Bar-Tel 1990; Merskin 2004). Demonization/dehumanization is a particularly extreme type of negative characterization and a well-established tool for justifying political violence, and thus merits its own category beyond more standard negative characterizations. Like #3, there are no responses in this category as it is not action oriented.

The next two levels (#5 and #6) represent the worst type of hate speech, as they refer to violence, either ascribed to the group's actions or about what should be done to the group (responses). Category #5 refers to literal violence that is nonlethal, either based on past/current/future actions or metaphorical/aspirational violence associated with the group. While literal references to violence can certainly increase hate and support for violence, research shows that even metaphorical violence can increase support for violence (Kalmoe 2014). Responses include incitement to nonlethal violence against the out-group. Category #6 is the most dangerous type of hate speech and either associates the out-group with past, present or future literal death, or incitement to kill the out-group, including calls for genocide against them.

Overall, the six categories fit into three buckets. Categories 1, 2, and 3 can be considered "early warning." While they can certainly increase hatred toward the out-group, they often fall outside traditional definitions of hate speech. Category 4 (dehumanization/demonization) is an extreme form of group defamation and a core typology of any hate speech definition. Categories 5 and 6 also generally fit into traditional definitions of hate speech, especially when they involve incitement through calls for violence and death against out-groups.

Methodology

The project employed a five-step process to derive a data set containing instances of hate speech in the media:

1. *Identifying sources and timeframe.* We identified and analyzed the top 10 conservative and liberal shows across cable news, radio, and YouTube (Katz 2018; Talkers N.D.; YouTube). Table 10.A1 displays the media figures, their shows, their platforms, and their audience size, for conservative and liberal shows, respectively. We defined the time period of study as the 14-week period from October 27, 2020, which was one week before the 2020 presidential election, to Jan. 27,

2021, which was one week after the president's inauguration. Only the first hour of each show was included in the study.

2. *Text collection and cleaning.* Content was gathered from a variety of sources including LexisNexis, YouTube, dedicated websites, and podcasts. Audio content was transformed into text by utilizing YouTube closed captioning. Transcripts were then cleaned to remove content.

3. *Semiautomated filtering.* This step derived a list of instances of hate speech. To accomplish this, we created a lexicon of approximately 300 subjects (that is, groups that were potential targets of hate speech) and a dictionary of approximately 8,000 keywords. The second step identified negative words and phrases (keywords), negative words and phrases that a speaker could associate with subjects. We employed original Python-based software (Kerchner and Littman 2019) to search the transcripts for each instance where a subject and a keyword were located within a five-word proximity. The product of this step was a table of potential hate speech instances, or Units of Analysis (UOAs), along with relevant metadata and the local context of each instance (see Table 10.A2).

4. *Human coding.* Human coders (tested for intercoder reliability) reviewed the table of potential UOAs; for each item, coders verified that the keyword applied to the subject and was semantically relevant; for instances deemed relevant, the coder also categorized the instance using the six-point hate speech intensity scale and decided if it was an example of rhetoric or response. In total, each coder had 11 options for each candidate UOA discovered by the automated filter, as outlined below in Table 10.2:

   To test for intercoder reliability, two coders separately coded 1,291 units generated by the system from a two-week pilot-study sample. This followed an extensive effort to refine the code book with two coders simultaneously coding earlier samples, clarifying ambiguities, and revising the code book until coders consistently reached the same coding outcomes at a rate of 93.5%, with Krippendorff's Alpha coefficient of 0.765; above 0.7 indicates reliable data findings (Lombard et al. 2002), as outlined in Table 10.A3.

5. *Analysis.* Descriptive analysis and data visualization were performed on the coded data to enable researchers to observe trends and meaningful features in the data related to the theme of this book, with particular focus on protected status groups that were targeted for hate speech by conservative media.

Table 10.2 Human Coding Options

Option #	Definition
1	Rejected potential UOA presented and could not find new UOA in text
2	Accept UOA presented and/or add new UOA; coded 1A—1 intensity, rhetoric (A)
3	Accept UOA presented and/or add new UOA; coded 1B—1 intensity, response (B)
4	Accept UOA presented and/or add new UOA; coded 2A—2 intensity, rhetoric (A)
5	Accept UOA presented and/or add new UOA; coded 2B—2 intensity, response (B)
6	Accept UOA presented and/or add new UOA; coded 3A—3 intensity, rhetoric (A)
7	Accept UOA presented and/or add new UOA; coded 4A—4 intensity, rhetoric (A)
8	Accept UOA presented and/or add new UOA; coded 5A—5 intensity, rhetoric (A)
9	Accept UOA presented and/or add new UOA; coded 5B—5 intensity, response (B)
10	Accept UOA presented and/or add new UOA; coded 6A—6 intensity, rhetoric (A)
11	Accept UOA presented and/or add new UOA; coded 6B—6 intensity, response (B)

Findings

Over the 14-week period of the study, over 33,700 potential UOAs were generated by the Python-based search of transcripts. Human coders reviewed these and identified 4,514 UOAs that were then allocated to the six-point hate speech intensity scale. Furthermore, 997 UOAs were added from the coder review of the extracts, adding up to 5,511 total UOAs. This study distinguished four different typologies of hate speech groups—protected status, foreign, profession/industry and other. This chapter focuses only on groups with protected status (or immutable qualities). From the 5,511 total UOAs, only 462 related to protected status groups. The UOAs referencing protected status and referencing all typologies combined are presented in tabular format in Table 10.A4.

When examining the findings by intensity, the majority of the UOAs for all typologies were negative characterizations (#3 on the intensity scale), which accounted for 69.5% of all UOAs across the six-point scale. Negative characterizations also accounted for the majority of cases for the protected status typology, representing 59.7% of UOAs. Collectively, #2

240 CONNECTIVE ACTION AND THE RISE OF THE FAR-RIGHT

and #3 account for over 90% of UOAs for all typologies, but 72% for protected status. This was because the most extreme types of hate speech (demonization/dehumanization, violence and death) were more prevalent for protected status groups vs other typology groups. Whereas these three hate-speech categories represented 7% of all UOAs for all typologies, they accounted for 28.8% of UOAs for the protected status group. This is a notable difference and suggests that hate speech is clearly more intense for protected status groups. The distribution of UOAs by intensity is shown in Table 10.A5 for UOAs referencing protected status typology and for all UOAs referencing protected status groups.

The top five protected status groups targeted for hate by rank in this study (Table 10.A6) are Blacks (33.6% of total), migrants (32.7%), Muslims (11.3%), women (10.2%), and LGBT+ (4.1%). When looking at these same findings segmented between conservative and liberal shows (Table 10.A7) that remarkably, over 90% of the negative and hateful rhetoric came from conservative shows even though the same volume of content was examined for each. When looking at the top five categories by conservative vs liberal shows, conservative shows accounted for 96.8% of such rhetoric relating to Blacks, 95.4% regarding migrants, 65.4% for Muslims, 93.6% for women, and 100% for LGBT+. These are all groups, of course, that are targets of right-wing media outrage narratives that from the perspective of the conservative dilemma, are used to distract conservative audiences from underlying issues of economic elite wealth concentration and inequality. The following section examines some of these outrage narratives in more detail for the top three groups—Blacks, migrants, and Muslims—based on a more detailed analysis of the media content used in the outrage narratives.

Blacks

From the 155 negative and hateful comments against Blacks, over 35% of them (55) suggested that they were violent (as shown in Table 10.A8). Associating Blacks with violence and crime, of course, is a well-established negative stereotype in the white American psyche going back centuries and the findings from this study show that it is still present either through direct association or via the proxy of the Black Lives Matter movement, which is used as a dog whistle to avoid direct attacks and utilize plausible deniability. The next three most widely used characterizations built on this theme with minor variations by referring to Blacks/BLM as thugs and criminals (17 references/11%), terrorists (13 references/8.4%), murderers (12 references/7.7%), and looters/thieves (10 references/6.5%).

Migrants

The second most-referenced protected status group in this study is migrants. The dominant negative attribute associated with migrants is that they are illegal (as shown in Table 10.A9). While the terms "illegal alien" and "illegal immigrant" are historically considered legal and accurate, they are nonetheless loaded terms that negatively connote migrants with illegality and therefore criminality, thus delegitimizing them to the majority in-group. While leading news outlets and the US federal government have stopped using the term, preferring more neutral terms such as "undocumented immigrant," it nonetheless remains popular within conservative media and audiences. Out of the 151 units of analysis identified in this study, 100 or 66% referred to migrants as illegal. This was followed by an even more sinister characterization, referring to migrants as flooding or invading the United States, which accounted for 23 or 15.2% of references. This type of characterization is a clear form of demonization, in which the group is presented as a threat to the majority group and is central to white supremacist notions of replacement theory, in which the majority fear having their cultural and demographic dominance replaced by inferior cultures and people. This "demographic determinism," as Andrew Thompson argues, in which groups associated with the political opposition appear set to form a demographic majority, inevitably lead to a rise of anti-democratic views and demographic backsliding (Thompson, this volume). Other leading characterizations equated migrants with murderers and criminals.

Muslims

The third most referenced protected status group for negative and hateful comments on conservative media were Muslims. This group was also highest among all the groups on the six-point scale, averaging 4.15/6 on conservative media. The most widely used negative/hateful characterization referred to Muslims as terrorists or violent (21/52 or 40.4%), as shown in Table 10.A10. This was followed by references to the group as radical/extremist/fundamentalist or militant at 12/52 or 23.1%. Other less common characteristics referred to Muslims as hating the US, Nazis, and stupid.

January 6th Capitol Insurrection

When examining the three most frequently cited protected-status groups before and after January 6, there is a clear pattern toward greater intensity after January 6 (as shown in Table 10.A11). This is particularly the case for Blacks where the average intensity increases from 3.73 to 4.24 and Muslims where the average increases from 3.96 to 4.67. For Blacks, there was a particularly notable increase in the #5 intensity category, which associates the group with violence or calls for violence against them. While #5 represented 21.4% of all UOAs before January 6, this increased to 37.9% after January 6, at least in part due to false claims suggesting that BLM was somehow involved with the January 6th Capitol insurrection.

Conclusion

The findings from this chapter and underlying study provide evidence to support claims that the conservative media, as a surrogate organization, were disproportionately focused on outrage narratives targeting protected status groups associated with their political opposition. This was demonstrated by the findings that showed conservative media to be the purveyor of negative and hateful rhetoric against protected status groups by a factor of 10 versus liberal shows covering the same amount of time (10 hours a day for each). Conservative media was particularly focused on Blacks and Migrants, representing 35.7% and 34% of their vitriol, respectively, and in both cases conservative media, in fact, represented over 95% of all negative/hateful rhetoric against these groups. Both groups were associated with violence and criminality.

In the case of Blacks, the BLM movement, which sought to raise awareness about police violence (and other discrimination) against Blacks, and which had high support in the African American community, was maligned as a violent, criminal, terrorist, and Marxist enterprise. In the aftermath of the January 6 attacks, this false narrative was further promoted by accusing BLM of having a role in the attack on the Capitol. In the case of migrants, there was a continuous and persistent focus on their illegality, followed by the much more sinister idea that they are flooding and invading the United States, thus creating a direct threat to the majority's power and established culture.

These narratives and cross-cutting issues, of course, have proven effective in motivating large segments of the population, who might otherwise be natural allies of the political left due to their difficult economic circumstances, to support conservative political parties who promise to fight for them against these groups and their alleged threats. While much focus in recent years has been on the role of digital surrogate organizations and the spread of hateful rhetoric on the internet and social media, this study shows that these trends predate the internet and social media and are also present over older forms of media, which continue to attract daily audiences in the tens of millions.

Appendix

Table 10.A1 Leading Conservative and Liberal Shows

Figure	Show	Platform	Audience Size (000s)
Conservative Shows			
Rush Limbaugh	The Rush Limbaugh Show	Premiere	15,500
Mark Levin	The Mark Levin Show	Westwood One	11,000
Glenn Beck	The Glenn Beck Program	Premiere	10,500
Mike Gallagher	The Mike Gallagher Show	Salem Radio Networks	8,500
Michael Savage	The Savage Nation	Westwood One	7,500
Hugh Hewitt	The Hugh Hewitt Show	Salem Radio Network	7,500
Dana Loesch	The Dana Show	Radio America	7,250
Tucker Carlson	Tucker Carlson Tonight	Fox News	4,330
Sean Hannity	Hannity	Fox News	4,310

continued

244 CONNECTIVE ACTION AND THE RISE OF THE FAR-RIGHT

Table 10.A1 *continued*

Figure	Show	Platform	Audience Size (000s)
Laura Ingraham	The Ingraham Angle	Fox News	3,620
Liberal Shows			
Thom Hartmann	The Thom Hartmann Program	WYD Media	7,000
Stephanie Miller	The Stephanie Miller Show	WYD Media	6,000
Cenk Uygur & Ana Kasparian	The Young Turks	YouTube	4,930
Rachel Maddow	The Rachel Maddow Show	MSNBC	3,500
Chuck Todd	Meet the Press Daily	MSNBC	3,814
Lawrence O'Donnell	Last Word with O'Donnell	MSNBC	3,062
Brian Williams	11th Hour with Brian Williams	MSNBC	2,176
Chris Hayes	All In With Chris Hayes	MSNBC	2,093
Ari Melber	The Beat with Ari Melber	MSNBC	1,894
Chris Cuomo	Cuomo Prime Time	CNN	1,671

Table 10.A2 Extract File Data Dictionary

Variable Name	Description
extract_date	Date/time the program was run
file	File name of the PDF where the instance was found.
show_date	Date of the show (extracted from the file naming schema)
show_id	Show ID (extracted from the file naming schema)
subject	Subject word found
subject_code	Subject code (used to group similar subject words together)
keyword	Keyword found (if present)
keyword_code	Keyword code (intensity score assigned in the keywords file)
keyword_id	Keyword ID (used to group similar keywords together)

Variable Name	Description
relevant?	Blank column to be used by the human coder to mark whether the match is semantically relevant in context
extract	Larger section of text around the window is provided, to provide the human coder with context (a default of a 20-word window was used)

Table 10.A3 Intercoder Reliability Findings

Percentage Agreement	Krippendorff's Alpha (nominal)	N Agreements	N Disagreement	N Cases
93.5%	0.765	1,207	84	1,291

Table 10.A4 Total Units of Analysis

Type	System Generated	System Relevant	System Added	Total UOAs
All typologies	33,783	4,514	997	5,511
Protected Status	33,783	337	125	462

Table 10.A5 Hate Speech Intensity

Type	1	2	3	4	5	6	Total
All typologies	24 (0.4%)	1,267 (23.0%)	3,831 (69.5%)	127 (2.3%)	140 (2.5%)	122 (2.2%)	5,511
Protected Status	1 (0.2%)	52 (11.3%)	276 (59.7%)	34 (7.4%)	62 (13.4%)	37 (8.0%)	462

Table 10.A6 Total Entries by Group Category

Group Typology	First	Second	Third	Fourth	Fifth	Other	Total
Protected Status	Black 155 33.6%	Migrant 151 32.7%	Muslim 52 11.3%	Women 47 10.2%	LGBT+ 19 4.1%	38 8.2%	462 100%

Table 10.A7 Top Protected Status Group Targets of Hate Speech in Conservative and Liberal Shows

Total Ranking	Conservative UOAs	Liberal UOAs	Conservative Intensity Scale Average	Liberal Intensity Scale Average
Black	150 (96.8%)	5 (3.2%)	3.82	N/A
Migrant	144 (95.4%)	7 (4.6%)	3.18	N/A
Muslim	34 (65.4%)	18 (34.6%)	4.15	3.67
Women	44 (93.6%)	3 (6.4%)	2.89	N/A
LGBT+	19 (100%)	0 (0.0%)	3.32	N/A
Other	28 (73.7%)	10 (26.3%)	2.89	3.30
Total	**419 (90.7%)**	**43 (9.3%)**	**3.44**	**3.65**

Table 10.A8 Black/BLM Characterizations

Characterization	Number of occurrences
Blacks/BLM are violent	55
Black people are/BLM is full of thugs and criminals	17
BLM is a terrorist group	13
Blacks/BLM are murderers	12
BLM loots/steals	10
BLM is like an unruly mob	8
BLM is Marxist/Communist/Radical	8
Black people are being killed	6
BLM hijacked the civil rights movement	5
BLM is indoctrinating children	4
Other	17

Other: BLM rioting forced the right to do Jan. 6; BLM lies; BLM should be criticized; BLM is bossy/demanding; Black people blame white people for their problems; BLM is racist; BLM hates America; BLM is fascist; BLM members are subhuman; Unclear

Table 10.A9 Migrant characterizations

Characterization	Number of occurrences
Illegal Alien/Immigrant	100
Migrants are flooding/invading the US	23
Migrants are murderers	11
Migrants are criminals	9
Migrants disrupt our way of life/society	2
Migration is a disaster	2
Other	4

Other: Migrants are bad people; Migrants should be deported; Migrants are brainwashed by the left/Democrats; Migrants come to the US in poor condition

Table 10.A10 Muslim characterizations

Characterization	Number of occurrences
Muslims are terrorists/violent	21
Muslims are radical/extremist/fundamentalist/militant	13
Muslims hate the US	3
Muslim are like hordes	2
Muslims are Nazis	2
Muslims are stupid	2
Other	9

Other: Muslims indoctrinate people; Islam is wrong; Muslims are angry; Muslims are like a mob; Muslims are racist; Muslims are scary; Muslims are losers; Muslims are brutal; Islam is a threat

Table 10.A11 Leading Protected Status Groups before and after January 6, 2021

Subject	1	2	3	4	5	6	Total UOAs	UOA Intensity
Black Pre Jan 6	0	12	37	7	18	10	84	3.73
	0.0%	14.3%	44.1%	8.3%	21.4%	11.9%	100%	
Black Post Jan 6	0	5	27	5	25	4	66	4.24
	0.0%	7.6%	40.9%	7.6%	37.9%	6.1%	100%	
Migrant Pre Jan 6	0	3	68	4	0	7	82	3.27
	0.0%	3.7%	82.9%	4.9%	0.0%	8.5%	100%	
Migrant Post Jan 6	0	8	49	1	1	3	62	3.07
	0.0%	12.9%	79.0%	1.6%	1.6%	4.8%	100%	
Muslim Pre Jan 6	1	1	9	5	5	4	25	3.96
	4.0%	4.0%	36.0%	20.0%	20.%	16.0%	100%	
Muslim Post Jan 6	0	0	0	4	4	1	9	4.67
	0.0%	0.0%	0.0%	44.4%	44.4%	11.1%	100%	

References

Bahador, Babak. 2015. "The Media and Deconstruction of the Enemy Image." In Julia Hoffmann and Virgil Hawkins, eds., *Communication and Peace: Mapping an Emerging Field* (pp. 120–132). New York: Routledge.

Bahador, Babak., Robert M. Entman, and Curd Knüpfer. 2019. "Who's Elite and How the Answer Matters to Politics." *Political Communication* 36 (1): 195–202.

Bar-Tel, Daniel. 1990. "Causes and Consequences of Delegitimization: Models of Conflict and Ethnocentrism." *Journal of Social Issues* 46 (1): 65–81.

Bartlett, Jamie, Jeremy Reffin, Noelle Rumball, and Sarah Williamson. 2014. "Anti-Social media." *Demos* 1 (51). https://www.demos.co.uk/files/DEMOS_Anti-social_Media.pdf?1391774638.

Benesch, Susan. 2013. "Dangerous Speech: A Proposal to Prevent Group Violence." Dangerous Speech Project. https://dangerousspeech.org/wp-content/uploads/2018/01/Dangerous-Speech-Guidelines-2013.pdf.

Benesch, Susan. 2014. "Defining and Diminishing Hate Speech. State of the World's Minorities and Indigenous Peoples." *Minority Rights International*: 18–25. https://minorityrights.org/wp-content/uploads/old-site-downloads/mrg-state-of-the-worlds-minorities-2014-chapter02.pdf.

Brewer, Paul R., Joseph Graf, and Lars Willnat. 2003. "Priming or Framing: Media Influence on Attitudes Toward Foreign Countries." *International Communication Gazette* 65 (6): 493–508.

Brown, Rachel Hilary. 2016. *Defusing Hate: A Strategic Communication Guide to Counteract Dangerous Speech.* https://www.ushmm.org/m/pdfs/20160229-Defusing-Hate-Guide.pdf.

Buyse, Antoine. 2014. "Words of Violence: 'Fear Speech,' or How Violent Conflict Escalation Relates to the Freedom of Expression." Human Rights Quarterly 36 (4): 779–797.

Carruthers, Susan L. 2011. *The Media at War.* Basingstoke, UK: Palgrave MacMillan.

Dower, John W. 1986. *War Without Mercy: Race and Power in the Pacific War.* New York: Pantheon Books.

Freelon, Deen. 2010. ReCal: Intercoder Reliability Calculation as a Web Service. *International Journal of Internet Science* 5 (1): 20–33.

Gagliardone, Iginio, Danit Gal, Thiago Alves, and Gabriela Martinez. 2015. "Countering Online Hate Speech." UNESCO Series on Internet Freedom. Paris. https://unesdoc.unesco.org/ark:/48223/pf0000233231

Hacker, Jacob S., and Paul Pierson. 2020. *Let Them Eat Tweets: How the Right Rules in an Age of Extreme Inequality.* New York: Liveright Publishing Corporation.

Hemmer, Nicole. 2016. *Messenger of the Right: Conservative Media and the Transformation of American Politics.* Philadelphia: University of Pennsylvania Press.

Horowitz, Juliana Menasce. 2021. "Support for Black Lives Matter Declined after George Floyd Protests, but has Remained Unchanged Since." Pew Research Center. September 27. https://www.pewresearch.org/fact-tank/2021/09/27/support-for-black-lives-matter-declined-after-george-floyd-protests-but-has-remained-unchanged-since/.

Howard, Jeffrey W. 2019. "Free Speech and Hate Speech." *Annual Review of Political Science* 22: 93–109.

Kalmoe, Nathan P. 2014. "Fueling the Fire: Violent Metaphors, Trait Aggression, and Support for Political Violence." *Political Communication* 31 (4): 545–563.

Katz, A. J. 2018. "Q3 2018 Ratings: Fox News Marks 67 Straight Quarters as No.1 Cable News Network; Hannity Becomes No.1 Basic Cable Series." *Adweek: TVNewser*, October 2. https://www.adweek.com/tvnewser/q3-2018-ratings-fox-news-marks-67-straight-quarters-as-most-watched-cable-news-network-hannity-becomes-no-1-basic-cable-series/378271.

Keen, Sam. 1991. *Faces of the Enemy: Reflections on the Hostile Imagination.* San Francisco: Harper & Row.

Kerchner, Daniel, and Justin Littman. 2019. "gwu-libraries/vopd: 1.2.1." *Zenodo*. https://doi.org/10.5281/zenodo.3526765.

Lepoutre, Maxime C. 2019. "Can 'More Speech' Counter Ignorant Speech?" *Journal of Ethics and Social Philosophy* 16 (3): 155–191.

Lombard, Matthew, Jennifer Snyder-Duch, and Cheryl Campanella Bracken. 2002. "Content Analysis in Mass Communication Research: An Assessment and Reporting of Intercoder Reliability." *Human Communication Research* 28 (4): 587–604.

Merskin, Debra. 2004. "The Construction of Arabs as Enemies: Post-September 11 Discourse of George W. Bush." *Mass Communication and Society* 7 (2): 157–175.

Saleem, Haji Mohammad, Kelly P. Dillon, Susan Benesch, and Derek Ruths. 2017. "A Web of Hate: Tackling Hateful Speech in Online Social Spaces." https://dangerousspeech.org/a-web-of-hate-tackling-hateful-speech-in-online-social-spaces/.

Talkers. n.d. "Top Talk Audiences." http://www.talkers.com/top-talk-audiences/.

Tucker, Eric. 2015. "How Federal Law Draws a Line between Freedom of Speech and Hate Crimes." *PBS News Hour*. December 31. https://www.pbs.org/newshour/nation/how-federal-law-draws-a-line-between-free-speech-and-hate-crimes.

United Nations. 1966. International Covenant on Civil and Political Rights. https://www.ohchr.org/en/professionalinterest/pages/ccpr.aspx.

Waltman, Michael S., and Ashely A. Mattheis. 2017. "Understanding Hate Speech." In *Oxford Research Encyclopedia of Communication*. Oxford: Oxford University Press. https://doi.org/10.1093/acrefore/9780190228613.013.422.

Wickham, Hadley. 2014. "Tidy Data." *Journal of Statistical Software* 59 (10): 1–23.

YouTube (n.d.) News and Politics Channels. https://www.youtube.com/channels/news_politics.

Ziblatt, Daniel. 2017. *Conservative Parties and the Birth of Democracy*. New York: Cambridge University Press.

Chapter 11
Demographic Determinism, Republican Identity, and Democratic Backsliding

Andrew Ifedapo Thompson

The theory of the conservative dilemma anticipates that conservative parties will have numerical disadvantages at the polls if they only give attention to economic issues that would favor the majority. This dynamic of the structure of these parties often leads conservative parties to give more attention to cross-cutting cleavage issues, many of which tend to be cultural or social in nature. One such effective cleavage issue is race, specifically racial animus. In this chapter I call to the increasing focus of the Republican Party on racial threat. Messaging from party elites call to it, and it is reflected in the party base (Mason 2015, 2016; Achen and Bartels 2016; Brown and Enos 2021, Thompson 2021). In this chapter I address one particular component of identity, race, and how it relates to perceptions of the GOP and attitudes toward American democracy at large.

Specifically, I argue that party leaders and other members have come to, wrongly, perceive the coming racial demographic changes in the US to inevitably support the Democratic Party.[1] This is what I call demographic determinism. From this perspective, I argue that a larger conclusion is drawn that threatens the function of American democracy. Republicans perceive the Democratic advantage to be set in stone. The influence of this idea lays a foundation in which the party is significantly more susceptible to influence by surrogate organizations that can effectively advance ideas of racial threat and, in turn, push the party away from commitments to democracy (Hacker and Pierson 2020). I conclude this chapter by showing that these deterministic views about US racial demographic change then led to anti-democratic views which facilitate democratic backsliding.

---

[1] Predictions about the changing racial demographics of the US are contested (Alba 2018; Levy and Myers 2021), making assumptions about the potential changes to parties even less reliable because of how parties make decisions and adapt to changing environments.

Andrew Ifedapo Thompson, *Demographic Determinism, Republican Identity, and Democratic Backsliding*. In: *Connective Action and the Rise of the Far-Right*. Edited by: Steven Livingston and Michael Miller, Oxford University Press. © Oxford University Press (2025). DOI: 10.1093/oso/9780197794937.003.0011

Role of Race in the Republican Party

The GOP has not always functioned and been perceived to be the party of white Americans. In earlier eras of its existence, it operated under a racially heterogenous banner (Heersink and Jenkins 2020; Hugey and Parks 2014). Since the civil rights movement and the shifting party coalitions that accompanied it, the Republican Party has steadily become the party of white Americans. It has advocated for issues pertinent to white Americans and engaged in the use of dog whistles (López 2015) to stir up the most racially resentful white Americans, among a host of other strategies. Recent examples abound.

Debate over the inclusion of critical race theory (CRT) in classrooms is one place in which a racial dog whistle has been used to stir support among Republicans (Anderson 2021; Smith 2021). Parents have expressed concern over their children being taught issues of race in classrooms across the country, which has since been described as CRT. As the title indicates, this topic takes a critical and self-reflective approach to race in the US (Taylor et al. 2009). Some parents have expressed reservations about its inclusion into curricula for their children, and this sentiment in some instances connects to ethnonationalist views of America (Tensley 2021; Kaufmann 2022). Republican elites throughout the country have taken up opposition to these curriculum changes and used them as a rallying cry for their Republican base. In the terms of the volume's organizing framework, critical race theory is a cross-cutting cleavage issue designed to mobilize white working- and middle-class voters.

Race is implicit within much of this debate and is likely a key motivator in the opposition to critical race theory, Americans who oppose CRT feel that the country is "getting away from them," as Parker and Blum note elsewhere in this volume, and is not displaying the "traditional values" that they are accustomed to (Haltiwanger 2021; Klingenstein 2020). It is clear that racial demographic change motivates some of these arguments; Americans see the country changing and the perceptions of it changing, and these views connect closely to senses of racial threat. Republican elites can and have exploited these anxieties about racial changes to stir up their base and encourage participation. Regarding the exploitation of these feelings, candidate for Virginia governor Glenn Youngkin asserted that he would ban CRT in the state in his first day in office through an executive order (Laughland 2022).

While these tactics have not been limited to the Republican Party—the Democratic Party has utilized similar tactics at times, such as with references to Black Americans as "super predators" (Bogert 2020)—they have a far greater frequency and magnitude in GOP messaging. There are numerous historical examples of these same strategies that elites have utilized, such as becoming more tough on crime and opposition to affirmative action.

A direct outgrowth of these tactics is a consolidated white conservative base of voters. White identity is also more closely connected to Republican Party identity, no doubt connected to these tactics and messaging. The party has increased in racial homogeneity over time, and especially since the 1960s when the Democratic Party came to be associated with the civil rights movement and other rights movements that some whites perceived as threatening to their dominant status. White Americans clearly dominate the party discussion both in terms of who leaders cater to, and who they most actively listen to. And this dynamic leads to a pernicious problem with the changing demographics of the United States—a partisan interpretation of the diversification of America.

Partisan Racial Demographic Change

Arguably since the 2000 Census, Republican Party elites have been aware of a disadvantage they have had, relative to the Democratic Party, in appealing to racial minorities. The party has used racial messaging for decades to activate their base which has led many Americans to perceive that it is a political party that is more oriented toward white Americans (Mendelberg 2001; Reny et al. 2019; Thompson and Busby 2021). However, for some time GOP leaders have been confident about the prospects of making a turn in the party's appeal to Americans of color:

> Republicans have argued that Democrats take Blacks and Hispanics for granted. Since President Bush's election, the GOP has been pulling out all the stops to create inroads into minority communities. Here in New York City, Republicans have taken responsibility for the highly visible economic changes in urban communities such as Harlem's 125th St. While Democrats still outnumber Republicans in New York a large block of voters share Republican values yet don't identify themselves as members of the GOP. The news of the first Republican convention to be held in New

York City may bring these "closet" Republicans out in the open. It's a good thing for the Republicans as they prepare themselves to show the world the GOP is diverse. (Racine 2003)

The coalition built by Barack Obama and his subsequent 2008 electoral win threw the proverbial wrench into these plans. Obama's presidency seemed to be clear evidence to the GOP strategists that they were at severe deficit in galvanizing people of color. Moreover, the 2008 election proved to be the election most determined by racial attitudes in history. On this, Tesler and Sears (2010) show that while Obama was boosted by racial liberals all throughout his campaign, he was also strongly opposed by racial conservatives in a consistent fashion. They assert, "The results presented in these chapters suggest that the hopes of some for a post-racial Obama era were far from a sure thing and probably even a long shot. Rather, if anything, American partisan politics could easily become increasingly organized by racial attitudes during the Obama presidency" (Tesler and Sears 2010, 9). This polarization along racial lines indicated that race was becoming a more salient point for both parties, likely in opposite directions. The Democratic Party could use positive discussions and signals of race to continue to galvanize racial liberals, while the Republican Party could push negative messaging about race to motivate and convince racial conservatives to support them.

This turn in the GOP was further accentuated by two events. The first event was the establishment and proliferation of the Tea Party movement. Ideologically, the Tea Party was greatly in favor of small government measures, but it also had a strong racial undercurrent (Parker and Barreto 2014). It was fervently oppositional to the Obama presidency, sometimes through dog whistles. And additionally, it used implicit racially tinged messaging about "makers and takers" in American society. This language referred to Americans who were worthy and unworthy of receiving support, based upon perceived qualities of hard work and Americanness (Williamson et al. 2011). This undercurrent in the early Obama-era ultimately led to a second event that was perceived to be a boon for Republican elites concerned about the party platform—the 2010 midterm elections.

The Democrats were shellacked in 2010, which was unquestionably a reaction to Obama (Busch 2011; Karpowitz et al. 2011; Weatherford 2012). Importantly, midterms draw a different population of voters than the general election, which happened to be a whiter, older, more conservative group of voters (O'Neil 2022). The GOP victory in 2010, in addition to growing Tea Party support and racially conservative motivations in opposing Obama, created a potential solution for the party moving into the future. The strategy that could work to compete with Democrats was more strongly in tandem with a white identity politics. It also was a direct reaction to perceptions and projections of racial demographic change that came to fruition around the same time. White Americans were losing their majority in the country, and some Republican elites could emphasize this as a rallying call.

Demographic Determinism and the Republican Party

Following the 2010 Census, demographers and other experts of Census data began calling a definitive coming shift in US racial demographics (Bowler and Segura 2011). This was the idea that by midcentury, whites would become a minority and people of color would become the numerical majority of the country. It has since been described as the majority-minority flip, or the browning of America (Sundstrom 2008). Within the context of the American experiment this was shocking news. It was presumed to eventually happen decades before, but these predictions were showing that the US was changing more rapidly than previously expected. The rapidity of these racial changes was compounded by assumptions about how they might affect politics.

Due to the politicization of race in America, the majority-minority flip also led experts to make inferences about the future of politics. The narratives that emerged in this period have had staying power in American political discourse. I call the idea *demographic determinism*. This notion is a deterministic view of partisan politics that anticipates racial demographic change will overwhelmingly benefit the Democratic Party. It is a simple, yet powerful idea: over time as Americans of color increase in size, the Democratic Party will be at an increasing advantage over the Republican Party because the party platform appeals more to people of color. Racial minorities are increasing in size, so electorally they will be able to exercise their influence more. The determinism also cuts in the opposite direction, in that whites are perceived to be more Republican, and therefore the GOP will be less able to win elections as the country diversifies—and importantly, there is nothing inherently white about the structure of the GOP. Because of this perceived developing numerical disadvantage, however, the party looks toward this as an incentive to develop into a white ethnonationalist party. Demographic determinism was not limited to party theorizing, this same prediction about the future changes to the country bled into scholarly speculation on future party changes.

> The demographic changes occurring in the US are nearly certain to reduce the proportion of the electorate that is White and Christian. As Teixeira, Frey, and Griffin (2015) report, "In 1980, the population of the United States was 80 percent White. Today, that proportion has fallen to 63 percent, and by 2060, it is projected to be less than 44 percent" (p. 2). At some point, the Republican coalition as currently defined will not be capable of winning national elections. This could lead to a revision of party coalitions that would introduce new cross-cutting identities, and therefore reduce polarization. (Mason 2018, 4)

As articulated in the passage by Mason, political inferences built on the racial demographic change of the US were essentially conjecture at the time. In the years that followed these Census projections, scholars of racial attitudes showed that these predictions were consequential in the minds of white Americans. Craig and Richeson show that the projection of the majority-minority flip leads to whites feeling a greater sense of racial threat, and increases their explicit and implicit racial bias, pro-white attitudes, and discriminatory attitudes (Craig and Richeson 2014a). In a separate set of studies, they also find that this same information causes an increase in support for the Republican Party and more expressed conservative policy support among white Americans (Craig and Richeson 2014b). A host of additional studies published around the same time show there to be robust senses of racial threat over the majority-minority flip felt among white Americans (e.g., Danbold and Huo 2015; Willer et al. 2016).

This scholarly turn in the applied study of racial threat reflected a shift in white American attitudes about diversification of the country. Around this same point in time, the GOP was experiencing an internal identity crisis about the changing demographic landscape that put the party at a crossroad. It could either deepen its connection to white identity or attempt to expand its outreach. This point of contention was brought out by demographic determinism. A consistent winning strategy for the party could either run in an expansive or restrictive direction. These theoretical perspectives were at odds, and the debate about which strategy was more effective has immediate bearing on the current conservative dilemma.

A Political Fork in the Road

The perception of demographic determinism put the Republican Party in a place where it needed to either expand its appeal or double down with its standing base. The *expansive party approach* was understood, and implied in previous eras of strategizing, but started to become a more viable idea as time went on. It recognized the diminishing numbers of white Americans and the idea of demographic determinism as advantageous. The expansive approach called for adjusting the GOP's messaging and policy framework in order to accommodate these forthcoming demographic changes. In short, it recognized that the party needed to draw in more racial minorities to win.

This perspective became especially salient after President Obama's reelection in 2012. For elites who favored the expansive party approach, Obama's victory was the canary in the coalmine for the direction of the country. Despite the success of the 2010 Midterm elections, there was not enough of a groundswell against Obama to substantively contest the new base of voters that the Democratic Party had motivated in this presidential election. The dynamic spelled great trouble for Republicans in the vein of demographic determinism—consistent losses and a decreasing electoral advantage. As such, the expansive party approach of the Republican Party was proposed immediately following this loss, in the 2012 GOP autopsy report days after the general election.

In the early pages of the report, party experts write:

> The nation's demographic changes add to the urgency of recognizing how precarious our position has become. America is changing demographically, and unless Republicans are able to grow our appeal the way GOP governors have done, the changes tilt the playing field even more in the Democratic direction....
>
> Public perception of the Party is at record lows. Young voters are increasingly rolling their eyes at what the Party represents, and many minorities wrongly think that Republicans do not like them or want them in the country. When someone rolls their eyes at us, they are not likely to open their ears to us. (Barbour et al. 2013, 9)

Party elites were keenly aware of how the GOP was being perceived among the American public. In the passages above they articulate the shifting sands of political culture in the US which they viewed to be closely aligned with the demographic changes. Later in this same report, they are even more explicit about their perceptions of the prospect of demographic determinism.

> In both 2008 and 2012, President Obama won a combined 80 percent of the votes of all minority voters, including not only African Americans but also Hispanics, Asians, and others. The minority groups that President Obama carried with 80 percent of the vote in 2012 are on track to become a majority of the nation's population by 2050. Today these minority groups make up 37 percent of the population, and they cast a record 28 percent of the votes in the 2012 presidential election, according to the election exit polls, an increase of 2 percentage points from 2008. We have to work harder at engaging demographic partners and allies. (Barbour et al. 2013)

This strain of Republican strategizing, when taken to its furthest extent is pro-democratic. It calls for the adjustment of the party platform to better accommodate a changing country. In other words, it seeks to appeal to the growing majority to win office. It legitimizes the democratic system of government by extending the party.

The other strategic narrative ran directly in the face of the expansive one. It was intentionally anti-democratic and probably most closely aligned with the dynamics of the worst-case-scenario for the conservative dilemma, one Ziblatt illustrates with his case study of the collapse of the Weimar Republic (Ziblatt 2017, Ch. 9). The restrictive approach emphasized a type of ethnonationalism to motivate the threatened white Republican base. It harkened to earlier years of American life and traditionalism. It described those "good ol' days" as an ideal that needed to be returned to fully realize the strength of the nation. It specified how "true Americans" needed to stand up in the face of social and cultural changes, which President Obama served as the figurehead for at the time, in order to prevent their status being threatened and their power from being subverted. At the time, this idea of taking back the country took the form of increased political participation. All the while this idea was catching fire, a separate, competing strain of thought among Republicans was being developed further and proposed. The Tea Party faction of the GOP helped shape the narrative behind this emergent platform (Blum 2020; and see Parker and Blum, this volume).

In sum, the restrictive approach to Republican strategizing was focused, not on expanding, but on doubling down in ethnonationalist appeals. These were meant to galvanize the white base. Within this view, despite the perception of demographic determinism, Republican elites aimed to motivate this base for the sake of winning elections. The restrictive perspective was not inherently pro-democratic. It was implicitly oriented toward stimulating conflict among white Americans; and, if necessary, could accommodate anti-democratic ideas. If racial minorities are growing in size, are viewed as oppositional to the GOP, and will be able to exercise more political power over time, then it might be necessary to the restrict their ability to participate to protect the GOP's interests.

This crossroad that the GOP found itself at reflects Ziblatt's theorizing about the two electoral solutions conservative parties can use to respond to the conservative dilemma. These are either adhering to the "rules of the (democratic) game" or adapting older, anti-democratic techniques to maintain power. The first approach, which aligns with what I define as the *expansive party approach*, Ziblatt articulates as formal party-building, and describes it as building "the machinery of hierarchical and mass competitive political parties and to win 'clean' elections" (2017, 35). The second solution follows the *restrictive party approach*. He writes that it was a strategy "to develop new informal techniques of electoral fraud, manipulation, clientelism and corruption that substituted for the 'old corruption' of deference and coercion" (2017, 34). In short, it is the party's way of posturing in democratic form, yet manipulating the rules in such a way to ensure that they can stay in power.

The 2016 GOP primaries were the battleground for these two perspectives. Marco Rubio and Jeb Bush were more representative of the expansive approach, seen as appealing more to Latinx voters who might be partial to the GOP's social conservative views. Conversely, Ted Cruz and Donald Trump represented the restrictive strategy as a strong reaction to racial demographic change. Cruz was less overt in emphasizing ethnonationalism, while Trump was clear in his platform.

The Trump victory in the primaries was an assertion of which of the two perspectives the party would use. It was vindication for the *restrictive party approach*. Again, taken to its furthest extent, this strategy could become anti-democratic. The senses of racial threat that Trump emphasized throughout his campaign and time in office served to motivate the white Republican base. Concerns about racial minorities exercising their power into the future was a potent force for increasing participation (Mutz 2018), but eventually these views could take on a life of their own. If the country was diversifying and the changes were seen to help the Democratic Party (which they were), then the partisan racial threat from these changes could sow less confidence in democracy as a system of government.

Party members want their party to win. If they perceive the electoral makeup of the country to be at a consistent and inevitable disadvantage, then they will likely become less supportive of the rules of the electoral game. In the lead up to the 2020 election, these doubts of the system were emphasized by President Trump among other conservative elites. In short, they refined the restrictive strategy. It was such a productive strategy that it led to a very strong connection between racial threat and anti-democratic attitudes (Bartels 2020).

I go further to evaluate the causal connection between these two sets of views. Through the 2020 election up until now, demographic determinism has been emphasized in strongly partisan ways among the GOP. To test for how it motivated anti-democratic ideas among Republican voters, I went about framing racial demographic change as something that would either help the Democratic Party or the Republican Party. Elites have emphasized that it will help Democrats, and so this is the salient narrative in the minds of Republicans. The central intention behind these studies is to determine whether racial threat motivates views about democracy among Republicans. I expect that when Republicans learn that their party will benefit from racial demographic change, which is the opposite of the demographic determinism narrative, they will express less racial threat *and* less anti-democratic views.

Causally Testing Demographic Determinism

I use a set of two preregistered vignette experiments where I make the party that is projected to benefit from the majority-minority flip explicit (Thompson 2022). After this, I assess the extent to which they elicit senses of racial threat and generate support for anti-democratic ideas among Republicans and Democrats. The baseline condition I use describes the majority-minority flip generally—which allows me to isolate the effects of each partisan frame.

In my first experiment, I analyze general senses of racial threat and anti-democratic ideas. Within the second, I use more granular measures of both concepts, particularly in the vein of threat from specific racial groups and

Table 11.1 Description of Experimental Conditions

Conditions	Description
1	Pure Control
2	Majority-minority flip
3	Majority-minority flip + Republican frame
4	Majority-minority flip + Democratic frame

degrees of support for policy that is overtly anti-democratic. Experiment 1 was conducted using the online vendor Lucid Fulcrum in April 2021 (N = 1,087). Experiment 2 was conducted with a representative sample through Forthright (formerly Bovitz, Inc.),[2] and is Census matched on gender, race, and region (N = 1,274).

Respondents provided consent, completed an attention check that filtered out inattentive participants, and then answered demographic items in the beginning of this survey.[3] Upon completing these pretreatment items, respondents were randomly assigned to one of the four conditions, three of which involve racial demographic change.[4] Two conditions are partisan frames of racial demographic change: one is a baseline condition for demographic change, and one is a pure control (see Table 11.1).

In both studies, I ultimately find that the frame that shifts the idea of demographic determinism (Condition #3 above compared to Condition #2) in favor of the GOP causes a decrease in the sense of racial threat and reduces anti-democratic views.

Experiment 2 expands on the goals of Experiment 1, testing the same stimuli of politically grounded views of anti-democratic attitudes. I use party-contingent items adapted from Graham and Svolik (2020).[5] I list the

---

[2] This survey platform has been utilized in a series of previous works (Druckman et al. 2013; Rothschild 2020; Bakker et al. 2020).

[3] As a second quality check, respondents also completed an open-ended question asking them to describe their community. Those who did not answer the prompt or provided an indecipherable response are excluded from the sample.

[4] I block randomize on party identification to provide sufficient and uniform statistical power across Republican and Democratic respondents.

[5] By party-contingent, I mean that respondents viewed a particular wording of the measure based upon their party identification.

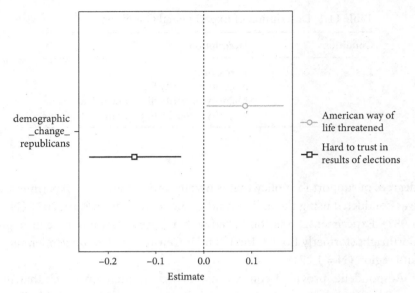

Figure 11.1 Effect of Republican demographic change frame on Republicans' anti-democratic attitudes.

adapted measures below, then provide a brief description of what they capture:

1) A proposal to reduce the number of polling stations in areas that support [Republicans/Democrats].
2) [Republican/Democratic] governors should prosecute journalists who accuse them of misconduct without revealing sources.
3) [Republican/Democratic] governors should ban far-right group rallies in state capitols.
4) [Republican/Democratic] governors should ban far-left group rallies in state capitols.

Within both of these studies, I show Republicans' senses of racial threat which emerge from racial demographic change are contingent on which party they expect to benefit from those changes. I confirm that the inference they make about the coming majority-minority flip is that racial minorities will mostly identify as Democrats. When they are told that Republicans will actually benefit from racial demographic change, this counteracts their racially threatened views.

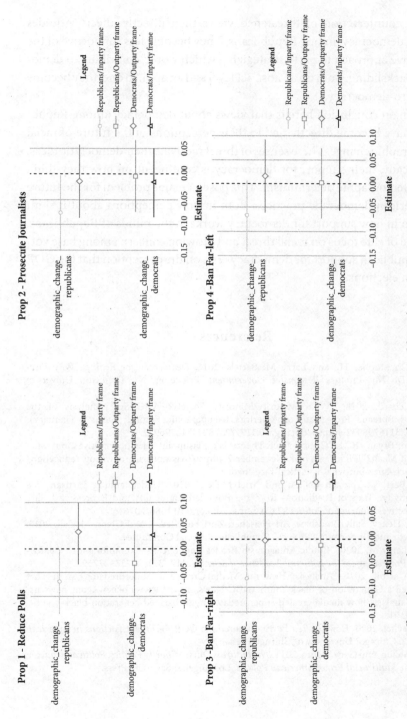

Figure 11.2 Effect of party demographic advantage frames on Republicans' anti-democratic attitudes.

Note: The baseline in each of these graphs is the general racial demographic change (Condition #2). This figure shows the results of these comparisons along with corresponding 95% confidence intervals.

This counteraction of threatened views then directly affects attitudes toward democracy among Republicans. They become less supportive of the restrictive approach to party strategizing which would contribute to democratic backsliding. Both on an abstract level and an applied one, they become more pro-democracy.

My main conclusion here is that views about democracy among Republicans have become directly tied to their perceptions of the future of racial demographic change. These senses of threat motivate their democratic ideas. Specifically, their support for democracy is contingent on how they think about demographic determinism. This poses a major problem for the future of American democratic practices. Both in how perceptions about it shift, but also in how support for democracy works in the minds of Republicans. Because of elite focus on racial threat and growing concern among base voters, Republican support for democracy rests on the perception that the GOP can win elections.

References

Achen, Christopher H., and Larry M. Bartels. 2016. *Democracy for Realists: Why Elections Do Not Produce Responsive Government.* Princeton, NJ: Princeton University Press.

Alba, Richard. 2018. "What Majority-Minority Society? A Critical Analysis of the Census Bureau's Projections of America's Demographic Future." *Socius* 4 (January): 2378023118796932. https://doi.org/10.1177/2378023118796932.

Anderson, Bryan. 2021. "Critical Race Theory is a Flashpoint for Conservatives, but what Does it Mean?" *PBS NewsHour,* November 2. https://www.pbs.org/newshour/education/so-much-buzz-but-what-is-critical-race-theory.

Bakker, Bert N., Yphtach Lelkes, and Ariel Malka. 2020. "Understanding Partisan Cue Receptivity: Tests of Predictions from the Bounded Rationality and Expressive Utility Perspectives." *Journal of Politics* 82 (3). https://doi.org/10.1086/707616.

Barbour, Henry, Sally Bradshaw, Ari Fleischer, Zori Fonalledas, and Glenn McCall. 2013. "Growth and Opportunity Project." Republican National Committee.

Bartels, Larry M. 2020. "Ethnic Antagonism Erodes Republicans' Commitment to Democracy." *Proceedings of the National Academy of Sciences.* 117 (37): 22752–22759.

Bogert, Carroll. 2020. "Analysis: How the Media Created a 'Superpredator' Myth That Harmed a Generation of Black Youth." NBC News. https://www.nbcnews.com/news/us-news/analysis-how-media-created-superpredator-myth-harmed-generation-black-youth-n1248101.

Blum, Rachel. 2020. *How the Tea Party Captured the GOP: Insurgent Factions in American Politics.* Chicago: University of Chicago Press.

Bowler, Shaun, and Gary Segura. 2011. *The Future is Ours: Minority Politics, Political Behavior, and the Multiracial Era of American Politics.* Los Angeles: Sage/CQ Press.

Brown, Jacob R., and Ryan D. Enos. 2021. "The Measurement of Partisan Sorting for 180 Million Voters." *Nature Human Behaviour* (March): 1–11.

Busch, Andrew E. 2011. "The 2010 Midterm Elections: An Overview." *The Forum*. 8 (4). https://doi.org/10.2202/1540-8884.1409.

Craig, Maureen, and Jennifer Richeson. 2014a. "More Diverse Yet Less Tolerant? How the Increasingly Diverse Racial Landscape Affects White Americans' Racial Attitudes." *Personality and Social Psychology Bulletin* 40 (6): 750–761.

Craig, Maureen, and Jennifer Richeson. 2014b. "On the Precipice of a 'Majority-Minority' America: Perceived Status Threat from the Racial Demographic Shift Affects White Americans' Political Ideology." *Psychological Science* 25 (6): 1189–1197.

Danbold, Felix, and Yuen J. Huo. 2015. "No Longer 'All-American'? Whites' Defensive Reactions to Their Numerical Decline." *Social Psychological and Personality Science* 6 (2): 210–218.

Druckman, James, Erik Peterson, and Rune Slothuus. 2013. "How Elite Partisan Polarization Affects Public Opinion Formation." *American Political Science Review.*107 (1): 57–79.

Graham, Matthew H., and Milan W. Svolik. 2020. "Democracy in America? Partisanship, Polarization, and the Robustness of Support for Democracy in the United States." *American Political Science Review.*114 (2): 392–409.

Hacker, Jacob S., and Paul Pierson. 2020. *Let Them Eat Tweets: How the Right Rules in an Age of Extreme Inequality*. New York: Liveright Publishing.

Haltiwanger, John. 2021. "Nearly Half of Republicans Say 'a Time Will Come When Patriotic Americans Have to Take the Law into Their Own Hands,' New Poll Shows." *Business Insider.* https://www.businessinsider.com/47-percent-gop-voters-patriots-take-law-own-hands-poll-2021-7.

Heersink, Boris, and Jeffery A. Jenkins. 2020. *Republican Party Politics and the American South, 1865–1968*. Cambridge: Cambridge University Press.

Hugey, Matthew, and Gregory Parks. 2014. "The Wrongs of the Right." *NYU Press* (blog). https://nyupress.org/9780814760543/the-wrongs-of-the-right.

Karpowitz, Christopher F., J. Quin Monson, Kelly D. Patterson, and Jeremy C. Pope. 2011. "Tea Time in America? The Impact of the Tea Party Movement on the 2010 Midterm Elections." *PS: Political Science & Politics* 44 (2): 303–309.

Kaufmann, Eric. 2022. "The New Culture Wars: Why Critical Race Theory Matters More than Cancel Culture." *Social Science Quarterly* 103 (4): 773–788.

Klingenstein, Thomas. 2020. "Preserving the American Way of Life." *The American Mind.* https://americanmind.org/memo/preserving-the-american-way-of-life/.

Laughland, Oliver. 2022. "Glenn Youngkin Attempts to Ban Critical Race Theory on Day One as Virginia Governor." *The Guardian*, January 16. https://www.theguardian.com/us-news/2022/jan/16/virginia-governor-glenn-youngkin-sworn-into-office-critical-race-theory.

Levy, Morris, and Dowell Myers. 2021. "Racial Projections in Perspective: Public Reactions to Narratives about Rising Diversity." *Perspectives on Politics* 19 (4): 1147–1164.

López, Ian Haney. 2015. *Dog Whistle Politics: How Coded Racial Appeals Have Reinvented Racism and Wrecked the Middle Class*. Reprint edition. Oxford: Oxford University Press.

Mason, Lilliana. 2015. "'I Disrespectfully Agree': The Differential Effects of Partisan Sorting on Social and Issue Polarization." *American Journal of Political Science* 59 (1): 128–145.

Mason, Lilliana. 2016. "A Cross-Cutting Calm: How Social Sorting Drives Affective Polarization." *Public Opinion Quarterly* 80 (S1): 351–377.

Mason, Lilliana. 2018. "Losing Common Ground: Social Sorting and Polarization." The *Forum* 16 (1): 47–66.

Mendelberg, Tali. 2001. *The Race Card: Campaign Strategy, Implicit Messages, and the Norm of Equality*. Princeton, NJ: Princeton University Press.

Mutz, Diana C. 2018. "Status Threat, Not Economic Hardship, Explains the 2016 Presidential Vote." *Proceedings of the National Academy of Sciences* 115 (19): E4330–E4339.

O'Neil, Aaron. 2022. "Voter Turnout in U.S. Midterms by Ethnicity 1966–2018." *Statista*. 2022. https://www.statista.com/statistics/1096123/voter-turnout-midterms-by-ethnicity-historical/.

Parker, Christopher S., and Matt A. Barreto. 2014. *Change They Can't Believe In: The Tea Party and Reactionary Politics in America*. Updated edition. Princeton, NJ: Princeton University Press.

Racine, Theresa. 2003. "Ready for a Switch? The Republican Party Wants Minorities to Make a Change." *Network Journal* 10 (6).

Reny, Tyler, Ali Valenzuela, and Loren Collingwood. 2019. "'No, You're Playing the Race Card': Testing the Effects of Anti-Black, Anti-Latino, and Anti-Immigrant Appeals in the Post-Obama Era." *Political Psychology*. 41 (2): 283–302. https://onlinelibrary.wiley.com/doi/full/10.1111/pops.12614.

Rothschild, Jacob E. 2020. "Identities, Interest Group Coalitions, and Intergroup Relations." *Politics, Groups, and Identities* 10 (1): 63–80.

Smith, David. 2021. "Trumpism without Trump: How Republican Dog-Whistles Exploited Democratic Divisions." *The Guardian*, November 6. https://www.theguardian.com/us-news/2021/nov/06/republicans-glenn-youngkin-joe-biden-democrats.

Sundstrom, Ronald R. 2008. *The Browning of America and the Evasion of Social Justice*. Albany: SUNY Press.

Taylor, Edward, David Gillborn, and Gloria Ladson-Billings. 2009. *Foundations of Critical Race Theory in Education*. London: Routledge.

Tensley, Brandon. 2021. "The Engineered Conservative Panic over Critical Race Theory, Explained- CNN Politics." CNN, July 8. https://www.cnn.com/2021/07/08/politics/critical-race-theory-panic-race-deconstructed-newsletter/index.html.

Tesler, Michael, and David O. Sears. 2010. *Obama's Race: The 2008 Election and the Dream of a Post-Racial America*. Chicago: University of Chicago Press.

Thompson, Andrew Ifedapo. 2021. "How Racial Threat Motivates Partisan Differences in Anti-Democratic Attitudes." APSA Preprints. https://preprints.apsanet.org/engage/apsa/article-details/6005bf249135b000189e7176

Thompson, Andrew Ifedapo, and Ethan C. Busby. 2021. "Defending the Dog Whistle: The Role of Justifications in Racial Messaging." *Political Behavior*. November. https://doi.org/10.1007/s11109-021-09759-x.

Thompson, Andrew Ifedapo, and Ethan C. Busby. 2022. "The Partisan Utility of Racial Demographic Change and Democratic Backsliding in the American Public." *APSA Preprints*. doi: 10.33774/apsa-2022-544lb.

Weatherford, M. Stephen. 2012. "The Wages of Competence: Obama, the Economy, and the 2010 Midterm Elections." *Presidential Studies Quarterly* 42 (1): 8–39.

Willer, Robb, Matthew Feinberg, and Rachel Wetts. 2016. "Threats to Racial Status Promote Tea Party Support Among White Americans." SSRN Scholarly Paper ID 2770186. https://papers.ssrn.com/abstract=2770186.

Williamson, Vanessa, Theda Skocpol, and John Coggin. 2011. "The Tea Party and the Remaking of Republican Conservatism." *Perspectives on Politics* 9 (1): 25–43.

Ziblatt, Daniel. 2017. *Conservative Political Parties and the Birth of Modern Democracy in Europe.* Cambridge: Cambridge University Press.

Chapter 12
Digital Death Spiral

How Analytics Hastened the Republican Party's Descent into Trumpism

David Karpf

At the 2020 Republican National Convention, the Republican Party decided not to adopt a policy platform. The party instead adopted a resolution stating that it "has and will continue to support [President Donald Trump's] America-first agenda." To be a Republican circa 2020, one must unequivocally support Trump. No other policy positions required.

In February 2022, the Republican National Committee (RNC) formally censured two Republican members of Congress—Liz Cheney of Wyoming and Adam Kinzinger of Illinois—for the act of agreeing to serve on the House Select Committee on the January 6th attack. The RNC described the January 6th Capitol attack in its censure resolution as "legitimate political discourse." A Republican circa 2022 can attempt to sack the Capitol building in support of Donald J. Trump and remain in good standing with the Party. But participating in an investigation of a plot to overthrow the government is grounds for expulsion.

How did the party of Reagan and Bush so quickly and completely become the party of Trumpism? It calls to mind Ernest Hemingway's description of bankruptcy ("How did you go bankrupt? Gradually, then suddenly"). The gradual forces—affective polarization, white racial resentment, the aftershocks of neoliberal policymaking, the fracturing of the media system, decreased trust in government, and the dissolution of elite governance norms—can be viewed across decades. The seeds of Trumpism sprouted for years, rendering the party increasingly vulnerable to takeover from an authoritarian demagogue. The trend among party surrogate organizations has long slanted toward illiberalism. A robust political science literature has developed around these themes (Mason 2018; Hacker and Pierson 2011, 2020; Ziblatt 2017; Levitsky and Ziblatt 2018).

David Karpf, *Digital Death Spiral*. In: *Connective Action and the Rise of the Far-Right*. Edited by: Steven Livingston and Michael Miller, Oxford University Press. © Oxford University Press (2025).
DOI: 10.1093/oso/9780197794937.003.0012

There is still more work to be done on the sudden side of the equation, though. The descent into Trumpism was not inevitable, nor did it appear contemporaneously likely. Its speed has come as a surprise. And one important part of the story of how Trumpism has attained such an ironclad grip on the Republican Party involves relatively recent changes in the digital media landscape. The Trump years have, not coincidentally, coincided with the rise of new forms of *digital listening* among news organizations, advocacy organizations, and political associations. Analytics-based feedback create reinforcement cycles that helped Trump capture the party infrastructure that in theory is intended to resolve Ziblatt's conservative dilemma (2017).

The descent into Trumpism is only in part a cautionary tale of how data analytics can be a corrosive social force in the absence of principled decision-makers. And if actors within the Republican Party network are going to overcome Trumpism, they will need to wrestle both with the long-term trends that made the Party vulnerable to Trumpism and with the short-term forces that cemented his control in such little time.

Some Background: Analytics and Digital Listening

I am drawing, in this chapter, from a set of theoretical and empirical observations that were published in my 2016 book *Analytic Activism: Digital Listening and the New Political Strategy*. The book suffered from unfortunate timing—it was written back when "President Trump" was still a late-night comedy punchline and published (in December 2016) just as the public was reeling against the newfound reality. It was not a book *about* Trump's victory or governance style. But, during the ensuing months, I had ample opportunities to distill relevant themes and warning signs from its pages.

The book discusses how "netroots" political associations incorporate data into their decision-making. Digital-first organizations like MoveOn.org and Color of Change face the same systemic constraints as legacy interest groups. Or to make the point in the language used in this volume, digital surrogate organizations face many of the same constraints as legacy ones. They attempt to build and marshal political interest, converting it into progressive power that can help them bend American politics toward (their vision of) justice. Their relative advantage comes through how they combine analytics and a culture of testing to help them gauge member interest, develop new tactics, and measure which of their political interventions are most effective. The crucial shift is that since they treat everyone on their email lists as members, they also treat online signals of member behavior as a type of participatory input. Rather than relying entirely on the instincts of professional lobbyists and campaigners to develop their tactics and strategies, they also analyze how members respond to their issue appeals to listen to their members' revealed preferences.

The organizations I studied in the book relied on a mix of *internal* and *external* analytics. Internal analytics are drawn from data that is generated by the organization's own interactions with its members and supporters (e.g., email open-rates and clickthrough rates, event attendance, survey responses, and donations). These data are nonpublic and subject to the direct control of the organization, allowing for a culture of testing that results in innovative new tactics. But internal analytics are also limited in scope by the organization's own existing activities and supporter base. External analytics, by contrast, come from third-party sources (data visualization of Twitter and Facebook trending topics, etc.). These data are either public or purchasable. External analytics tend to be of lower quality, and it does not allow for testing or experimentation, but it offers a window into public dialogues and political activity beyond the scope of the organization's existing work.

Conservative advocacy organizations are absent from the book. This was by design and by necessity. As I had noted in a previous book, *The MoveOn Effect*, American conservative activist leaders have repeatedly attempted and failed to build their own equivalents to the progressive netroots in the United States (Karpf 2012). From an organizational ecology perspective, there are good reasons to treat the left and the right as distinct islands—progressive organizations hire the same staff, who attend the same trainings and work on the same political campaigns. They appeal to the same major donors and activate overlapping supporter-bases in response to the same political opportunities. Conservative activist organizations are ecologically walled off from this progressive ecosystem. There is no staff exchange or shared base of practitioner knowledge. The political opportunity structure, the donor base, the hybrid media incentives, and the cultural assumptions based on past organizational victories and defeats all diverge. Rather than attempting to compare across the two sides (one of which I had established the research relationships necessary for deep field work, the other of which viewed me with hostility and distrust), I focused my attention on describing and explaining how digital listening is conceived, structured, and deployed within the context of progressive political advocacy and activism.

The final two chapters of the book offer a warning of sorts. Among the netroots political associations that were pioneering this new form of digital listening, there was much talk of so-called vanity metrics. Vanity metrics are numbers that are easy to measure but are only loosely related to the organization's real strategic goals. These organizations that rely heavily on data for decision-making also look askance at anyone who insists they are "trusting the data" or "letting the data decide." Digital listening can be a valuable input for improving strategic decisions, but analytics cannot and should-not be a substitute for strategic vision.

Behavioral economist Dan Ariely (2010) once remarked that "you are what you measure." The corollary warning in *Analytic Activism* is: "You probably *aren't* what you have trouble measuring" (Karpf 2016). And since power and success are far harder to pin down than vanity metrics like list-growth and fundraising, there is a danger to legacy organizations struggling to embrace analytics that they will let the data lead them astray by optimizing for what's easy instead of what's important.

It strikes me that one of the traps we collectively fell into during the Trump years bears all the hallmarks of analytics-without-leadership. We became trapped in a perpetual feedback loop where elite organizations go haywire through the self-rationalization that they are "giving the people what they want," based on the narrowest, most easily obtained metrics of what people want with no broader vision of their purpose, or of what democracy requires.

I suspect it had unique impacts on the network of party surrogates that have historically been tasked with navigating the conservative dilemma for the Republican Party. What is lost when a party fundamentally built around contradictory impulses—attracting a majority electoral coalition while simultaneously promoting the economic interests of a narrow elite—is handed tools that are radically effective at measuring popularity but not importance? Who gets to decide within such a party network which values (liberal or illiberal) are worth optimizing for? In other words, party leaders without vision or principles, save doing the bidding of their billionaire backers, will latch onto whatever "cross-cutting cleavage issue" that works, irrespective of its impact on democracy. It seems to reveal a win-at-all-costs tactical philosophy that is ethically bankrupt.

272 CONNECTIVE ACTION AND THE RISE OF THE FAR-RIGHT

I am proposing that the frame of digital-listening-gone-awry can helpfully reveal a handful of the immediate phenomena that have cemented Trumpism's hold on the Republican Party network and can perhaps be of use in crafting solutions moving forward.

With that background out of the way, let us discuss the unexpected rise and ironclad ascendency of Trumpism.

The 2016 Primary: Schrodinger's Audience

With the gift of hindsight, it can be easy to forget just how shocking it was that Donald Trump managed to win the 2016 Republican nomination.[1] This simply wasn't how past presidential primary campaigns had *worked*. Trump's initial rise in the polls was easy to discount. When he announced his campaign for the presidency in the summer of 2015, he faced a crowded field of opponents who lacked his immediate name recognition. Thanks to his decades of experience as a reality television star and a tabloid fixture, Trump entered the race with overwhelming name recognition, but no credentials as a credible government leader or Republican policymaker. Trump lacked party support and, at least in those early months, was covered skeptically by *Fox News*. It wasn't until Breitbart, with then CEO Steve Bannon at the helm, started encroaching on Fox's market share among key conservative demographics that Fox News got on the Trump train (Benkler et al. 2017, 52).

The established literature on presidential primaries strongly indicated that through myriad informal mechanisms, party leaders had the necessary soft power to determine presidential nominations. (In the words of the best-known work on the subject, "The Party Decides").[2] Nonserious candidates of Trump's ilk frequently attain a brief polling lead during the "invisible primary" months but then fall victim to a cycle of "Discovery-Scrutiny-Decline" (Sides and Vavreck 2014) that brought voters back toward serious, party-backed nominees. This was a well-known pattern in the literature—so

---

[1] This section is adapted from a May 4, 2016 blog post, "Schrodinger's Audience: How News Analytics Handed America Trump" that was previously available at http: civichall.org/civicist/schrodingers-audience. The Civicist blog later shut down and the post is now only accessible through the Internet Archive: https://web.archive.org/web/20160508140337/ http://civichall.org/civicist/schrodingers-audience-how-news-analytics-gave-america-trump

[2] Interestingly, Hacker and Pierson's (2011) explanation for GOP backsliding is based on the conclusion that American political parties no longer decide because of the misguided reforms in the 1970s that gave voters more power. See Cohen et al. (2008).

well-known that political scientists like me felt abundantly confident treating Trump's late-2015 levels of support as a mirage. (I routinely joked in those months that were Trump to win a single primary, it would be as shocking to American political scientists as the fall of the Soviet Union had been for Kremlinologists. That joke, suffice to say, aged poorly.)

Something went awry with the Discovery-Scrutiny-Decline cycle in late 2015. Media gave Trump's longshot candidacy the same sort of initial coverage we would expect. And then the coverage just never abated. The media spotlight never left Trump. Opposing campaigns kept waiting for the normal shifting in media coverage, and it simply never arrived. Nick Confessore and Karen Yourish conducted an analysis of media coverage in the Republican Primary (Confessore and Yourish 2016). They found that Donald Trump received more than six times as much media attention as his closest rival, Ted Cruz. Trump received the equivalent of $1,898,000,000 in free media attention, compared to his $10 million in paid television advertising. Cruz received $313 million in free media coverage, versus $22 million in paid advertisements. Jeb Bush, the early frontrunner, spent $82 million on ads and received $214 million in free coverage. Marco Rubio, another well-funded challenger, spent $55 million on ads and received $204 million in free coverage. Trump simply dominated the media spotlight, like no outside challenger ever had before. Why?

The simplest explanation is ratings. CBS chairman Les Moonves famously remarked that Trump's candidacy "may not be good for America, but it's damn good for CBS" (Collins 2016). Conservative *New York Times* columnist Ross Douthat likewise noted that Trump was "such a gift to our industry" (Klein 2016). And this is all doubtless true. Trump news, Trump articles, and Trump hot-takes all performed better than Kasich articles, Bush news, and Rubio hot-takes. Trump made the 2016 Republican Primary *entertaining* in a way that his opponents could not.

Certainly, the candidate himself deserves some credit for this media strategy. Trump skillfully applied the narrative sensibilities of reality television to the presidential race. If nothing else, he was a masterful showman.

But it bears noting that ratings have, historically, been an inexact metric. Herbert Gans (2004, 229) noted in his classic study *Deciding What's News* that journalists "had little knowledge about the actual audience and rejected feedback from it. Although they had a vague image of the audience, they paid little attention to it." News organizations in the broadcast media era had no way of knowing in granular detail which stories, topics, and candidates

274 CONNECTIVE ACTION AND THE RISE OF THE FAR-RIGHT

were the most popular. They developed and institutionalized newsgathering routines in the absence of these feedback loops.

Nick Denton, when he was CEO of Gawker.com, once proclaimed that "probably the biggest change in internet media isn't the immediacy of it, or the low costs, but the measurability" (Petre 2015). By 2016, all media outlets had transitioned online, and they all had begun making use of sophisticated analytics dashboards from companies like Chartbeat to track, monitor, and judge which stories were the most popular. Some of these analytics were made public, through "most read," "most emailed," "trending," or "related" sidebars on media sites. Others are tracked internally, as a tool to aid editorial judgment. One crucial difference between the 2016 election and previous elections was the way that media organizations, for the first time, could measure and judge just how much more popular the Donald Trump stories were than all of the other stories.

The thing to keep in mind here is that *the act of measuring a process also changes that process.* Newsroom analytics sent a signal to journalists and their editors (Trump stories bring in more traffic than Bush/Cruz/Walker/Carson/Rubio/Kasich stories). And this signal gets wrapped into modified news routines (people seem to be demanding more Trump. Let's keep up the Trump coverage). The result is a positive feedback loop, in which Trump's endless media dominance becomes a justification for further commentary about Trump's dominance. This is a longstanding insight within the field of political communication, dating back to Kurt and Gladys Lang's classic study of television-crowd interactions at the MacArthur Day Parade (Lang and Lang 1953). Media does not reflect political behavior; it *refracts* political behavior.

In a world with digital media, but less analytics, the 2016 primary would have unfolded differently. Trump would still have been the same showman. He would still have the same instincts, and the same Twitter skills, and the same press conference behavior. But journalists and their editors would have been less attuned to the immediate feedback of Trump's daily ratings effects, and this would have led them to spread their coverage more evenly (as they always had in the past). Perhaps Trump still would have bested his competitors. Trump was a unique celebrity candidate, with a special talent for turning subtext into text. And he benefited from a crowded field that included a never-ending series of strategic pratfalls by his opponents. (If only Jeb Bush had been as formidable as he initially seemed on paper; if only some candidate other than universally disliked Ted Cruz had been in second place when candidates were being winnowed from the field and trying to find a suitable anti-Trump consensus pick.) But it is also quite possible that had media coverage in the 2016 primary more closely resembled media coverage in previous election years, Donald Trump might have gone through the same discovery-scrutiny-decline cycle of previous longshot candidates who lacked institutional support.

It is a phenomenon reminiscent of Schrodinger's cat. Outside the realm of quantum mechanics, Schrodinger's cat is treated as a reference to how the act of observing a phenomenon can change the phenomenon itself. The growth of newsroom analytics in 2016 resulted, in a sense, in Schrodinger's audience. The act of observing reader/viewer behavior resulted in a feedback loop that changed audience behavior and contributed to the rise of Trumpism.

The Trump Presidency: The Ratings Will Continue Until Morale Improves

Reflecting on the Trump years, Les Moonves's comment from 2016 sounds like an ominous warning: Trump may not have been good for America, but he was good for news ratings. And this raises a vexing problem: By what metrics should Trump and the media be judged? Consider whether Trump's time in office was a historic success, or an abysmal failure. Trump boasts few policy achievements but appointed a lot of judges to lifetime positions. His administration was historically plagued by self-inflicted scandals, but few of his lieutenants are serving prison sentences. He was impeached twice by the House but convicted neither time by Senate. His party lost control of the House of Representatives in the 2018 election despite a lopsided, gerrymandered map tilting the election heavily in their favor, but his party also gained two Senate seats. The economy improved during his tenure, until it collapsed during his mismanagement of the COVID-19 pandemic. He was constantly in the news, but never received majority support in presidential approval polls. He told more demonstrable lies than any president in history, but every one of those lies was treated as a news event. There is no objective, mutually agreed-upon standard by which presidential performance is judged. There are norms and traditions for how such things are judged by historians, political scientists, pundits, public officials, and international peers. But these norms and traditions have proven to be costless to

276   CONNECTIVE ACTION AND THE RISE OF THE FAR-RIGHT

discard. If we measure a presidency by total volume of news clippings, then Trump was the most successful president in history. If we measure a presidency by policy accomplishments, public approval, stability of domestic and international institutions, or minimization of preventable deaths among the citizenry, then he ranks among the absolute worst.

Within the Republican Party network, the lack of strategic agreement about the party's broader goals and vision—what Republicans intended to *achieve* through governance, and how such achievements might be measured—has been a fundamental impediment to any cohesive resistance to Trumpism. (The party's sole consistent policy stance appears to be tax cuts for the wealthy.) Trump is constantly in the news, upsetting liberal opponents, and raising money. Those all *seem* like vanity metrics—easy to count, but with no real relationship to effective governance or long-term policy success. But if the Trumpist wing of the party rejects all alternate metrics that paint Trump's presidency in a less-flattering light, then these easily countable elements can act as evidence that Trumpism is actually quite popular. (Just look at the rally attendance!) Out of this process flows the kinds of issues that according to Ziblatt's model serve to distract the national conversation, keeping it focused on the latest outrage rather than on substantive policy considerations, such as massive social and economic inequality, environmental catastrophe, and growing international instability.

For political reporters, a central conundrum of the Trump years was that the president was bad for the news as fourth estate, but great for the news business. Trump inspired distrust of the news media, and violence against reporters. He lied on camera and insisted that video clips of his press comments were "fake news." If the purpose of a free press is to perform a monitorial/watchdog function—to "comfort the afflicted and afflict the comfortable"—then the press was clearly weakened by the Trump years. But if the purpose of political news organizations is to garner clicks, likes, and subscriptions, then Trump was fantastic, and the news media emerged stronger than ever. Once again, it all depends on what variables we measure, what data we listen to.

The tension between these competing imperatives—the democratic ideal of watchdog journalism versus the impulse to build and monetize audiences—helped to define political journalism throughout the Trump years. Whether it was Rachel Maddow breathlessly promoting the latest scandal that was sure to bring down Trump, CNN finding a Trump supporter for every panel in the hopes of a viral argument breaking out, or mainstream reporters softening their coverage so they wouldn't lose access to key Trump officials, the high-traffic impulse consistently won out over the democratic-ideals impulse.

One moment that stands out as exemplary was the January 6, 2019 interview between Anderson Cooper and Alexandria Ocasio-Cortez (AOC) on *60 Minutes*. Cooper pointedly asks AOC, "Do you believe President Trump is a racist?" to which she replies "Yeah . . . no question." Cooper, recognizing a potentially viral moment, feigns shock and asks, "How can you say that?" *60 Minutes* had its teaser, and the clip became the center of public discourse for a day or so. The interview was good for the news *business*. Nearly a year earlier, Anderson Cooper himself had stated on air that President Trump's remarks were clearly racist—"not racial. Not racially tinged. Racist." It was a moment of clarity that spotlighted the media's role in defending civic values and standing as a watchdog. In interviewing AOC, it was almost as though Cooper had forgotten his own public commentary on Trump's words and actions (Ryan 2018).

Political news during the Trump administration often bore a resemblance to a sitcom from the 1990s, where each individual episode was self-contained. The same characters recurred, with the same tropes and catchphrases. But the events of one episode did not impact later episodes. Sitcoms used to be written this way because TV writers could not expect audiences to follow every episode closely. Political news during the Trump era behaved this way because the constant drumbeat of holding a brazen authoritarian accountable for his transgressions—reminding viewers every week that the corruption scandals were ongoing, and the people implicated in them were still in charge—wasn't the best way to drive ratings.

This phenomenon was tragically on display during the early months of the COVID response. Donald Trump held daily press briefings where, alongside spreading medical misinformation (suggesting, at one point, that people could cure COVID by injecting bleach and sunlight into their bodies), he routinely insisted that we had "turned a corner" and were just two weeks away from ending the pandemic. Digital listening by the press and by conservative surrogate organizations were mutually reinforcing, narrowing the objectives that they measured themselves by and actively pursued. The Trump press conferences were an exercise in trying to win the next news cycle. The long, hard work of organizing logistics for a national pandemic response strategy went completely unaddressed.

The trouble is that the measures of success that are most easily accessible—clicks, ratings, views, political donations, public approval ratings—are often at cross purposes with how we actually think success ought to be measured. The most effective political journalism is not the reporting with the highest click rates. The most effective presidents are not the ones who sell the most merchandise or hold the largest rallies. And within the Republican Party network, the further trouble is that Trump's perpetual media dominance created its own feedback effect. Clearly, whatever he was doing must have been working—just listen to those crowds or tune in to the conservative media ecosystem! (Benkler et al. 2017). Republican Party officials like Paul Ryan and Mitch McConnell could, in theory, have reined Trump's authoritarian instincts in. They were the individuals best positioned to defend longstanding governance norms and establish boundaries for what the Republican Party would stand for. But Republican political leadership proved to be fickle, less concerned with providing a bulwark for American democracy (which is important, but hardly easy to observe) than they were with giving the conservative base what they wanted (which could be measured through analytics readily at hand). Party surrogate organizations became enthralled by the Trumpist wing of the Party because the Trumpist wing's successes could be so easily measured.

The 2020 Election: What Should Campaigns Optimize For?

The 2020 election must be judged with an asterisk, given how the COVID-19 pandemic affected every aspect of public and private life. We cannot know how the Trump and Biden campaigns would have operated in an otherwise normal election cycle. But there are still some key lessons we can draw from how the Trump campaign used analytics to refine and optimize its tactics.

For over a decade, Republican political operatives had tried and failed to build a Republican equivalent to the Democratic fundraising website ActBlue.com. ActBlue is a fundraising portal, founded in 2004, that provides easy-to-use small donor fundraising support to local, state, and national Democratic campaigns. It is also used by Political Action Committees and grassroots volunteers. The site is simple, cheap, and flexible. Republicans, recognizing the Democrats fundraising infrastructure advantage, have tried every election cycle to build their own ActBlue. Due to a variety of coordination problems (Republican elites like to control who can receive funding,

Republican consultants make a lot of money through online fundraising fees and rationally seek to guard their turf, etc.), they have never succeeded (Karpf 2012). In 2020, Republicans finally solved the problem. The Trump campaign spearheaded the development of WinRed.com and sent clear marching orders that all Republicans would be expected to use it.

WinRed managed to raise colossal sums of money—$1.9 billion—from Republican small donors in 2020. It was arguably the biggest technological successes of the cycle. But when the dust settled, *how* they raised that money became a subject of sustained inquiry. Reporter Shane Goldmacher of the *New York Times* broke the story in April 2021 about the deceptive fundraising practices that the Trump campaign pioneered in partnership with WinRed (Goldmacher 2021). Over the course of the campaign, Trump's digital fundraising team deployed increasingly aggressive, deceptive tactics to trick Trump supporters into donating far more than they intended. By prechecking a "make it weekly" box in the donation form and by repeatedly decreasing the size of the fine print to mask that intended one-time donations would be charged as recurring donations, the Trump campaign cannibalized its small-donor fundraising pool. According to Goldmacher's reporting, "In the final two and a half months of 2020, the Trump campaign, the Republican National Committee and their shared accounts issued more than 530,000 refunds worth $64.3 million to online donors." The Biden campaign, by comparison, issued 37,000 online refunds totaling $5.6 million over that same time period.

At the time of this writing, multiple states' Attorneys General are pursuing lawsuits against WinRed. WinRed, the RNC, and the Trump campaign maintain that they did nothing wrong. Gerrit Lansing, WinRed's president, told the *Times* that "Donors are the lifeblood of G.O.P. campaigns" and boasted of the company's customer support (Goldmacher 2021). Jason Miller, a Trump campaign spokesman, suggested that 530,000 refunds was small in the grander scheme of things: "Our campaign was built by the hardworking men and women of America, and cherishing their investments was paramount to anything else we did" (Goldmacher 2021).

WinRed's fundraising tactics are a twisted, hall-of-mirrors version of the organizational practices I documented in *Analytic Activism*. The Trump campaign's fundraising operation had a clear goal and established metrics: raise as much money from supporters as possible. It ran controlled experiments to see which fundraising appeals would be the most effective. It listened to supporters by monitoring their behavior, and it fine-tuned its fundraising appeals in response. The result: the less clear it is that intended one-time donations will be recurring donations, the more recurring donors you will sign up!

Of course, the shocking part of this example is its combination of audacity and shortsightedness. WinRed is, in Ziblatt's framework, a key surrogate organization within the broader Republican Party network. It is supposed to bridge between the interests of economic elites and the broader electoral coalition. The purpose of an electoral campaign is not to raise the most money or sell the most merchandise. The purpose of an electoral campaign is to win a majority of votes! The avid Trump supporter who defaults on his credit card because the campaign charged him seven times what he could afford to donate presumably becomes less likely to cast a ballot, volunteer for the campaign, or give to future Republican candidates.

But here, once again, we can see the logic of analytics, stripped of any strategic leadership or human judgment. The goal of the campaign's *fundraising* team is to raise as much money as they can. Adding a prechecked recurring donation box does lead to an immediate fundraising boost. Burying the text of that box so supporters are less likely to notice it provides a further boost. The rash of fraud complaints, the angry supporters, the legal troubles, and the front-page news stories are all someone else's problem, to be dealt with in another time and place. WinRed is a digital surrogate; it is optimized to raise money, not win elections or protect the interests of the party's grassroots supporter base. The Trump campaign and WinRed optimized for maximizing fundraising because that was what they were built to do.

The surprising thing is that as we headed into the 2022 election, WinRed continued to be a major part of the RNC's electoral infrastructure. The company defrauded half a million Republican donors and was still internally hailed as a triumph.

The result is a mutually reinforcing system that continuously rewards the Trumpist wing of the party. WinRed becomes a leverage point in intraparty competition—Republican candidates who want to mount a primary challenge and stand up against the party's slide into authoritarianism face the additional hurdle of potentially being denied access to a core campaign infrastructure. Liz Cheney, for instance, had no fundraising page on WinRed for the contested 2022 Wyoming Republican Primary. Her campaign hired an alternate vendor that specialized in digital fundraising for churches and nonprofits instead.

Digital surrogate organizations—media outlets, elected officials, and conservative activist networks—use digital listening and testing to rapidly identify salient cultural grievances on social media. Partisan activists, organizations, and party elites test which topics and frames generate the most engagement, which in turn plays an agenda-setting role for mainstream media outlets. While none of these activities are entirely new—the roots of conservative surrogate organizations fanning the flames of cultural grievance to hold a cross-class coalition together stretches back many decades—the result is an acceleration of the illiberal tendencies among conservative parties that democracies have historically struggled to keep in check.

The Deeper Currents: If You Stand For Nothing, What Will You Fall For?

Analytics-based feedback loops are not the primary *cause* of the Republican Party's rapid descent into authoritarianism and ethnonationalism. They are, rather, an accelerant. A party with stronger leadership or a more robust moral core would be far less vulnerable to optimizing for what generates clicks and cash, as opposed to actually governing. Yet of course the logic of the framework used to organize this volume would tell us that conservative parties such as the GOP face a dilemma, especially in the face of extreme social and economic inequality. To win elections, they must, with the assistance of allied organizations, form a cross-class coalition based on emotive nonmaterial issues such as race, xenophobia, nationalism, and religious bigotry. As Ziblatt notes (2017), this is a dangerous game. The issues that allow for the formation of a cross-class coalition are volatile and subject to adoption by more extremist elements in society. The very solution to the conservative dilemma contains the seeds of authoritarianism and democratic backsliding. These seeds were planted long ago. Before Trump and Breitbart there was the Tea Party, and Fox News, and Karl Rove, and the Club for Growth, and Rush Limbaugh, and Newt Gingrich. Parker and Blum elsewhere in this volume describe this point, as does Feldstein.

Republican digital fundraising is built upon the rusty foundations of Republican direct mail fundraising—a cathedral constructed by Richard Viguerie, whom Jeffrey Berry (1999) once artfully described as a "one man tragedy of the commons." In "The Long Con," historian Rick Perlstein (2012) has thoroughly documented the grand history of conservative elites treating their grassroots supporters as suckers.

Limbaugh and Fox News spent decades moving the center-of-gravity within the Republican Party network from think tanks and elected officials toward radio shock jocks and television personalities. They stoked conservative audiences' fears, tested political messages, and pushed their listeners to become an angry, vocal base that punished all forms of good governance behavior from political elites. In so doing, the Republican Party has also moved away from adopting actual policy stances in favor of a politics of cultural grievance.

One way the Trumpian majority within the Republican Party network exercises control is through the threat of well-funded primary challenges to any Republican who does not offer full-throated support. This, too, has a long pedigree. It was a well-worn tactic throughout the Tea Party years and was introduced into mainstream Republican Party politics by the Club for Growth in 1998. Conservative political associations spent decades punishing any Republican elected official who failed their latest purity test. Eventually that same tactic was turned against the people who had gained power by deploying it. There is no defining policy that unites the party anymore, nor is there any reward for individuals who adhere to basic liberal-democratic values. There is just a race to show fealty to the party and hatred of the Democratic opposition. Republican elites have focused their analytics on vanity metrics—a party with no platform has no deeper governance objectives.

Likewise, Limbaugh and Fox News spent decades turning conservative talk radio and conservative broadcast news into partisan theater. They lacked the fine-toothed analytics tools that have now taken hold in newsrooms, but is it any wonder that the trend in conservative media has been toward high-click outrage content, with no consideration of journalistic values? Those values left the premises long before Trump showed any political ambitions.

Tucker Carlson (at least until his show was abruptly cancelled by Fox News) has been able to take advantage of a complex mix of external and internal analytics to identify the precise topics, frames, and status threats that will keep his viewers tuning in (Confessore 2022). But Carlson does not stoke white fear because the data forces him to do so—he stokes white fear because that is the audience that his network has chosen to cultivate for decades. The party of Reaganism became the party of Trumpism gradually, step by step, as party elites abandoned any pretense of prioritizing effective governance over short-term partisan gain. The seeds of Trumpism were planted when Newt Gingrich declared a state of total war against Bill Clinton and the Democrats in Congress, for their grand sin of being the opposition party. They were planted by Tom Delay pushing extreme gerrymanders to solidify Republican control of the House regardless of what the voters think. They were planted by Mitch McConnell declaring that his main objective in 2009 was to make Barack Obama a one-term president. There were planted by Ted Cruz, who engineered a government shutdown in symbolic protest against funding the Affordable Care Act. The Party elites spent decades standing for no core principles in particular. Is it any wonder that the intraparty opposition to Trump proved so fleeting?

Conclusion: A Democracy, If You Can Keep It

Let us return now to where this chapter began. The Republican Party has fallen. It embraces the insurrectionists and banishes elected officials who take their oath of office seriously enough to investigate an organized attack on the seat of government. The Party spiraled into authoritarianism gradually and then all-at-once.

Viewed from a certain angle, none of this comes as a surprise. *Of course* they censured Elizabeth Cheney and Adam Kinzinger! Cheney and Kinzinger were contributing to bad news cycles. Bad news cycles are bad for the Party, bad for fundraising, bad for clicks and shares. And *of course* they called the insurrection "legitimate political discourse!" Focusing on the insurrection leads to bad news cycles. Those insurrectionists are also donors and supporters. The real enemies are the people voting for the other side. This line of thinking is anathema to a functional, healthy democracy. But it is easy to optimize for. And lacking any leadership or moral core, it is the line of thinking that Republican Party leaders have adopted.

The stark problem here is that *only the Republican Party can fix the Republican Party*. The realities of gerrymandering and partisan geography make it practically impossible for Democrats en masse to "vote the bums out of office," at least in the short term. The echo chamber of the conservative media ecosystem protects Republican elites from feeling any social shaming from mainstream or progressive media. The conservative takeover of the Supreme Court ensures that there will be no legal deus ex machina protecting the foundations of democracy. If American democracy is going to eventually be repaired, it is going to require the anti-Trump wing of the Republican Party to stand for some higher purpose than winning the next news cycle, raising the most money, and gaining seats in the next election. That higher purpose cannot be easily optimized for. It requires moral clarity and commitment to shared norms and understandings. It requires, in other words, human leadership.

Analytics is not the cause of the Republican Party's slide into authoritarianism. It has been an accelerant. But it is also, I think, an illustrative one. Trumpism is tremendously effective at optimizing for attention, outrage, and partisan support. It is fundamentally corrosive to democratic governance and civic life.

The Republican Party can only begin to repair itself if it chooses to optimize for some deeper governance values. And the fourth estate can only live up to its democratic role if it prioritizes its role as watchdog over its role as intermediary between advertisers and potential customers. Digital listening can harm a democracy or help a democracy. It can exacerbate or help ameliorate the conservative dilemma. It depends on what the party leadership and their surrogates choose to value.

References

Ariely, Dan. 2010. "You Are What You Measure." *Harvard Business Review*, June 2010. https://hbr.org/2010/06/column-you-are-what-you-measure.

Benkler, Yochai, Robert Faris, and Hal Roberts. 2017. *Network Propaganda: Manipulation, Disinformation and Radicalization in American Politics*. New York: Oxford University Press.

Berry, Jeffrey. 1999. *The New Liberalism*. Washington, DC: Brookings Institution Press.

Cohen, Marty, David Karol, Hans Noel, and John Zaller. 2008. *The Party Decides: Presidential Nominations Before and After Reform*. Chicago: University of Chicago Press.

Collins, Eliza. 2016. "Les Moonves: Trump's Run is 'Damn Good for CBS.'" *Politico*, February 29. https://www.politico.com/blogs/on-media/2016/02/les-moonves-trump-cbs-220001.

Confessore, Nicholas. 2022. "How Tucker Carlson Stoked White Fear to Conquer Cable." *The New York Times*, April 30. https://www.nytimes.com/2022/04/30/us/tucker-carlson-gop-republican-party.html.

Confessore, Nicholas, and Karen Yourish. 2016. "$2 Billion Worth of Free Media for Donald Trump." The Upshot blog, *New York Times*, March 15. https://www.nytimes.com/2016/03/16/upshot/measuring-donald-trumps-mammoth-advantage-in-free-media.html.

Gans, Herbert. 2004. *Deciding What's News: A Study of CBS Evening News, NBC Nightly News, Newsweek and Time*. Evanston, IL: Northwestern University Press.

Goldmacher, Shane. 2021. "How Trump Steered Supporters Into Unwitting Donations." *New York Times*, April 3. https://www.nytimes.com/2021/04/03/us/politics/trump-donations.html.

Hacker, Jacob, and Paul Pierson. 2011. *Winner-Take-All Politics: How Washington Made the Rich Richer and Turned Its Back on the Middle Class.* New York: Simon & Schuster.

Hacker, Jacob, and Paul Pierson. 2020. *Let Them Eat Tweets: How the Right Rules in an Age of Extreme Inequality.* New York: Liveright.

Karpf, David. 2012. *The MoveOn Effect: The Unexpected Transformation of American Political Advocacy.* New York: Oxford University Press.

Karpf, David. 2016. *Analytic Activism: Digital Listening and the New Political Strategy.* Oxford: Oxford University Press.

Klein, Ezra. 2016. "Ross Douthat on Lord of the Rings conservatism, Donald Trump, and writing for liberals." *Vox.com*, January 27. https://www.vox.com/latest-news/2016/1/27/10852856/ross-douthat-trump

Lang, Kurt, and Gladys Lang. 1953. *Television and Politics.* London: Transaction Publishers.

Levitsky, Steven, and Daniel Ziblatt. 2018. *How Democracies Die.* New York: Broadway Books.

Mason, Lilliana. 2018. *Uncivil Agreement: How Politics Became Our Identity.* Chicago: University of Chicago Press.

Perlstein, Rick. 2012. "The Long Con: Mail-order Conservatism." *The Baffler*, November. https://thebaffler.com/salvos/the-long-con.

Petre, Caitlin. 2015. "The Traffic Factories: Metrics at Chartbeat, Gawker Media, and The New York Times." Tow Center for Digital Journalism. May 7. http://towcenter.org/research/traffic-factories/.

Ryan, Josiah. 2018. "Anderson Cooper: 'The sentiment the President expressed today is a racist sentiment.'" CNN, January 11. https://www.cnn.com/2018/01/11/politics/cooper-trump-sentiment-racist-cnntv/index.html.

Sides, John, and Lynn Vavreck. 2014. *The Gamble: Choice and Chance in the 2012 Presidential Election.* Princeton, NJ: Princeton University Press.

Ziblatt, Daniel. 2017. *Conservative Parties and the Birth of Democracy.* New York: Cambridge University Press.

Chapter 13
Conclusion

Steven Livingston and Michael Miller

In the wake of Donald Trump's improbable victory in the 2016 presidential election, scholars, pundits, politicians, and ordinary citizens alike sought explanations. How had someone best known as a reality television personality, someone who had never held elected office and who had shown little interest in or understanding of national and global issues, become President of the United States? According to some reports, even Trump didn't expect to win the 2016 election (Wolff 2018). What happened?

In the search for answers, attention turned almost immediately to speculation about the role of social media. This in itself was surprising. For most of the preceding 20 years, digital technologies had been heralded as "liberation tech"—tools for smiting autocrats and fostering democracy (Diamond 2010). Yet views changed after the Brexit vote and Trump's election, and social media quickly came to be understood as a threat to democracy. This was especially true when social technologies were leveraged by foreign adversaries. Seemingly overnight, trolls and bots in St. Petersburg, Beijing, and Tehran were spinning up newly perceived realities designed to weaken public resolve, sow panic, deepen distrust of government institutions and of other citizens, and even throw elections. These were not unfounded concerns (Chen 2015).

By examining fluctuations in troll farm content associated with slower output on Russian holidays, Columbia University researchers found evidence that Russian internet trolls influenced the betting odds for the 2016 US presidential election (Almond et al. 2022). Another study found that changes in levels of candidate support were preceded by corresponding changes in IRA retweet volume (Ruck et al. 2019. See also Badawy et al. 2018; Grinberg et al. 2019; Howard et al. 2018; Isaac and Wakabayashi 2017). In other words, variations in public opinion were predicted by variations in Russian-directed Twitter content. Social media seemed to have a direct and significant impact in what people believed, and how they voted. And it

Steven Livingston and Michael Miller, *Conclusion*. In: *Connective Action and the Rise of the Far-Right*. Edited by: Steven Livingston and Michael Miller, Oxford University Press. © Oxford University Press (2025).
DOI: 10.1093/oso/9780197794937.003.0013

CONCLUSION   287

wasn't a small problem. One notable study characterized the Russian disinformation campaign as a "firehose of falsehood" (Paul and Matthews 2016). The sheer volume and variety of disinformation simply overwhelmed people's capacity to discern reality. One prominent political communication scholar concluded that Russian disinformation was responsible for Trump's election (Jamieson 2018).

Until it wasn't.

In a 2023 study, New York University's Center for Social Media and Politics found that Russian Twitter campaigns during the 2016 presidential race had, in fact, reached only a small number of highly partisan Republican users who were already firmly committed to Donald Trump. As the study concluded, there were "no measurable changes in attitudes, polarization, or voting behavior among those exposed to this foreign influence campaign" (NYU 2023). The effort to clear up the confusion around the 2016 presidential election and the role of social media has itself become quite confusing.

Whatever the correct conclusion concerning social media and the 2016 election, one thing is clear: the presidential election that year set into motion a research trajectory predicated on a largely undertheorized set of causal hypotheses. The standard individual-level media effects research trajectory assumes that democratic decay is, principally, the result of individual-level cognitive effects associated with variations in social media (and sometimes in combination with conventional media) content. In this telling, content has an alarming capacity to suck unwary users down a proverbial disinformation and conspiracy theory rabbit hole (Sutton and Douglas 2022; Pierre 2020; Tang et al. 2020). Indeed, the proposition embraces something akin to the old hypodermic needle or magic bullet model of media effects that emerged in the early part of the twentieth century. These early models attempted to account for the effects of socially disruptive new technologies— including "talking films" and radio (Katz 1957). The social anxieties that emerged with the introduction of new technologies in the early twentieth century also led to the creation of research and civic engagement organizations that were dedicated to buttressing the defenses of average citizens against the ill-effects of propaganda. In 1937, for example, the influential Institute for Propaganda Analysis was created to analyze media content effects. "The institute received considerable public attention because of the widespread fear that without critical education about propaganda, citizens of the emerging unstable mass society could not withstand the onslaught of

288 CONNECTIVE ACTION AND THE RISE OF THE FAR-RIGHT

subversive mass media messages" (Bryant and Zillmann 2009, 11). Several books about the threat propaganda posed to average citizens were published, with Alfred McClung Lee and Elizabeth Briant Lee's (1939) *The Fine Art of Propaganda* perhaps the most noteworthy example.

Similar anxieties emerged around the effects of social media platforms, especially following the 2016 election. The opening lines of a highly influential report published by the William and Flora Hewlett Foundation captured the premise succinctly: "While the problems of disinformation, misinformation and propaganda are not new, certain aspects of modern technology and communications appear to be contributing to a rapid polarization and democratic deterioration in the U.S. and abroad." The report continued, "in combination with social media, [disinformation, misinformation, and propaganda] come to play in increasing polarization and tribalization, thereby weakening our democratic systems" (Born and Edington 2017, 4). After framing the problem in this way, the report goes on to offer several potential solutions, including "improving journalistic quality," identifying and "holding accountable creators of disinformation and misinformation," "providing support and advice to the major platforms," and "improving fact checking and citizen media literacy" (Born and Edington 2017, 17). Technological problems called for technical solutions.

It is worth stressing that framing the causes of democratic backsliding in this way does indeed capture important aspects of the problem, while failing to account for others. Our goal has been to take stock and assess the strengths and limitations of the implicit framing concepts that shaped the initial response to the seemingly sudden crisis of democracy in America and elsewhere in the world. How a problem is framed leads to privileging particular solutions. If the problem is understood *exclusively* as a corrupted information environment due to nefarious actors found online, then the proper solutions involve strengthening the signal and reception of good information. In parallel, this understanding favors cognitive science-inspired research testing the merits of different adjustments to the signal. What are the limits to this approach?

Consideration of the effects of the most extreme degree of material inequality in a century, the consequences of centuries of systemic racism, the consequences of decades of neoliberal attacks on authoritative institutions, the existential crisis of climate collapse, the growing threat of nuclear annihilation, or the risks posed by automation and "deaths of despair"—these

CONCLUSION   289

issues tend not to make their way into the post-2016 research paradigm. Rather than look outward to power structures in society, research turned to assessing the cognitive effects of media content on individuals.

This isn't surprising, given the composition of the experts interviewed in the Hewlett report. The list of informants included prominent political science and cognitive science researchers, staff members and the leadership of several other foundations, and tech corporation executives. Not on the list of experts were historians, sociologists, political scientists, or philosophers who could have offered a broader analysis of the causes of democratic decay in the twenty-first century. No one from the well-established democracy scholarship community, such as Daniel Ziblatt, Nancy Bermeo, or Steven Levitsky, were interviewed for the report. Nor were scholars from V-Dem or Freedom House interviewed. And the experts who *were* interviewed were presented with questions such as, "How/to what extent is online disinformation/propaganda directly affecting the performance of US democracy?" and "Are citizens polarizing because of exposure to biased information or are polarized citizens seeking out biased information—How strong is causality?" (Born and Edington 2017, 39). Given the roles and expertise of the informants and given the thematic content of the questions asked of them, the report's conclusions are not surprising.

The Hewlett Foundation report may not have been unique in terms of its framing, but it was certainly consequential. It appears to have galvanized the philanthropic community in an effort to address democratic backsliding understood as the result of online disinformation (O'Hara and Nelson 2020, 2). Endeavors to combat disinformation, misinformation, and propaganda by the philanthropic community, as well as by the United States government between 2016 and 2021, were extraordinary. According to one accounting, a little under $71 million had been distributed to a handful of universities in the United States, think tanks, and to the Social Science Research Council.[1] This is probably a conservative estimate (Knight Foundation 2019).

---

[1] The authors wish to thank Kelly Born for sharing her PowerPoint presentation containing these figures. For the sake of full disclosure, the authors of this chapter, who are also the coeditors of this book, were, respectively, the lead author of a proposal that brought a $5 million Knight Foundation grant to the George Washington University to establish the Institute for Data, Democracy, and Politics (IDDP), while the second author and coeditor was, at the time, a program officer with the Social Science Research Council (SSRC). The SSRC has received multiple grants from the Knight Foundation. Furthermore, both the SSRC and IDDP grants have covered the costs of the workshop that brings together the scholars contributing to this book. We are grateful for this generous support.

Whatever the total, this was an extraordinary commitment to supporting dis/misinformation research.[2]

And to be sure, researching online disinformation is essential, as several of the chapters in this volume attest. Yet without factoring in social context, technocentric explanations fail to offer a robust explanation of democratic backsliding, just as the institutionalist's explanations fall short when offered without awareness of the effects of digital platforms on social mobilization. What we have presented is a *connective action* understanding of an institutionalist framework for explaining backsliding. The seeds of such an understanding are already in place. Foundations large and small have supported a wide array of initiatives that go beyond standalone technocentric arguments, including the SSRC working group represented in this volume (see for example Daniels 2020; Bennett and Livingston 2020).

But the great bulk of the funding has gone toward technocentric research. The weight of so much money on a single hypothesis—or related set of hypotheses, all centering on social media content's presumed effects on *individuals*—has pulled research almost entirely in a technocentric direction. As Deen Freelon and Chris Wells put it so cogently, the research focus on "fake news," "misinformation," "disinformation," "media manipulation," "coordinated inauthentic behavior," and "propaganda" has become "*the* defining political communication topic of our time, given the massive media attention, reams of scholarship, and unprecedented funding opportunities devoted to it" (Freelon and Wells 2020, emphasis in the original). Seventy million dollars put to the service of "creating a new discipline" around big data and computer science shoved consideration of the effects of social and economic power structures in society to the side. Put another way, many scholars lost sight of the *political* in political communication research. It is as E. E. Schattschneider said of the new positivist political science of his day: it was "a mountain of data surrounding a vacuum" (Schattschneider 1969, 8).

This mirrors developments in the social sciences in post–World War II period. A handful of major foundations supported the development of a more scientific basis of the social sciences. At the time, the social sciences "were often dismissed as unscientific, and for that were excluded from the newly created National Science Foundation (NSF)" (Geiger 1988). Beardley

---

[2] SSRC's Disinformation Research Mapping Platform, MediaWell, was designed with precisely this goal in mind. That work, which one of this volume's coeditors worked closely on, was supported by a coalition of foundations, including Ford, Hewlett, Knight, Democracy Fund, and S. D. Bechtel.

Rumi, a pioneering early twentieth-century statistician and the director of the Laura Spelman Rockefeller Memorial, a precursor to the Rockefeller Foundation, concluded that it was "necessary to develop social science and social scientists within the universities before one could expect a body of reliable knowledge for application to social problems" (Geiger 1988, 316). To be useful and legitimate, social science needed to emulate the natural sciences and be applied to the task of finding technical solutions to technically understood social problems.

Seventy years later, foundation leaders spoke of creating a "new discipline" for the study of disinformation and democracy: "There is a need for innovative approaches that recognize the complexity of these challenges by joining computational sciences, social sciences and the humanities" (Knight Foundation 2019). But with the preponderance of research firmly rooted in technocentric research assumptions, the weight of research leaned in the direction of social media network analyses and cognitive modeling of disinformation effects. Soon, computer scientists, some of whom were attracted to disinformation studies for the first time because of the availability of funding at a scale that nearly matched research support found in the tech sector, started investigating political science problems, though without the benefit of available institutionalist insights. Patterns will simply emerge from the data. Theories that might explain the patterns didn't seem all that important to some (Pigliucci 2009).

Without question, technology-oriented explanations can offer important insights (Benkler et al. 2018). Yet on its own, a focus on technology cannot produce a more complete explanation of democratic backsliding. For example, if Facebook, Twitter, and other social technologies are responsible for democratic backsliding, we must explain why the top five most stable liberal democracies in the world in 2022—Sweden, Denmark, Norway, Costa Rica, and New Zealand—are also among the countries with the highest internet penetration and social media adoption rates (V-Dem Institute 2022, 10; Kepios 2022). The technocentric model must also clarify how social media explains the long-term decline in trust in state institutions among the Western nations, a trend that began in the 1960s and 1970s (Pew Research Center 2015). Something more is needed to explain democratic backsliding. As Samuel Woolley notes, more complete explanations require "the combination of social, economic, and political problems that spurs manipulative uses of social media in the first place" (2020, 7). This book has tried to take Woolley's point to heart.

292 CONNECTIVE ACTION AND THE RISE OF THE FAR-RIGHT

We have drawn on the insights of the connective action literature *and* on the older institutionalist scholarship devoted to sussing out the relative weight to be given to social, economic, and political factors when trying to explain democratic consolidation and backsliding. The emergence and health of the middle class, the degree of social and economic inequality, the nature of civic organizations and their relationship to the state and to political parties, and the strength of parties must be taken into consideration, as must the role of digital platforms in the organization of publics. We have relied on the conservative dilemma model of democratic consolidation or backsliding and the connective action model of public mobilization in our efforts to create a more robust democratic backsliding model. Here is what we have discovered.

A Political Communication Model of Democratic Backsliding

Here is what we've put forward as an important corrective to recent efforts to explain democratic backsliding. First, social technologies, and digital platforms more generally, broaden the range of what is reasonably understood to be a civic or social movement organization. Ziblatt's (2017) original formulation of party surrogate organizations includes civic associations, business enterprise (such as newspaper groups and their owners), and interest organizations (such as agrarian leagues). Just so long as they helped a conservative party redirect attention to cross-cutting issues, Ziblatt is largely agnostic on the question of organizational forms. Hacker and Pierson (2020), in their helpful application of Ziblatt's model to the contemporary Republican Party in the United States, do not change Ziblatt's historical understanding of a surrogate organization in any fundamental way. In their analysis, important GOP surrogates include donor networks of billionaires and corporations, single issue groups like the National Rifle Association, and cultural institutions such as Evangelical churches and the Catholic Church. These are all important examples of *conventional* surrogate organizations.

In the digital era, surrogate organizations are more varied in form and consequential in operation. Here, too, we have only skimmed the surface of other disciplinary literatures, as Bennett and Segerberg note when discussing the "communication as organization" thesis (2014, 1449). As Bennett and Livingston describe in Chapter 1, the conceptual framing chapter to this volume, digital surrogate organizations or networks bring substantially different properties to the question of democratic backsliding.

The institutionalist literature offers ambivalent assessments of the role played by civil society organizations in democracy (Armony 2004; Almond and Verba 1963). Some scholars regard robust civil society organizations as foundational elements of democracy while others have understood them to be sources of destabilization and autocracy (Bermeo 2003). Jacob Hacker and Paul Pierson capture the ambivalence well. On the one hand,

> Parties may find these outside groups useful surrogates. This is particularly true of conservative parties since they face the tricky challenge of broadening their mass appeal while maintaining their allegiance to economic elites. Depending on the nature of the alliance between the party and outside groups, these relationships may be limited and intermittent, or deep and lasting. (2020, 23–24)

To broaden the party's appeal, surrogates promote emotively engaging yet potentially destabilizing cross-cutting cleavage issues that usually involve racial, gender, ethnic, religious, or nationalist status threats. We will come back to this point in just a moment. In one form or another, cross-cutting cleavage issues involve some form of the following narrative: "They are threatening Us." "They are out to get you and your way of life." Several of our contributors have reported this in their contributions to this volume. In fact, as recent sociological research has demonstrated, various status threats have coalesced around a volatile brew of Christian nationalism, white supremacy, and Identitarianism (Gorski and Perry 2022; Stewart, 2025). As Hacker and Pierson put it, "In a worst-case scenario, the party falls into a spiral of weakening control over the most extreme elements of its coalition." As a result, "Reliance on surrogates can thus lead a party down the path to extremism" (Hacker and Pierson 2020, 24).

This takes us to the core concern of our investigation: If *conventional* surrogate organizations carry such risks, "digital surrogate organizations" deepen the threat to democracy. If routinized communication constitutes organization, and if recommendation algorithms amplify outrage, conspiracy theories, and disinformation, at an organizational level social technologies are destabilization engines, or as Max Fisher calls them, chaos machines (2022). What we've seen in this volume is a model of far-right connective action that gives voice and agency to extremist activists dedicated to the destruction of liberal democracy. We have emphasized the effects of digital networks on the nature of organizations and social mobilization, rather than on individual psychological effects resulting from exposure to social media content. As we note in the preface, the institutionalist democracy research literature is ambivalent about the role of civil society organizations in democracies. Under certain conditions, civil society organizations can destabilize democracy (Almond and Verba 1963; Berman 1997a, 1997b; Bermeo 2003; Bermeo and Nord 2000; Newton 2001). Far-right connective action removes some of that ambivalence, but the cost of certainty is greater anxiety about the viability of democracy.

In digital space, boundaries between the party, some of its surrogates, and issues collapses. The distinction between cross-cutting cleavage issues and surrogate organizations disappears. "Routine patterns of online communication" *are* the organization. Digitally enabled organizations such as QAnon, in turn, become elements of hybrid organizational forms that involve other more conventional surrogate organizations, such as news channels. In some circumstances, the party is but a node in a hybrid network of powerful conventional surrogates such as the Koch Foundations *and* digital surrogates that emerge around the latest conspiracy. As a result, the GOP and other conservative parties are left with less control over fundraising, candidate selection, or issue agendas (Bergengruen and Wilson 2022).

For instance, a self-described Christian crowdfunding site called GiveSendGo raised millions of dollars for the Proud Boys, a violent group that played a prominent role in the January 6th insurrection (Wilson 2021; see also Newhouse 2019). Sometimes after more mainstream online fundraising platforms have refused, it has taken up a variety of right-wing causes, including a legal defense fund for Kyle Rittenhouse, the right-wing vigilante who killed two Black Lives Matter protesters in 2020. It has also raised funds for those charged in crimes related to their involvement in the January 6th insurrection. It also raised in excess of $9 million in support of the "Freedom Convoy" campaigns by Canadian truckers in 2021–2022. But hybrid surrogate networks are not only digital. Since 2016, a different sort of billionaire donor to far-right causes has emerged. The older economic libertarian donors like Charles Koch were still there, of course, but a new more radical, social-issues-oriented donor began to emerge (Weaver and Learner 2023). Donors such as Peter Theil bankroll far-right nationalists, as he did in J. D. Vance's successful 2022 Senate campaign (Sargent 2022;

see also Mac and Lerer 2022). In addition to political campaigns, Theil has reportedly met with white nationalists and has embraced a neo-monarchist blogger popular among the "post-liberal" right (Gais 2021; Pogue 2022).

What is the upshot of all this? The combination of extraordinary amounts of available donor money and digital affordances makes it difficult for conservative parties to police their own ideological borders. This is what makes far-right connective action so threatening to conventional conservative parties and to liberal democracy.

There is a second important closing thought. The institutionalist backsliding paradigm correctly draws attention to social and economic conditions when assessing the stability of democracy. The dilemma itself emerges from the unique challenges faced by any party that aligns itself with economic elites while simultaneously competing in a democracy that requires broad public support in elections. Following the 2024 elections, the Democratic Party is facing its own conservative dilemma moment. As much as the Republic Party, it has become ensconsed with economic elites (Schleifer November 27, 2024). At its root, the dilemma is borne of tensions found between democracy and concentrations of wealth. According to the logic of the model, for democracy to survive, social and material inequality must remain subordinate to distractive cleavage issues. Otherwise, the conservative party's wealthy core constituency—the wealthy and party allies—might lose confidence in their ability to remain competitive in elections and resort to taking more undemocratic measures. The great irony of Ziblatt's (2017) model of democratic stabilization is that in the face of dire economic and social conditions the best course of action is to distract national debate from the most pressing issues confronting a nation and a majority of its citizens. Resolving the dilemma requires subterfuge, a reorientation of national conversation away from inequality and to alternative cleave issues. And what issues are these?

They are issues rooted in identity threats, including race, gender, ethnicity, and nationalism. Put differently, cross-cutting issues stoke racism, misogyny, and bigotry toward non-normative gender expression and jingoism. So understood, democracy is perched on a powder keg with political pyromaniacs striking matches left and right. It is easy to see that when formulated in this way the emergence of digital technology upends the delicate balance between having just enough threat induced rage to keep desperate citizens distracted from their own lived material conditions to having too much rage, a rage that spills over into extremist violence. The paradox of the

CONNECTIVE ACTION AND THE RISE OF THE FAR-RIGHT

conservative dilemma model is that it defines success as a continuation of an unsustainable status quo of grief and misery.[3]

A central feature of the status quo is wealth and income inequality. According to data from the US Federal Reserve, at the end of 2021 the top 1% of households in the United States held about a third (32.3%) of the country's wealth. Meanwhile, the bottom 50% held only 2.6% of the wealth. And the disparities are growing. By 2023, over 7% of U.S. households had an annual income under $15,000 (statista 2023). And by 2024, the top 10% of households held 67% of total household wealth. The bottom 50% of households held only 2.5% of total household wealth (Hernández Kent and Ricketts 2024). The combined net worth of the 400 richest Americans in 2020 was $3.2 trillion, up from $2.7 trillion in 2017 (Bloomberg Billionaire Index n.d.). During the COVID-19 pandemic alone, the wealth held by billionaires in the US increased by 70% (Picchi 2021). It is difficult to think clearly about such an extraordinary concentration of wealth because the numbers at this scale are difficult to comprehend. Despite all of this wealth, many billionaires continue to shirk their responsibilities as citizens. A 2019 study found that the average effective tax rate paid by the richest 400 families (0.003% of the population) in the US was 23%, while the rate paid by the bottom half of American households was 24.2% (Saez and Zucman 2019). Our broader point can be illustrated by a photograph of Donald Trump's 2025 inauguration. Seated in the front row were three of the richest persons in human history: Mark Zuckerberg ($218 billion), Jeff Bezos ($249 billion), and Elon Musk ($447 billion), along with other billionaires, including nominated cabinet members. The personal net worth of Zuckerberg, Bezos, and Musk alone is greater than the GDP of any U.S. state except California, Texas, New York, Florida and Illinois (Padilla and Sullivan 2025).

Measured in other ways, the working class shoulder a greater part of the burdens of citizenship. As the *Baltimore Sun* put it in describing combat fatalities in Iraq by service members from Maryland, "No one from Bethesda, Potomac (median family income of $200,000 in 2021) or Columbia was among those from the state who died in Iraq. Instead, young soldiers from places like Elkridge, Port Deposit (median family income of $50,833 in 2021) and Waldorf gave their lives" (Bowman 2005). The wealthy do what they will, and the poor suffer what they must.

---

[3] Ziblatt of course is not advocating for such a democracy. Rather, he argues that economic elites are the key determining factor behind democratic consolidation or backsliding.

CONCLUSION   297

Predatory corporate capitalism is another part of the status quo. Since the beginning of the pandemic, a great deal of research attention has been paid to anti-vaccine propaganda, and for good reason. Confidence in vaccines is certainly affected by pernicious online disinformation charlatans (Frenkel 2021). But these purveyors of online misinformation and disinformation have had help in undermining public confidence in the pharmaceutical industry. Purdue Pharma has *knowingly* addicted hundreds of thousands of Americans to OxyContin, a move that led to tens of thousands of deaths (Keneally 2019). And Purdue wasn't alone. Walgreens and CVS, two of the largest US pharmacies, agreed in 2023 to pay more than $10 billion to several states in a settlement of lawsuits brought against them by several states' attorney generals. Walmart also agreed to pay more than $3 billion. And four pharmaceutical companies—Johnson & Johnson, AmerisourceBergen, Cardinal Health, and McKesson—agreed to collectively pay $26 billion in February (Archie 2022). OxyContin overdoses are a small part of the wave of "deaths of despair" that sociologists Anne Case and Angus Deaton write about in their description of the social devastation wrought by modern neoliberal capitalism (Case and Deaton 2020a). In 2018 alone, some 158,000 people in the United States died from suicide, drug overdoses, or chronic liver disease caused by alcohol consumption, compared to 65,000 in 1995 (Case and Deaton 2020b). Predatory corporate greed is a part of the lived experience of people in the material world, the status quo.

The status quo also includes an epidemic of police violence. In 2022 police killed at least 1,176 people around the country, making it the deadliest year on record. From 2013 when data were first collected to 2022, 11,119 people have been killed by police officers in the United States. In 2022, 24% of those killed were Black people, many of them men, while only 13% of the US population is Black. From 2013 to 2022, Black Americans were three times more likely to be killed by US police than white people. In some cities, the disparities were worse. According to Mapping Police Violence, in Minneapolis where George Floyd was murdered by police officers, Black residents are 28 times more likely to be killed by a police officer than are white residents (Mapping Police Violence 2022).

These conditions, these material realities notwithstanding, the outrage engines that draw attention to the threat du jour keep cranking out the hits, from immigrant caravans to critical race theory, from drag queen reading hours to vague assertions of "wokeness." Meanwhile, almost 34 million Americans were "food insecure" in 2022, including nine million children

(Hampton 2022). According to the Board of Governors of the Federal Reserve System annual survey of financial well-being of American families, 40% of Americans would struggle to pay an unexpected $400 expense (Grover 2022). The leading cause of bankruptcy in the United States is unpayable healthcare costs. And for those who own a home, this vital source of personal financial security is put at risk by the costs of healthcare. Ninety percent of those who had unpaid medical expenses and who had homes took out a second mortgage to pay their medical bills (Wood 2017). To understand the roots of public rage, political communication scholars must look outward to the world. Social media platforms certainly stoke the flames, but they didn't start the fire.

To survive, a democracy must address the basic needs of its citizens. All of them.

References

Almond, Douglas, Xinming Du, Alana Vogel. 2022. "Reduced Trolling on Russian Holidays and Daily US Presidential Election Odds." *Plos One*, March 30. https://journals.plos.org/plosone/article?id=10.1371/journal.pone.0264507

Almond, Gabriel, and Sidney Verba. 1963. *The Civic Culture: Political Attitudes and Democracy in Five Nations.* New York: Sage Publishing.

Archie, Ayana. 2022. "CVS and Walgreens Agree to Pay $10 Billion to Settle Lawsuits Linked to Opioid Sales." NPR, December 13. https://www.npr.org/2022/12/13/1142416718/cvs-walgreens-opioid-crisis-settlement.

Armony, Ariel C. 2004. *The Dubious Link: Civic Engagement and Democratization.* Stanford, CA: Stanford University Press.

Badawy, Adam, Emiliano Ferrara, and Kristina. Lerman, 2018. "Analyzing the Digital Traces of Political Manipulation: The 2016 Russian Interference Twitter Campaign." *2018 IEEE/ACM International Conference on Advances in Social Networks Analysis and Mining.* doi: https://doi.org/10.1109/ASONAM.2018.8508646.

Benkler, Yochai, Robert Farris, and Hal Roberts. 2018. *Network Propaganda.* New York: Oxford University Press.

Bennett, W. Lance, and Steven Livingston. 2020. *The Disinformation Age: Politics, Technology, and Disruptive Communication in the United States.* New York: Cambridge University Press.

Bennett, W. Lance, and Alexandra Segerberg. 2013 (2014 Kindle). *The Logic of Connective Action: Digital Media and the Personalization of Contentious Politics.* New York: Cambridge University Press.

Bergengruen, Vera, and Chris Wilson. 2022. "'Free' Crowdfunding Site Linked to Right-Wing Causes Generates a Windfall for Itself." *Time*, March 3. https://time.com/6150317/givesendgo-trucker-convoy-canada-profits.

Berman, Sheri. 1997a. "Civil Society and Political Institutionalization." *American Behavioral Scientist* 40 (5): 562–574.

Berman, Sheri. 1997b. "Civil Society and the Collapse of the Weimar Republic." *World Politics* 49 (3): 401–429.

Bermeo, Nancy G. 2003. *Ordinary People in Extraordinary Times*. Princeton, NJ: Princeton University Press.

Bermeo, Nancy G., and Philip Nord. 2000. *Civil Society Before Democracy: Lessons from Nineteenth-Century Europe*. Lanham, MD: Rowman & Littlefield.

Bloomberg Billionaire Index. n.d. https://www.bloomberg.com/billionaires/.

Born, Kelly, and Nell Edington. 2017. "Analysis of Philanthropic Opportunities to Mitigate the Disinformation/Propaganda Problem." The William and Flora Hewlett Foundation. https://www.hewlett.org/wp-content/uploads/2017/11/Hewlett-Disinformation-Propag anda-Report.pd.

Bowman, Tom. 2005. "Iraq War Casualties Mostly White, Working Class." *Baltimore Sun*, October 30. https://www.baltimoresun.com/news/bs-xpm-2005-10-30-0510290288-story. html.

Bryant, Jennings, and Dolf Zillmann. 2009. "A Retrospective and Prospective Look at Media Effects." In Robin L. Nabi and Mary Beth Oliver, eds., *The Sage Handbook of Media Processes and Effects* 9–17. Thousand Oaks, CA: Sage Publishing.

Case, Anne, and Angus Deaton. 2020a. *Deaths of Despair and the Future of Capitalism*. Princeton, NJ: Princeton University Press.

Case, Anne, and Angus Deaton. 2020b. "American Capitalism is Failing Trump's Base as White Working-Class 'Deaths of Despair' Rise." NBC News, April 14. https://www. nbcnews.com/think/opinion/american-capitalism-failing-trump-s-base-white-working-class-deaths-ncna1181456.

Chen, Adrian. 2015. "The Agency." *New York Times*, June 2. https://www.nytimes.com/2015/ 06/07/magazine/the-agency.html?_r=0.

Daniels, Alex. 2020. "Hewlett Commits $50 Million to New Effort to Rethink How Capitalism Should Work." *Chronicle of Philanthropy*, December 8. https://www.philanthropy.com/ article/hewlett-commits-50-million-to-new-effort-to-rethink-how-capitalism-should-work.

Diamond, Larry. 2010. "Liberation Technology." *Journal of Democracy* 21 (3): 69–83.

Fisher, Max. 2022. *The Chaos Machine: The Inside Story of How Social Media Rewired Our Minds and Our World*. New York: Little, Brown.

Freelon, Deen, and Chris Wells. 2020. "Disinformation as Political Communication." *Political Communication* 37 (2): 145–156.

Frenkel, Sheera. 2021. "The Most Influential Spreaders of Coronavirus Misinformation Online." *New York Times*, July 24. https://www.nytimes.com/2021/07/24/technology/ joseph-mercola-coronavirus-misinformation-online.html https://www.nytimes.com/ 2021/07/24/technology/joseph-mercola-coronavirus-misinformation-online.html.

Gais, Hannah. 2021. "White Nationalist Who Met with Peter Thiel Admired Terrorist Litera-ture." Southern Poverty Law Center. March 18. https://www.splcenter.org/hatewatch/2021/ 03/18/white-nationalist-who-met-peter-thiel-admired-terroristic-literature.

Geiger, Roger L. 1988. "American Foundations and Academic Social Science, 1945–1960." *Minerva* 26 (3): 315–341.

Gorski, Philip S., and Samuel L. Perry. 2022. *The Flag and the Cross: White Christian Nationalism and the Threat to American Democracy*. New York: Oxford University Press.

Grinberg, Nir, Kenneth Joseph, Lisa Friedland, Briony Swire-Thompson, and David Lazer. 2019. "Fake News on Twitter During the 2016 U.S. Presidential Election." *Science* 363 (6425): 374–378.

Grover, Michael. 2022. "What a $400 Emergency Expense Tells Us About the Economy." Fed-eral Reserve Bank of Minneapolis. June 11. https://www.minneapolisfed.org/article/2021/ what-a-400-dollar-emergency-expense-tells-us-about-the-economy.

Hacker, Jacob S., and Paul Pierson. 2020. *Let them Eat Tweets: How the Right Rules in an Age of Extreme Inequality*. New York: Liveright.

300 CONNECTIVE ACTION AND THE RISE OF THE FAR-RIGHT

Hampton, Olivia. 2022. "The Hidden Face of Hunger in America." NPR, October 2. https://www.npr.org/2022/10/02/1125571699/hunger-poverty-us-dc-food-pantry.

Hernández Kent, Ana and Lowell R. Ricketts. 2024. "The State of U.S. Wealth Inequality." Federal Reserve Bank of St. Louis." October 22. https://www.stlouisfed.org/community-development-research/the-state-of-us-wealth-inequality

Howard, Philip N., B. Ganesh, Dimitra Liotsiou, John Kelly, and Camille François. 2018. "The IRA, Social Media and Political Polarization in the United States, 2012–2018." *Project on Computational Propaganda, Working Paper.* https://comprop.oii.ox.ac.uk/research/ira-political-polarization/.

Isaac, Mike, and Daisuke Wakabayashi. 2017. "Russian Influence Reached 126 million Through Facebook Alone." *New York Times*, October 30. https://www.nytimes.com/2017/10/30/technology/facebook-google-russia.html.

Jamieson, Kathleen Hall. 2018. *Cyberwar: How Russian Hackers and Trolls Helped Elect a President.* New York: Oxford University Press.

Katz, Elihu. 1957. "The Two-Step Flow of Communication: An Up-To-Date Report on an Hypothesis." *Public Opinion Quarterly* 21 (1): 61–78.

Keneally, Meghan. 2019. "US Opioid-Related Deaths Have Quadrupled in Past 18 Years, Affecting Young Adults and Northeast the Most." ABC News, February 22. https://abcnews.go.com/Health/us-opioid-related-deaths-quadrupled-past-18-years/story?id=61236140.

Kepios. 2022. "Digital 2022 Global Overview Report." https://datareportal.com/reports/digital-2022-local-country-headlines?utm_source=DataReportal&utm_medium=Country_Article_Hyperlink&utm_campaign=Digital_2022&utm_term=New_Zealand&utm_content=Yearbook_Promo.

Knight Foundation. 2019. "Knight Invests $50 million to Develop New Field of Research Around Technology's Impact on Democracy." July 22. https://knightfoundation.org/press/releases/knight-fifty-million-develop-new-research-technology-impact-democracy/

Lee, Alfred McClung, and Elizabeth Briant Lee 1939. *The Fine Art of Propaganda: a Study of Father Coughlin's Speeches.* New York: Harcourt, Brace and Company.

Mac, Ryan, and Lisa Lerer. 2022. "The Right's Would-Be Kingmaker." *New York Times*, February 14. https://www.nytimes.com/2022/02/14/technology/republican-trump-peter-thiel.html

Mapping Police Violence. 2022. "2022 Police Violence Report." https://policeviolencereport.org/

Newhouse, Alex. 2019. "From Classifieds to Crypto: How White Supremacist Groups Have Embraced Crowdfunding." Center on Terrorism, Extremism, and Counterterrorism, Middlebury Institute of International Studies. https://www.middlebury.edu/institute/sites/www.middlebury.edu.institute/files/201906/Alex%20Newhouse%20CTEC%20Paper.pdf?fv=9T_mzirH

Newton, Kenneth. 2001. "Trust, Social Capital, Civil Society, and Democracy." *International Political Science Review* 22 (2): 201–214.

NYU. 2023. "Exposure to Russian Twitter Campaigns in 2016 Presidential Race Highly Concentrated, Largely Limited to Strongly Partisan Republicans." NYU. January 9. https://www.nyu.edu/about/news-publications/news/2023/january/exposure-to-russian-twitter-campaigns-in-2016-presidential-race-.html.

O'Hara, Amy, and Jodi Nelson. 2020. "Combatting Digital Disinformation: An Evaluation of the William and Flora Hewlett Foundation's Disinformation Strategy. Hewlett Foundation. https://hewlett.org/wp-content/uploads/2020/10/Final-Hewlett-evaluation-report-on-disinformation-.pdf.

Padilla, Ramon and Shawn J. Sullivan. 2025. "Trump's Inauguration was Packed with Some of the World's Richest People." USA Today. January 21. https://www.usatoday.com/story/graphics/2025/01/21/trump-inauguration-ultra-rich-musk-bezos-zuckerberg/77858780007/

Paul, Christopher, and Miriam Matthews. 2016. "The Russian 'Firehose of Falsehood' Propaganda Model: Why it Might Work and Options to Counter it." RAND Research Report, PE-198-OSD. doi: https://doi.org/10.7249/PE198.

Pew Research Center. 2015. "Trust in Government: 1958–2015." November 23. https://www.pewresearch.org/politics/2015/11/23/1-trust-in-government-1958-2015/.

Picchi, Aimee. 2021. "The New Gilded Age: 2,750 People Have More Wealth than Half the Planet." CBS News, December 7. https://www.cbsnews.com/news/wealth-inequality-billionaires-piketty-report/.

Pierre, Joseph M. 2020. "Mistrust and Misinformation: A Two-Component, Socio-Epistemic Model of Belief in Conspiracy Theories." *Journal of Social and Political Psychology* 8 (2): 617–641.

Pigliucci, Massimo. 2009. "The End of Theory in Science?" *EMBO Reports* 10 (6). https://doi.org/10.1038/embor.2009.111.

Pogue, James. 2022. "Inside the New Right, Where Peter Theil is Placing his Biggest Bets." *Vanity Fair*, April 20. https://www.vanityfair.com/news/2022/04/inside-the-new-right-where-peter-thiel-is-placing-his-biggest-bets.

Ruck, Damian J., Natalie Manaeva Rice, Joshua Borycz, and R. Alexander Bentley. 2019. "Internet Research Agency Twitter Activity Predicted 2016 U.S. Election Polls." *First Monday* 24 (7). https://firstmonday.org/article/view/10107/8049.

Saez, Emmanuel, and Gabriel Zucman. 2019. *The Triumph of Injustice: How the Rich Dodge Taxes and How to Make Them Pay*. New York: Norton.

Sargent, Greg. 2022. "Why a Secretive Tech Billionaire is Bankrolling J. D. Vance." *Washington Post*, May 5. https://www.washingtonpost.com/opinions/2022/05/05/peter-thiel-bankrolling-jd-vance-reactionary-nationalism/.

Schattschneider, Elmer. E. 1969. *Two Hundred Million Americans in Search of a Government*. New York: Holt, Rinehart and Winston.

Schleifer, Theodore. 2024. "What's a Democratic Billionaire to Do Now?" The New York Times, November 27. https://www.nytimes.com/2024/11/27/us/politics/democratic-donors-reid-hoffman-democracy-alliance.html

Statista. 2023. "Percentage Distribution of Household Income in the United States in 2023". https://www.statista.com/statistics/203183/percentage-distribution-of-household-income-in-the-us/.

Sutton, Robbie M., and Karen M. Douglas. 2022. "Rabbit Hole Syndrome: Inadvertent, Accelerating, and Entrenched Commitment to Conspiracy Beliefs." *Current Opinion in Psychology* 48 (December). https://www.sciencedirect.com/science/article/pii/S2352250X2200183X

Tang, Lu, Kayo Fujimoto, Muhammad (Tuan) Amith, Rachel Cunningham, Rebecca A. Costantini, Felicia York, Grace Xiong, Julie A. Boom, Tao Tao. 2020. "'Down the Rabbit Hole' of Vaccine Misinformation on YouTube: Network Exposure Study." *Journal of Medical Internet Research* 23 (1). https://www.jmir.org/2021/1/e23262/.

V-Dem Institute. 2022. "Democracy Report 2022: Autocratization Changing Nature?" https://v-dem.net/media/publications/dr_2022.pdf.

Weaver, Courtney, and Sam Learner. 2023. "Far-Right Republican Receive Millions from New Class of Debt Hardliners." *Financial Times*, March 4. https://www.ft.com/content/998f0ff9-e78f-415c-8bc4-c431dded76bc.

Wilson, Jason. 2021. "Proud Boys and Other Far-Right Groups Raise Millions via Christian Funding Site." *The Guardian*, April 10. https://www.theguardian.com/world/2021/apr/10/proud-boys-far-right-givesendgo-christian-fundraising-site.

Wolff, Michael. 2018. *Fire and Fury: Inside the Trump White House*. New York: Henry Holt and Company.

Wood, Ed. 2017. "Health Care Costs Number One Cause of Bankruptcy for American Families." American Bankruptcy Institute. https://www.abi.org/feed-item/health-care-costs-number-one-cause-of-bankruptcy-for-american-families.

Woolley, Samuel. 2020. *The Reality Game: How the Next Wave of Technology Will Break the Truth*. New York: Public Affairs, The Hachette Group.

Ziblatt, Daniel. 2017. *Conservative Parties and the Birth of Democracy*. New York: Cambridge University Press.